MACROECONOMIC INSTABILITY
IN POST-COMMUNIST COUNTRIES

Macroeconomic Instability in Post-Communist Countries

JACEK ROSTOWSKI

CLARENDON PRESS · OXFORD
1998

Oxford University Press, Great Clarendon Street, Oxford OX2 6DP
Oxford New York
Athens Auckland Bangkok Bogota Bombay
Buenos Aires Calcutta Cape Town Dar es Salaam
Delhi Florence Hong Kong Istanbul Karachi
Kuala Lumpur Madras Madrid Melbourne
Mexico City Nairobi Paris Singapore
Taipei Tokyo Toronto Warsaw
and associated companies in
Berlin Ibadan

Oxford is a trade mark of Oxford University Press

Published in the United States
by Oxford University Press Inc. New York

A catalogue record for this book is available from the British Library

Library of Congress Cataloging in Publication Data
Rostowski, Jacek.
Macroeconomic instability in post-communist countries/
Jacek Rostowski
p.   cm.
Includes bibliographical references (p.360)
1. Economic stabilization–Europe, Eastern.   2. Economic
stabilization–Former Soviet republics.   3. Europe, Eastern–
Economic policy–1989-   4. Former Soviet republics–Economic
policy.   5. Post-communism–Economic aspects–Europe, Eastern.
6. Post-communism–Economic aspects–Former Soviet republics.
7. Finance–Europe, Eastern.   8. Finance–Former Soviet republics.
I. Title.
HC244.R595   1998   339.5'0947–dc21   97-30583
ISBN 0-19-829048-9

Typeset by J&L Composition Ltd, Filey, North Yorkshire

Printed and bound in Great Britain by Biddles Ltd, Guildford & KingsLynn

*To all those who worked tirelessly to undo
Lenin's legacy, and in particular to
Leszek Balcerowicz and Yegor Gaidar.*

PREFACE

Many of the chapters of this book were written in response to the practical problems thrown up by the transformation of the post-Communist countries into market economies (the earliest, Chapter 2, in 1988). Some, for example Chapters 2, 3, 8, 9, and 10, were written with specific policy makers and specific problems in mind. In the case of Chapter 2, the intended audience was the leadership of the democratic opposition in Poland, who had no power in 1988, but did already have significant influence over Polish public opinion. Other chapters were reviews of the transition experience regarding particular issues, as they presented themselves at the time (Chapters 4, 7, 11, and 12). None of these chapters have been corrected as far as their contents are concerned, although minor changes intended to improve style and clarity have been introduced in some cases. This abstention from revision was intended to give the reader the flavour of the debates at the time. Chapter 14 has been extensively restructured to make the argument clearer without, however, changing either the analysis or the data that was used in the original draft. The remaining chapters were written for this book. I have also added an introductory overview of the problem of macroeconomic instability during the transformation (Chapter 1), as well as introductions to each of the three Parts of the book. The intention of these is to allow me to qualify, and indeed retract, some of the analysis in the chapters which either the unfolding of the story, access to better data, or work by colleagues have shown to be mistaken.

This book could not have been written without the encouragement and tolerance of my wife Wanda, or without the intellectual inspiration and stimulation which I received from many colleagues and friends. I would like to mention in particular: Mark Allen, Anders Åslund, Andrew Berg, Leszek Balcerowicz, Peter Boone, Marek Dąbrowski, Yegor Gaidar,

Stanisław Gomułka, Richard Layard, Kálmán Mizsei, Vitali Naishul, Jeffrey Sachs, Ljubo Sirc, Sergei Vassiliev, Stanisław Wellisz and Jan Winiecki. I also want to express my gratitude to the late Peter Wiles for bringing me to the study of comparative economic systems and teaching me an economics which is not blind to politics and institutions and to Jeffrey Sachs for showing me that deep moral earnestness need not be in the least bit grey. Finally, I am grateful to my father who brought me up to believe that markets are indissolubly linked to individual freedom. Nora Krokovay was extremely efficient and helpful in working long hours on the final draft of the book.

CONTENTS

LIST OF FIGURES

LIST OF TABLES

LIST OF ABBREVIATIONS

CBR	Central Bank of Russia
CESMECON	private Belgrade consulting firm
CIS	Commonwealth of Independent States
CMEA	Council for Mutual Economic Assistance
CNG	credit for non-government
EBRD	European Bank for Reconstruction and Development
EBFRP	Enterprise and Bank Financial Restructuring Programme
FSU	former Soviet Union
IEG	inter-enterprise credit
IED	inter-enterprise debt
IMF	International Monetary Fund
LDC	less-developed country
NAIRU	non-accelerating inflation rate of unemployment
NBY	National Bank of Yugoslavia
ND	New Dinar
NDA	net domestic assets
NIC	newly industrializing country
NMP	net material produce
OD	Old Dinar
OECD	Organization for Economic Co-operation and Development
PCE	post-communist economy
RCE	reforming communist economies
SCB	state commercial banks
SOE	state owned enterprise
STE	Soviet-type economy
TIP	Tax based incomes policy
WPC	warehousing and payments company

I

Introduction

Macroeconomic Instability in Post-Communist Countries, Suggested Causes and Proposed Cures

1. Historical Background

The destruction—or collapse—of a world system is bound to be cataclysmic, and the collapse of the world socialist system which is playing itself out at present across twenty eight countries is no exception.[1] Indeed, the very fact that these twenty eight states were only nine in 1990, shows the scale of the changes. That this collapse has occurred without a major war has tended to obscure what is happening: the political, social and economic relations which governed these societies are all being simultaneously changed in a fundamental way. This by way of admission that there is much that lies outside our understanding as economists, and that it is likely to become particularly important in times and places such as those studied in this book. In such a context, the presence of macroeconomic instability is hardly surprising. Yet, it is the job of economists to try to identify the specific causes of economic phenomena, even—or maybe particularly—when they are caught up in the whirlwind of history.

The instability affecting the post-communist economies (PCEs) has manifested itself throughout the region in the form of both very large falls in statistically measured output and in very high rates of inflation. Table 1 shows peak inflation rates and output troughs (as compared to 1989). However, the

most striking regularity in the data is that the number of countries in which inflation has fallen below 50 per cent per annum (and remained below that level), keeps increasing. Seventeen out of 26 countries had achieved this level of inflation by 1995. Equally, the number of countries which are experiencing some economic growth is also increasing, with the number of such countries having reached fourteen by 1995. Thus, extreme macroeconomic instability is itself a transitional phenomenon.

As of early 1996 we can roughly divide the PCEs into two groups, the successful and the unsuccessful (Table 1). There are also a number of countries which are on the borderline. In the successful countries, after an episode of (very) high inflation, the rate of change of prices has been brought down to the low tens of per cent per annum, and it remains on a downward trend. Among the unsuccessful, inflation remains above 50 per cent per annum, and there is little certainty that there will not be a renewed inflationary explosion in spite of current successes in reducing inflation. The successful countries have also experienced recovery in measured output, some almost returning to pre-transition levels. In the unsuccessful group, output was still falling in 1995. In the borderline countries, either inflation was still relatively high (e.g. Bulgaria), or output was still falling (e.g. Georgia). Table 2 shows how many countries have succeeded in achieving economic growth or a rate of inflation below 50 per cent per annum in each sub-region. In order to make comparisons across sub-regions, the number of successful countries since the commencement of the transition in that sub-region is given. The transition is taken to have started in Central Europe in 1990, in ex-Yugoslavia in 1991 (the end of the Serbo-Croat War) and in the FSU in 1992. Table 2 thus shows that success is fairly evenly spread across sub-regions. From this and from the general improvement in both inflation and output in the region, we can conclude that the borderline countries, and indeed the unsuccessful, may be expected to join the successful ones in due course.

After discussing the main schools of thought as regards the causes of macroeconomic instability in Sections 2, 3, and 4, the political roots of this instability are described in Sections 5 and 6.

Table 1 Key macroeconomic indicators for the post-communist economies 1989–95

	1995 inflation[a]	Peak inflation per cent per annum	1995 GDP, 1989=100	Growth in GDP since trough (per cent)	Output trough 1989=100	Private sector/GDP mid-1994[b]
SUCCESSFUL						
Albania	5	239 [92]	75	26	60 [92]	50
Armenia	45	10996 [93]	37	10	34 [93]	40
Croatia	3	1150 [93]	84	3	82 [93]	40
Czech Republic						
	10	52 [91]	85	7	79 [93]	65
Estonia	22	954 [92]	74	12	66 [93]	55
Hungary	28	32 [91]	86	5	82 [93]	55
Latvia	23	958 [92]	54	3	52 [93]	55
Lithuania	30	1175 [92]	42	7	39 [93]	50
Poland	23	640 [89]	97	19	81 [91]	55
Romania	30	296 [93]	81	8	75 [92]	35
Slovakia	10	58 [91]	84	10	76 [93]	55
Slovenia	10	247 [91]	94	13	83 [92]	30
UNCERTAIN						
Bulgaria	50	339 [91]	75	4	72 [93]	40
Georgia	25	7380 [94]	17	—	17 [95]	—
Kirgyzstan	25	1771 [92]	43	—	43 [95]	30
Macedonia	10	1935 [92]	53	—	53 [95]	35
Moldova	20	2198 [92]	42	—	42 [95]	20
Serbia-Montenegro[c]	120	$3.72*10^{13}$ [93]	54	13	47 [93]	—
UNSUCCESSFUL						
Azerbaijan	100	1788 [94]	35	—	35 [95]	20
Belarus	260	1994 [93]	54	—	54 [95]	15
Kazakhstan	60	2567 [92]	44	—	44 [95]	20
Russia	145	2318 [92]	49	—	49 [95]	50
Tadjikistan	240	7344 [93]	40	—	40 [95]	15
Turkmenistan	2500	9750 [93]	63	—	63 [95]	15
Ukraine	150	10155 [93]	43	—	43 [95]	30
Uzbekistan	155	910 [92]	82	—	82 [95]	20

[a] All inflation rates are annual, point to point, date indicates year.
[b] Rough EBRD estimate, *Transition Report*, 1994.
[c] *Source*: Chapter 4, and *Ekonomska Politika*, 1995–6, various issues.

Source: K. Bartholdy, Table 1, p. 525.

Section 7 draws conclusions from the rest of the book for the debates described in this chapter.

There are three main schools of thought on the causes of macroeconomic instability in PCEs:

1) structuralist/vulgar Keynesian
2) gradualist
3) radical reformist

Table 2 The spread of economic stabilization

	Year 2	Year 3	Year 4
Inflation below 50% per annum:			
CEE	1	4	5
ex-Yugoslavia	0	1	2
FSU	2	4	7
TOTAL	3	9	14
GDP growing:			
CEE	—	1	3
ex-Yugoslavia	–	1	3
FSU	–	4	4
TOTAL	–	6	10

Source: as Table 1.

Each of these has a number of variants, four of which we will touch upon: 'evolutionary gradualism' (a variant of 2), and the 'supply-side', 'demand-side', and 'statistical artefact' explanations (all of which are variants of 3). Each diagnosis corresponds to a class of policy prescription, although the mapping is not one to one. Thus, structuralists and vulgar Keynesians may propose either populist or state interventionist policies (Section 2), while gradualists may propose either various kinds of interventionist policies (e.g. market building interventionism or market constraining interventionism),[2] or evolutionary ones. Radical reformists will tend to support some kind of 'shock therapy', though again not in all sectors (I myself would be more gradualist than most gradualists as regards financial sector reform).

2. Vulgar Keynesian and Structuralist Explanations of Macroeconomic Instability

The vulgar Keynesian approach[3] is mainly an explanation of the fall in output (believed to be very much a real rather than a statistical phenomenon) rather than of the high inflation in the region, and its proponents do not usually concern themselves with the latter (e.g. Bhaduri and Laski, 1993). The central thesis

is that output has fallen—it is claimed catastrophically—because of the anti-inflationary policies pursued by govern-ments. These have resulted in a sharp reduction in aggregate demand (e.g. as a result of the elimination of reduction in budget deficits), which in turn has caused output to fall. The fact that countries such as Russia or Ukraine, which maintained massive budget or quasi-budget deficits[4] during the first few years of the transition, have experienced falls in statistical out-put which are far larger than those in countries (such as Poland or the Czech Republic) which have pursued more consistent anti-inflationary policies, is simply ignored (Table 1).

For a theory of post-communist inflation which is more or less consonant with the vulgar Keynesian approach, we have to turn to structuralism. A commonly held view throughout the region before the beginning of the transition was that the highly monopolized nature of industry made a stabilization impossi-ble. This is a version of the structuralist belief common in developing countries (and particularly in Latin America), that—whatever the case in the rest of the world—inflation in one's own country is a monopolistic phenomenon. Such struc-turalism lies at the root of both populism and of much 'inter-ventionist gradualism' as policy prescriptions. The former exists in both Latin America and post-communist countries, the latter is largely restricted to Eastern Europe.

In the post-communist countries, as in Latin America, struc-turalism often goes together with the following additional propositions:

1) administrative increases in the prices of basic inputs such as oil are said to be the proximate cause of inflation (monopo-lists faced by such increases cannot be prevented from passing them on to consumers by a mere shortage of demand);

2) for this reason restrictive monetary and fiscal policies cannot stop inflation, though they may cause output to decline;

3) obversely, loose monetary and fiscal policies are not responsible for inflation and can help to sustain (expand) output;

4) the effective way to control inflation is to control prices administratively.

One can thus see that the step from structuralism (points 1 and 2) to populism (points 3 and 4) is a short one. A country with a fundamental mispricing of certain key goods (such as oil in the case of Russia) should thus either do nothing except print more money (the populist prescription)[5] or else undertake a long programme of—more or less planned—industrial restructuring (the interventionist-gradualist prescription).[6] A 'big bang' which is based on rapid liberalization and (largely orthodox) shock stabilization, then fails simply because it has to (points 1 to 4), or succeeds at too high a cost (as, it is claimed, has been the case in Poland and Czecho-Slovakia).

However, the difference between supposedly unavoidable failure (e.g. Russia) and excessive cost depends, according to the structuralists, largely on the degree of monopolization of the economy. As a result, the difference between orthodox market economists and structuralists is more than meets the eye. Many market economists believe that the cost of stabilization in previously 100 per cent full employment economies such as PCEs depends partly on the non-accelerating inflation rate of unemployment—the NAIRU (Chapters 2 and 3)—and this depends in turn on the level of rigidity in the economy, of which the degree of monopolization in the non-traded sector of the economy can be an important part. The difference between the two approaches depends therefore partly on suggested solutions: market economists see rapid liberalization as a way of reducing rigidities and thus the NAIRU quickly, structuralists tend rather to believe in rapid growth or planned industrial restructuring.[7]

3. Gradualism

Gradualism is a policy prescription rather than a diagnosis, but the former must flow from the latter. More extreme 'glacial' gradualists may differ little from vulgar Keynesians. They often claim that stabilization based on monetary and fiscal policy cannot succeed because 'the market does not yet work' in transition economies. A long preparatory period of building market institutions is therefore necessary. Tax reform, demo-

nopolization, financial sector development, enterprise and industrial restructuring by government, even privatization can—and have been—claimed to be essential prerequisites for a successful macroeconomic stabilization based on monetary and fiscal policy.

These issues are addressed in Chapter 2, where it is argued that high levels of aggregate demand—and in particular generalized excess demand—strengthen the hand of the very producer groups which stand to loose from the structural and institutional reforms which are, indeed, necessary to reduce the costs of stabilization. Macroeconomic stabilization therefore needs to precede structural reforms, and not the other way round. This is not just because inflation is a process which, waiting for no man, feeds on itself and of itself causes output to fall (Chapter 4), but above all for strategic-political reasons. The interest groups opposed to economic reform need to be dealt a shattering blow at the very beginning of the battle for reform, and that blow is macroeconomic stabilization.

Moderate gradualists accept the need to stabilize at the beginning of the transition 'where necessary' (e.g. Portes, 1993). However, they believe that the fall in output (which is largely real in their view), has been due to major economic policy mistakes. These involve both macroeconomic policy errors and a failure to undertake a number of structural or institutional reforms sufficiently quickly. Since the moderate gradualists are professional economists, the criticism they levy at transition policy as it has been practised in PCEs is detailed and technical. As Portes (1993) writes 'serious, operational policy is about detail'. The problem with this apparently reasonable approach is that the details differ sharply from country to country, and yet the overall picture across twenty eight countries clearly has considerable consistency. If avoiding large falls in industrial output during transition is a matter of getting the detailed policies right, why has not one out of the twenty eight countries succeeded?

It seems inadequate to attribute the supposedly real and supposedly avoidable falls of upward of 25 per cent in industrial production which have been observed in PCEs to 'a

combination, the weights differing among countries, of excessive monetary contraction (beyond that needed for stabilization, at least if devaluation had not overshot) with the inadequacy of supply response . . .' as Portes (1994) does. This will not account for Hungary (1990—3), where output decline has been correlated with real appreciation rather than with real depreciation, or for the countries in the FSU and the Balkans which have failed to stabilize, but which have nevertheless suffered massive falls in statistical output (Table 1).[8] Portes (1993) of course also blames a lack of '(s)tructural reform—in property rights, lending discipline, managerial motivation, and much else . . .', but on the same page he admits that '(i)t is impossible to do everything at once', and it is in the same paper that he states that 'where necessary' stabilization must come at the beginning of the transition. Portes therefore fails to convince that the output falls which occurred, if real, were avoidable—except in some abstract world in which it was indeed possible to do everything at once! The problem with moderate gradualism is that it is too modest: by claiming that it is the details of policy that have caused the supposed economic disaster in the post-communist world, it renders itself powerless before the very uniformity which requires explanation.[9]

Guillermo Calvo and Fabrizio Coricelli (1992*a*, 1992*b*, 1993), whom one might also classify as moderate gradualists, face the same problem. Stabilization is necessary but has been too harsh in its implementation, it is claimed. This view becomes less convincing as more and more countries stabilize with much the same results as Poland (and usually worse results, as far as output is concerned). However, Calvo and Coricelli are more consistent than most moderate gradualists in that they do propose a radically alternative macroeconomic policy: prices could be held down through the use of subsidies so as to sustain the real value of credit (1993). Indeed, there is a strand in gradualist thinking which is quite as bold as that of the 'shock therapists', particularly as far as policy prescriptions are concerned.[10]

Evolutionary gradualism[11] springs from a view of the economy which is almost diametrically opposed to that of most moderate gradualists, who tend to constructivism (indeed inter-

ventionism, if not etatism). Economic transition should be gradual not because a great deal of institution and market building[12] needs to precede liberalization, but rather because all long existing institutional setups have a degree of legitimacy and efficiency. They should therefore not be reformed, but should rather be allowed to evolve. On this view it is *excessively rapid* institutional reform which, by suddenly removing the distortions and rigidities of the old system has severed many economic links between actors and led to the output depression.

It is indeed probable that, in many areas, evolution could lead to more rapid institutional change than the forced institutional reform from above which both moderate gradualists and radical reformers tend to favour. An example is the remarkable speed and quality of private sector development in Poland, discussed in Chapter 14. Nevertheless, the idea that access to below cost-price inputs (and presumably to cheap central bank credits also) is a kind of customary right, and that such rights should not be confiscated but can only be traded away, leaves unanswered the question of what to do when such rights can only be maintained at the cost of increasing burdens on other members of society. This is in fact what has happened throughout the region. The old privileges could no longer be financed by tax revenues, because of a collapse in tax discipline, and had to be paid for by the inflation tax (whose incidence is quite different from that of the conventional taxes which it replaced).[13]

The evolutionary gradualist perspective is important, however, because it highlights the point that the motivation of many politicians in instituting shock therapy has been to save the post-communist state from disintegration by drastically pruning its functions. From this perspective gradualists and radical reformers are brothers under the skin, disagreeing only on the ability of the state to intervene successfully in the economy and on the need for it to do so, while some Hayekians like Naishul (1994) actually welcome the loss of the state's ability to perform many of the functions (such as policing or banking supervision) which are considered normal in Western capitalist countries.

4. Radical Reformist Explanations for Macroeconomic Instability

Supporters of rapid reform and stabilization explain the fall in output in three main ways:

1) the demand-side explanation—the need for unemployment to be increased to (or above) the NAIRU (e.g. Chapter 2);

2) the supply-side explanation—the need to change the entire product mix of the economy (e.g. Gomulka, 1993*a*);

3) the statistical artefact explanation—the fall in output was far smaller than official statistics suggest, and—to the extent to which it was real—was mostly due to exogenous factors such as the collapse of the CMEA (e.g. Berg and Sachs, 1992).

The demand-side view starts from the premise that in PCEs actual unemployment had to rise to the NAIRU to prevent inflation from accelerating, and needed to rise above the NAIRU to reduce inflation, to the extent to which stabilization policies were not credible. Since all socialist countries—with the exception of China and Yugoslavia—had zero unemployment, they all had unemployment rates below the NAIRU. Since labour and other factor markets were highly rigid, NAIRU was likely to be high compared to Western market economies, and the rate of unemployment needed to reduce inflation could be even higher. High inflation in these countries has therefore resulted from the failure to raise unemployment sufficiently.[14]

Output has fallen as a result of the fall in employment (though value added at world prices need not necessarily have declined). The prevalence of firms dominated by employees or paternalistic managers means that employment is not reduced as much as it would be for any given fall in demand in a market capitalist economy. As a result, for a given NAIRU, demand must be reduced by more than it would be in a capitalist economy to achieve the same reduction in employment and inflation. Output therefore falls more than employment, and therefore labour productivity also falls. All this is discussed at length in the Introduction to Part 1 and in Chapter 2.

In addition, a number of mechanisms ensure that if an economy starts off from a situation of excess demand for certain

important categories of assets, then eliminating this state of affairs is likely to lead to a period of overshooting in the other direction. A well-known example of such a mechanism is the increase in the demand for the domestic currency which occurs on stabilization. The obverse of this phenomenon is the fall in demand for goods and services which occurs while real balances are being re-built (Chapter 9). Two additional mechanisms of the same kind which are specific to post-communist economies result from the fact that excess demand feeds on itself (Kornai, 1980). The first occurs because actors hoarded goods which were persistently in short supply due to underpricing. When the shortages disappeared, these stocks had to be run down (Berg and Sachs, 1992). The second occurs because of the unwinding of the forced substitution which existed under the regime of generalized excess demand (see the Introduction to Part 1 for a lengthier discussion of these issues).

The supply-side view is very well summarized in Gomulka (1993*a*): 'As the relative prices of energy and other inputs increase a great deal, some production processes become loss making and have to be discontinued. Superimposed on these changes are demand shifts related to the shrinkage of the defence sector and CMEA trade. Owing to the presence of various rigidities, substantial resources become permanently useless or idle until redeployed and/or improved . . .'[15] Since all these micro adjustments are large and necessary, the post-reform recessions are inevitable . . . [This necessitates] the application of macroeconomic policies, which ensure that aggregate demand falls a great deal, and falls quickly, to the level of much reduced sustainable aggregate supply'. Failure to do this sufficiently energetically is the fundamental source of high inflation in the region.

Both the above explanations for macroeconomic instability during transition regard falls in output as real and significant in size, if inevitable. The third radical reformist view denies that large falls have taken place in those countries which have implemented reform vigorously,[16] and that such real falls as have occurred have been due to exogenous factors such as the breakdown of the CMEA trading system. At the heart of the

argument lies the problem of how the national incomes of communist countries before the transition should have been measured, particularly given tht both money and relative prices did not clear markets. The case when money prices fail to clear markets (repressed inflation) is obvious: before price liberalization the measure of GDP based on factor incomes will overstate true GDP, because factors are being paid more than they are worth, and are unable to spend all of the income which they wish to. Although repressed inflation before the transition undoubtedly resulted in exaggerated measures of declines in real incomes (see Berg and Sachs, 1992, for Poland), there are too many countries for which it is implausible given the pre-transition level of shortages and the size of the fall in GDP, for instance Czechoslovakia and Hungary, for this explanation to be accepted as general.

Figure 1 illustrates the problem: the service sector is repressed, with both the controlled price ($P_o{}^s$) below the equilibrium price and supply set by planners ($Q_o{}^s$) below the equilibrium level of output which would maximize social surplus. Price and supply are free in manufacturing, and forced substitution towards manufacturing results in the demand curve for manufactured goods at D_o. Output at $Q_o{}^m$, and $P_o{}^m$ will clear the market.[17] Measured GDP is $P_o{}^s Q_o{}^s + P_o{}^m Q_o{}^m$ (it is assumed that there are no intermediate inputs). Under these circumstances there is no acceptable way of measuring true GDP. However, if we price the two goods at the marginal utility they give consumers at given levels of output, then 'true' GDP can be thought of as $P_2{}^s Q_o{}^s + P_2{}^m Q_o$. When prices of services are freed, the demand curve for manufactured products shifts in to D_1, and meassured GDP in manufacturing falls from $P_o{}^m Q_o{}^m$ to $P_1{}^m Q_1{}^m$. However, 'true' GDP in manufacturing changes from $P_2{}^m Q_o{}^m$ to $P_1{}^m Q_1{}^m$, which can be either a reduction or an increase depending on whether the elasticity of demand is greater than or less than unity. Similarly, 'true' GDP in services goes from $P_2{}^s Q_o{}^s$ to $P_1{}^s Q_1{}^s$, which can also be either an increase or a reduction. However, irrespective of whether 'true' GDP has increased or fallen, the output levels $Q_o{}^s$ and $Q_o{}^m$ fail to maximize social surplus and therefore has to be considered inferior

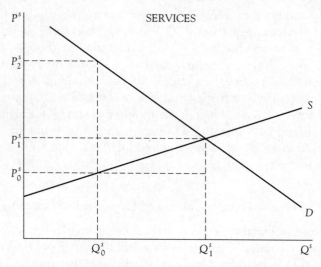

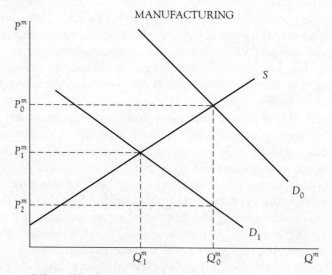

Figure 1   *Effects of liberalization on output*

to $Q_1{}^s$ and $Q_1{}^m$. Moreover, if the increase in 'measurable' GDP in the service sector from $P_0{}^s Q_0{}^s$ to $P_1{}^s Q_1{}^s$ fails to be measured in fact, then measured GDP will decrease even though 'true' GDP may have increased, and social welfare will have increased.[18] A relevant example of the problems associated with using official statistics to measure changes in GDP is given in Chapter 14: a doubling in the number of shops in Poland in 1990–1 (and an unparalleled improvement in their quality) was reflected in an increase in measured GDP generated in internal trade of 8.6 per cent!

5. Domestic Political Causes of Macroeconomic Instability

The root political cause of macroeconomic instability in PCEs is democratization. From this spring all the other political evils which have contributed both to inflation and the statistical falls in output. The centrally planned system was based on fear of the ruling communist party and its secret police, of which the planning commission in each country was only a technical support service. When democratization caused the fear to disappear the fundamental mechanism on which the economic system was founded—that orders from above were obeyed—ceased to operate.

Hayek (1986) argued that an economic system in which the bulk of activity was directed by the state could not operate in conjunction with a democratic political system. The conflicts which arose when markets were not available to resolve millions of problems of resource allocation and income distribution in an apolitical way, could only be solved by a dictatorship. Hence Hayek's warning that continued expansion of state direction of the economy in the West would lead to dictatorship. The marketizing revolutions which swept Eastern Europe from 1989 show that the link also works the other way. The fall of the communist dictatorships required the adoption of market mechanisms. This was the only way to make the economy function, however imperfectly, under the new political conditions. This was the prime cause of the 'jump to the market', and not the influence of dogmatic liberal economists at home or the

IMF abroad. It is no accident that it is Turkmenistan and Uzbekistan which have made the least progress towards a market economy. China shows that dictatorship is consistent with marketization, but Eastern Europe demonstrates that democracy requires it.

It is the failure to understand this basic point which lends some gradualist proposals their surreal air. The weakening—sometimes the disintegration—of the state which accompanied the fall of communism was a fact, whether one lamented or welcomed it. For instance, the idea that such states could, let alone should, carry out active industrial policies effectively in the early years of transition, can only be entertained by those who have never seen the proposals for such policies drafted in the Ministries of Industry in the region (e.g. Ministry of Industry, 1990), and much the same applies to anti-monopoly policy.

The weakening of the communist dictatorships had clearly traceable economic effects. Thus, in Poland—with its strong trade union tradition—the first thing to go was wage discipline. In June 1989, two months before the communists surrendered power, statistical real wages were 42 per cent higher than they had been two years before. Since productivity had not increased this was merely the expression of a severe monetary overhang (Berg and Sachs, 1992). In the Soviet Union, where managers were politically stronger than workers, from 1989 enterprises were largely ignoring the central planning authorities and engaging in barter-based market relationships. Democratization also led to the economic fragmentation of the USSR well before its political dissolution, as newly elected Republican authorities created export barriers as a way of 'protecting the domestic market' under conditions of generalized excess demand. The same process was well under way between the Oblast'i of the Russian Federation at the time Gaidar implemented price liberalization, and put an end to this threat to the political unity of Russia (Chapter 7). Across the region the relaxation of taxation discipline increased budget deficits and stoked inflationary pressures (Chapter 12).

6. *International Political Causes of Macroeconomic Instability*

Democratization caused the demise of the Soviet empire, and this meant that first the USSR, and then Russia, were no longer willing to subsidize—through the supply of cheap raw materials—first the former satellites (from 1990), and then the former Republics of the Soviet Union (from 1992). These subsidies were worth some 3 per cent of Central Europe's GDP (Gomulka, 1993*a*), and many times this figure in the non-Russian republics of the USSR and Bulgaria. The removal of the subsidies was a powerful exogenous shock, causing a severe fall in output throughout the region, and strong inflationary pressures in those countries which failed to adjust demand to the fall in supply.[19] Similarly, by putting an end to the strategic rivalry with the West, democratization eliminated the bulk of domestic demand for military hardware in the former Soviet block, causing what was effectively a second massive negative exogenous shock, this time on the demand side.[20]

In addition to such real shocks, the dissolution of the USSR caused chaos in the fiscal, monetary, payments, and trade systems of the successor states (see Chapters 7 and 9). In Yugoslavia—the only country not to be much affected by the events in the former Soviet Union (FSU)—democratization also led to political disintegration and war, with much the same effects in terms of ruptured economic links and a shift in the structure of output, only in this case *towards* military hardware (see Chapter 4).

At the same time the newly free countries of Central and Eastern Europe and the FSU found that, if they were to establish their economic independence and provide a sound basis for their political independence, they first had to thoroughly liberalize and marketize their economies and stabilize their currencies. The reason was the dependence of a significant part of their economies, particularly in manufacturing, on subsidized Russian raw materials. Given the terms of trade shock resulting from Russia's understandable unwillingness to continue subsidizing foreign and independent countries (be it through underpricing or through payments deficits), domestic demand for

imports from Russia had to be reduced and hard currency earnings to pay for these imports had to be increased. This required:

1) a sharp reduction of raw materials, and particularly energy, subsidies;

2) macroeconomic stabilization to reduce domestic aggregate demand and thus reduce the demand for imports and increase the supply of exports;

3) generalized price liberalization to achieve structural adjustment on the supply side (above all an increase in exports to non-CMEA and non-FSU countries).

The need to establish economic independence by paying one's way in a new market-based international economic order played an important part in convincing politicians that marketization and stabilization were necessary. This was particularly the case in Poland, the Baltics and Slovenia.[21] Countries where the attachment to national independence was weaker, such as Ukraine or Belarus, found it harder to obtain a political consensus for rapid reform. A third group consists of countries such as Croatia, Georgia and Serbia-Montenegro, which were at war, and like many such countries suffered from very high (and even true hyper-) inflation. In their case what was decisive was not a lack of desire for independence, but an inability to achieve stabilization because of the fiscal pressures resulting from war. At the same time Russia was caught in the vice of sharply declining oil production, which fell from 516 million tonnes (516mt) to 399mt between 1990 and 1992. In response, in 1991 the USSR cut Russia's oil exports—mainly to Eastern Europe—from 156mt to 91mt. The policy was continued by an independent Russia in 1992, with a further reduction of exports to non-FSU countries to 66mt. However, in 1993 in spite of a further sharp decline in oil production, exports increased to 82mt, at the expense of domestic and FSU consumers.[22] Thus, the USSR and then Russia were exporting economic reform, first to Central and Eastern Europe, then to the Baltics (which were subjected to energy blockades in 1992 and 1993), and finally to the rest of the FSU.[23] The decline in oil production was also a force for reform within Russia itself, as oil prices

needed to be raised and domestic demand curtailed to induce energy conservation and to make room for exports.

This is the context in which we should view the collapse of intra-CMEA trade. The Central and East European countries were faced with a Soviet Union which was determined to sell its raw materials for hard currency at world prices, but which was incapable of creating an efficient mechanism by which its importers could obtain hard currency and thus buy from Eastern Europe (e.g. foreign currency auctions or a degree of convertibility). The Central and East Europeans could either continue with state barter-based trade (excluding raw materials), in which case they would have run a large trade surplus with the USSR, running up positive balances with which they could buy little or nothing, or they could do what they actually did: shift to hard currency trade at world prices for all goods. Moreover, the continuation of state organized barter trade would have meant the isolation of the CMEA traded sector (both imports and exports) from the world market prices whose importation into PCEs was so important (Portes, 1993). In fact it can be argued that the Central Europeans went too far in trying to sustain CMEA trade. In 1990 the Poles subsidized it to the tune of 2 per cent of GDP, and similar schemes existed in Czecho-Slovakia and Hungary.

7. Macroeconomic Instability and Policy during the Transition to Capitalism

Three main themes are addressed in the ensuing chapters: the causes of macroeconomic instability in PCEs, as regards both output and inflation; the design of stabilization/liberalization programmes; and the role of financial (and particularly banking) systems in stabilization and transition.

The general tendency of PCEs to suffer from high inflation is explained in terms of the operation of the NAIRU in full employment economies in Chapter 2. In the special case of Serbia-Montenegro in 1993–4 (Chapter 4), what was probably the second fastest hyperinflation in history resulted from the attempt by the authorities to finance the war at a level far in

excess of their ability to raise conventional taxes. A classical hyperinflationary spiral ensued, with inflation undermining conventional tax revenue through the Tanzi-Olivera effect. Chapter 8 describes how inflationary expectations can lead to a temporary inflationary bubble if enterprises increase the trade credit they extend to each other, even in the absence of an expansion of the money supply.

A number of mechanisms responsible for the falls in employment and statistical output are discussed. The most important is the need for unemployment to rise to, or above, the NAIRU so as to reduce inflation (Chapter 2). However, failure to stabilize inflation does not necessarily allow output losses to be avoided. One can see this clearly in the case of Serbia-Montenegro in 1993, where the hyperinflation led to severe output contraction and massive shortages, even in the presence of free prices (Chapter 4). The fall in output in this case seems to have been partly due to the loss of information about relative prices carried by nominal prices, as a result of the noise caused by the hyperinflation.[24] Also, the need for the banking system to begin allocating credit on the basis of commercial criteria for the first time in forty—or in the case of the former Soviet Union seventy—years from the first day of the stabilization programmes causes an unavoidable 'credit crunch', with consequences for output in the traditional state sector (Chapter 5). Chapter 9 describes the mechanism by which a sharp devaluation (necessary if a country is to accumulate sufficient international reserves to run a currency board) will simultaneously lead to inflation and depression.[25] It is shown in Chapter 8 that if inflationary expectations have caused a trade credit explosion above the sustainable level, then a failure to validate this through an increase in nominal money can be sufficient to cause a sharp fall in output. Finally, it is suggested in Chapter 6 that in the medium term in labour-managed firms, statutory wage controls can lead to a reduction in output, as workers reduce their effort, so as to increase real wages/effective hours worked.

As regards policy, there is an evolution from general consideration of stabilization in Chapters 2, 3, 4, and 7, to specific

aspects of such policies in subsequent chapters. Thus, Chapter 2 argues that stabilization must precede structural policies aimed at increasing the efficiency of the economy, since the interest groups which have most to lose from marketization are strengthened by excess demand and high inflation. In the absence of a government which has the political strength to stabilize, the legalization of dollarization is advocated, as this limits the authorities' ability to fix prices administratively or to obtain purchasing power through the printing press. In Chapter 3, shock rather than gradual stabilization is advocated, based on the need to change expectations rapidly in order to reduce the costs of stabilization. The benefits of orthodox and heterodox shocks are discussed, with the conclusion that orthodox shocks, in which exchange rates are fixed but wages (and particularly) prices are free, are to be preferred. It is also proposed that currency boards and balanced budgets should be written into the new constitutions of the region. In Chapter 4, the Serbo-Montenegrian episode shows that when real money balances have shrunk to minuscule levels due to very high inflation tax, stabilization based on introducing convertibility at a fixed exchange rate is very effective in the short term, even in the absence of any expectations that the state budget would be balanced. This casts doubt on the Sargent (1986*a*) approach to stabilization, in which the expectation of budget balance is central to the achievement of credibility (and thus success) for a stabilization programme. The reasons for the failure of the 1992 attempted stabilization in Russia are analyzed in Chapter 7. Apart from insufficient radicalism, the main problems were the non-existence of certain key state institutions (customs borders, monopoly over domestic money creation) and the depth of the Russian economy's structural difficulties, which may have doomed any macroeconomic policy to failure in the short term.

At the level of more specific policies, Chapter 6 reviews the arguments for and against wage controls during stabilization in PCEs. Chapter 8 deals with the inter-enterprise debt explosion which was a key factor in inducing Gaidar to retreat from stabilization in 1992. Securitization of the debt (without any

government guarantee, explicit or implicit) is proposed as a solution, but only when doing nothing is either politically or economically unfeasible. In Chapter 9 we propose a mechanism for a smooth decoupling of a country (in this case Latvia) from the rouble zone through the introduction of a secondary domestic currency to circulate in parallel to the hyperinflating rouble. It is also proposed that the new stable currency should be administered through a currency board type of system. Chapter 10 examines the dilemmas which are likely to confront a country once macroeconomic stabilization is achieved. In particular the problems arising out of the growth in money supply as a result of the increase in the money multiplier are discussed. This increase also augments the post-stabilization bad debt problem. Chapter 12 analyses the sources of the post-stabilization fiscal crisis in Czecho-Slovakia, Hungary, and Poland, and concludes that Hungary must cut back its social provision sharply, while the Czech Republic, Poland and Slovakia need to avoid its expansion.

Five chapters address financial, and above all banking sector issues in the transition. Chapter 5 considers the 'credit crunch' explanation of the post-communist fall in statistical output. It is argued that a credit crunch is an unavoidable part of the transition, because a stabilization/liberalization requires banks to begin to allocate credit commercially from one day to the next, unless bank credit is abolished by combining debt forgiveness with the introduction of 100 per cent reserve banking. This theme of the usefulness of gradualism in launching the banking sector on the path of commercial credit allocation is further addressed in Chapters 9, 10, and 11. Chapters 9 and 11 contain proposals for the creation of maximally stable monetary and banking systems.[26] Chapter 10 discusses the monetary control and bad debt problems which result from re-monetization after successful stabilization. Chapter 13 assesses to what extent German-type universal banks are suitable for the PCEs, and concludes that—as long as state ownership of banks, high inflation, and a tendency to state interventionism at the micro level persist—they are not. Chapter 14 examines the link between shock macroeconomic stabilization and structural

change, taking the rapid development of the private sector in Poland as an example.

NOTES

1. We include the no longer existing GDR and the not yet existing Bosnia in the total.
2. A good example of the difference between these is the attitude towards monopolies: a 'market building interventionist' will favour a strong anti-monopoly policy (e.g. Portes, 1993), while a 'market constraining interventionist' will favour the creation of strong industrial groups to act as national champions.
3. This label is not intended to be pejorative, although it is meant to recall 'vulgar Marxism'. Like the latter the 'keynesianism' espoused by its proponents is of a very simple variety, which at least has the merit of giving a very clear policy prescription.
4. Via non-commercial central bank lending to state enterprises.
5. Populists the world over often believe that stimulating growth will solve structural problems by enabling the growth of the 'right' activities, and thus reducing the relative importance of the 'wrong' ones. In post-communist countries there has been a strand of populist thought suggesting that loose macro-economic policy would help restructuring by encouraging private sector development. It is also often argued (by gradualists as well as populists) that enterprise restructuring is impossible if credit is tight, so that restructuring on the basis of market signals *requires* loose macro policy.
6. As we have seen, more moderate gradualists will wish to restructure by demonopolizing, more interventionist ones will wish to create large holding companies which can become national champions.
7. Although monopoly is presumably very bad—since it causes inflation—structuralists have rarely been found to advocate energetic anti-trust policy. Monopolies seem to be thought of as somehow inherent in the technological structure of the economy, and thus unavoidable. Moderate gradualists (e.g. Nuti and Portes, 1993) are more consistent in this respect.
8. One must leave out of account, of course, those countries which have undergone civil or foreign war, such as Armenia, Azerbaijan, Georgia, and Tadjikistan. Portes himself admits that Hungary does not fit his scheme: the similar level of output fall in that country requires us to 'go back to country specificities'! The Hungarians did *other* things wrong: 'the self inflicted wave of bankruptcies and the debt service burden . . .'. What an interesting coincidence.
9. An important exception is the stress Portes (1993) lays on the collapse of trade between the countries of the Council for Mutual Economic Assistance (CMEA). However, he quite mistakenly claims that the dangers this entailed were underestimated by reformist governments.

I can personally testify to endless government meetings on the subject, at least in Poland. However, there was little that the governments of the former satellites could do (see Sect. 6). Trade was bound to collapse once the Soviets demanded payment in hard currency at world prices for their raw materials, but failed to create an international payments mechanism for their trade with former satellites and republics.

Indeed, foreign trade seems to be altogether a rather unfortunate area for moderate gradualists. Thus Portes (1993) argues for 'a uniform (or possibly cascading) tariff at a significant level' which 'would give more time to adjust'. Indeed, here he is less sophisticated than other commentators who have called for degressive tariffs, which would be automatically reduced over time. Yet on the previous page he claims that excessive devaluation of the currency in Poland and Czecho-Slovakia was a serious policy error, apparently unaware that digressive tariffs and undervaluation at a fixed exchange rate are largely equivalent (with the difference that devaluation stimulates exports as well as providing temporary protection to import substitutes). Even more surprising, while excessive devaluation is blamed (correctly) for the 'post-stabilization inflation' in Poland, the mechanism through which this occurs is supposedly that the devaluation enabled domestic firms to exercise their monopoly power in the traded goods sector—as if perfectly competitive producers of traded goods would not have raised their prices to world levels!

10. Examples are: the socialization (or alternatively the forgiveness) of all debt (Begg and Portes, 1992; Calvo and Frenkel, 1991); a generalized employment subsidy (Akerlof et al., 1991); 100 per cent reserve banking (McKinnon, 1991; Rostowski, Chapter 12).

11. I would include Murrell (1992), Naishul (1994), and Pejovich (1994) in this group.

12. Usually to be done by the state itself.

13. However, the right to use foreign currency, which Naishul (1994) and Rostowski (Ch. 2 and 10) favour, would limit the state's ability to use the printing press to finance such acquired rights.

14. Portes (1994) is therefore right to speak of '. . . advisers who believed in the endemic macroeconomic disequilibrium of socialist economies . . .', though he should add the words: 'under conditions of free prices and, initially, zero unemployment'.

15. This is perfectly consistent with the operation of the demand side mechanism resulting from the unwinding of forced substitution described above.

16. Most of those who hold this view would exclude the former GDR from this statement.

17. One could have the more complicated case in which prices in manufacturing are fixed, so that there is excess demand in this sector as well. In this case, the excess demand in services is assumed to be larger

and 'primary', in the sense that it is this demand which spills over and causes excess demand in manufacturing.

18. Such a failure to measure the growth of the service sector may occur because under communism the statistical service was not oriented to measuring consumer services for ideological reasons (they were considered to be non-productive), or because much of the service sector involves 'grey' activity due to tax evasion. In our example, before price liberalization there are no 'visible queues' for goods, but only 'invisible queues' for services (e.g. cars which remain unrepaired for a very long time). Thus no account is taken of the deadweight loss resulting from the resources which go into queuing, and which are analyzed by Berg and Sachs (1992).

19. See Bruno and Sachs (1985) on the effects of failing to adjust to negative external supply shocks and of trying to offset them through an expansion of demand.

20. Exogenous to the economic system, though not to the transformation process as a whole.

21. In the last case *vis-à-vis* Serbia.

22. If supplies to FSU states had been maintained at their 1990 level of 163mt, then either exports would have had to have fallen from 156mt to nine million tonnes, or domestic consumption would have had to have fallen from 227mt to 80mt, or some combination of the two.

23. Russia's growing disinclination to supply oil without payment lies behind Ukraine's new-found enthusiasm for reform in the autumn of 1994.

24. Since output increased after stabilization and long before sanctions against Serbia-Montenegro were relaxed, it is legitimate to conclude that the fall in output was partly due to the hyperinflation itself.

25. Let us assume that the domestic elasticities of supply and demand for importables and exportables are such that devaluation leads to an increase in the supply of import substitutes which is equal to the fall in the demand for exportables, while the balance of trade improves by the sum of these two changes. Total real expenditure on tradeables remains constant, while nominal expenditure on tradeables increases, since their prices rise due to the devaluation. If the nominal domestic money supply remains constant and the velocity of circulation does not increase, then demand for non-tradeables must fall.

26. The first in the context of the introduction of the new national currency in Latvia, and the second more generally for the region as a whole.

PART ONE

Crisis and
Stabilization in
Central Europe

Introduction
to Part One

Chapter 2 was written at a time when it was generally assumed that communist parties would continue to govern, however weakened, in Eastern Europe and the Soviet Union for some time to come. The aim was to show that macroeconomics made the reformist communist goal of 'full employment market socialism' unattainable. This goal was, incidentally, shared by Solidarity, the only powerful anti-communist opposition movement in the region at the time of writing.[1]

This explains the quite limited nature of the proposals made regarding anti-inflationary policies, foreign trade liberalization, and privatization. I believed stabilization of national currencies to be unattainable by the weak and illegitimate communist governments of the region, so that the best way to provide emerging markets in the East with a stable currency was thought to be dollarization. I expected current account convertibility to remain unattainable, and foreign trade liberalization to consist mainly of free access to the world market for private sector exporters and for importers having access to foreign currency (in what were expected to be highly dollarized economies). The sale of state enterprises was excluded as politically unfeasible, with the expansion of private business coming solely from private sector development.[2]

However, the essential dilemma regarding the sequencing of reforms emerges clearly from the chapter: to what extent should policies be directed first at making the economy more flexible, so as to reduce the costs of stabilization? In Chapter 2 this is formulated as the question of how to sequence supply side measures, aimed at reducing the NAIRU, and demand side measures aimed at reducing inflation. This is the question which lies at the heart of what was to become the debate between 'shock therapists' and 'gradualists', with the gradual-

ists tending to stress the high costs of stabilization in an unreformed economy in which a number of markets function imperfectly or not at all, while the shock therapists have stressed the costs of allowing very high inflation to persist.

The argument for stabilizing first is put clearly: the vested interests which lose as a result of the supply side policies are the very producer groups whose power is enhanced by high levels of demand. Stabilization thus not only halts inflation but, by creating excess supply, it makes it easier to impose the structural changes which are required. Obviously, those measures which can be taken before or simultaneously with stabilization should be, but the idea of a 'shock' stabilization/liberalization package of the kind which was implemented in Poland only nine months after Chapter 2 was written was quite foreign to economists specializing in the area at the time (April 1989).[3]

At the core of Chapter 2 lies a simple expectations-augmented Phillips curve model of the macroeconomy: if, in a market economy, actual unemployment is below the 'natural' or non-accelerating inflation rate of unemployment (the so-called NAIRU) then inflation will accelerate (Fig. 2). Since all communist economies—with the exception of China and Yugoslavia—had zero unemployment (the 'communist economy rate of unemployment' or CERU), their economies were bound to face explosive inflation once prices and wages were freed. Furthermore, as a result of the distortions in the allocation of resources which result from high inflation, inflation would be more costly in real (employment and output) terms the more marketized the economy had become. Marketizing reforms could only be successful, therefore, if they were accompanied by stabilization, and given the pervasiveness of rigidities and distortions in the early transition, this was likely to require very high rates of unemployment.

From today's perspective, the most striking features of Chapter 2 are its extreme pessimism as regards the levels of unemployment which I expected to accompany stabilization, and my excessive caution as regards the amount and speed of the economic changes which were thought possible. In the countries which have succeeded in stabilizing (i.e. in which inflation is on a downward trend), unemployment in no case exceeds 17 per cent

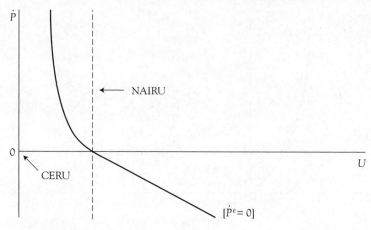

Figure 2   *The Phillips Curve*

of the labour force, as compared with the 25–40 per cent anticipated in Chaper 2, and with the 22 per cent currently (1994) in
Spain. In some countries which have stabilized successfully, the
level of unemployment is well below 5 per cent (e.g. the Czech
Republic, Estonia and Latvia). At the same time, practically no
mention was made in Chapter 2 of what has turned out to be a
universal consequence of the post-communist economic
changes: massive falls in statistically measured industrial output
and GDP.

Some of the reasons why unemployment might not need to
exceed the NAIRU during stabilization are discussed in Chapter
3 (Section 6).[4] Nevertheless, the question remains as to why the
actual level of unemployment turned out to be so much lower
than the anticipated NAIRU? There seem to be two main reasons. First, even if in the medium term inflation is independent
of the level of unemployment (i.e. the Phillips curve is vertical at
the NAIRU), in the short term inflation may depend not so
much upon the level of unemployment as on the rate of change
of that level, as it is this variable which may determine employees' perception of the likelihood of their becoming unemployed
themselves (Figure 3). The second explanation is that far more
was done much faster in making the supply side of the economy

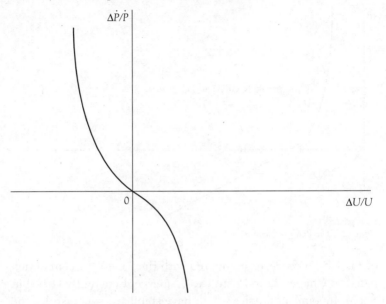

Figure 3   *The effect of changes in unemployment on changes in inflation*

more flexible, and thus reducing the NAIRU, than I thought was possible at the time Chapter 2 was written.

One mechanism which links the fall in output with the Phillips curve approach is the property rights structure of state owned enterprises (SOEs) in most PCEs. Given the absence of owners who are both interested and capable of maximizing profits, the available revenue from reduced sales after stabilization will tend to be shared among existing employees. This will reduce unemployment for any given level of real aggregate demand.[5] However, whatever the property rights arrangements, in order to achieve any given reduction in the rate of inflation, the level (or rate of increase) of unemployment must be the same, i.e. it must be such that employees fear that by attempting to achieve a higher level (or rate of increase) of nominal wages they run an unacceptable risk of becoming unemployed themselves. If many firms are under strong employee influence, then a given rate (or reduction in the rate) of inflation will require a greater reduction in real aggregate demand below CERU, and

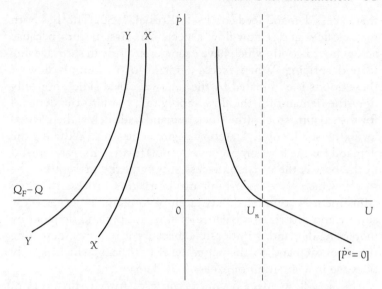

Figure 4   *Impact of property rights on output with a given Phillips curve*

will therefore entail a higher drop in output.[6] Fig. 4 shows this result, with the fall in output in the left-hand half of the diagram $(Q_F - Q)$ given by the line XX under private property and by YY under unclear property rights or labour management.

Outside the Phillips curve framework, output declines were caused by a number of mechanisms which ensure that if an economy starts off from a situation of excess demand for certain important categories of assets, then eliminating this state of affairs is bound to lead to a period of overshooting in the direction of excess supply. A well-known example of such a mechanism is the increase in the demand for the domestic currency and the fall in demand for goods which occurs on stabilization (Chapter 3). If the authorities try to soften the ensuing recession excessively by an over generous increase in the money stock, then inflationary expectations can revive reducing the demand for money, and reigniting the inflation. The line between a costless and a failed stabilization can be a very thin one.

A mechanism which is specific to communist economies is

that excess demand feeds on itself (Kornai, 1980). This has both a stock-flow and a flow-flow aspect. The first occurs because actors hoard goods which have been persistently in shortage due to underpricing. When excess demand for the supply flow of these goods is eliminated by the removal of subsidies, not only does the demand for the flow supply fall, but also the demand for the existing stocks (the stock demand) falls below their actual level (the stock supply). Actors begin to de-stock, reducing the demand for the flow supply (and output) further. Excess demand in the past is the cause of excess supply in the present via the stocks which have been built up. Until this process of stock adjustment is completed, any attempt to eliminate excess flow supply and return to a balance of flow supply and demand by increasing demand is impossible, because it requires increasing the stock demand to the actual level of stocks, which is only possible in a situation of excess flow demand.

The flow-flow effect occurs because of forced substitution. Flow demand for underpriced good A is displaced onto good B. The elimination of excess flow demand for A as a result of price liberalization leads to a fall in flow demand for B. The relative price of B falls so that a part of B producing capacity becomes unprofitable. Flow demand for B can only be increased to equal flow supply—given existing capacity in industry B—if excess flow demand for A were re-established (Chapter 1, Fig. 1).

The first draft of Chapter 3 was written during August–September of 1989.[7] Because there was now a non-communist government in Poland, which benefited from a high degree of legitimacy which allowed it to stabilize the macroeconomy, Chapter 3 was far more concerned than Chapter 2 had been with discussing the relative advantages of different techniques of stabilization. The chapter argued in favour of a shock stabilization, on the grounds that this would reduce the costs in terms of unemployment: a sudden regime change leads to a change in expectations (and a downward shift in the short-run Phillips curve), so that unemployment need not exceed the NAIRU. Nevertheless, the idea that stabilization can be cost-

less in employment terms in Eastern Europe was rejected, on the grounds that prior to reform these economies had zero unemployment, and that therefore actual unemployment was unsustainably well *below* the NAIRU.

In order to achieve such a sudden shift to a non-inflationary regime, the chapter argued for a strong pre-commitment by the authorities to both balanced budgets and an irrevocably fixed exchange rate. It was suggested that the best way of achieving this was through writing these commitments into the constitution. With the advent of new non-communist governments in at least some of the countries of the region, new constitutions were required, and I viewed this as an opportunity to create a stable framework for making macroeconomic policy during the transition. In fact, such a 'constitutional' approach has only been adopted in Estonia—and only very partially at that. Estonia has written the full backing of its high-powered money with international reserves into its Central Bank Law in 1992, following the example of Argentina in 1991 (see Chapter 11). The only countries which have succeeded in both maintaining budget balance (at least on paper) and avoiding devaluation from the beginning of the transition until 1996 were Czecho-Slovakia and its successor the Czech Republic (see Chapter 12), Estonia, and Latvia.[8]

The question of whether stock stabilizations should be orthodox or heterodox is also discussed in Chapter 3. The latter are distinguished by the use of price and wage controls as well as the tight monetary and fiscal policy which are part of orthodox stabilizations. It is because of the incompatibility of price and wage controls with marketization that I expressed a definite preference for orthodox stabilizations—particularly in the context of PCEs. Combining wage controls with freeing prices, which has been adopted in many PCEs, was discussed.[9] This hybrid of the orthodox and heterodox approaches was justified on the grounds that there are no real owners in the state sector who would try to resist wage pressures (for this reason I considered that such controls should be limited to SOEs). This is a justification which I now consider dubious (see Chapter 6). However, I still believe that wage controls may be useful as a

form of pre-commitment by government, in much the same way as a fixed exchange rate regime.

In Chapter 3 fixed exchange rates are considered as compatible with orthodoxy. There is, of course, an important difference between fixing exchange rates temporarily, so as to reduce the velocity of circulation in the initial months of a stabilization programme, which is the way fixed exchange rates have been used in heterodox programmes, and fixing the parity of the currency permanently, as happened when in the 1920s Austria, Germany, Hungary, and Poland returned to the gold standard, and as I advocate in the paper. It is pointed out, however, that if the initial exchange rate results in a large real undervaluation of the domestic currency, then inflation will take place after the beginning of the stabilization, as domestic prices approach world prices, even if the budget is balanced and there is tight control of domestic sources of money creation. The fear expressed in Chapter 3 is that this 'world price pull inflation' will cause a persistence of inflationary expectations such that inflation revives, and the fixed exchange rate itself may then become unsustainable. The question of how to ensure that the exchange rate which is chosen at the beginning of the stabilization can be maintained indefinitely is one which is returned to in Chapters 9 and 11.

Chapter 4 discusses the extreme case of the Serbo-Montenegran hyperinflation of 1993–4. This was probably the second fastest in history, far exceeding the German hyperinflation of 1923. It provided a rare opportunity to observe directly the microeconomic effects (and costs) of hyperinflation. The Serbo-Montenegran episode also shows clearly how inflationary financing is not a sustainable policy, due to the Tanzi-Olivera effect on real tax revenues and of the output destroying action of the inflation itself. Finally, the episode shows that when real money balances have shrunk to minuscule levels due to very high inflation tax, stabilization based on introducing convertibility at a fixed exchange rate is very effective in the short term, even in the complete absence of expectations that the state budget will be balanced. This casts serious doubt

on the rational expectations approach to stabilization (e.g. Sargent 1986*a*).

The question of whether an output reducing credit crunch is avoidable in post-communist stabilizations is discussed in Chapter 5. It is suggested that quite far-reaching institutional changes, and not merely policy measures, would be needed if the impact of such credit crunches was to be sharply reduced. Chapter 6 reviews the arguments for and against wage controls during stabilization in PCEs, an issue which is first considered in Chapters 2 and 3. It concludes that most arguments in favour of such policies are weak, but that they may be useful as a way for governments to pre-commit to stabilization, and that they seem to have performed this role in Poland in 1990–1.

NOTES

1. An anecdote underlines the political sensitivity of the subject. When in July 1989 a summary of Chapter 2 appeared in the Solidarity weekly 'Solidarność', a passage in which I mentioned the *possibility* that expansion in private sector employment would be so considerable that no unemployment would result was changed—without my agreement—so as to turn that eventuality into a *probability*. This was the decision of the Editor-in Chief himself, Tadeusz Mazowiecki, who was to become the first post-war non-communist Prime Minister of Poland within six weeks, and whose government it was which was to institute the first 'shock therapy' programme in the region.

2. This has in fact proved the main source of privatization of the economy after the fall of communism in Poland and probably Hungary, although not in Russia, the Czech Republic, Eastern Germany and Lithuania.

3. As a result, I laid insufficient stress on currency convertibility and trade liberalization as ways of eliminating monopoly power in the traded goods sector almost at one stroke.

4. Ch. 3 was written in August–September 1989, i.e. before the path-breaking Polish 'big bang' stabilization/liberalization programme. The possible role of a high level of policy credibility in reducing the amount of unemployment which accompanies stabilization is mentioned in Ch. 2 [Sect. 4]. Little stress was laid on this, however, as the communist governments then in power were not thought capable of generating such credibility.

5. Indeed, it is interesting that SOEs have succeeded in sacking large numbers of workers in spite of their property rights structure, even

in those countries (such as Poland) where workers councils and trade unions are most powerful.
6. I am grateful to Richard Layard for this point.
7. The paper was sent as a kind of overview of available policies to Leszek Balcerowicz, the Deputy Prime Minister of Poland in the first non-communist government in the region, who had just been put in charge of that country's economy. It was revised somewhat in early 1990, before its publication, already after the beginning of Poland's shock stabilization/liberalization programme.
8. Slovakia and in 1992 in the FSU.
9. In the corrections to the paper introduced in 1990.

2

Market Socialism is Not Enough: Inflation *vs.* Unemployment in Reforming Communist Economies

1. Introduction

All the market socialist economies are facing high or hyperinflation. Rates of inflation for 1988 were 17 per cent for Hungary and 20 per cent for China, 60 per cent for Poland and 195 per cent for Yugoslavia. The implications for the whole of Eastern Europe and the Soviet Union are profound. Poor East European economic performance is widely seen as being due to the inefficiency of the traditional centrally administered economic system, which manifests itself in its inability to generate intensive as opposed to extensive growth or produce exports that would be competitive on world markets (particularly important given the high debt levels of many East European countries), and the high level of material intensity which the system exhibits. Market socialism is often seen as a way of increasing efficiency. If, as appears to be the case, full employment market socialism is an intrinsically inflationary system, and if inflation is destructive of economic efficiency (and indeed political stability) under market socialism, then the introduction of market socialist reforms is an insufficient solution to the economic problems of communist countries. The question then arises: what other, or additional, measures are needed to cure these countries' economic ailments? Some tentative proposals are discussed at the end of this chapter.

Those who argue that inflation has few negative effects in reformed communist economies claim that in these countries productive decisions and the allocation of resources are still

overwhelmingly determined by administrative rather than market mechanisms. Therefore inflation, which is merely a market phenomenon, has little effect on production or investment. This argument has to be taken seriously. Certainly, as far as Hungary and Poland are concerned, we have considerable evidence that outside consumer goods markets most resources are allocated administratively (Kornai, 1986; Rostowski and Auerbach, 1986; Gomulka and Rostowski, 1984). One can certainly imagine an economy in which production is so tightly 'informally centrally administered' that money in the intra-industry sector, though formally active, is in fact passive (as it is formally in the traditional Soviet-type economy). Only in the consumer goods sector and in the labour market would money be truly active. In such an economy inflation would, as a result of a lack of synchronization of wage and price changes, merely add an additional element of unpredictability to the shifting pattern of shortages which STEs experience. In such a case, inflation would pose little threat to the realisation of the efficiency gains which it is hoped the introduction of market socialism would generate, simply because market socialism had not really been introduced.

This argument is largely irrelevant. Even if inflation has few real effects in the reformed socialist economies because market socialism has not in fact been introduced, the problem of how to deal with inflation once market socialism was introduced still remains (unless it were claimed that the introduction of market socialism by itself somehow abolished inflationary pressures). Secondly, those who support the view that market socialism has not in fact been introduced in these countries often also lay stress on the growth of the private sector as the source of much of the economic improvement that has taken place. There can be little doubt that in the absence of an alternative, foreign, currency (of which more below), inflation must harm the efficiency of the private sector. Thirdly, the political effects of inflation are clearly very real in the countries concerned. Because it proceeds unevenly, rapid inflation causes people acute anxiety with regard to their absolute and relative standard of living, undermining the legitimacy of government, which is

perceived as having failed in one of its primary duties. Fourthly, there is evidence that inflation does indeed have real economic effects in all the countries concerned. Thus the role of the exchange rate in stimulating Polish exports to hard currency markets is admitted even by sceptical observers such as Gorynia and Otta.[1] One of the main problems they point to is that while inflation proceeds comparatively smoothly, devaluation occurs in discrete jumps, upsetting enterprises' ability to calculate costs and profits in the absence of forward currency markets. That a similar mechanism operates in China is indicated by General Secretary Zhao's proposal in the summer of 1988 to devalue the Renmibi by 50 per cent, while increasing wages by only 20 per cent, in a policy package aimed at stimulating exports.[2] As regards Hungary, (Kornai, 1986), in an overview which is generally very sceptical about the importance of market forces in that country, states that 'the well known dynamic process of the price-cost-wage spiral . . . can do much harm to the core of decentralisation; to financial discipline and rational calculation based on prices and profits. Inefficiencies can be comfortably covered up by passing over cost increases to the buyer'. Finally, Kornai points out that inflation hampers the introduction of marketizing reforms. First, it creates a situation in which marketization and inflation are linked in the public mind and, more insidiously, by the very fact that it disrupts rational calculation, it allows bureaucrats to claim that markets cause evident misallocations of resources.

2. Causes of Inflation under Market Socialism

Although the Western literature regarding inflation under 'managerial' (i.e. non-Yugoslav) market socialism is small, the debate regarding the causes of inflation in capitalist market economies can be, with certain adjustments, applied to market socialism. Explanations of inflation under market socialism can be grouped in the following main 'families': the historical; the mainstream or 'accelerationist'; and the cost-push. Almost all of what follows concerns the countries of 'managerial' market socialism: China, Hungary, and Poland (if economic *perestroika*

is actually implemented, the USSR will also belong to this group). Yugoslavia is referred to only when points arising from the discussion also seem relevant to that country. There is a very large literature on the causes of inflation both in labour managed economies in general, and in Yugoslavia in particular. It is not my purpose here to enter into that debate.

We call 'historical' those explanations which stress transient phenomena as the causes of inflation, and view the full employment market socialist system itself as not being intrinsically inflationary. To this family belongs the argument (Kornai, 1986) that it is the policy of consumer price increases pursued by the Hungarian authorities with the aim of reducing consumption to improve the balance of payments in the 1980s which is responsible for the increase in inflation in that period. To this family also would belong the view that inflation under market socialism is a hangover from the previous (Soviet-type) economic system. The idea is that when the Soviet-type system, with its high level of excess demand on consumer goods markets, is liberalized (particularly with regard to wage and price-setting autonomy for enterprises), there is bound to be a period of price adjustment, which in the real world will not be instantaneous. There is, however, an important difference between the two 'historical' explanations given above: the first is 'country-specific', while the second will apply to all economies moving from a Soviet-type system to market socialism. Both, however, reject that view that 'full employment managerial market socialism' as it exists at present is intrinsically inflationary.

We shall not discuss the policy implications of country-specific historical explanations, as that would require analysis of the economic policy and institutions of each country. Also, the generalized nature of high inflation under managerial market socialism (although we have only three cases, we do have a 100 per cent correlation!) provides at least a prima facie case for an explanation common to all. The predictions of the 'hangover' hypothesis are clear: inflation should die out as market clearing prices spread through the economy after the introduction of market socialism. The policy implications are that nothing need be done, except to take care that inflation does not

become institutionalized through a wage-price-cost spiral (for instance through indexation, either official or informal). In fact, inflation has tended to increase, rather than decrease, over time in all the market socialist countries. The only exception is Poland, where, following 100 per cent inflation in the first year after the reformed system was introduced, prices having adjusted after a period of extreme repressed inflation (Nuti, 1985), there was declining inflation for the subsequent three years. Since 1985, however, inflation has increased steadily from a low of 15 per cent, and reached 60 per cent in 1988. The historical explanations of which we are aware are therefore found to be unsatisfactory either because they are insufficiently general, or because they are empirically wrong.

The 'accelerationist' explanation maintains that each market economy has a natural or 'non-accelerating inflation rate of unemployment' (NAIRU). Any attempt to bring the actual rate of unemployment below this natural rate leads to accelerating inflation. If the actual rate is at the natural rate, inflation will be stable, either at a positive or zero rate (Friedman, 1981). The natural rate itself is determined by structural factors, such as the degree of trade union power, redundancy and unemployment benefits, the flexibility of housing or training markets, and so on. Since unemployment is effectively zero in all three countries, the actual rate must be below the natural rate (which in all existing capitalist market economies is positive and between about 2 per cent and 10 per cent in advanced countries). Accelerating inflation is thus the result to be expected. Looking at the inflationary mechanism at the microeconomic level, the effective absence of bankruptcy means that workers are never in danger of pricing themselves out of their jobs. Wage increases are automatically validated by government either through the direct provision of subsidies to loss-making enterprises (often in the form of cheap credit which they are not expected to repay), or through the relaxation of price controls on an enterprise's output. The maintenance of a generalized regime of excess demand (i.e., shortage on most goods and factor markets), means that such a relaxation of price controls is equivalent to an increase in the liquidity of the enterprise

concerned. Whether the maintenance of generalized excess demand results mainly from monetary or fiscal policy, and indeed whether the two kinds of policy can be meaningfully separated under the particular institutions of market socialism, is a secondary question.

The cost-push explanation lays stress on very similar factors (monopoly, trade union power, etc.). The difference is that whereas in the accelerationist model they determine the natural rate of unemployment, in cost-push explanations they are seen as structural factors that facilitate the exertion of cost-push pressure on prices (Wiles, 1973*a*). As a result, the prescriptions implicit in the two approaches differ significantly. Cost-push theorists, though they would support the weakening of anti-competitive elements in the economy, tend to believe that there are severe limits to such competition encouraging policies, and that political solutions to the problem of inflation are necessary and possible. Thus a prices and incomes policy (whether tax-based, compulsory or voluntary) introduced either by consensus or by a strong government could halt, or at least stabilize, inflation at a lower cost in terms of unemployment than would a purely demand-contractionary policy (be it monetary, fiscal, or a combination of both).

From a cost-push perspective, therefore, political factors, such as the lack of legitimacy of governments, or their weakness, become relevant economic variables. There is thus a certain kinship between the cost-push and the country-specific historical explanations. It could be argued by supporters of the cost-push theory that there is no necessary relationship between weak and/or illegitimate government and market socialism. A strong or legitimate government in a market socialist country might be able to avoid high inflation, and near to full employment market socialism would then not be inevitably inflationary.

Historically, however, market socialism has led to inflation, and inflation has caused a weakening of government in market socialist economies. Thus although the Polish government was politically weak at the time of the introduction of market socialism in 1982, and market socialist reforms were in part

an attempt by that government to increase its authority by improving economic performance and creating political space into which it could co-opt certain elements of the opposition, the acceleration of inflation from 1985 has again weakened that government. In the Yugoslav, Hungarian, and (most recently) Chinese cases, on the other hand, government weakness developed after the introduction of market socialism (and more or less in line with the acceleration of inflation). Thus the historical record leads one to conclude that government authority cannot be used to stop cost-push inflation once it begins because inflation itself undermines government authority.

Whether or not market socialism caused government weakness (via inflation), it is a historical fact, and one which anti-inflationary policy has to take into account, that in Hungary, Poland, Yugoslavia, and even China we have fairly weak, and largely illegitimate, governments. The prospects for the taming of inflation through an exertion of government authority or the creation of consensus are therefore bleak. The overthrow of existing regimes and their replacement by legitimate governments is also unlikely. The conditions for a political solution to cost-push inflation, even if such a thing existed in principle, do not seem to be present in practice in the market socialist countries.

Moreover, market socialism and prices and incomes policies are incompatible in principle. The way in which the economic bureaucracy uses its powers over price and wage formation to induce enterprises to execute its wishes rather than to follow the dictates of the market is very well documented (Kornai, 1986; Gomulka and Rostowski, 1984). The same incompatibility between a properly functioning market economy and bureaucratically administered prices holds in capitalist market economies. But under capitalism the prices and incomes bureaucracy starts out small, and the damage it can do is initially also small. Market socialist countries inherit huge bureaucracies from their Soviet-type past, and the damage these can do is correspondingly great.

3. *The Sequence of Supply and Demand Side Policies*

Both accelerationists and believers in cost-push would agree that rigidities of the kind described in the previous section should be removed. Believers in cost-push consider that this would in itself significantly reduce inflationary pressures. Such pressures as remained could be contained by some form of prices and incomes policy. Accelerationists, while believing that inflation is always and everywhere a demand-driven phenomenon, would agree that the removal of rigidities would reduce the cost in terms of unemployment of abolishing inflation. The remaining policy question, therefore, is the matter of sequence: should inflation be controlled first (be it through monetary, fiscal, or incomes policy), with microeconomic rigidities coming second; should it be the other way round; or should both sets of problems be tackled simultaneously? Here we are once again entering upon poorly researched territory, where political instinct seems as important as economic analysis. Indeed, it may be that the answer depends in large measure on the particular political circumstances of the country concerned.

Most Western government and IMF practice indicates a belief that inflation must be tackled first. The reasoning seems to be that the high levels of demand which accompany inflation increase the strength of the supplier groups (trade unions, cartels, local authorities) which are the main vested interests opposed to the supply side measures needed to increase the flexibility and competitiveness of markets. It seems reasonable to suppose that the power of supplier groups is directly related to the level of aggregate demand, since the demand for their own products will be related, in most cases, to aggregate demand in a positive way. The higher the demand for a particular producer group's product, the greater the number of people affected by interruptions in the supply of that product (as a result of a strike, for instance), and the greater the social pressure (usually on the authorites) for that interruption to be terminated. Indeed, this may be why the cost-push solution to inflation of a prices and incomes policy has had comparatively

little success, as it often generates excess demand for the products of those very groups whose vested interests (in the form of anti-competitive practices) the government wishes to attack.

This does not mean that a government which was particularly strong could not proceed in a different way, and introduce competition and flexibility-enhancing measures as the first part of its anti-inflationary policy. Strength can come from extremely wide support for the economic policies of the government or from the ability to repress opposition successfully. Power (or consensus) could be used to implement measures aimed at reducing the cost in terms of unemployment of the demand-contractionary policies directed against inflation, either previous to or simultaneously with such policies. The consensus approach to anti-inflationary and structural adjustment policies has been fairly successful in a number of small democratic West European countries such as Austria and Sweden. In principle, a strong dictatorship should be able to proceed in the same way. However, this proposal would seem to suffer from the same weakness as the political approach to cost-push inflationary pressures discussed in the previous section: the regimes in the countries we are discussing are not sufficiently strong or legitimate to pursue such a policy successfully, with the possible exception of the Chinese. A straightforward attack on producers' vested interests is therefore likely to be impossible.

4. The Natural Rate of Unemployment in Market Socialist Economies

Nevertheless, the question of whether it is possible to introduce supply side measures which would mitigate the impact of demand-contractionary policies on unemployment is crucial for two reasons: first, the populations of these countries are likely to be highly sensitive politically to mass unemployment, as they have had little or no experience of it for over three decades;[3] secondly the rate of unemployment required to bring inflation under control in these countries is likely to be much higher than it was in Western Europe. Econometric estimates of

natural rates of unemployment confirm that those economies which are comparatively flexible have low natural rates compared to those with rigid labour and other markets. Thus, according to OECD estimates (Flanagan, 1987), during 1983–7 the natural rate of unemployment for Japan was 2.5 per cent, for the three large continental West European countries and the United States it was 6.3 per cent (unweighted average), and for the United Kingdom in 1981–3 it was 9.4 per cent. Since the market socialist countries are evidently off their long-run Phillips curves (with close to zero open unemployment), we can have no idea of their natural rates of unemployment. Nevertheless, casual empiricism would suggest that the number and importance of rigidities is at least several times as great as in the United Kingdom. If we assume that natural rates are roughly proportional to rigidities, then natural rates of unemployment of 20–30 per cent do not seem unreasonable. Such a range finds some support from Chinese studies, which place rural under-employment at 30–40 per cent of the labour force and industrial under-employment at one third (Reynolds, 1987), and Mencinger's (1983) study of Yugoslavia, which gives under-employment of 19 per cent in 1982, on top of open unemployment of 10 per cent. It is unclear whether even strong dictatorships could survive unemployment rates of 20–30 per cent in countries which have little experience of unemployment, and three of the regimes are far from strong.

What is more, according to the accelerationist view, the natural rate of unemployment is only sufficient to achieve stabilization of inflation, and even higher levels of unemployment are needed if inflation is to be reduced. Furthermore, it is far from certain whether inflation can be stabilized at rates of 15–20 per cent (the current rates in China and Hungary), let alone at rates of 60–195 per cent (Poland and Yugoslavia). A case could be made that inflation has to be fairly low, say below 5 per cent (to judge by the practice of most OECD countries), if its tendency to accelerate is to be halted. The argument runs as follows: higher rates of inflation are more variable in absolute terms (if not in proportion to their longer-term averages), which causes them to be more destructive of businesses and indivi-

duals' ability to make rational calculations. This development increases the natural rate of unemployment, so that if inflation was initially stable it accelerates over time (Friedman, 1978). The experience of most Western countries has been that the actual rate of unemployment must temporarily exceed the natural rate (as estimated in the OECD studies described above) by about one third for inflation to be reduced below 5 per cent (from initial inflation rates of 6–20 per cent). If natural rates of unemployment in market socialist countries are indeed 20–30 per cent, the actual rates of unemployment needed to tame inflation may be 25–40 per cent.

It has been claimed (Sargent, 1986b; Matthews and Minford, 1987) that if a government achieves a high degree of credibility for its determination (and ability!) to disinflate, the cost in terms of unemployment will be much lower, as actors adjust their inflationary expectations, and therefore behaviour, downwards so as to avoid the costs (losses for employers, unemployment for workers) of predicting the future incorrectly. On this argument, if governments in market capitalist countries had succeeded in convincing actors of their determination to disinflate earlier, the actors would not have had to find out the reality of that commitment the hard way, and bankruptcies and unemployment could have been far lower. If the governments of market socialist countries could achieve a high degree of credibility for their anti-inflationary policies, the cost in terms of unemployment could be considerably lower than the extremely high rates suggested above. The question is whether governments in these countries are likely to achieve a higher degree of credibility than did those in the West. Prima facie this seems unlikely, first because of the socialist ideology these governments are associated with, and secondly because the record of two (the Polish and Yugoslav) in permitting inflation is far worse than was that of Western governments in the 1970s, while that of the other two (the Hungarian and Chinese), is about as bad as that of the most inflationary governments in the OECD in the 1970s (the UK and Italy).

On the other hand, there is some Western evidence that, at least in countries in which labour markets are not very competitive,

such as most of Western Europe (but not the United States), natural rates of unemployment may increase as actual rates increase (Blanchard and Summers, 1988; Layard and Nickell, 1986). One of the explanations given for this 'outward drift' in the natural rate is that the unemployed lose skills and hope, reducing their own desire to work and that of employers to hire them. This suggests that initially somewhat lower levels of unemployment than is suggested above may be sufficient to stabilize inflation. Even so, the number of rigidities in the market socialist economies is so large, and the credibility of anti-inflationary policy is likely to be so low, that very high levels of unemployment will in any case be needed to stabilize inflation, even initially—they will simply be somewhat smaller than they would otherwise have been. In the longer term, moreover, natural rates of unemployment would increase in the market socialist economies, as they have in Western Europe, unless policies aimed at making the long-term unemployed more active in the labour market, through training schemes for instance, were implemented. It is vital, however, that such schemes should not undermine the credibility of the anti-inflationary commitment of the authorities. However, doubt is cast on Blanchard and Summers' argument by the most recent British experience.[4] Compared with 1979, when inflation as measured by the consumer expenditure deflator was 10 per cent and unemployment was 5 per cent, in the first quarter of 1989 inflation was 5.5 per cent and unemployment was 6.5 per cent. This evidence is compatible either with vertical or downward sloping long-run Phillips curves, but certainly not with a permanent outward drift in the natural rate of unemployment as a result of high actual unemployment during the Thatcher years. The British experience is particularly important because of the stress placed on it by Blanchard and Summers (1988) themselves.

Of course, we do not *know* what the shape of the long-run Phillips curve is in the market socialist countries, although this is extremely important for policy. If Phillips curves were downward sloping, allowing a reasonably long-term trade-off between inflation and unemployment, stabilization of infla-

tion—but still at very high rates—might be possible while keeping unemployment at socially (just) acceptable levels (say 15 per cent). The question of the shape of the long-run Phillips curve in these countries cannot be resolved however, because with unemployment close to zero, the economy has to be off the long-run Phillips curve, so that it is impossible to determine whether that curve is negatively or positively sloped, vertical, or even horizontal. Nevertheless, most Western studies of capitalist market economies suggest that long-run Phillips curves are positively sloped (inflation and unemployment rising together) or vertical (Cukierman, 1983). It is therefore up to those who believe that a stable long-term trade-off could exist in the market socialist countries to argue the case.

5. Conventional Supply and Demand Side Measures against Unemployment and Inflation

There is certainly no shortage of inflexibilities in the countries with which we are concerned. The first is the highly monopolized industrial structure inherited from the centralized administrative system (Kornai, 1986), although this is less the case in China, where the central economic administration's tendency to create giant enterprises could not overcome the vast size of the country. It has proved impossible to offset the high degree of monopolization through competition from imports. This is only partly because of debt problems. Even China, which has no debt problem, is not prepared to let its import pattern be determined by market forces (Srinivasan, 1987). More generally, the absence of bankruptcy and the prevalence of subsidy and excess demand mean that the intensity of competition is low, and exporters are not very successful on world markets. This in turn makes the authorities unwilling to allow unrestricted competition from imports within the country. The monopolistic structure of industry cannot be eroded because both entry and exit are bureaucratically controlled (Kornai, 1986, for Hungary). Control of entry makes it very hard for enterprises, state or private, which observe high profits in a particular sector to set up in competition. Control of exit, mainly via government

subsidies to well-established loss makers, means that the risk for a new entrant not approved by the bureaucracy is increased. Secondly, the geographical mobility of labour is low because of the very extensive restrictions in the housing market (see Rostowski, 1989*a*, for the situation in Poland).

The situation is more complex as regards skill mobility. In Hungary, labour supply responds rapidly to changes in differentials between enterprises (Kornai, 1986), and labour turnover is quite high, so one would expect skill changes in response to changing differentials also to be high. In general wage differentials are low, and this seems to be a result that the market itself generates, as a consequence of generalized excess demand (Winiecki, 1988). In that case low skill mobility would be a consequence rather than a cause of inflationary pressures. It would remain, however, an important way in which inflation could adversely affect the efficiency of the economy and the competitiveness of its exports. In China, of course, there is no free market among the core of permanent employees in state enterprises (Korzec, 1988).

The supply side measures required flow directly from these rigidities: the breaking up of large monopolistic enterprises and the creation of new enterprises to compete with the old; the introduction of a free international trade regime; the creation of a proper housing market based on owner occupation or market clearing rents; the creation of a labour market where it does not exist (China), and the acceptance of frictional unemployment where that does not exist (all three countries). This list is, of course, far from exhaustive. Some of these measures will be easier to introduce than others. Monopolistic cartels (such as the *zrzeszenia* in Poland) of enterprises that could in fact function independently can be broken up quite easily, as can the monopolistic system of material supply (*pośrednictwo obowiązkowe*, in Poland) where it persists. But some of the monopoly was 'built into' the technology of factories. When investment options were considered under the Soviet-type system there was a bias towards larger, integrated, technological solutions. Given the low rate of net capital formation in Poland and Hungary (2.5 per cent and 4 per cent respectively), there is little

possibility of creating new socialized enterprises which would compete with the giants. There is also serious difficulty in creating a free regime in international trade (which would include a floating exchange rate) until inflation is brought under control, as on top of everything else, enterprises would have to contend with a high volatility of costs and exchange rates in making economic calculations. As a result international competition probably cannot be used to increase the flexibility of the economy *previous* to demand-contractionary measures aimed against inflation.

However, a certain degree of trade liberalization would be both possible and desirable if it were introduced *simultaneously* with anti-inflationary policies. Various half-way houses to free trade are discussed below under the headings of privatization and 'dollarization'. The creation of a proper housing market is both desirable and possible, and (Rostowski, 1989a; Kornai, 1986) the first steps in this direction are occurring. So is the creation of a labour market in China (Korzec, 1988), and frictional unemployment has been accepted in China (Reynolds, 1987) and Hungary, where there is talk of there being 200,000 unemployed (4 per cent of the labour force) by 1990 (Rupnik, 1988). All the same, it seems unlikely that measures which aim at tackling the problem of rigidities on the supply side of the economy head-on can be introduced on a sufficient scale previous to the introduction of demand-contractionary policies.

On the demand side, the most important task facing governments is the re-establishment of control over the creation of money. This is made difficult by the fact that the introduction of market socialism requires the creation of a commercial and investment banking system which will facilitate the flow of funds from cash-rich enterprises and individuals to investment-opportunity-rich ones. Market socialism is incompatible with a monopoly of credit, because there would then be only one view of the profitability of an undertaking—effectively a central planning of capital flows, leading to central planning of all investment not financed through ploughback. In practice, banking decentralization has taken the form of a hiving-off of commercial and investments banks by the central bank, which

under the traditional Soviet-type system is a monobank. The central banks in Yugoslavia and China have as yet failed to develop the skills required to control the overall creation of credit without controlling its allocation at the micro level (Chow, 1987; Gedeon, 1987). In Hungary it is still too early to evaluate the operation of the new banking system, which was introduced only in 1986. In Poland a commercial banking system has not yet been established. Also, effective techniques for forecasting and controlling government expenditure have yet to be developed (Naughton, 1987, for the case of China), although this is likely to be easier. This is not to suggest that the problems of controlling inflation are *merely* technical, but even if inflation is always and everywhere a monetary phenomenon, then it remains true that the control of the money supply is always and everywhere a not insignificant technical problem.

6. Unconventional Measures

6.1. Privatization

Many of the institutional changes suggested in this section have already been introduced to some extent in one or other of the market socialist economies. These useful beginnings need to be extended rapidly if the supply side flexibility of these economies is to be increased. By privatization we mean, first, the removal of the disabilities which affect the private sector, effectively preventing entrepreneurs from undertaking a vast number of activities in these countries, and secondly, the introduction of stable regulations (e.g. tax legislation) for the private sector. We do not, in this first stage of privatization, consider the selling-off of socialized sector assets to the private sector to be politically feasible (although leasing of socialized factories to private entrepreneurs has happened on a significant scale in China, and is beginning in Poland).

Privatization is important if the flexibility of these economies is to be increased. Even in a profit-oriented market socialist enterprise the speed of response to changing market conditions is reduced by: (a) the monopolistic power such an enterprise

often has; (b) the unwillingness of the workforce, which is often highly organized in trade unions and self-management councils, to accept rapid change; (c) the knowledge of both management and workers that they are likely to be bailed out by government subsidies. Opening up almost all fields of economic activity to private entrepreneurs means effectively reducing barriers to entry, and therefore the degree of monopoly, because first, given similar regulations it is likely to take less time to set up a new private firm; secondly, as noted, private firms are likely to respond faster to changes in market conditions; and thirdly, a larger number of private than socialized firms are likely to be brought into existence to satisfy a given demand (it will usually be easier for a bureaucratic 'founding organ', a ministry or local authority, to create one large new enterprise than many small ones). The presence of opportunities for private sector activity in most branches of the economy will act as a buffer against unemployment. The private sector can absorb workers cast onto the labour market as a result of bankruptcies of inefficient and highly subsidized socialized firms. Greater scope for private economic activity will allow a larger reduction in subsidies for a given level of unemployment, and as a result less pressure on government expenditure and the budget deficit. The danger is that, as the importance of the private sector grows, the state in its desire to avoid unemployment will be as lax towards the private sector as it now is with respect to the socialized sector. There is some sign of this happening already in Poland, with lax criteria for the allocation of credit to the private sector and negative real interest rates. This is why 'dollarization' (the freedom for individuals and enterprises to use hard foreign currency) is so important, given the authorities' lack of will to control inflation.

Probably the least controversial measure is the privatization of the housing market so as to increase geographical mobility. In both Hungary (Daniel, 1985) and Poland (Rostowski, 1989*a*) there are owner-occupied sectors (both flats and villas), both in the countryside and the towns. These sectors are growing, if slowly. There is also a sector of largely illegal, sublet dwellings. In Poland a new law, operative from 1 January 1988, has made it

legal for private owners, of whom there are quite a few, to let dwellings (which have been vacated after that date, or are newly built) at market rents to tenants who will have no security of tenure.[5] Given the notorious inefficiency of the socialized building enterprises, and the fact that individuals cannot in practice contract with these firms to build private dwellings (and probably would not wish to if they could), the growth of the private construction sector is important. In Hungary 55.5 per cent of new dwellings were built privately in 1984, and in Poland the figure for 1986 was 31 per cent.

The sectors in which privatization is likely to have the greatest impact on the responsiveness of the economy to supply and demand conditions are services and manufacturing. Already in Hungary and Poland a large proportion of all repair services are provided by private entrepreneurs. The most significant change in recent years has been the growing share of the private sector in the provision of services to socialized enterprises (Rostowski, 1989a, for a description of this phenomenon in Poland). Since repairs of capital goods can be a substitute for the purchase of new ones from monopolistic suppliers, growing private provision of repair services increases the degree of competition in the economy. An increase in the private sector's still very small share in manufacturing, particularly of intermediate goods and components, would increase the flexibility of the economy directly. An important side effect would be the probable increase in the variety of intermediate goods produced. A larger share for the private sector might also increase the average intensity of labour, which is often said to be very low in the socialized sectors of these economies and to be quite high in the private sector.

The most important step, however, is the opening up of international trade, particularly outside CMEA, to the private sector. There are three reasons for this. First, the main barrier to the expansion of private sector firms is the control of many of their inputs by the socialized sector, a problem which also affects private agriculture. Free access to world markets would allow private entrepreneurs and farmers to circumvent this barrier. Second, with a skilled labour force, which is often

underworked, badly managed, and unsuitably organized into giant firms in the socialized sector, it seems probable that all three countries have an unexploited comparative advantage in some of the goods that small-scale, private, fairly labour-intensive, low- to medium-technology firms could produce, ranging from custom-made intermediate wood and plastic products to computer software. Of particular significance is the extremely low average wage in all three countries, even at the official rate of exchange. In Poland this is about $120 per month, with earnings in the most favoured sectors, such as coal mining, of about $300 per month (Kowalski, 1987). This is one-fifth to one-tenth of the levels in the industrialized West, and is competitive with middle-developed countries such as Mexico. Third, access to world markets by the private sector would be one of the ways in which 'dollarization' of the economy could proceed even more rapidly than it is doing at present in Poland and Yugoslavia (see below).

Finally, these economies should be made more open to foreign capital. This would combine the benefits of privatization and of access to the world market with a knowledge of Western ways of doing business. Although all three countries have joint venture legislation, only China has many thousands of joint ventures operating. Hungary has 180 joint ventures and Poland has over 600 private foreign companies, the so-called 'Polonia' firms. Although a radical liberalization of the regime governing foreign capital in these two countries has taken place in the past few years, it remains to be seen whether this will be sufficient to attract inward investment on a larger scale.

6.2. Dollarization

'Dollarization' means the substitution of hard (Western) currency for the domestic currency as the medium of exchange, and above all as the store of value, in a large part of the domestic economy, so that the country effectively adopts a dual currency system. The phenomenon is known from many countries suffering from hyperinflation, Argentina at present and Israel in the early 1980s being examples. Dollarization is, at present, only relevant to the two market socialist countries

which are affected by hyperinflation—Poland and Yugoslavia. China and Hungary have the possibility of bringing inflation and excess demand under control, and then moving on to convertibility of the domestic currency. Although the present author is not optimistic as to their likely success, dollarization is very much a cure of last resort. Dollarization is made easier in Poland and Yugoslavia by the fact that both countries have large numbers of their nationals working abroad. These send home remittances if they are permanently domiciled abroad, or return home with their accumulated hard currency earnings after periods of temporary, often illegal, work in the West.

The advantages of 'dollarization' are, first, that enterprises and individuals are provided with a currency (or currencies) whose value is more or less constant, thus reducing the degree of risk involved in economic calculations. In this way one of the main real costs of inflation, and one which probably increases the natural rate of unemployment, is avoided. Second, enter-prises (both socialized and private) are able to import what they need directly from the outside world, without having to go through the lengthy process of obtaining approval for hard currency from the central authorities (usually the central bank). Not only are such decisions taken slowly, but their quality is likely to be lower than that of decisions taken by the enterprises directly affected. The current system in Poland of hard-currency retention quotas and auctions is a halfway house to the full dollarization discussed here.[6]

By 1987 in Poland the majority of savings deposits and cash held by the population were in hard currency (valued at the black market rate of exchange) (Rostowski, 1989*b*). If inflation continues to gather pace, this proportion will increase further, as individuals and private businesses switch to currencies which devalue far less (if at all), for use as stores of value and even media of exchange for larger transactions (such as house, car or machinery purchases). Many private businesses have used hard currency as their unit of account for years. Current inflation and shortages (due to repressed inflation) have also led many socialized enterprises to insist on part payment in hard cur-

rency in both Poland and China, and such practices can be expected to expand if inflation accelerates further.

Acceleration of inflation can be expected to lead more actors to opt out of the inflationary economy in a multi-currency system. In such an economy, if exchange rates between currencies are flexible, then Gresham's law does not hold. Indeed, the better money (the one which is less inflation-ridden and whose purchasing power is less impaired by shortages of goods due to controls on prices which it is used to denominate) will displace the worse (Hayek, 1976). A government which finances a budget deficit caused mainly by widespread subsidies to loss-making enterprises by printing money will find that people paid in the domestic currency are facing more and more transactions which have to be carried out in hard currency, and that the free-market value of the domestic currency is falling. Inflation thus becomes self-limiting. As more and more of the non-subsidized activities switch into hard currency, the pool of profitable activities which take place in the domestic currency, and which are effectively taxed by the printing of money to pay for the subsidies to loss makers,[7] will constantly decline. As the 'inflation-tax base' declines, the 'inflation-tax rate' increases, speeding up the process by which profitable activities switch to the hard currency economy. In the end only loss-making activities would be financed in the domestic currency. Once this situation was reached the domestic currency would have literally no value.[8] The authorities could therefore be expected either to pursue a less expansionary monetary policy before this stage was reached, or to prevent certain profitable activities from switching to the hard currency economy by administrative decree, which would be a form of direct impost upon them. As long as most of the profitable part of the economy used hard currency, it would be fairly visible who was paying the inflation tax. This might lead to countervailing political pressure, or to the profitable domestic currency sector simply being smaller than it otherwise would have been.

Dollarization of necessity involves a cost: the 'seigniorage', which is paid to the suppliers of the hard currencies. For dollars and marks to circulate in Poland and Yugoslavia they have to be

obtained—ultimately from the central banks of the United States and West Germany. They can only be obtained in exchange for goods and services, yet they are then used for exchange, and as stores of value, by Polish or Yugoslav residents, so that they are not used to purchase US or West German goods. Naturally, a single dollar may circulate many times a year, thus facilitating transactions worth several times its value in that period. Nevertheless, the cost of seigniorage remains, whereas countries whose governments are capable of providing their citizens with a stable currency do not have to pay it. Seigniorage costs already represent a significant amount. In Poland probably some $7 billion are held by the population in hard currency bank accounts and cash (Rostowski, 1989b), an increase of some $5 billion since 1982, or $700 million per annum, which is between 0.5 per cent and 1 per cent of GNP per annum in purchasing power parity terms. However, in the absence of a successful anti-inflationary policy, the attempt to do without a second, 'hard' currency would lead to even higher costs due to the disruption of economic activity which would be caused by a hyperinflation from which there was no easy shelter.

7. Conclusion

The high and hyperinflation that market socialist economies are experiencing does matter economically and politically. Inflation is destructive of enterprises' and individuals' ability to make economic calculations, so that its disruptive effects become more severe as the economy is reformed in a market direction and relies less on administrative control. Western evidence, limited as its use inevitably is, suggests that whatever the proximate causes of inflation in the market socialist countries (e.g. government policy to raise consumer goods prices so as to reduce consumption for international payments reasons in Hungary), the underlying reason is the maintenance of the actual rate of unemployment far below the natural rate. Given the extremely high degree of rigidity in these economies the natural rate of unemployment could well lie in the range of

20–30 per cent. Since it is far from certain whether inflation can be stabilized at rates of 60–195 per cent (such as exist in Poland and Yugoslavia), the actual rates of unemployment required in these two countries to bring inflation under control could be considerably higher. Unemployment at these levels may be politically unacceptable in countries which have had very little experience of unemployment over the past four decades (excepting Yugoslavia).

Practice in most countries faced with high rates of inflation has been to address the problem of inflation first by the use of demand-contractionary policies (both monetary and fiscal), before trying to reduce the impact of such policies on unemployment through supply side policies. The reason for this may be that high demand increases the economic power of the producer interests which are most concerned to impede supply side reforms. In a situation in which the natural rate may be extremely high, however, it is important to consider what policies, if any, can be undertaken before the 'deflationary shock' is brought about, so as to reduce the cost of bringing inflation under control.

Conventional policies, such as increasing the degree of domestic and foreign competition and the degree of geographical labour mobility are limited in their scope, either because of historically inherited conditions (e.g. gigantism built into the technology of plants or the unavailability of investment resources because of current crisis conditions), or because they can of their very nature be taken only after inflation has been tamed to some extent (e.g. introducing a regime of free international trade). We therefore propose a number of unconventional measures, some of which are merely extensions of policies that have already been tried as an *ad hoc* attempt to increase the flexibility or rationality of the economy in one or other of the market socialist countries. The first of these is privatization, by which is meant the right of private entrepreneurs to compete on equal terms with socialized enterprises in a particular sphere of activity. This is the easiest way of increasing competition in domestic markets. To prevent the private sector from being constrained in its development by the

unavailability of domestic suppliers and the discrimination against private sector customers that socialized suppliers often practise, it is important that the private sector be allowed to trade freely on the world market, retaining almost all its hard currency earnings from exports.

'Dollarization', or the legalization of the use of hard currencies in domestic transactions, should be introduced in the two countries (Poland and Yugoslavia), which are already suffering from hyperinflation. The benefits of this are that individuals and enterprises (both private and socialized) have access to currencies that retain their value and which allow them to compare domestic costs with those on world markets. 'Dollarization' would also make inflation self-limiting to some degree. The higher the rate of inflation, the larger the sphere of activity that actors would choose to carry on in hard currency, and thus the less the impact of inflation on the real economy. This would be an accelerating process. As the number of activities affected by inflation declined, the 'inflation tax' on these activities for a given budget deficit would have to increase, inducing activities to switch even more rapidly to the hard currency economy.

The implications of this paper for countries which are just embarking on market socialist reforms, such as the USSR, are grave. The process is likely to be far longer, far more economically and politically disruptive, and the end result far less like anything that one can call socialism, than the optimistic visions painted by reform economists would lead one to suppose. If marketization is like the curate's egg, unfortunately, it would seem that it has to be eaten whole.

NOTES

This chapter was first published in *Communist Economies*, vol. 1, no. 3, 1989. The author wishes to thank Paul Auerbach, Geoff Davison and George Hadjimatheou for their extremely useful comments on an earlier draft of this paper.

1. M. Gorynia and W. Otta, 'Czy przedsiębiorstwa muszą aeksporto-wać?', *Życie Gospodarcze*, 9, 1988.
2. J. Mirsky, *The Observer*, 31 July 1988.
3. Urban unemployment reached a peak of 2.3 per cent in China in 1983

according to official figures. Reynolds (1987) suggests that the true level may have easily been twice as high, but even this is very low by Western standards. Within a few years this unemployment was officially eliminated by the simple expedient of making migration to the cities far harder, and ordering enterprises to hire the unemployed.

4. S. Brittan, 'A realistic target for price stability', *Financial Times*, 11 May 1989.

5. *Dziennik Ustaw*, 21, 1987.

6. At present the mechanism in Poland works as follows: exporting enterprises are allowed to retain a certain proportion of hard currency earnings (the so-called retention quotas) which they are then free to sell on an inter-enterprise auction market, at clearing prices. Second, the state sells some of the hard currency it has allocated to imports to the highest bidding enterprises. Some of these funds are earmarked for the purchase of particular raw materials and components (Rostowski, 1989b).

7. Inflation evidently imposes a tax on people foolish enough to have kept the domestic currency as a store of value when real interest rates are negative. Those who use it as a unit of account suffer (i.e. are taxed) because the variability of inflation at high rates makes this less useful. Those who use it exclusively as a medium of exchange suffer increased transactions costs resulting from the need to get into and out of the currency before and after each exchange.

8. The only impediment to this situation arising is that profit-making activities would have to obtain the domestic currency to pay their taxes, which would generate demand for that currency. If taxes were perfectly index-linked (which would be impossible if the domestic currency were used for very few purposes), or if they were assessed in hard currency on hard-currency incomes at the free market rate of exchange, then an exogenous fall in the value of the domestic currency (caused, for instance, by a wage increase to state employees), would be partly offset as taxpayers demanded more of the currency to meet their higher bills. If tax payments were the only purpose for which domestic currency was required by profitable activities in the economy, then the free market exchange rate would be stable, whatever the emission of money by the state. But this implies that everything of significance in fact happens in the hard currency. The state cannot run a real budget deficit (unless it borrows hard currency), as government expenditures as well as taxes are really denominated in hard currency. People receiving payment from the state in domestic currency immediately change it for hard currency to purchase goods and services not provided by the state. The formal denomination of state revenues and expenditures in the domestic currency is merely a fig-leaf for national pride.

3

Stopping Very Rapid Inflations in Reforming and Post-Communist Economies

1. Introduction

What are the conditions necessary for stopping very rapid inflations in reforming and post-communist economies (RCEs and PCEs)?[1] The question is of considerable importance, as two reforming communist economies, Yugoslavia and Poland, are already suffering from very rapid inflation (about 1,500 per cent and 400 per cent in autumn 1989), while the other two, China and Hungary, are suffering from high inflation (30 per cent and 20 per cent, respectively). The implications of the experience of moderate inflation in advanced capitalist countries for RCEs and PCEs has been dealt with in Chapter 2. Here we shall draw on the experience of very rapid inflation of nine market capitalist economies and of two RCEs, as well as examining the implications of the specific institutional structure of RCEs and PCEs for the stopping of very rapid inflation. Five of the experiences of very rapid inflation took place in the early 1920s in Austria, Germany, Hungary, Poland, and the Soviet Union, while six took place in the 1980s in Argentina, Bolivia, Brazil, Israel, Mexico, and Vietnam.[2] In seven cases the very rapid inflation was successfully tamed, but in two (Argentina and Brazil) it was still continuing at the time of writing (the cases of Mexico and Vietnam are still unresolved). The limited number of cases available for examination (eleven) means that conclusions will, in many cases, be tentative and will lack scientific status. However, all the cases have one characteristic in common: where stabilization was successful, the inflation was

either completely stopped or dramatically reduced very suddenly, usually during a matter of a few weeks or, at most, months.

In every case, except one, in which very high inflation was successfully stopped, an initially very large budget deficit was eliminated extremely rapidly (in a matter of a few months). The one case in which the deficit was not eliminated almost simultaneously with the stopping of the inflation is Austria in 1922, when it took another two years before the budget was balanced (Sargent, 1986*a*). It may therefore be sufficient if the deficit is sharply reduced, indicating the authorities' willingness to deal with the problem. Maybe more important in the Austrian case, stopping of the inflation was accompanied by Austria signing an internationally binding protocol by which, in exchange for a large international (mainly British) loan, Austria committed itself not to finance its budget deficits by the printing of money (advances of notes from the Austrian Central Bank to the state), but only through voluntary lending by the population or foreigners. At the same time, Austria accepted a Commissioner General appointed by the League of Nations who was to monitor the fulfilment of Austria's commitments. Thus, although the budget was not balanced immediately, conditions were created which made credible the commitment to do so in a non-inflationary way (i.e. not via the printing of money) in the medium term. Israel is a similar case (Helpman and Leiderman, 1988). It succeeded in reducing its domestically financed budget deficit by about three quarters to 2.6 per cent of GNP in 1986. This reduced the rate of inflation from about 380 per cent per annum in 1984 and the first three quarters of 1985 to about 30 per cent per annum in the last quarter of 1985 and 1986. However, even 2.6 per cent of GNP is a significant budget deficit by most conventional measures, and given the past inflationary history of the country the failure to eliminate the deficit completely in subsequent years has resulted in the persistence of inflation at a high level (25–30 per cent per annum) during the 1980s. In the USSR the budget deficit was reduced far more gradually. The share of the deficit financed through emission fell from 85 per cent in the first quarter of 1922, to 20 per cent

in the second quarter of 1923, to 5 per cent for the whole of the fiscal year 1 October 1923–30 September 1924 (stabilization took place in the first quarter of 1924) (Rostowski and Shapiro, 1992). The theoretical foundations for the belief that elimination of the budget deficit is the key to stopping inflation has been stated most clearly by Sargent (1986b).

However, the most convincing evidence of the key importance of budget deficits in generating hyperinflation is the fate of countries which have attempted to stop very rapid inflations without eliminating, or at least sharply reducing, their budget deficits. The Austral and Cruzado plans in Argentina and Brazil are particularly instructive (Helpman and Leiderman, 1988; Dornbusch and de Pablo, 1989; Cardoso and Fishlow, 1989). This is not to deny that a given budget deficit may be consistent with a number of different rates of very high inflation, depending first on the degree to which inertial inflation has been built into the system through indexation of nominal variables in the economy, and due secondly to the Laffer curve, which exists for inflation tax revenue. Increasing inflation first increases and then decreases the inflation tax it generates, so that there are at least two rates of inflation wich correspond to a given achievable budget deficit, except for the highest achievable deficit (Bruno, 1988). This helps to explain the often weak statistical relation between budget deficits and inflation in countries with high inflation (Helpman and Leiderman, 1988).[3] Furthermore, in every case in the 1980s, the reduction of the budget deficit was helped by the so-called Tanzi effect: as inflation fell, the benefit to taxpayers from delaying their tax payments was also reduced.

2. Monetary and Fiscal Constitutions and Policy

The four capitalist stabilizations of the 1920s were accompanied by important reforms of the monetary system. In every case a new central bank was created which was forbidden by statute to do the following:

(1) to lend to the government at all except on the security of an equal amount of gold and foreign assets (Austria and

Hungary), or not to lend the government more than a certain fixed amount (Germany and Poland);

(2) to fail to cover its note issue with certain minimal proportions of gold, silver, foreign earning assets, and commercial bills, i.e. domestic earning assets (Austria, Hungary, and Poland), or not to issue more than a fixed number of notes (Germany, see Sargent, 1986*b*).

In the Soviet Union, although no new central bank was created, a parallel 'fully backed currency', the *chervonets*, was introduced in October 1922, five quarters before stabilization finally succeeded. This currency was allowed to circulate simultaneously with the hyperinflating currency, the *sovznak*, the emission of which continued to be used to finance the budget deficit. At least one quarter of the issue of *chervontsy* had to be backed by gold and stable foreign currency, while the rest was backed by short-term bills, other short-term obligations, and easily marketable goods (Baykov, 1946). In February 1924 the issue of the *sovznaki* was discontinued, effectively ending the previous inflationary monetary system.

To what extent, then, is reform of the monetary system a necessary part of stopping very rapid inflations? At a theoretical level the answer is that implicit in Sargent and Wallace (1986). The creation of a new monetary system, exhibiting the characteristics described above, ensures that the budget has to be balanced in the long run, and not by monetary emission (which is banned by the new 'monetary constitution'). As a result the population's confidence in the currency is restored, and inflation stops. The creation of a new 'fiscal constitution' banning budget deficits, as suggested by Buchanan (1989), would have the same effect if it were credible, as it would remove the need for monetary emission. What is more, the reforms of the monetary system described by Sargent (1986*a*), which were introduced in the 1920s in countries suffering from hyperinflation, were clearly constitutional in nature. A gradual tightening of monetary policy or a gradual balancing of the budget would stop very rapid inflation just as well in the end but, argues Sargent (1986*b*), it would probably happen at a greater cost in terms of unemployment. This is because there

would be a period when the new policies were in force but not credible. Decisions based on the continuation of previous policies would be made by economic actors, and this would lead to the bankruptcy of some of the firms concerned and the loss of employment by some of the workers involved.

Whether an 'anti-inflationary constitution' would be helpful, and which constitution—the monetary or the fiscal—should be adopted depends on whether such a constitution is credible, and if so, which version is the more credible, i.e. which constitution the population is more likely to believe will not be violated. In the 1920s the countries concerned had adopted a system of fiat money after the Great War to deal with the extremely difficult situations they faced, either as defeated powers (Austria, Germany, Hungary), or as newly created or post-revolutionary states (Austria, Hungary, Poland, the Soviet Union). For much of pre-war living memory, however, they had been on the gold standard. Thus a return to a system of backed money was easily understood and believed by the population.[4] The situation in the 1980s is completely different. All countries are on a fiat money system, so it is not surprising that neither in Israel nor in Bolivia, the two successful cases of the mid-1980s, was there a reform of the monetary system. Rather there was a very sharp change in monetary and fiscal regime. The former consisted in diminishing the budget deficit sharply, while the latter involved nominal credit ceilings and/or positive real rates of interest. Adopting a backed money system or a 'fiscal constitution' would not have corresponded to anything in people's experience.[5]

Constitutional change is not therefore necessary for taming very high inflations. Nevertheless, it seems likely that in PCEs, where the need for change in political and economic systems is widely accepted (e.g. to implement democracy and widespread privatization), the simultaneous introduction of an anti-inflationary constitution (be it monetary or fiscal or both), could greatly facilitate the taming of very high inflation by adding to the credibility of stabilization programmes. In RCEs such as the USSR which are undergoing, or are likely to undergo rapid change, monetary and fiscal constitutions

could provide a stable framework for policy debates. They would thus allow the population a few key reference points for their economic decisions, as well as—possibly—nipping the danger of hyperinflation in the bud.

3. What Kind of Constitution for Reforming and Post-Communist Economies

Accepting that Sargent's arguments in favour of sudden change in the 'rules of the game' are convincing, what kind of change do RCEs and PCEs suffering from very rapid inflation need? The purpose of constitutional change is to establish rules (either on the monetary or fiscal side) which suddenly impose an end to the policies which caused inflation, and which are seen to do so. However, a constitution outlawing inflationary policies may be of little use if there are other elements of the economic system which are intrinsically inflationary. Indeed, if these other elements are basic to the system, a constitution which contradicts them is likely to remain a dead letter.

I have argued elsewhere (Chapter 2) that the RCEs and PCEs existing in China, Hungary, and Poland are intrinsically inflationary. The reason is that these are partly marketized economies which have abandoned the traditional Soviet-type anti-inflationary mechanisms of permanent and ubiquitous centralized price and wage setting, but which still do not allow any significant unemployment. (This has changed in Poland since the beginning of 1990.) With many prices free, excess aggregate demand causes price inflation, including that of administered prices. Rising free prices cause the relative prices of price controlled goods to fall, increasing shortages of these goods and increasing subsidy payments which have to be paid out to producers of these goods as costs rise. A failure to increase controlled prices only leads to larger subsidy payments, and thus greater budget deficits and faster inflation in the uncontrolled sector. As long as the authorities' commitment to full employment persists it is impossible to eliminate excess aggregate demand while maintaining price flexibility in a large part of the economy. In other words, in microeconomic terms we can

say either: (a) enterprises are very rarely allowed to go bankrupt, or (b) that enterprises have soft budget constraints (Kornai, 1979). Both of these statements come down to the observation that persistently loss-making enterprises (but not only such enterprises) are saved by subsidies, preferential credit, access to inputs in short supply, or exemption from price control. Whichever way we look at it, workers cannot price themselves out of jobs and managements cannot bring about the bankruptcy of their firms either by paying excessive wages or by overinvesting (Topiński, 1989 on the latter point). The macroeconomic equivalent of these microeconomic statements is that the actual rate of unemployment in PCEs and those RCEs which have a large sector in which prices are market determined is (probably far) below the natural rate. This leads inevitably to accelerating inflation, which is inhibited for certain periods by prices and incomes policies (i.e. by a temporary return to central planning of prices and wages).

A constitution aimed at stopping inflation in RCEs and PCEs would therefore not only have to have a monetary or fiscal element, but also a systemic one. This would have two aspects: (1) at the macroeconomic level the acceptance that unemployment, probably (though not necessarily—see Section 6) on a very large scale, will occur as a result of stopping very rapid inflation; (2) at a microeconomic level the creation of a system by which persistently loss-making enterprises go bankrupt automatically. Bankruptcy should become a natural economic process, rather than the exceptional political process it is at present. It is interesting to note that during the stabilization in the USSR, enterprises which ran short of money and credit were temporarily closed down. However, it is unclear to what extent such a system, incorporating these changes could be considered meaningfully socialist.

Furthermore, the constitution would have to incorporate changes in the banking system. The banking system in RCEs and PCEs does not have the normal two-tier (central bank/commercial banks) structure. It is a somewhat decentralized variant of the standard Soviet-type monobank system. The so-called commercial banks are state-owned, and were pre-

viously branches of the state monobank. They have been hived off by administrative decree and been given a nominal independence, which is much like that of so-called independent state enterprises in these economies. Since the directors of these commercial banks are appointed by the central bank or the Ministry of Finance, they mostly carry out the instructions of these institutions. Until now these instructions have usually been to save any enterprise in serious danger of bankruptcy by proving credit on non-commercial terms (this has been particularly the case in Yugoslavia and Poland). Since the credit is effectively non-returnable, merely insisting that the real interest rates charged to enterprises on loans be positive, as is usually required in IMF stabilization programmes, is insufficient. The authorities can easily get around such a prohibition by instructing the banks to supply additional credit, so as to effectively capitalize interest payments. This has largely been the Yugoslav experience in the 1980s. Some economy-wide nominal credit target would therefore appear to be necessary.

Wood (1989) claims that in Vietnam during 1988 and 1989 the demand for credit seems to have been successfully constrained merely by the setting of extremely high real interest rates, which runs counter to our argument. However, the main reason for the reduction in demand for credit seems to have been the belief by borrowers that such high rates could not persist, and the possibility of suspending wage payments without having to declare bankruptcy when enterprises run out of money. This latter institutional arrangement does not exist in the more advanced RCEs and PCEs, whereas the 'putting-off' response of borrowers suggests that very high credit formation may resume as soon as interest rates have fallen to expected levels.

There would also, therefore, have to be a banking system element in the anti-inflationary constitution. What should this element be? There are two possibilities. We shall start with the one which is more in keeping with the spirit of market socialism.

3.1. Credit Revaluation and Creation Rules

A key problem associated with standard IMF stabilization packages is that positive real interest rates at very high rates

of inflation entail the repayment of a large proportion of the principal of outstanding loans in real terms. If inflation is 100 per cent during the year, then with a real interest rate of 3 per cent the nominal interest that has to be paid on a loan of zl.1,000 is zl.1,060. This would in effect mean repayment of over 50 per cent of the principal of the loan in real terms, which would hinder most èconomic undertakings with longer gestation periods. To avoid this result the following rules could be imposed on state commercial banks by the central bank: (1) principal owed to banks is indexed so that it maintains its real value; (2) a positive nominal rate of interest is charged over and above this. Thus if inflation was 100 per cent during the year, then a loan of zl.1,000 becomes one of zl.2,000 after a year. Nominal interest rates are then charged on the new index-augmented amount, so that if the interest rate agreed was 3 per cent zl.60 must be paid.[6] At the same time the central bank has the following conditions imposed upon it by the constitution: (1) the mass of outstanding credit (including the increase due to indexation) must not grow faster than the nominal growth rate of the economy planned for the period concerned; (2) the rate of interest on bank credit should be set so as to equalize the supply of credit under (1) with demand for it. The main problem is rule (1) imposed on the central bank. How does one constitutionally guarantee that the forecast for the nominal growth rate of the economy (i.e. effectively, at very high rates of inflation, a forecast of the rate of inflation) for the coming period is set sufficiently low? If it is not set sufficiently low, rule (1) becomes a mechanism for perpetuating inflation at whatever rate is 'forecast'. A second problem regards how the central bank is to allocate credit creation among the 'commercial' state banks. This is an efficiency problem rather than a macroeconomic one but it is none the less important for that.

3.2. Bank Privatization

Complete privatization of the commercial banking system would create the normal two-tier system. It would then be sufficient to adopt a standard monetary or fiscal constitution.

It is important, however, that no state-controlled banks run on a non-commercial basis should remain.[7]

4. *What Kind of Fiscal or Monetary Constitution?*

In relation to the adoption of a *fiscal constitution*, the main question is whether budget deficits should be abolished immediately, or whether a transitional period of a few years should be allowed. Under normal circumstances there would be something to be said for a gradual introduction of balanced budgets. If the remaining deficit were financed by debt, one could argue for pushing some of the cost of adjustment onto later years, when, as a result of the economic improvement brought about by the stopping of very high inflation, society would be better able to bear them. The problem is that in current circumstances in RCEs and PCEs it is very unlikely that a deficit could be financed by borrowing (and if it were this could only be at a very large risk premium). Monetary emission would have to be used. If the additional money were held voluntarily as a result of increased demand for money following on a belief that inflation had really been stopped, then the deficit would be financed by voluntarily paid seigniorage, and there would neither be a tax on holding money nor further inflationary pressure. The problem is that it is almost impossible to predict what the increase in the demand for money resulting from the stopping of inflation will be. A mistake could result in a short-term persistence of inflation, which could then undermine the credibility of the whole anti-inflationary policy.

As described above, one of the key elements in stopping the hyperinflations of the 1920s was a change in the monetary system, replacing fiat money by backed money. Such a *monetary constitution* can be a substitute for a prohibition of budget deficits, but would it be suitable for RCEs and PCEs today? A backed, or 'inside' money system would imply a ban on additional fiat money being created. The state, the population, and the commercial banks could only obtain additional money from the central bank in exchange for foreign currency, bullion, and foreign negotiable assets (bonds and shares). The advantage

of such a system is that the population itself sets the supply of money equal to the increased demand for it which occurs after the stopping of very rapid inflation. There is thus no danger of a miscalculation by the authorities as to the amount of the increase in the demand for money, resulting in either over or under supply.[8]

What is more, the population can easily finance such adjustments in their portfolios, because of the very large amount of foreign currency held during very rapid inflations. In October 1923, at the height of the German hyperinflation, the value of foreign currency in circulation was at least equal to and perhaps several times the real value of domestic notes (Sargent 1986*a*). In Poland already in 1987, with inflation only at 25 per cent, hard-currency savings accounts were more than equal to those denominated in zloty, and hard-currency notes in circulation were about three times the value of zloty notes, both figures estimated at the black market rate of exchange (Rostowski, 1986*b*). It is worth noting that the state continues to obtain seigniorage for the creation of money in a backed money system. It receives foreign currency, bullion, etc., in exchange for the product of its printing presses. If the state pursues a very conservative fractional reserve policy, so that although the domestic currency is not 100 per cent backed—it is, let us say, 30 per cent backed—the state can still either spend or lend part of its seigniorage income abroad, and still be able to convert domestic currency into foreign currency or bullion on demand.

The disadvantage of a backed money system is that it requires that the price of the domestic currency in terms of one other asset, over whose supply the state has no control, should be fixed. This other asset can be bullion or the currency of a state which pursues a tight anti-inflationary policy (West Germany or the USA would be suitable in today's circumstances). This means that backed money is incompatible with a floating exchange rate. It also means that the danger of setting the exchange rate of the domestic currency at too low or too high a level in terms of the desired external current account position remains. Overvaluation will lead to balance of payments deficits

followed either by speculation against the domestic currency as the credibility of the fixed exchange rate is undermined, or to recession. Undervaluation will lead to a deterioration in the terms of trade and current account surplus, which may not make sense for an RCE or PCE if it is simultaneously reforming its foreign investment rules so as to encourage inward direct capital investment.

Very large undervaluation could also lead to an 'inflationary bubble' (i.e. a temporary continuation of inflation at rates which are higher than could be sustained in the long run). The standard argument is that fixing the exchange rate of a hyperinflating currency causes a sharp fall in the velocity of circulation, because of a large increase in the demand for domestic money as people become convinced that the domestic currency is as good to hold as foreign currency. Although such a 'velocity effect' is likely to hold as long as the fixed exchange rate is credibly defensible (i.e. low), there will also be offsetting import substitution and export effects. Enterprises are likely to increase purchases of domestic inputs which have now become cheaper, and may also exchange foreign currency accumulated under the previous foreign exchange retention quota system for domestic currency for the same purpose, generating a kind of 'internal export effect'. Finally, exports are likely to increase sharply as they have in Poland in the first part of 1990. All of these expenditure switching effects could have a large impact on the domestic price level. In a regime change it is impossible to say which effect, the velocity effect or the expenditure switching effects, will be the stronger. But one can say that the more undervalued the domestic currency at the time when the exchange rate is fixed, the larger will be the expenditure switch-ing effects, and thus the more rapid and persistent will be the inflation in the bubble. The danger is that rapid and persistent inflation in a bubble may cause inflationary expectations to revive, and thus undermine the stabilization.

The likelihood of making a mistake when setting the exchange rate is somewhat smaller in those RCE and PCEs such as Poland, which have well-developed free hard-currency markets which would provide some guide to the correct rate.

However, it could be argued that, in countries without internal convertibility and/or without a unified exchange rate (and this latter condition held in Poland before 1990), the number of unknowns is too great for the equilibrium exchange rate to be guessed at with confidence, with the consequence that a direct move to a backed money system (which makes subsequent changes in the exchange rate very difficult) would be foolhardy. The implication is that convertibility at a uniform, but flexible, rate of exchange should precede stabilization. This would allow the distortions caused by the absence of convertibility or the presence of a multiple exchange rate system to be eliminated before the choice of the correct permanently fixed rate of exchange had to be made. Inconvertibility of the currency and/or a multiple exchange rate system mean that different prices are distorted from world prices in differing degrees and indeed in different directions, which makes the choice of an equilibrium exchange rate particularly difficult. This consideration is even more relevant to those RCEs and PCEs which have neither internal convertibility nor uniform exchange rates.

If the fixed exchange rate undervalues the domestic currency considerably, this would result in a large increase in the government's hard-currency reserves, helping to balance the budget (government income from seigniorage) and thus increasing confidence. This could go a long way to counteracting the effects of the inflationary bubble on expectations.

Undervaluation of the domestic currency is not therefore likely to be a serious threat to the ultimate success of the stabilization programme. It could, of course, involve quite high real costs, if foreigners and domestic owners of hard currency rushed to buy up most of the land and/or capital stock of the country, and because of its effects on the current account and terms of trade. Such costs will be greater, the greater the original undervaluation of the currency. Possibly even more important, a very large undervaluation could set in train very sharp equilibrating responses, mainly in the form of an inflationary bubble and large fluctuations on the current account, which could lead to overshooting of equilibrium

values for many variables (e.g. the real exchange rate). However, some degree of undervaluation and its associated costs would be worth bearing to achieve stabilization.

In every case except one (Poland in 1924) stabilization involved obtaining significant external assistance, either in the form of a large foreign loan, in the form of aid, or in the form of a reduction in foreign claims against the country concerned.[9] What is more, a stabilization loan allows a country adopting a backed money system to set a fixed exchange rate which does not have to be excessively low (for the purpose of avoiding a run on the currency), thus avoiding the costs described above.

The question remains whether a fixed exchange rate policy pursued by an RCE or PCE would be credible. The answer must surely be: not much more credible than a balanced budget policy pursued by that same country! Nevertheless, a monetary constitution may have one, not insignificant advantage. If the authorities change the rate at which the central bank exchanges domestic for foreign currency, this will be immediately visible. On the fiscal side there are all sorts of ways of slowly departing from budget balance without it being absolutely clear what is happening (extending the length of the period over which the budget must balance, creating 'extra budgetary funds', etc.).

The conclusion would thus seem to be that whereas a banking element and a systemic element in a new anti-inflationary constitution are necessary conditions for success, there is no guarantee that either a fiscal or a monetary constitution would be respected by the authorities or be credible under the conditions obtaining in RCEs and PCEs. The answer to the question whether RCEs and PCEs should adopt a fiscal or a monetary constitution is therefore likely to be 'both'! In a situation in which the inviolability of the constitution is far from certain, multiplying constitutional safeguards seems the best strategy. If all constitutional safeguards should prove unavailing, the only solution would be the complete abandonment of the domestic currency, as suggested in Chapter 2. The disadvantage of such a policy is that seigniorage is then received by the foreign government rather than the domestic one.

5. Orthodox vs. Heterodox Policies

All the stabilizations of the 1920s were 'orthodox', as was the stabilization in Bolivia. The four remaining attempted stabilizations of the 1980s were all heterodox, but only that in Israel was successful (it is too early to say whether those in Mexico and Vietnam will prove successful). The orthodox approach consists in: (1) moving rapidly to balance the budget and re-establishing control over the creation of money[10] (either through monetary targets, or a monetary constitution; (2) raising prices of state supplied utilities (e.g. transport or electricity) so as to reduce the budget deficit and limit excess demand for these goods; and, (3) the removal of all controls on prices, interest rates, imports, and capital movements, and a general liberalization of goods, financial, and labour markets. The purpose of this widespread liberalization is to increase the elasticity of the supply side of the economy, reducing the natural rate of unemployment, and therefore with it the unemployment rate at which inflation is stopped (Chapter 2). The heterodox approach is the same as regards points (1) and (2) above, but it differs fundamentally as regards point (3). Instead of removing price and wage controls, the heterodox approach involves imposing a price and wage freeze for a limited time (after the price increases under (2) above have been imposed). The idea of price controls is to act directly on the expectations of workers and employers (Fischer, 1988). If the government adopts a low inflation policy and that policy is not believed by employers (in RCEs and PCEs these would have to become independent, bankruptable, state or private enterprises) or by workers, then the outcome will be a recession and low inflation. If the government's policy is credible the result will be low inflation without a recession (see Chapter 6). Fischer argues that in countries with a history of failed stabilization programmes the likelihood that the policy will be credible is small. Price controls assure actors that inflation will be low, at least for a time. During that time they have the opportunity to convince themselves that the so-called fundamentals (i.e. fiscal and monetary policy) are indeed con-

sistent with the maintenance of low inflation. The question remains, however, whether the whole stabilization package is credible in the slightly longer term if it is sustained by prices and wage policies which are known to be only temporary.

Without entering further into the debate on the relative merits of the two approaches in LDCs, it should be noted that RCEs and PCEs differ from LDCs in an important respect: they are economies which are moving away from near total centralized administration, because of the huge efficiency costs of that system. Price and wage controls must slow down the process of marketization and industrial restructuring which is vital for RCEs and PCEs. Moreover, because of their command-planning past, RCEs and PCEs often have large economic bureaucracies, so that price control is likely to be much more detailed than in LDCs and thus more onerous and destructive of such markets as exist. For this reason price controls should be avoided during stabilizations in RCEs and PCEs. The question of wage controls is somewhat more complicated. The absence of real owners who would resist wage pressure by the workforce in the state sector in RCEs and PCEs suggests that wage policies limited to that sector may be justified during stabilizations, although minimum rates of return on capital in the state sector are likely to be superior instruments in the longer term. The real question, however, is whether governments are strong enough to sustain wage controls in the face of fairly buoyant demand. If they are not, then wage policies will be breached, causing the likely collapse of stabilization programmes. The absence of wage controls causes authorities to rely more on demand management policies, with the result that unemployment is likely to be higher, which weakens the bargaining position of supplier groups such as trade unions and increases the probability that the stabilization programme can be sustained in spite of the opposition of such groups (Chapter 2), although higher unemployment may also reduce the will of the authorities to stick with the programme.

6. Can Reforming and Post-communist Economies avoid Unemployment while Stopping Very Rapid Inflation?

It is evident that the answer to this question must be 'no', if all unemployment is to be completely avoided. The reasons for this have been described above in Section 4. What we are concerned with here is whether unemployment can be kept very low in RCEs and PCEs while stopping very rapid inflation. Sargent (1986a) makes the point that the increase in unemployment can be very much smaller than would be predicted by estimations of short-run Phillips curves, if people are convinced that the rules of the game have changed, and that the economy will in effect move suddenly to a much lower short-run Phillips curve (Sargent himself does not use the expectations augmented Phillips curve apparatus). Fischer (1988) says: 'Only two years after it was first done, it is now a commonplace that with the fundamentals in place, virtually costless stabilization is possible.' To what extent does experience bear out these views, and how applicable are they to RCEs and PCEs?

Of the eight successful stabilizations, only in Germany, Israel, and the USSR was there no significant increase in unemployment (in the case of Hungary there is no data available for the pre-stabilization period, while the case of Mexico is too recent for proper judgement to be possible).[11] In Germany and the Soviet Union, employment and output actually increased (in Germany output rose by over 40 per cent in 1924 compared with 1923, the year of the hyperinflation). In Israel unemployment rose only very slightly, from an average of 6.6 per cent in the first three quarters of 1985 to 7 per cent in the last quarter of that year and 1986. In Austria, Bolivia, and Poland, output and employment fell. In Austria, unemployment trebled from 38,000 in October 1922 to 117,000 in January 1923 after which, although it fell somewhat in January 1924, it continued rising in 1925 and 1926, when it reached 208,000 in January (Sargent, 1986a). In Poland, industrial unemployment increased by roughly 50 per cent from 1923 to 1924 (the years before and after the stabilization), from 86,000 to 128,000. In Bolivia, official GNP fell by 6.3 per cent in 1986 after the stabilization.

However, the German, Soviet, and Bolivian cases are rather special. In Germany, 1923 was the year of the French occupation of the Ruhr, and of enormous disruption to production resulting from it. In Germany, the hyperinflation itself was also responsible for the decline in output. By making it very much harder to use money as a unit of account, hyperinflation sharply reduces the efficiency of the economy, which can lead to increased unemployment. Unemployment rose from 3 per cent of unionized workers to 25 per cent between June 1923 and November (the height of the hyperinflation and the time when stabilization occurred). After stabilization, unemployment fell, but only to about 8–12 per cent, in the middle of 1924, much higher than the average of 4 per cent recorded in the first half of 1923. In the Soviet Union, the period after 1921 was one of recovery from war, revolution, and civil war, and the increase in production that accompanies the re-establishment of elementary order in a society. The result was increasing production throughout 1922–5, largely independently of what was happening in the monetary sphere. In Bolivia, the whole of the 1980s are a period of a collapse of the tin industry and of a transfer of economic activity from the official economy, registered in GNP statistics, to the production of cocaine, which is not. Official GNP fell 21.3 per cent between 1981 and 1985 (i.e. before the stabilization, see Helpman and Leiderman, 1988). Thus in all three countries special factors, unrelated to the macroeconomic issues with which we are concerned, were at work.

Experience would therefore seem to indicate that stabilization is likely to lead to an increase in unemployment and a fall in output, unless hyperinflation has already caused unemployment to increase, in which case stabilization may cause it to decline, though not necessarily immediately (for this to happen the credibility of the stabilization must become secure). However, even when the increase in unemployment is large, as in the cases of Poland and Austria, it is nowhere near as great as might be expected from normal short-term Phillips curve-type estimations. Sargent's point, that people adjust to the change in the rules of the game very fast, seems to be borne out.

Nevertheless, Fischer's claim that almost costless stabilization

can be achieved thanks to heterodox policies is far more doubtful. In the first place, Germany, which had the same kind of
result as Israel, applied a totally orthodox approach. Secondly,
it is possible to interpret the Israeli experience, like the German
one, as stabilization causing the levelling off of unemployment,
which had already been rising as a result of the disruption of the
economy due to the very rapid inflation.[12] Finally, because of
the special factors at work in that country, i.e. the shift to the
cocaine economy, the Bolivian example cannot show (as is
claimed by Fischer) that, at least in the 1980s, orthodox policies
have to lead to higher unemployment than heterodox ones.

To summarize, it is likely that an economy will avoid moving
very far to the right of the natural rate of unemployment (along
the short-run Phillips curve) during a disinflation from very
high rates of inflation. This is because the change in the rules
of the game, which is probably an essential part of any successful stabilization policy at very high rates of inflation, has to be
very visible and therefore causes a rapid downward shift in the
short-term Phillips curve on which the economy finds itself.
This does not mean, however, that any economy can disinflate
while remaining at a level of unemployment which is below the
natural rate. Even Israel, which is supposedly the great example
of 'costless disinflation', remained at a rate of unemployment of
7 per cent which, given what we know of the experience of
other market economies (Chapter 2), is likely to have been fairly
close to its natural rate of unemployment. The implications for
RCEs and PCEs are clear. All of them are at an actual rate of
unemployment far below their natural rate (Chapter 2). As a
result any stabilization is bound, in their case, to involve an
increase in unemployment at least to the natural rates for their
economies. In the case of RCEs and PCEs stabilization cannot
be costless in terms of unemployment.

Some economists claim that unemployment could be kept
very low in RCEs and PCEs if stabilization is accompanied by a
very far-reaching liberalization and marketization of the economy. It is said that there are huge areas of unsatisfied demand in
RCEs and PCEs, mainly in consumer goods, foods, and services
(including many services which are supplied at present very

inadequately by the state, such as medicine and health), and that the expansion of these sectors in response to private demand would soak up almost all of the labour released by the contraction of loss-making firms (expected to be mainly in heavy industry). While it is doubtless true that a far-reaching marketization and liberalization of RCEs and PCEs, which would need to incorporate a far-reaching programme of privatization, would help to reduce the natural rate of unemployment and thus the cost of stabilization, such supply-side measures cannot be introduced very fast. A period of high unemployment should therefore be expected immediately after stabilization (Chapter 2).

It should also be remembered that some of the jobs which exist at present in the private sector are likely to be lost during a stabilization. This is because they have been created during a period of high inflation and shortage. When the macroeconomic environment changes, the conditions which brought them into existence will disappear. An example is the various arbitraging firms whose profits derive from their privileged access to scarce material inputs in the state sector, or to state sector customers for imported computer and other hardware (the state sector firms having been prevented from buying the imports themselves because of restrictions which are aimed at combating some of the consequences of excess demand). Both reasons for their existence would disappear as a result of real liberalization of the economy.

However, the most important reason for the likely appearance of large-scale unemployment is that RCEs and PCEs face two simultaneous problems. The first is very rapid inflation. The second is the existence of very large areas of the economy which are overdeveloped, given both the needs of the domestic economy and their international competitiveness.[13] Most economists believe that industry in general, and the huge heavy industrial sector built up in the Stalinist period in particular, are the main structural problems facing RCEs and PCEs (Winiecki, 1987), although the generalized absence of market prices makes it very hard to be sure just where RCEs and PCEs' true comparative advantage lies. In principle, stabilization and the restructuring of the economy are two separate problems.

Budgets can be balanced and monetary constitutions adopted without cutting subsidies to unprofitable industries, which can be financed out of increased taxation or cuts in other govern-ment programmes such as health or defence.

In practice, this would be very undesirable economically. The structural adjustment which is required is a real one, and the need for it exists irrespective of whether stabilization occurs. Avoiding the restructuring is also probably quite unfeasible politically, once people know who is actually getting the sub-sidies, and how large they are. In RCEs and PCEs the vast majority of savings in government expenditure to balance the budget are likely to, and should, come from the elimination of subsidies to various kinds of economic activity. This is likely to lead to large-scale unemployment because the RCEs and PCEs suffer from what could be termed a 'restructuring overhang'. Whereas market capitalist economies have been adjusting to various changes in the world economy, such as the increased cost of energy or the rise of the newly industrializing countries (NICs), in a continuous way for the last thirty years, RCEs and PCEs have hardly done so at all. The introduction of full-blown market mechanisms, including an abolition of import restric-tions and the introduction of full convertibility of the currency at a single exchange rate, is therefore bound to lead to wide-spread real dislocations and the bankruptcy of many firms in RCEs and PCEs. Although the unemployment this restructur-ing will cause will be eliminated eventually, it will take time.

7. Conclusion

Assuming a low credibility of governments in RCEs and PCEs, I believe that the kind of change in 'policy regime' which would be required to convince the population that the rules of the game have really changed, so that stabilization of very high rates of inflation could be achieved, requires a number of constitutional amendments. These would entail not only a fiscal constitution outlawing budget deficits but also a monetary constitution trans-forming the national currency from fiat money into backed and inside money. Theoretically, either a monetary or a fiscal con-

stitution should be adequate to achieve stabilization in a market capitalist economy, but given the need for maximum credibility and verifiability for the anti-inflationary policy, both are needed in RCEs and PCEs suffering from very rapid inflation.

Furthermore, there would have to be a systemic component to the anti-inflationary constitution. This would have a micro-economic dimension and a macroeconomic one. At the microeconomic level, 'automatic' bankruptcy of persistently loss-making enterprises would have to be introduced. This means that such enterprises, which were unable to obtain loans on commercial terms from the banks, should go bankrupt as a matter of course (as opposed to the present practice by which bankruptcy is an exceptional and political decision). At the macroeconomic level, RCEs and PCEs would have to accept that unemployment, possibly on a large scale, will be the inevitable side-effect of stabilization. A banking component of the anti-inflationary constitutional changes is also needed, to prevent state-owned banks from being able to lend unlimited amounts of credit to loss-making enterprises, thus undermining the monetary, fiscal, and systemic changes.

On the other hand, we conclude that price controls, in spite of the arguments put forward by supporters of 'heterodox-shock' anti-inflationary policies, are particularly dangerous in RCEs and PCEs because these are only emerging from the command planning system, and have very large bureaucracies which are likely to use such controls to stifle the growth of markets and maintain their power over the economy. Foreign aid is very helpful in stabilization programmes, particularly when these involve transferring to a backed money system or adopting convertibility with a fixed exchange rate.

Although it is true that in general the level of unemployment may fail to rise in a market economy suffering from very high inflation if stabilization policy is introduced in such a way that the population is convinced that the rules of the game have changed completely, it does not follow that RCEs and PCEs can stabilize their economies without large-scale unemployment. A successful stabilization involves changing people's expectations to such a degree that the economy moves suddenly down its

long-run Phillips curve, as the short-run Phillips curve on which it finds itself shifts down. As a result there may be no need to move along the short-run curve to points to the right of the natural rate of unemployment. In fact, only two countries (Germany and Israel) saw minimal or negative increases in unemployment during stabilization of very high inflation, and in the case of Germany this was probably due to special factors. Be that as it may, nothing will allow a country to achieve stabilization while maintaining unemployment above the natural rate, even if the population is entirely convinced that the rules of the game have changed completely. RCEs and PCEs are therefore faced with the absolute necessity of accepting unemployment at their natural rates if they are to stabilize.

We find unconvincing the claim that expansion of the private sector is likely to soak up most of the unemployment generated by the slimming down of unprofitable state enterprises (i.e. that natural rates of unemployment in RCEs and PCEs are very low). Parts of the private sector itself exist because of inflationary conditions, and are likely to suffer when these disappear. While it is doubtless true that a far-reaching marketization and liberalization of RCEs and PCEs (which would need to incorporate extensive privatization), would help to reduce the natural rate of unemployment and thus the cost of stabilization, such supply-side measures cannot be introduced very fast. Socialist countries, including RCEs and PCEs, have been slow to adapt to changes in the world economic environment and as a result have a restructuring overhang, i.e. a stock of uncompetitive enterprises which will have to be closed down quickly. The creation of new ones will occur, but it will take time.

NOTES

This chapter was first published in *Jahrbuch der Wirtschaft Osteuropas*, Band 14, no. 2 (1990), 31–52. It grew out of the policy debate in *Solidarnosść circles in the summer of 1989, after the semi-free elections of June. An early draft was written in September for Leszek Balcerowicz when he became Deputy Prime Minister and Minister of Finance. The author wishes to thank Paul Auerbach, Geoff Davison and two anonymous referees for very useful comments on an earlier draft of this chapter.*

1. I prefer this term to 'market socialism', as it allows one to avoid the 'model vs. muddle' question. In this chapter I am concerned with examining the muddle.

2. The first four capitalist cases have been described in the seminal article by Sargent (1986a), and the second four in a wide range of articles, including Helpman and Leiderman (1988). The stopping of the Soviet inflation of the 1920s is described in Davies (1958) and Baykov (1946), while the Vietnamese is described in A. Wood (1989).

3. This weak correlation also occurs because of uncertainty about the timing of stabilization programmes (which would reduce the budget deficit), or about the financing of a larger proportion of the deficit through emission, which can cause expectations of future inflation to vary in a way quite unrelated to the current budget deficit.

4. The Soviet case is unclear. On the one hand backed money was well remembered and understood, on the other the Bolshevik authorities were probably considered untrustworthy guardians of the value of the currency (as indeed they proved to be in the 1930s).

5. Although it can be argued that full internal convertibility of the domestic currency plus a permanently fixed exchange rate is the modern equivalent of an 'inside' or 'backed' money system. In all four examples from the 1980s there was an attempt to fix, or at least manage, the exchange rate (in the cases of Israel and Bolivia with a fair degree of success). However, there was no suggestion that the fixing of the exchange rate would be permanent.

6. This suggestion is based on discussion with S. Kawalec.

7. State-owned banks, such as the French, which are run on a truly commercial basis do not pose a fundamental problem.

8. The importance of this aspect of post-inflationary stabilization should not be underestimated. Thus in Austria during the hyperinflation between January 1921 and August 1922, the note circulation of the central bank increased only 39 times, while prices increased 110 times, the difference being accounted for by an increase in the velocity of circulation resulting from the flight from money caused by the hyperinflation. Between September 1922 and December 1923 retail prices increased by 8.8 per cent, while the note circulation of the central bank increased by more than three times. A similar scale of adjustment occurred in all the cases of successful stopping of very rapid inflation, both in the 1920s and in the 1980s.

9. In the cases of Austria and Hungary, foreign loans were obtained as well as there being a permanent reduction in the claims of the victorious allied powers against these two countries. In the case of Germany, foreign claims for war reparations were sharply and permanently reduced under the Dawes plan. In the case of Israel, the United States supplied interim emergency aid of $1.5 billion for a limited period (one and a half years) which was equivalent to about 4 per cent of GNP for the period concerned. Bolivia receives aid equivalent to about 5 per

cent of GNP continuously as part of the aid it gets as one of Latin America's poorest countries.

10. In principle, from a truly orthodox point of view, either of these instruments should be sufficient. However, in this sense, even in the 1920s only Austria followed a truly orthodox policy.

11. Although employment and output were unaffected by the stabilization in Mexico, the heterodox policy of freezing domestic prices, wages, and the exchange rate (at too high a level) has resulted in a dramatic deterioration in the external accounts which makes it likely that the policy will not prove sustainable, and a fall in output and employment is likely in 1990 (Wharton, 1989).

12. Unemployment rose from 4.5 per cent in 1983 to 5.9 per cent in 1984, to 6.6 per cent in the first three quarters of 1985 and 7 per cent in the last quarter of 1985 and in 1986.

13. Once the economy becomes open and will have a currency convertible at a single exchange rate these two criteria will become one.

4

Hyperinflation and Stabilization in Serbia-Montenegro, 1992–1994

1. Introduction

The Serbo-Montenegrian[1] hyperinflation of 1992–4 is the second fastest in history. In January 1994, the culminating month of the hyperinflation, consumer prices increased 310 million per cent per month, compared with a maximum monthly rate of 30 thousand per cent per month in the great German hyperinflation of 1923.[2] The average monthly inflation rate was 1,660 per cent exceeding Greece, 1943–4 (1,070 per cent) and Germany, 1922–3 (320 per cent), and second only to Hungary II, 1946 (360,000 per cent per month).

The stabilization of January 1994 was based on the introduction of convertibility for the domestic currency at a fixed exchange rate. The success of the stabilization is striking, given that there was no intention to balance the budget: the original version of the programme forecast a budget deficit of 15 per cent of GDP, or *thirty-eight times* the pre-stabilization domestic money supply. There was thus no possibility of financing the deficit through borrowing. Also, it was stated clearly that base money creation would be used to finance the deficit. Yet in spite of these manifest weaknesses in the design of the programme, it was initially highly successful, with consumer prices falling 8.7 per cent in the first four months. This experience casts doubt on Sargent's (1986*a*) argument that balanced budgets are necessary to establish the credibility which is needed for stabilizations to succeed.

The work below is the result of a research trip undertaken to Serbia in early February 1994.[3] The original aim of the research was to examine the microeconomic effects of a true

hyperinflation (e.g. purchasing, price, and output setting behaviour of actors).[4] Anecdotal evidence on this subject was
gathered, and is presented in Section 3. Section 2 analyses the
process of acceleration of the hyperinflation, and the conse-
quent theoretical and policy conclusions which can be drawn.
Section 4 describes and assesses the 24 January 1994 stabilization programme (the so-called Avramovic programme).

2. The Process of Hyperinflationary Acceleration

Monthly inflation rates are given in Table 3. The first thing to
note is that the Serbo-Montenegrian hyperinflation was
remarkably long, lasting 22 months as conventionally measured
(inflation of over 50 per cent per month). Only Nicaragua
(1987–91, 48 months) and China (1947–9, 26 months) were
longer (Sachs and Larrain, 1993).[5] It thus lasted significantly
longer than its closest competitors in terms of speed (Hungary
II 12 months; Greece 13 months; Germany 16 months).

A number of 'step increases' in the rate of inflation seem to
have occurred: beginning 1992, second quarter 1992, January
1993 and August 1993. In November 1993 the exponential
inflationary explosion began. The remarkable thing, in a way,
is how late this happened (sixteen months after conventionally
measured hyperinflation began).[6]

Two forces drove the Serbo-Montenegrian hyperinflation:
sharply declining real balances, which meant that the inflation

Table 3 Serbia-Montenegro: average monthly and actual monthly rates of inflation

1991		6.5	1993	M5	223.7
1992	Q1	36.7		M6	341.1
	Q2	68.2		M7	432.9
	Q3	61.3		M8	1,790.5
	Q4	49.6		M9	692.2
1993	M1	101.3		M10	1,150.0
	M2	194.0		M11	22,180.0
	M3	263.1		M12	283,833.0
	M4	96.8	1994	M1	310,000,000.0

Source: Ekonomska Politika various issues.

tax base was declining, so that ever higher inflation rates were required to obtain the same inflation tax revenue (Table 4); and, a powerful Tanzi-Olivera effect, which sharply reduced the real value of conventional taxes (although not all the data sets available point to this latter effect).

Thus at the end of the hyperinflation the total real domestic money supply amounted to less than $4 per capita in Serbia-Montenegro. This means that on average the total domestic money supply may have been changing hands as often as twice a day at this time.[7] Such a fall in real money balances is exactly what Cagan (1956) predicts. As the cost of holding money—the expected inflation rate for cash and the expected inflation rate minus the expected nominal interest rate for deposits—increases, real money balances decline and the velocity of circulation increases.

The surprising thing is that, in spite of this collapse in real money balances, seigniorage revenue has been estimated as having remained remarkably stable, oscillating around $140 million per month, close to the level achieved in 1992 when the rate of inflation was far lower (CESMECON, 1993*b*). In other words, even at the extraordinary inflation rates registered in Serbia-Montenegro in 1993–4, the inflation-tax Laffer curve does not seem to have bent backwards.

Moreover, seigniorage remained stable at inflation rates far above the 500 per cent per annum which, it has been claimed, has been the seigniorage maximizing inflation rate in modern Latin American episodes. However, this result does confirm simulation results for Israel by Bufman and Leiderman (1992). Also, it suggests that the theoretical puzzle in Bruno and Fischer

Table 4 Dinar money balances in US$ equivalents (end of period in millions of $)

1990	4,000
1991	1,500
1992	450
1993 VI	125
1993 XII	40

Source: CESMECON 1993*b* and 1994.

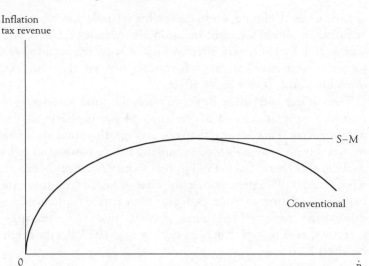

Figure 5   *The inflation tax Laffer Curve in Serbia-Montenegro*

(1990), by which points on the downward sloping part of the inflation-tax Laffer curve are stable, may in fact be empirically unimportant. However, there are serious difficulties with the data (see Appendix I).

The second engine of the hyperinflationary process in Serbia-Montenegro has been the Tanzi-Olivera effect. Hyperinflation severely reduced the real value of conventional tax revenues, so that even with a given level of seigniorage, government expenditure has declined sharply as a share of GDP (and has declined even more sharply in real terms, as GDP itself has fallen).[8]

According to CESMECON, the process of erosion of real tax revenues seems to have accelerated during 1993: conventional tax revenues in the last quarter of the year were running at an annualized rate of $700 million (Table 5). The authorities attempted to offset the Tanzi-Olivera effect by shortening the period of tax collection. Thus the weighted average of the delays in cashing fiscal revenues was 20 days in the first quarter of 1993, 15 days in the second quarter, 10 days in the third quarter, and 5–10 days in the fourth quarter.[9] In the first three

Table 5 Serbia-Montenegro: Conventional tax revenues 1991–93 (millions of US$)

	1991	1992	1993
January	—	214	144
February	—	327	114
March	—	230	144
April	1048	174	226
May	722	170	101
June	710	179	104
July	761	196	57
August	456	173	63
September	423	247	90
October	471	303	85
November	375	295	35
December	421	256	62
Average	599	230	102
TOTAL	5387	2764	1225

Source: CESMECON estimates provided to the author.

quarters of the year the shortening of the tax collection period just offset the acceleration of inflation, and about 50 per cent of the real value of tax revenue was lost in each of these quarters. In November the loss was between 59 per cent (five day delay) and 83 per cent (ten day delay), and in December the loss was between 71 per cent and 95 per cent. The monthly estimates of real conventional tax revenue given in Table 5 seem to confirm this. However, there are serious problems with the data, with a number of competing estimates of the main fiscal magnitudes (see Appendix 1).

3. The Microeconomics of Hyperinflation in Serbia-Montenegro

This section is concerned mainly with price setting, choice of means of payment, and the real effects of hyperinflation. Inevitably, it is largely based on anecdotal (rather than systematic) evidence.

One can distinguish a number of different sectors of the Serbo-Montenegrian economy as regards means of payment and price setting behaviour. The first was the so-called 'green market' where farmers sell food and alcohol. Here prices were set in Deutsche Marks throughout 1992 and 1993. Those

wishing to pay in Dinars had to pay at the current street market rate of exchange, possibly with a mark-up. At the other extreme there was the 'official economy', consisting of all large shops, whether state, socially owned or private, all large businesses (non-financial and financial, also state, socially owned and private),[10] and transactions between the state and the rest of the economy. In this sector all official transactions were effected by the use of cheques.[11] In between was the host of small private businesses (e.g. shops, taxis), which theoretically had the obligation to accept payment in Dinars and by cheque, but where compliance might be difficult to enforce.

3.1. A Model of Hyperinflationary Shortage in the Retail Sector

A number of phenomena occurred, especially during the second half of 1993, which show that at these kinds of inflation rates the price mechanism can break down, with important and costly real effects. The most important was the appearance of widespread shortages. These were initially due to the misguided price freeze which the authorities introduced in late August 1993.[12] However, shortages were not eliminated in 'official sector' shops after prices were freed in October. This was because prices were rising so rapidly that it was often impossible for retailers to buy the same real volume of goods with the proceeds of a given day's sale as had been sold (i.e., the inflation rate over the turnover period exceeded the sales margin).[13] As one would expect, in response to accelerating inflation, prices were set for shorter and shorter intervals: until October this was usually once a week, then it increased to twice weekly, ending with twice daily price changes in small shops in January 1994 (see Weiss, 1993, for a discussion of these issues with regard to other countries).

However, large shops and supermarket chains felt unable to change their prices more than once daily because they did not have bar code systems. As a result, changing prices in the middle of the day could have led to a severe risk of till fraud, as employees could have registered sales at the lower morning prices and put the difference in their own pockets.[14] These shops responded in a number of ways. The first was to reduce

the number of goods which they sold. One large supermarket chain reported that in October–November 1993 it was actually selling only cheese, eggs, pasta, bread, and milk, and that from about 10 December 1993 it sold only bread and milk. The reason for this reduction in variety was stated to be that it made it easier to avoid loss in real terms. Perishable foods were discontinued, while non-perishables either had their prices set at intentionally prohibitive levels or were withdrawn from sale and kept in warehouses. The same supermarket chain increased the frequency of its purchasing strategy meetings from daily to twice daily at the end of November 1993,[15] showing that even when prices are completely free, hyperinflation causes many of the symptoms of a shortage economy to appear.

We can account for this behaviour by extending the standard (s,S) price adjustment model (e.g. Dixit, 1993). Sellers set a nominal price N for a certain period of time T. At the beginning of T the real value of N is S. As inflation proceeds the real value of N declines, when it reaches s the seller increases N such that the real price should return to S. Thus S and s are the upper and lower bound of the real price which sellers charge for the good. Sheshinski and Weiss (1993) have shown that the greater the costs of price adjustment the rarer are price adjustments, and in consquence, the larger are the price adjustments made. Also, the faster the inflation rate the more frequent the price adjustments. However, what has been observed for the first time in the Serbo-Montenegrian experience is that—for a given technology—there is an absolute limit to the frequency of price adjustments, and therefore to the shortness of the period T during which the nominal price N remains constant. In what follows we assume that $T_t = T_{min}$. Under these circumstances, if s is the lowest price that a seller will accept, because below that price he cannot replace the unit at its future expected wholesale price, then accelerating inflation will cause S_t to rise, while s remains constant:

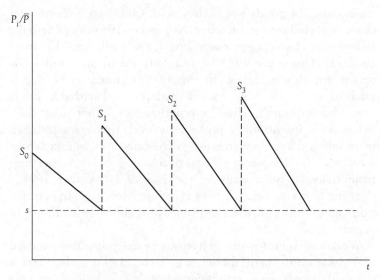

Figure 6   *Hyperinflation: nominal price adjustments and evolution of real prices*

If S is the highest real price at which consumers will buy any of the good concerned, then with S rising above S* for more goods as inflation increases, ever more goods will spend ever more time at real prices at which they will not be bought (i.e. at effectively prohibitive prices).

If S_t is far greater than S*, which is only slightly greater than s, then the real price will be in the range S* − s (when both buyer and seller are willing to engage in the trade) for only a small part of the period for which the good is exhibited for sale. If there is a carrying cost C, then if C > profit from sales when the real price is in the range S* − s, it will not be worth the seller's while to offer the good for sale at all. Such a result is likely in the situation described above, where S_t is far greater than S*, which is only slightly greater than s—unless a very large number of units can be sold during the window of opportunity when the real price is in the range S* − s. Thus as inflation accelerates beyond the level at which the frequency of price adjustments can be increased, there will be more and more goods actually withdrawn from sale by retailers.

We can model the behaviour of retailers somewhat differently, but with the same result, if we assume that actual inflation involves a stochastic element. As before, the range $S^* - s << S_t - S^*$. The actual rate of inflation P determines the rate at which the real price decreases. Let there be rational expectations, so that $P = P^e + u_t$. If retailers are risk averse, then the greater the standard deviation (σ_{ut}) relative to the range $S^* - s$, the smaller the likelihood that the good concerned will be sold in shops accepting the domestic currency. Since the variability of inflation increases with the inflation rate (Engle, 1983; Taylor, 1981), this phenomenon can be expected to increase with inflation:

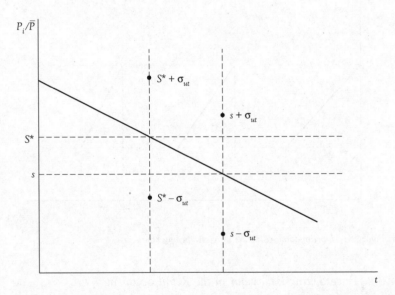

Figure 7   *Hyperinflation: evolution of real prices and shortages*

The second tactic was to reduce the length of opening hours. The supermarket chain already quoted reduced its opening hours from twelve to seven per day. There were two reasons given for this: first, there was less time for the fixed prices the shop had set to fall far below the highest prices which consumers were prepared to pay; second, the repricing of goods

every day required a significant amount of time. Although the prices of most goods were intentionally set at prohibitive levels at this time, nevertheless, with inflation so rapid many of these prices had to be updated daily to remain prohibitive.

This behaviour can be explained quite easily using the previous framework. If real prices of many goods are in the range $S_t - S^*$ for much of the day then profits can be increased by closing the shop for the time when this is true, if it is costly to keep the shop open. The time T_t which the shop was kept open would then decline as inflation increased:

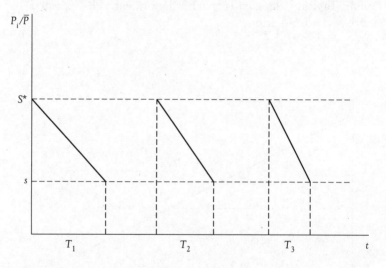

Figure 8   *Hyperinflation: reduction in retail opening hours*

3.2. Price Setting Behaviour in the Retail Sector in Serbia-Montenegro

In Serbia-Montenegro the situation was made worse for official sector retailers by the obligation they had to accept cheques, since these took a number of days to clear. They responded by setting prices which were a considerable margin above those in the small shops (which had different prices for cheque and cash transactions). The result was that the large shops were only used by those paying by cheque.

As late as October the relative prices of various goods were apparently changed in the large shops from time to time, but from November all prices were adjusted proportionally on the basis of the next day's expected exchange rate. By January 1994 the supermarket chain mentioned earlier reported using the following formula to set the next day's price:

(1) $P_{t+1} = PDM*e_{t+1}*(P_t - {}_3)$

In other words, the next day's price was today's Deutsche Mark price times the next day's expected opening exchange rate *TIMES* today's price index relative to that of three days before. Such a pricing formula could lead to an inflationary bubble, particularly if households' expectations are adaptive and if the demand for real balances depends strongly on expected inflation.

In the context of the microeconomic pricing decisions we are discussing, it is the daily, and not the monthly inflation rate which is relevant. Taken on a daily basis the acceleration of inflation appears far smaller, and allows us to understand how it was that any kind of money based economic activity remained possible.

One important question to which it was unfortunately impossible to obtain a clear answer was the extent to which inflation during the day was a continuous phenomenon, and to what extent it was discrete. Much of the folklore of hyperinflation assumes a continuous process, for example the famous anecdote that in Germany in 1923 it made sense to buy two beers at once when in a bar, as the second beer became warm

Table 6 Serbia-Montenegro: average daily inflation rates in 1993–94 (per calendar day)

April	2.6	September	7.0
May	3.7	October	10.1
June	5.3	November	19.4
July	5.5	December	27.3
August	10.1	January	62.0

Source: as Table 3.

more slowly than its price increased. However, such anecdotal evidence as was obtained tended to indicate that even at the dizzying rates of January 1994, in Serbia-Montenegro most prices were set for an appreciable period of time (e.g. one working day, or half a working day). Beyond a certain point, the acceleration of inflation led merely to larger discrete price increases, with a significant reduction in working hours to make inter-temporal arbitrage to the disadvantage of the seller more difficult.

In the small business sector prices were generally set twice a day, on the basis of the black market exchange rate. Even this allowed arbitrage, as holders of hard currency waited until the exchange rate moved (apparently this was usually around midday), bought dinars, and then rushed to buy goods as quickly as possible, before their prices rose in response to the new exchange rate. One example of continuous pricing which proves the rule of its absence, is the case of taxis. These set their meters in notional units and were then informed by their dispatchers what price to charge on the basis of the current exchange rate. Obviously, this was impossible for most businesses, which did not have access to up to the minute information on the exchange rate.[16]

The practical difficulties of continuous price adjustment for most businesses explains both prohibitive pricing and the physical withdrawal of goods, and the use of actual foreign currency (rather than merely pricing in foreign currency which was also formally illegal). The first point is of considerable theoretical and policy importance. It explains why a sufficiently rapid hyperinflation can lead not only to the misallocation of resources (e.g. Rostowski and Shapiro, 1992), but to the breakdown of the market mechanism, just as price control does. As regards policy, it is important to note that the pervasive shortages of the second half of 1993 in Serbia-Montenegro only began to disappear with the introduction of the stabilization programme at the end of January 1994. Second, if stabilization is impossible, then the preservation of the market mechanism in extreme hyperinflations of the Serbo-

Montenegrin kind requires the legalization of the use of foreign currencies which are stable.[17]

3.3. *The Financial Sector*

The hyperinflation debauched the financial system almost entirely.[18] The Serbo-Montenegrin financial system consists of two sectors: socially owned banks and private banks. The socially owned banks had most of their balance sheets composed of foreign currency positions which were frozen (partly as a result of sanctions). As regards unfrozen positions, on the asset side these banks had a small amount of Dinar cash, some foreign currency cash, and some Dinar loans and overdrafts (the Dinar positions being quite small at the black market exchange rate). On the liabilities side, capital (in Dinars) represented 1–2 per cent of the balance sheet, there was a small amount of Dinar deposits and some Dinar refinance credit from the National Bank of Yugoslavia.

The socially owned banks thus performed three main functions during the hyperinflation: (1) together with the SPP they provided the country's payments system; (2) they were a conduit for the allocation of vastly subsidized credit by the NBY to non-financial businesses; (3) they were the means by which some businesses and households could use overdraft facilities to reduce their inflation tax burden, and effectively share in seigniorage.[19]

On the other hand private banks responded to the hyperinflation by borrowing dinars from the socially owned banks on

Table 7 Serbia-Montenegro: balance sheet of a typical socially owned bank

Assets	Liabilities
1. Foreign currency (FC) deposits with NBY (frozen)	1. FC deposits of population (frozen)
2. FC loans to non-govt (frozen)	2. Refinance credit in FC (frozen)
3. FC cash	3. Capital (dinar)
4. Dinar cash	4. Dinar refinance credit
5. Dinar loans and overdrafts	5. Dinar deposits
6. Real estate etc.	

the inter-bank market, and buying foreign currency. The profits from these transactions had swollen their capital base. Dinar loans and cash were a small part of their assets. Such business as was conducted was with enterprises: above all the granting of dinar loans for working capital to exporters, accompanied by security (usually the equivalent of the whole amount borrowed) in foreign currency. Firms which borrowed, often maintained deposits with the same private banks. Thus the private banks shared in seigniorage to a significant extent, but performed few other functions towards the end of the hyperinflation. This was particularly so after the crash of the Dafina Bank, an outrageous Ponzi operation, which undermined households' confidence in private banks.

3.4. Other Non-financial Sectors

A phenomenon which has been noticed in a number of the faster hyperinflations, is the fall in output which accompanies these episodes (Rostowski, 1992). Serbia-Montenegro follows the same pattern, with industrial production falling at an accelerating rate as inflation itself has accelerated. The falls in industrial production were: 17.6 per cent in 1991, 22.9 per cent in 1992 and 37 per cent in 1993 (Madzar, 1993, and CESMECON, 1994). It can be argued that the primary cause of the fall in output in Serbia-Montenegro are the UN sanctions to which the country is subject. However, the fact that industrial output stabilized after the ending of the hyperinflation—with February being the first month in which it did not fall when seasonally adjusted—suggests that we may be dealing with something of wider significance.

A number of mechanisms have been proposed to explain how hyperinflation could cause output to fall. The first is that the inflation causes 'noise' which makes it harder to interpret price changes as being relative or not. As a result the allocation of resources is less efficient, and the true value of output falls (Auerbach, Davison and Rostowski, 1992). However, it is unclear why such a fall, while truly costly, should show up in the industrial output statistics. A second suggestion is that the dramatic fall in the value of real balances inevitably means a

roughly equivalent fall in real credit.[20] The problem is that often a large part of seigniorage is actually transferred to non-financial businesses in the form of cheap central bank credits, so that on a flow basis industry is actually obtaining additional liquidity at the expense of households (Layard and Richter, 1994).

Observation of the Serbo-Montenegrian hyperinflation suggests two additional possible mechanisms. The first is an extension to the non-retail sector of the process we described in Section 3.1. The greater the range of products one produces, the greater the risk that one will fail to reprice them all adequately, and that one will sell some at below replacement cost. One way of dealing with this problem is to reduce the range of one's products.[21] If goods are not perfect substitutes in production, this will lead to a fall in output. The second point is that once hyperinflation reaches Serbo-Montenegrian levels, domestic money is held exclusively for transaction purposes. Production requires undertaking transactions, which requires the holding of domestic money. Engaging in production thus means exposing oneself to the inflation tax, which thus becomes a tax on production.

That inflation itself was reducing output is indicated by the fact that industrial production recovered quite sharply after stabilization (Section 4.3). It is worth noting that neither of the last two mechanisms, which may have acted to depress output during the hyperinflation, would have operated if the use of foreign currency, so-called currency substitution, had been legal (Rostowski, 1992).

3.5. The State

An interesting phenomenon is the way the state tried to offset the Tanzi-Olivera effect not only by reducing tax payment periods, but also by increasing tax rates. Payroll taxes were increased to 222 per cent. There was a 3 per cent tax on the value of all payments made by cheque. The result was that by the end of the hyperinflation tax rates were totally unsuited to a non-inflationary environment, and needed to be very sharply reduced if the economy was not to find itself on the wrong part

of the conventional tax Laffer curve. This added a further dimension of uncertainty to any attempts at estimating budget revenues for 1994.

4. The Stabilization Programme

The Avramovic programme in its initial form of January 1994, stood the usual principles of stabilization on their head. Normally, when stabilizing hyperinflations it is considered vital to eliminate the monetary financing of the budget deficit, while a significant degree of discretion is usually maintained in the creation of credit for non-government (CNG) by the banking system.[22] In the Avramovic plan, on the contrary, money creation was initially reserved exclusively for financing the budget deficit, while expansion of CNG and the creation of deposit money unbacked by central bank liabilities[23] was made almost impossible. Furthermore, the budget deficit foreseen by the plan was massive: 14 per cent of GDP in 1994, or about thirty eight times the money supply at the time of stabilization.

As often occurs in hyperinflations, by January 1994 the international reserves of the central bank, small though they were, were worth several times the domestic money supply. Reserves were about $200 million, while the domestic money supply was less than $40 million. Introducing convertibility and fixing the exchange rate was thus safe, if further money creation was simultaneously brought under control. Convertibility at a fixed exchange rate could be expected to increase the demand for money very sharply, effectively eliminating the inflation overnight, as long as the fiscal fundamentals were in place.[24]

In fact, however, the fiscal fundamentals were in no way in place, and far from the National Bank of Yugoslavia (NBY) being made independent, it was openly stated that emission would be used to finance the massive budget deficit. Thus, both of the conditions which Sargent (1986a) considers to have been vital in bringing the hyperinflations of the 1920s to

an end, were violated in Serbia-Montenegro in 1994. It is this which makes the episode so important.

As we shall see in Section 4.1, the stabilization programme in its original form (and possibly even after the March 1994 amendments) was clearly unsustainable. According to rational expectations, a stabilization which is bound to break down at a future point in time should not succeed even temporarily: expected failure at time T implies that rational actors should run on the domestic currency at time $T-1$, which implies that the stabilization should fail at $T-1$, which means that the run should happen at $T-2$, and so on until we reach $T-i$, the moment at which the stabilization begins. The Serbo-Montenegrian experience therefore suggests that the benefits from the use of a (temporarily) stable currency outweigh the risk of loss at some uncertain point in the future from the holding of that currency.[25]

As a further twist, instead of proceeding in the standard way and fixing the exchange of the Old Dinar (OD), the NBY stopped creating ODs on 18 January 1994, and began to emit convertible New Dinars (ND) on 24 January.[26] Old Dinars initially continued in circulation, supposedly at a floating exchange rate against the ND (see Appendix 2).

4.1. *The Two Versions of the Fiscal Programme*

The fiscal side of the stabilization programme was initially presented in the Three Institutes Report (January 1994).[27] However, the programme was fundamentally revised in the final form which was passed by the Serb Republican Parliament in April 1994.

As compared with the estimated out-turn for 1993, the initial version of the fiscal programme planned only a slight reduction in government expenditure for 1994, a large increase in conventional tax revenue, and the persistence of a very large— though sharply reduced—budget deficit:

Table 8 Consolidated budget of Serbia-Montenegro 1992–94 (in US$ billions)

	1992[a]	1993[b]	1994[c] 1st half	1994[c] 2nd half	1994[c] whole
Revenue	3.7	2.7	1.7	2.0	3.7
Expenditures	5.3	5.5	2.5	2.7	5.2
Deficit	1.6	2.8	0.8	0.7	1.5

[a] Estimate.
[b] Forecast based on an estimate of the first 10 months of 1993.
[c] First half forecast, second half guess.
Source: Three Institutes (1994).

Achieving low inflation while at the same time maintaining a budget deficit of about 14 per cent of GDP[28] was only possible on the assumption that the economy had been so demonetized through hyperinflation that it would willingly accept the $130 million of NDs which needed to be printed each month of the year to finance the budget deficit. In November 1993 the OD money supply was the equivalent of less than $4 per person (Section 1), so it is perhaps not too surprising that this was initially indeed the case. The question was how long such rapid remonetization could continue. In Poland and Russia, which have also experienced hyperinflations recently, the domestic money supply still does not exceed 20 per cent of GDP. But in these countries the hyperinflations were far smaller, and domestic money supply never fell below 10 per cent of GDP, whereas in the Serbo-Montenegrian case it fell to below 0.5 per cent of GDP.

It seems that in Serbia-Montenegro one should not rely on the ratio of domestic money to GDP rising above 10 per cent. On CESMECON's and the Three Institutes' figure for GDP of some $11 billion, this would give about eight months of deficit finance at the rate proposed in the initial Three Institutes version of the plan. In that case the population was likely to have been unwilling to increase its real balances at the rate required much beyond late summer.[29] AFter that date the authorities would have faced either a resumption of high inflation, or would have had to undertake a very sharp fiscal correction of

some 14 percentage points of GDP on a flow basis. This is considerably more than the correction achieved in Poland in the first half of 1990, which amounted to some 8 percentage points of GDP on a flow basis.

Such a sequencing of the stabilization seems perverse from the political point of view. The experience of other countries indicates that people are prepared to accept much hardship to bring an end to the chaos of hyperinflation, but that the willingness to bear costs evaporates fairly quickly. The 'front loading' of pain typical of IMF adjustment programmes is eminently rational politically. The initial version of the Avramovic programme violated this political rationality, giving people the benefits of relief from hyperinflation 'up front', and requiring them to pay the price further down the line.

A number of other features of the initial fiscal plan were striking and indicated the same 'jam today' approach: first, the Three Institutes estimate of government expenditure in 1993 was far higher—at $5.5 billion–than that which is consistent with CESMECON's estimates based on monthly data ($2.2 billion). If CESMECON's monthly data is to be believed,[30] then the AVramovic plan originally programmed for a threefold increase in government expenditure compared with the last quarter of 1993 (Tables 3 and A1). Assuming that the plan's estimates regarding revenues were correct, a hardly miserly 1.8-fold increase in real expenditures compared with 1993 would have allowed the general government accounts to be balanced, and would have promised a better chance of long-term success.

On the revenue side there was no serious programming in the initial version of the programme: it was merely stated that the increase in government revenue (compared to the estimated out-turn for 1993 as a whole) would come in equal proportions from: (1) a reversal of the Tanzi-Olivera effect; (2) new measures; and (3) a Laffer-curve effect resulting from a reduction in the extremely high tax rates which had been introduced in order to offset the Tanzi-Olivera effect.

In April 1994 the new government of the Republic of Serbia slashed general government expenditures in the Republic by 30 per cent from the ND6.7 billion which had been projected by

the Three Institutes to ND4.8 billion. Since the Federal Budget remained largely unchanged, total general government expenditure was reduced by slightly over 20 per cent.[31] Projected general government revenue was also revised down by about ND500 million. As a result the deficit of the general government of Serbia-Montenegro should be halved from about ND2.5 billion to ND1.2 billion (from about 14 per cent of GDP to about 6.5 per cent of GDP).

This indicates a shift of fiscal policy towards a stance more usual in stabilizations. Indeed, the NBY stated in May 1994 that it will not finance the budget deficit after July 1994. Nevertheless, even under the new fiscal programme, the size of the deficit is still not negligible. It would imply a remonetization leading to a domestic money to GDP ratio of about 7 per cent—which should be within the bounds of safety. However, this would only be the case on the assumption that monetary policy remained unchanged which, as we shall see, has not been the case.[32]

4.2. Monetary Policy

As described earlier, the ND currency was at first (until March 1994) exclusively introduced into circulation by being used to finance government expenditure. Some of this returned to the government in the form of tax revenue, but the monthly deficit constituted almost the only source of NDs for the economy. This permissiveness as far as the fiscal channel for the injection of NDs is concerned was initially combined with an extraordinarily restrictive regime for the banking system. Banks were only allowed to lend in one of two cases: (1) if they obtained refinance credit from the National Bank of Yugoslavia (NBY), and this was only possible against a hard currency deposit of 100 per cent of the sum borrowed; and (2) on the basis of time deposits of over one month. As the share of time deposits remained very small, the money multiplier remained close to one, and the banking system was close to 100 per cent reserve banking (see Chapter 11). The purpose of this policy was simply to reserve almost all of the proceeds of remonetization for the budget.

In March 1994, however, there was a fundamental shift in monetary policy by which commercial banks were allowed to extend credit on the basis of short-term deposits. Moreover, the new reserve ratios which were introduced at that time were very low, given the circumstances of a very recent hyperinflation.[33] As a result, whereas the total amount of high powered money was still only about ND720 million at the end of March 1994, of which about ND340 million was cash and about ND380 million was commercial bank deposits at the NBY, commercial bank credits to non-government had increased to about ND800 million. This means that deposits at commercial banks were about ND1.1 billion, and broad ND money was about ND1.2 billion, or already some 7 per cent of GDP.[34] The fundamental question remains, however, whether the loosening of monetary policy of early March has not been so great that the very significant tightening of fiscal policy which occurred in mid-April will prove insufficient to save the programme.[35] Indeed, by September 1994 the ND was trading at a 40 per cent discount to the official rate.

4.3. Initial Results of the Stabilization Programme

From the beginning of the programme to June 1994 consumer prices fell by 8.7 per cent. To mid-March the consumer price index declined by 0.4 per cent. However, this conceals enormous differences in the components of the index. Whereas goods prices declined by 13.5 per cent the cost of services increased by 57.4 per cent, as the authorities increased utilities tariffs and slashed subsidies.

As regards production, industrail output is reported to have increased compared to the same month of 1993 by 12 per cent in February and by 22 per cent in March (*The Economist*, 7 May 1994). Adjusted for the number of working days in the month, the increases were 0.1 per cent in February and 9.4 per cent in March.[36] Not only was this the first such increase for over four years, but it was also far from marginal. It brought the seasonally adjusted level of industrial output back to the level of September 1993, i.e. before the ravages brought about by the hyperinflationary explosion of the autumn. The key question is

Table 9 Serbia-Montenegro: price increases during the first two months of stabilization (%)

Services	57.4
Education and culture	62
Housing (rents and heating)	30
Transport and telecoms	20
Financial	−20
Goods	−13.5
Foodstuffs	−32
Beverages (incl. alcohol)	−41
Tobacco	0
Non-foodstuffs	−6.9
TOTAL	−0.4

Source: Advisers to the Serbian Government.

what the source of this growth was. Clearly little had changed as far as Serbia's external relations are concerned: sanctions were in place exactly as before.[37]

There are a number of possible sources for this real improvement, all of which are linked to the ending of the hyperinflation. The first is what can be termed the 'Calvo effect', resulting from the increase in real credit accompanying the remonetization which followed stabilization. And indeed, real credit did increase from the equivalent of some ND50 million at the end of the hyperinflation to some ND800 million at the end of March. The problem with this interpretation is that we know that no new credit for non-government was created in Serbia-Montenegro until March 1994. We therefore have to explain the beginning of the recovery in February, when there could have been no 'Calvo effect'. The alternative explanations for the February recovery are all related to the termination of the mechanisms which depressed output during the hyperinflation (Section 3.4). These mechanisms are: (1) the fact that the inflation tax is a tax on production, because in a hyperinflation the domestic money is only held to effect transactions and production requires that one engage in transactions in the domestic currency (if currency substitution is forbidden); (2) the reduction in the range of goods sold by risk averse retailers will cause a fall in output if capital, labour, and other factors cannot be perfectly elastically reallocated to the production of goods

which continue to be sold; (3) information noise regarding relative prices.

5. Conclusion

The history of the Serbo-Montenegrian stabilization is the story of the successive abandonment of the unconventional elements in the Avramovic programme. By early February the ND to OD exchange rate was effectively fixed, so that there never really was a bi-paper standard in the country. In March and April 1994 the stabilization programme was further changed in ways which brought it closer to conventional programmes: fiscal policy was made more restrictive and monetary policy was made looser with the re-introduction of fractional reserve banking (with quite low reserve ratios).

The reason for the tightening of the fiscal stance seems to lie mainly in Serbia's international position. The initial programme was built on the assumption that there would be peace in Bosnia by the summer of 1994, that sanctions would be lifted, and indeed that an IMF stand-by facility could be negotiated shortly thereafter.[38] The main purpose of the programme was therefore to enable the Milosevic group to survive politically until the summer of 1994. This was to be done by allowing the government to recover its ability to command resources, which had been ravaged during the hyperinflation by the destruction of the real value of conventional tax revenue through the Tanzi-Olivera effect. However, the NATO ultimata of February and April 1994 seem to have brought about a more realistic view in Belgrade. It was no longer sufficient to be able to maintain the machinery of government functioning through to the summer. A recurrence of hyperinflation before the end of the war had to be avoided at all costs. And since the war might not end in the foreseeable future, policy had to aim at permanent—rather than at temporary—stability. As regards the longer term success of the stabilization, one can only say that the welcome fiscal tightening seems to have been more than compensated by excessive monetary loosening. Nevertheless, whether the Avramovic plan is successful or not in the medium

term, the fact that it worked initially is of both theoretical and policy importance.

APPENDIX 1: Differing Estimates of Monetary and Fiscal Magnitudes

There are a number of difficulties with the data. CESMECON use the US$ value of the change in the broad money supply as their measure of seigniorage, on the grounds that banks have been instructed to grant loans by government, and that such directed credit cannot be distinguished from the credit of the NBY, particularly as banks have issued such informally directed credit even in the temporary absence of refinance from the NBY. If this is true of most bank credit then it would be correct to treat all bank liabilities as if they were Central Bank liabilities. Conventionally defined seigniorage from the creation of central bank money has of course been significantly smaller than real broad money creation (on the CESMECON figures it averaged about $80 million per month (Table 10)), but it too exhibits no clear downward trend for the (shorter) period available, apparently confirming the stability of seigniorage levels at extremely high inflation rates in Serbia-Montenegro.

Another problem arises from the fact that the data is obtained

Table 10 High-powered and broad money growth in Serbia-Montenegro, 1993

	Real increases in:	
	High-powered money	Broad money
January	$54m	$77m
February	$86m	$109m
March	$65m	$126m
April	$154m	$277m
May	$35m	$105m
June	$91m	$149m
July	$120m	$197m
August	$60m	$147m
September	$53m	$119m
October	—	$149m
November	—	$134m

Source: CESMECON 1993*b* and calculations by CESMECON provided to the author.

by taking the monthly increases in nominal broad (or high powered) money and deflating by the average informal market exchange rate for the month. However, if the bulk of government expenditure takes place on two days, in the middle of the month and at the end of the month,[39] then if the average exchange rate for the month is used to calculate the dollar value of seigniorage, an insufficiently depreciated exchange rate may be being used to deflate nominal money.[40]

In fact when we make this adjustment, broad seigniorage falls from an average of $144m/month to $113m/month. However, at this lower level, seigniorage appears to remain stable in spite of the extraordinary acceleration of inflation.[41] Table 11 shows two estimates of 'broad seigniorage'. The first is CESMECON's, and deflates the increase in nominal broad money by the average black market exchange rate for the month. The second deflates the same nominator by the average exchange rate on the 15th day of the month and the last day of the month.

Thus on the basis of two different monthly estimates, 'broad seigniorage' seems to have remained roughly constant almost to the very end of the hyperinflation. Moreover, CESMECON's estimates of monthly 'broad seigniorage' (1993a and 1994) show it as roughly constant at about $1.7bn on an annual basis for 1992 and 1993. Also, their estimates of the annual budget deficits (Table 12), show seigniorage either constant or actually increasing—from

Table 11 Serbia-Montenegro: estimates of 'Broad Seigniorage' (increases in broad money), 1993

	CESMECON	Rostowski
January	$77m	$59m
February	$109m	$79m
March	$126m	$90m
April	$277m	$223m
May	$105m	$81m
June	$149m	$131m
July	$197m	$198m
August	$147m	$117m
September	$119m	$67m
October	$149m	$95m
November	$134m	$106m
AVERAGE	$144m	$113m

Source: CESMECON 1993b, data provided by CESMECON and author's calculations based on exchange rates in *Ekonomska Politika* (various issues).

1991 to 1992—over the years as inflation accelerated far in excess of the 500 per cent per annum, which has been claimed to be the seigniorage maximizing rate of inflation on the basis of Latin American experience.

There are also serious conflicts between the available estimates of the fiscal magnitudes, and also conflicts between these estimates and the estimates of seigniorage which we have just discussed. The estimates below are adjustments by CESMECON of official figures and official estimates:

Table 12 Serbia-Montenegro: public sector finances 1990–93

	% of GMP[a]		
	Expenditures	Deficit	Revenues
1990	49	3	46
1991	60	21	39
1992	60	37	23
1993	43	28	15
	in US$ billion[b]		
	Expenditures	Deficit	Revenues
1990	11.3	0.7	10.6
1991	11.4	4.0	7.4
1992	8.4	5.2	3.2
1993	4.7	3.1	1.6

[a] Gross Material Product, which is about 90 per cent of Gross Domestic Product.
[b] GMP for Serbia and Montenegro (the present FRY) was $23 billion in 1990 and $19 billion in 1991. It is estimated as being $14 billion in 1992 and $11 billion in 1993 (CESMECON 1993*a*).

Source: CESMECON 1993*b* and 1994.

However, the so-called 'Three Institutes'[42] give results which are in general very different. Although both sources show a sharp decline in conventional tax revenues between 1992 and 1993, in the 'Three Institutes' data there is effectively no Tanzi-Olivera effect in operation, as the share of conventional tax revenue in GDP remains constant between 1992 and 1993, in spite of point to point inflation during the year increasing from 22 times in 1992 to 3,750,000,000,000 times in 1993:

Table 13 Consolidated budget of Serbia-Montenegro 1992–93 (in US$ billions)

	1992	% GDP	1993	% GDP
Revenue	3.7	26	2.7	25
Expenditures	5.3	39	5.5	50
Deficit	1.6	11	2.8	26

Source: Table 8 and GDP estimates from Table 12.

This is particularly surprising as the 'Three Institutes' lay great stress on the reversal of the Tanzi-Olivera effect as a key component of the stabilization programme they set out in the same document in which the above data are presented.

However, a further complication is that the figures for the budget deficit given in Table 12 are noticeably larger than the estimates of annual 'broad seigniorage' given by CESMECON itself, let alone those for 'narrow seigniorage' which would be the right definition to use here (Table 10). If we make these two adjustments (i.e. take narrow seigniorage of about $1 billion as correct for both 1992 and 1993), then government expenditure in 1993 should only have been about $2.6 billion,[43] and not the $4.7 billion given by CESMECON itself. Similarly, expenditures in 1992 should have been only about $4 billion, and not $8.4 billion.

The difference between the three estimates, two of which have been made by the same organization, shows just how hard it is to have confidence in any statistics under hyperinflationary circumstances. It should therefore act as a warning against technically complex econometric work by outside researchers or by those working many years after the episode (unless the authors have by some extraordinary piece of luck been able to examine the quality of their data scrupulously).

However, on both sets of CESMECON figures there is a collapse of real government expenditures in 1993 (either from $8.4bn to $4.7bn, or from $4bn to $2.6bn). This fall would explain the adoption of the stabilization programme of January 1994, and also the greater willingness of the Serb leadership to make concessions in Bosnia in the winter of 1994. According to official statistics transfers to the Serb Republic of Bosnia and the Serb Republic of Kraina were equivalent to 12.7 per cent of the GMP of Serbia-Montenegro. But the collapse of real government expenditures in 1993, and particularly towards the end of the year, suggests that the SRB and SRK were getting little material support in real terms by the end of the hyperinflation.

The conflict between different estimates of seigniorage also unfortunately makes it impossible to place Serbia-Montenegro in an international context. Layard and Richter (1994) have pointed to the 25 per cent share of seigniorage in Russian GDP during the current high inflation as being quite exceptional by international standards. They claim that generally this level never exceeds 10 per cent of GDP. Even if we accept 'broad seigniorage' calculated using the average monthly exchange rate as the appropriate measure, we have three significantly different values for each year for Serbia-Montenegro. On the basis of CESMECON's annual data regarding the budget deficit[44] (Table 12), seigniorage during 1991–3 was about as large in Serbia-Montenegro as it has been in Russia (and in 1992 it was far larger). According to the annual data regarding the deficit given by the Three Institutes (Table 13), seigniorage was far smaller than in Russia in 1992, but reached Russian levels in 1993. Finally, if we take CESMECON's direct monthly calculations of seigniorage and relate them to the GDP given by CESMECON (1993a), we find that the shares were about 13 per cent in 1992 and 16 per cent in 1993.[45] The present author has somewhat more confidence in the monthly figures than in the annual ones. However, if the annual figures should be confirmed, they would suggest that former socialist countries can sustain far higher shares of seigniorage in GDP. If this were so, it would require detailed examination.

APPENDIX II: *The role of the 'old dinar' after stabilization*

One of the strangest aspects of the programme is the fate of the Old Dinar. Old Dinar creation by the NBY ceased on 18 January 1994. The exchange rate of ODs continued to increase on the money market, however, from 7 million per Deutsche Mark on 18 January to 15 million on 21 January. It then declined to 13 million on the 24 January and 12 million on the 26 January 1994, which is the level at which it has remained since. Old Dinar cash has disappeared from circulation, apparently due to covert withdrawal by the authorities, but a not insignificant amount of OD deposits remained in existence.[46] Formally Serbia-Montenegro was on a bi-paper standard, with two domestic paper currencies which floated against each other, with the exchange rate between the two currencies being set by the market. Taxes were to be paid in the currency in which the taxable transaction was effected. However, the ND was the 'superior' currency, in that taxes on

transactions carried out in ODs could be paid in NDs, while the opposite was not the case (the same held for private debt, see below). This required the authorities to set a ND/OD exchange rate for tax payments in NDs on OD transactions, and this probably accounts for the rock solid stability of the 'market' rate of 12 million OD/ND.[47]

It is unclear why the authorities kept the OD in existence, and why they kept up the fiction that it was a separate independent currency. It may be that the authorities doubted that stabilization would succeed, and kept the OD in reserve, for use in financing the budget deficit in such an event. In any case, the role of the two currencies in the Serbo-Montenegrian stabilization has been quite different than in Russia in 1923–4, where the stable domestic currency (the chervonets) was issued via State Bank credits to non-government, while the hyperinflating treasury note (the sovznak) was used to finance the budget deficit (Rostowski and Shapiro, 1992).

One quite interesting problem has emerged as a result of the maintenance of the OD in existence. Interest rates rose through January 1994, to reach a peak of 1,114,400 per cent per month on 24 January 1994.

Thus, if ODs worth the equivalent of DM 1 million were

Table 14 Interest rates on the Belgrade money market for Old Dinars Jan.–Feb. 1994

	Daily	Monthly		Monthly	Annual
06.01	28.64	191,091	31.01	14.13	388.4
10.01	30.22	275,514	04.02	16.82	519.6
11.01	30.55	297,268	09.02	18.52	690.3
12.01	30.75	311,396	15.02	19.74	794.8
13.01	30.97	327,008	18.02	16.61	548.6
14.01	31.45	365,433	23.02	16.61	548.6
17.01	32.67	482,538	24.02	12.51	319.6
18.01	33.30	555,432	25.02	4.37	68.3
19.01	35.11	833,148	01.03	4.37	68.3
20.01	36.12	1,041,388	02.03	2.00	27.2
21.01	36.25	1,070,818	08.03	2.00	27.2
24.01	36.43	1,114,400	09.03	0.79	10.0
25.01	36.40	1,107,483	10.03	0.40	5.0
26.01	35.83	977,274	31.03	0.40	5.0
27.01	10.78	241.6			

Source: Trziste Novca i Kratkorocnih Hartija od Vrednosti, Beograd [The Belgrade Money and Short-term Credit Market].

borrowed on 21 January 1994 for ten working days, then the equivalent of DM 27.5 million needed to be repaid at the end of that period.[48] And this does not apply exclusively to the inter-bank market: banks were charging non-bank customers similar rates, and were offering similar rates to non-bank customers on CDs. If we assume that, in total, the equivalent of DM 20 million was lent on similar terms by the banks, and that an equivalent amount was borrowed by them (again on similar terms) then if the average 'expansion factor' on these sums was 10—instead of 27—then the banks could at present owe and be owed some DM 200 million, even though officially the OD money supply is said to be under the equivalent of DM 50 million.[49]

Banks were therefore desperately short of ODs: on the money market in early February demand for ODs exceeded supply by 15–20 times. This helps to account for the continuing rise in OD money market rates we see in Table 14, from 241 per cent p. a. on 27 January 1994 to 759 per cent p. a. on 15 February 1994. Since no ODs were being created by the NBY, we can be sure that these rates were not due to any doubts as to the credibility of the stabilization of the OD relative to the ND (on which interest rates were about 20 per cent per annum), but simply to a desire by borrowers to pay off OD liabilities bearing interest rates set before 27 January 1994 as quickly as possible.

NDs were legal tender for the settling of OD debts, at the current exchange rate of 12 million to one, almost from the begin-ning of the programme (although the opposite was not the case).[50] However, given the initial unavailability of NDs to the financial system—because NDs were only paid out to finance salaries and pensions—it was in practice impossible for borrowers to take advantage of this provision during the first half of February. Dur-ing 1–15 February total turnover on the Belgrade money market was 1,932,000 ODs and 125,000 NDs (both in ND terms). During 16–28 February the relevant figures were 529,000 ODs and 2,600,000 NDs.

NOTES

The first draft of this chapter appeared in the Discussion Paper series of the *Centre for Economic Performance, London School of Economics* no.213, in November 1994. Significant (though not hyper) inflation returned in Serbia-Montenegro in November 1994, with prices increasing by 120 per cent (December to December) during 1995.

1. This episode took place in the Federal Republic of Yugoslavia, which

consists of Serbia and Montenegro. We use the term Serbia-Montene-gro so as to avoid confusion with the Yugoslav high inflation of 1989, which occurred in the Socialist Federal Republic of Yugoslavia before the break-up of that country in 1991, in spite of the linguistic infeli-cities that ensue. The present FRY has a federal government and two republican governments, with the whole under the political control of Serbia. Federal institutions, such as the National Bank of Yugoslavia are, of course, referred to by their official names.

2. The two hyperinflations which were faster at their apogee are Hungary II (1946) which attained 419 quadrillion (10^{13}) % per month, and Greece (1944) which attained 855 million % per month.

3. Two weeks after the beginning of the stabilization programme.

4. One can think of hyperinflation as the economic analogue of a particle accelerator. A number of economic phenomena not encountered under normal conditions can be observed during hyperinflations. For instance, in hyperinflations different forms of money come to perform different functions (Rostowski and Shapiro, 1992). It says something about the (weakly) empirical nature of economics that I was (to my knowledge) the only foreign economist to conduct a research trip to Yugoslavia at this time.

5. Sachs and Larrain, quoting Cagan (1956) cite Russia 1921–4 as lasting 26 months. Contemporary sources (e.g. Young, 1925) give 10 months.

6. We can see this if we compare Germany in 1923, where the process became exponential ten months after hyperinflation began:

1921		7.7
1922	H1	12.4
	H2	28.9
1923	H1	53.6
	M7	285.8
	M8	1,162.3
	M9	2,436.8
	M10	29,524.8
	M11	10,128.6
	M12	73.8

(*Source*: Sargent, 1986*a*.)

7. Since annual GDP is estimated at $11 billion (CESMECON, 1993*b*), and total transactions are usually about twice GDP, daily transactions (assuming 300 working days per year) will have been about $65 million. However, if half of all transactions were effected in foreign currency the velocity of circulation will only have been once a day (i.e. 300 times a year). With inflation at 80 per cent per day a significantly slower velocity is unlikely.

8. Largely as a result of sanctions, but hyperinflation has also contrib-uted to the fall in output, as is shown by the output increases which have occurred upon stabilization and before the lifting of sanctions (see Sect. 4.3).

9. CESMECON, 1994.

10. Of the old Illyrian-type businesses which used to be in 'social owner-ship' some 36% have been transformed into state owned enterprises and 40% have been privatized.

11. Cash payments to an entity in this sector had to be passed through that entity's account by means of the state payments system the SPP.

12. It only reduced inflation from 19 times in August to 8 times in September.

13. The turnover period in such a situation lasts from the moment of sale of an item to the moment of purchase of its replacement (this last being defined as the moment at which the money used for the purchase is received by the seller of the good).

14. Information from the Managing Director of C-Market, a chain of 200 private supermarkets.

15. It also reported working its purchasing staff far harder at this time.

16. Since this was a black market rate it could not be broadcast by radio stations, although taxis could use CB to obtain this information immediately from their dispatchers.

17. See Rostowski (1992) for other arguments in favour of currency substitution.

18. The following is based on an account by Dr Zivkovic of CESMECON.

19. The last point is the only one which is specific to Serbia-Montenegro. For Eastern Europe, Yugoslavia had a high level of development of personal banking services, with every employed person having a bank account. Under hyperinflationary conditions it was advantageous to build up an overdraft as the punitive interest rates which were charged were still massively negative in real terms. In Serbia-Montenegro cheques are printed with the maximum amount for which they can be written on them. The issuing of such cheques to an individual in excess of the amount on his account was therefore in effect the granting of an overdraft to them.

20. I am grateful to Guillermo Calvo for this suggestion.

21. Note that Deutsche Mark pricing and using the spot exchange rate may not be adequate with inflation rates of 30–80 per cent per working day, unless one has the black market exchange rate on ticker tape!

22. See Sargent (1986a) for the classical justification of this approach.

23. Through the increase in the money multiplier which usually accompanies stabilization—see Ch. 10.

24. The real problem facing the authorities would then be by how much to increase the money supply without reigniting the hyperinflation, while at the same avoiding massive depression (see Ch. 9).

25. The difference between risk and uncertainty is important here: if the probability of collapse (risk) of the exchange rate at all points of time is known, the effect will be the same as if the time of collapse was known with certainty. On the other hand, if there is genuine uncertainty as to when the collapse will happen (although certainty that it

will happen at some time), then the reasoning forbidding a temporary stabilization, as outlined in the text, does not hold.

26. At a fixed rate of exchange of 1ND = 1 DM. Although the ND is formally only 'internally' convertible according to the law (i.e. it is convertible for current account transactions and for capital account transactions as long as the foreign currency involved remains within the country), in practice because of sanctions current account trans- actions must take place offshore, undermining the whole idea of internal convertibility. Thus, imports involve either the export of foreign cash, or the transfer of foreign currency to the banking system of a country breaking sanctions (such as Cyprus), after which the currency is used to finance imports into Serbia-Montenegro. Export proceeds are also likely to be held abroad, so that they can then be used to finance imports. The ND is therefore effectively fully con- vertible from the Serbo-Montenegrian point of view. Clearly, however, this is not the case as far as the international community is concerned.

27. Avramovic was the head of the team which wrote this report, and Avramovic confirmed to the present author that the figures contained in the report embodied his intentions as of early February 1994.

28. On CESMECON's assumption of a GDP of $11 billion. Other insti- tutes tend to assume a lower GDP.

29. That the authors of the programme may have had similar doubts from the very beginning is indicated by the fact that the plan for the first half of 1994 is claimed to be a projection, while that for the second half is admitted to be a guesstimate.

30. And preferred over its annual data (as I suspect it should).

31. Since Montenegro accounts for only 7 per cent of general government in the whole Federation, any changes in its budget made little differ- ence.

32. Furthermore, there is some lack of clarity regarding the state of the fiscal accounts during the first two months of the programme. Whereas the three state budgets were in balance during this period, ND370 million were added to the money supply through the 'fiscal channel'. It is unclear to what extent this was a deficit due to the extra budgetary Health Fund, and therefore properly part of the deficit of general government, and to what extent it merely represented the state's practice of depositing money in commercial banks, rather than at the NBY. To the extent to which it was the former, then the general government deficit wil have been very close to the levels projected in the initial fiscal programme, and which was—as we pointed out above—dangerously high.

33. Sight deposits—14 per cent; deposits up to 1 month—9 per cent; deposits of 1–3 months—5 per cent; over 3 months' deposits— 3 per cent.

34. Nevertheless, as late as mid-May no discount window had yet been opened at the NBY for NDs, although the NBY did discount ND50

million of commercial paper directly (this was not rediscounting—the money did not pass through the commercial banks).

35. A worrying aspect of current Serbo-Montenegrian policy making is the way the authorities talk of the money being created to finance the budget deficit being 'backed' by the international reserves of the NBY. This would indeed be true if the original monetary system, with 100 per cent reserve banking, had been maintained. In that case, all money would have consisted of NBY liabilities, and if the NBY had enough foreign assets to back these there would be no reason for disquiet, even if the NBY liabilities were being issued to finance the budget deficit. However, once fractional reserve banking is re-introduced, a very significant part of the total money supply consists of commercial bank liabilities. If the currency is convertible (as the ND is) then the NBY's international reserves must be thought of as backing for the whole of the broad money stock, and not just for that part of it which represents liabilities of the NBY. With the NBY's international reserves standing at about ND0.5 billion and the broad money supply being about ND1.4 billion at the end of March 1994, it is very much a matter of judgement whether there is any significant scope for further money creation in the absence of *increasing* international reserves.

36. Information obtained from advisers to the Serb government.

37. In September 1994 flights to Serbia were allowed for the first time, but all other sanctions remained.

38. Avramovic in conversation with the author.

39. This is when government salaries and pensions are paid out. it is also when enterprises pay wages (which is relevant if we treat the whole of the real value of the increase in broad money as seigniorage).

40. The more obvious question of whether the failure of seigniorage to decline is due to the use of 'dollars' (i.e. when we deflate by the exchange rate) rather than 'real old dinars' (i.e. when we deflate by the price index) can be answered in the negative: from September the rate of depreciation of the OD exceeded the rate of inflation quite significantly (CESMECON, 1994).

41. This need not have been the case if devaluation accelerated at an exponential rate from the second half of one month to the second half of the following month after September 1993.

42. Institute of Economics, Faculty of Economics and Institute of Economic Sciences, all in Belgrade. All were involved in devising the Avramovic stabilization programme, and thus had access to unpublished official data. On the other hand, this may have inhibited them from drawing certain conclusions.

43. $1.6 billion of tax revenue, and $1 billion of seigniorage.

44. Since no borrowing was possible the whole of the deficit had to be financed by seigniorage.

45. In fact, by using broad seigniorage we are taking something which has to be larger than the budget deficit, which is what the annual estimates gave us.

46. Deposits comprised three quarters of OD M1 at the end of October 1993, and this share had risen sharply during the year. So even if total OD money supply amounted to less than $40 million, most of this was deposit money.
47. The rate itself seems to have been based on the OD/DM market rate two days after the introduction of NDs on 26.1.94.
48. On 21 Jan. 1994 the exchange rate was 15 million OD/DM.
49. Prof. Nebojsa Savic, Ekonomski Institut, Beograd.
50. They could also have retroactively reduced OD interest rates on previously agreed contracts to a sensible level on 24 Jan. 1994 when the ND was introduced. This has been done many times in Latin America and is known as the 'tablita'. The Serbo-Montenegrian case shows once again that it is easy to avoid learning from others' experience!

5

Stabilization and the Banking Sector: Switching from Bad to Good Credit in Post-Communist Economies

1. Introduction

Before the beginning of the transition to capitalism all credit in Central Europe and the Soviet Union was 'systematically bad', in the sense that it was not allocated on the basis of commercial criteria, and therefore there was no reason to suppose that, once ordinary market conditions were established, any particular loan could be serviced and ultimately repaid by the borrower. Bad credit of this kind is not really an asset belonging to the lender, but rather a transfer to the borrower,[1] occurring at the expense of either the lender or of those financing the lender (the lender's lenders). To the extent that a part of any credit could be serviced and repaid, this was accidental, and to the extent that servicing is enforced, could be thought of as a random tax on particular borrowers.

The badness of credit before the transition had different causes in economies which were centrally administered right up to the loss of power by the communists, and in those in which some degree of market relations already existed. Albania, Bulgaria, Czechoslovakia, the German Democratic Republic, and Romania belonged to the first group; Hungary, Poland, the Soviet Union, and Yugoslavia to the second. In the first group credit was allocated on the basis of planners' preferences, which had no correspondence to commercial criteria. Sometimes credit was supplied to compensate state owned enterprises (SOEs) for a syphoning-off of profits, which was

intended to prevent the SOEs from accumulating inventories (Schmieding, 1991).[2]

In the second group, rapid inflation and sharply negative real interest rates had a similar effect. When loans are granted under such abnormal circumstances it is almost impossible to know which of them could be serviced and recovered under normal market conditions. Furthermore, in semi-market socialist systems of this kind, the Central Bank effectively acted as a guarantor of all bank and inter-enterprise loans (Calvo, 1991). Such implicit full credit insurance was sufficient in itself to ensure the badness of credit by maximizing moral hazard. Thus a key component of the transition to market capitalism is the transformation of systemically bad credit into systemically good credit.[3]

2. Microeconomic Aspects of Switching from Bad to Good Credit

The reasons for wishing to eliminate 'bad credit' early in the transition are self-evident: bad credit is a transfer to the borrower, moreover it usually takes place at the expense of the state or of holders of money (i.e. savers, if it is financed by the inflation tax). It is thus both the reason for the persistence of soft-budget constraints for SOEs and a source of inflation. Since it occurs outside public and/or parliamentary control bad credit is allocated in a less accountable way than are budgetary subsidies, and is therefore even less desirable than these.

What then stands in the way of switching from bad to good credit? We first examine the case of the centrally administered economies of the first group, as this allows us to avoid the additional complicating question of high inflation at the moment of the switch over. The main problem with a sudden switch is that banks which have never made such choices before, suddenly have to decide which enterprises they will continue financing, and which they will cut off from credit. They are likely to make many mistakes. The costs of the switch are therefore likely to be high, with viable enterprises having to curtail their activity, and even being liquidated, while continued lending to unviable enterprises undermines the capital base of

the commercial banks, leading either to the failure of certain banks or to their recapitalization—of which more below.

On the other hand, it is not easy to imagine a 'gradualist' solution to the problem of the switch from good to bad credit—after all, banks either are or they are not responsible for the loans they make. Yet it is in this area that the costs of 'shock therapy' are likely to be particularly high, as almost completely inexperienced institutions are given the *duty* to decide about the allocation of savings in the economy. There seem to be two ways out of this acute dilemma: global debt write-off and inflation.[4]

The first of these had been proposed by Begg and Portes (1993) and Schmieding (1991). Proponents of this approach stress the economic irrationality of the initial allocation of credit under central planning, point to the risk of liquidation of economically viable enterprises and of the bankruptcy of a significant number of banks, and therefore propose the writing-off of all bank debt inherited from the previous regime. Furthermore, it is claimed that inherited bad credit will contaminate the new, potentially good, credit, because banks, unable to bankrupt existing unviable borrowers due to the effects of such a move on their capital base, may allow such borrowers to capitalize interest and roll over principal payments due (so called 'evergreening'). This deprives new, potentially far better borrowers from access to credit. Once the bulk of bank assets consists of such bad credits, the true financial position of the banks will come to light, and the bad credits will have to be written off in any case. There may also be a moral contamination: if some borrowers see that others do not service their debts, they too will develop this habit. Since meeting one's liabilities lies at the heart of the capitalist order, it is the very essence of the new system which is undermined.[5]

The Begg-Portes-Schmieding solution faces two key problems. The first is that it posits the feasibility of a credible, once and for all, debt forgiveness which does not lead to moral hazard. The forgiveness of all debt at a stroke is no less likely to undermine debt service discipline—and thus the basis of the new capitalist order—than is the *ad hoc* failure to enforce debt

servicing by the many debtors who are in financial difficulties. Such a *deus ex machina* may be somewhat more believable in an economy which up to the beginning of the transformation was highly centrally administered, such as Czechoslovakia or the GDR, and where there was no discernible market rationale for the distribution of credit. It is very doubtful if it could exist in an economy such as Hungary or Russia, which has been trying to shift from a kind of market socialism plagued by soft budget constraints to a true market economy, and in which enterprises are co-responsible for their debts, since they had actively lobbied for credit under the old regime.

A more serious weakness of the proposal is that it treats the bad debt problem as if it were a stock problem exclusively, whereas it is in fact both a stock and a flow problem. The flow aspect arises from the lack of credit allocation skills in the commercial banks at the beginning of the transformation, from the property rights structure of both banks and their main customers the SOEs, and from certain cultural factors such as a relatively high level of corruption among bank staff. The existence of a flow problem is confirmed by the Polish experience, which shows that there are about as many qualified loans among credits issued to new private sector borrowers as there are among those made to the old SOE customers of the banks (Kawalec, Sikora, and Rymaszewski, 1993; and Gomulka, 1993*b*, Table 4).

There are two possible solutions to the flow problem, after the stock problem has been resolved through a global debt write-off. The first, suggested among others by Schmieding (1991), is to admit foreign banks onto the domestic market at the very beginning of the transition, since they have the requisite skills, traditions and property rights structure. Since foreign banks are not burdened with bad debts, their entry has been opposed in a number of PCEs—particularly in Russia—by the domestic banks, on the grounds that they would 'cherry pick' the best customers. However, after a global debt write off this argument would not hold. As regards the relative competitiveness of Western banks, the former GDR is the sole example of massive entry of Western banks onto the domestic market of a

PCE, and a study of the quality of new lending there should be most instructive. Polish experience is said to show that Western banks have not performed very much better than domestic banks. Of course, in some countries the entry of Western banks on a large scale is unfeasible for political rather than rational economic reasons (e.g. as a result of the political power of the domestic banks, which are determined to maintain their monopoly position, as has been very much the case in Russia).

The second solution to the flow problem is to abolish fractional reserve banking (Chapter 11, and McKinnon, 1992). Having to hold 100 per cent of their liabilities as reserves at the central bank, commercial banks would be unable to lend, and so would be unable to accumulate bad loans. This would allow banks to concentrate on their primary function as suppliers of payments services to the economy. Subsequently, a gradual reduction in required reserve ratios below 100 per cent would allow banks to learn by doing, as the economic volatility succeeding the collapse of communist power died down.

3. Macroeconomic Aspects of Switching from Bad to Good Credit

Inflation helps to solve the problem of the stock of bad credit inherited from the centrally administered system. But it does so at the cost of maintaining the flow of bad credit, and by ensuring that when inflation is brought under control, the problem of the stock of bad credit will re-emerge as a result of positive real interest rates, without there having been much progress in solving the flow problem. Nevertheless, it seems that the inflations which have everywhere accompanied the economic transition have been due, in part, to the desire of the authorities to evade the bad credit problem.[6]

3.1. The 'Credit Crunch' Hypothesis

The potential role of bad credit in generating inflation is clear. Let us imagine a PCE in which the banking system finances the purchase of inventories. Loans are granted only for the purchase of real inventories, and have to be repaid once these have been utilized in the production process. However, once this

happens new loans are obtained to purchase new inventories. Unless there is some anchor, such as a limit on total nominal credit or a positive real interest rate, then credit, money, and prices can increase indefinitely. This is so even though no firm receives 'excessive credit', because each firm individually can fully repay its loans by liquidating its stock of inventories.[7] What we have is a post-communist version of a banking system applying the 'real bills' doctrine. As is well known, under such circumstances the price level is indeterminate. Credit thus becomes a money (or inflation) machine. As we have seen, once inflation is high and real interest rates are sharply negative, all credit is 'systemically bad': as long as such circumstances persist most loans, however badly allocated, are likely to be repayable.

What stands in the way of 'switching off' this machine? The machine can be deactivated either by introducing positive real rates of interest (together with the requirement that interest on bank loans should not be capitalized), or by having a nominal domestic credit limit (Calvo, 1991). But in post-communist economies the additional consequence of deactivating the machine is that—for the first time—banks have to select which customers to continue lending to, and which to cut off from credit. Since the banks concerned have never previously had to make such decisions they are likely to make many mistakes, with the result that a large part of bank credit will be revealed as bad in the accounting sense (i.e. it will be revealed that borrowers cannot service it, see Fig. 9 where the shortening in the length of the balance sheet by 30 per cent in Fig. 9B as compared with Fig. 9A indicates an equivalent reduction in total real assets, while nominal magnitudes remain constant).

Stabilization thus transforms systemically bad credit into credit which is bad in an accounting sense (i.e. openly bad). The danger is that the possible ensuing insolvency of the banking system as in Fig. 9B will lead to a recapitalization of the banks which, unless the way in which banks operate is changed, will lead to new bad credits, new recapitalization, and so on. If this were to happen, bank recapitalization would become the new money machine. Thus the two events, switching to commercially

A: before stabilization/liberalization

ASSETS	LIABILITIES
RESERVES 300	CENTRAL BANK CREDIT 300
CREDIT (all systemically bad) 300	DEPOSITS 270
	CAPITAL 30

B: after stabilization/liberalization and a 50% increase in prices

ASSETS	LIABILITIES
RESERVES 300	CENTRAL BANK CREDIT 300
CREDIT 300 - - - - - - - - - - - - bad in an accounting sense 90	DEPOSITS 270
	CAPITAL 30

Figure 9 *Consolidated balance sheet of commercial banks before and after price liberalization*

based credit allocation and macroeconomic stabilization, are aspects of a single process: without stabilization banks will not start to allocate credit commercially (they need to believe that previous conditions under which real interest rates were highly negative have come to an end), but unless banks begin to allocate credit commercially, stabilization may fail because of the need to recapitalize the banks.

Calvo and Coricelli (1993) have pointed to the decline in real credit which accompanies price liberalization as a cause of the sharp drops in industrial output in post-communist economies. The solution they have proposed is that stabilization be accompanied by a 'one-off' increase in nominal central bank credit— so that total real credit will not decline (and possibly even increase).[8] However, this solution presents a number of problems:

1) *As long as the credit machine operates, SOEs are beneficiaries of a net flow of real funds from the rest of the economy (mainly households).* This is because before stabilization negative real interest rates and the creation by the central bank of a flow of new nominal credit which is directed to the SOEs, mean that during high inflation the SOEs are the main beneficiaries of the inflation tax, which is paid by holders of money. Stabilization, by introducing positive real interest rates on loans, stops or even reverses this flow of real funds, with the banking system (and thus, in PCEs, indirectly the budget) being the main beneficiary, with households also benefiting from the reduction in the inflation tax, though probably to a lesser extent. Unless other taxes can be increased sufficiently to maintain the subsidies to the SOE sector, which has not proved possible during the transition (Chapter 12), stabilization is bound to entail a deterioration in the real financial situation of SOEs as a whole.[9] This in turn is likely to lead to a decline in the output of SOEs.[10] Thus the Calvo and Coricelli proposal can only solve the problem of the stock of credit, but it cannot solve the problem of the continuous flow of additional credit, which is what SOEs really need if they are to maintain output at pre-stabilization levels.

2) *The proposal is vulnerable to a lack of credibility* vis-à-vis *both borrowers (assumed to be mostly enterprises) and deposit holders*

(assumed to be mostly households). If the former believe that the credit expansion is not truly once and for all, they will act on the assumption that more nominal credit will be available in the future. Thus, the cost to society in terms of output and employ-ment of disappointing these expectations will remain high. Moreover, deposit holders also have the power to frustrate policy makers' altruistic intentions. If they do not believe in the once and for all nature of the increase in the money supply which accompanies the once and for all increase in credit, then they will refuse to increase the real value of the money balances which they hold. They will do this by failing to reduce the velocity of circulation of money, so that the intended once and for all increase in nominal money will be offset by an equivalent increase in the price level. As a result, real credit also will fail to increase, since bank assets cannot increase in real terms if bank liabilities remain the same. The authorities will then be faced with the choice of either sticking to their announced policy, and refusing to increase nominal credit in the face of continuing inflation, even though this results in the very reduction of real credit which they wished to avoid, or alternatively, they can increase nominal credit, confirming the expectations of those who doubted the once and for all nature of the earlier nominal credit increase.

3) *Banks would misallocate much of any once and for all nominal credit increase.* As a result, they would soon be obliged to increase their lending margins and shorten their balance sheets, so as to improve their capital/asset ratios, bringing about the very 'credit crunch' the policy was designed to avoid (only somewhat later). Thus, for any given level of the banks' capital base, the greater the one off increase in bank credit, the greater the level of bad debt and the greater the need for credit retrench-ment subsequently (Fig. 10 where the real value of total assets remains constant—represented by the length of the balance sheet—while the nominal value increases by 50 per cent). There-fore, the proposed increase in bank credit would need to be accompanied by a government funded increase in the capital of (state owned) banks. The question then is whether a stabilization programme which began with an increase in central bank credit

A: before stabilization/liberalization

ASSETS	LIABILITIES
RESERVES 300	CENTRAL BANK CREDIT 300
CREDIT (all systemically bad) 300	DEPOSITS 270
	CAPITAL 30

B: after stabilization/liberalization, a 50% increase in the nominal value of central bank credit

ASSETS	LIABILITIES
RESERVES 450	CENTRAL BANK CREDIT 450
CREDIT 450 – – – – – – – – – – – – bad in accounting sense 135	DEPOSITS 420
	CAPITAL 30

Figure 10 *Consolidated balance sheet of commercial banks before and after price liberalization and an increase in nominal credit*

and commercial bank capital could be credible, or whether it would be more likely to be perceived as providing finance for the bad old habit of crediting loss makers.

4. Conclusion

One way of mitigating these phenomena is to combine stabilization with global debt write-off *and* the introduction of a very high (possibly even 100 per cent) reserve requirement in the banking sector. The SOE sector will then lose its net inflow of funds, but will not suffer a real net outflow as it has in some stabilizing PCEs.[11] Very high reserve requirements have the additional advantage that they reduce the problem of getting banks to loan efficiently by sharply reducing the amount of lending that banks can undertake. In the limiting case of 100 per cent reserve requirements the problem is altogether avoided, because all bank lending is abolished.

NOTES

1. This does not, of course, mean that no loans could be repaid. Credit was 'systemically bad' in communist economies in two senses: the first is that there was nothing in the procedure of credit allocation which gave reason to suppose that any particular loan could be repaid; the second is that therefore a large, but unknown, proportion of loans would not be able to be repaid. It is this latter proportion which constitutes a transfer to the borrower.
2. If planners believed an enterprise to be accumulating excess inventories they could reduce its credit, something which could not be done as easily with its own funds.
3. A significant number of loans may be recoverable given normal market conditions even when credit is 'systemically bad', and vice versa, many loans may be unrecoverable even when credit is systemically good. The difference depends on whether there exist the mechanisms requiring and enabling banks to select loans which will be good under normal market conditions.
4. There may also exist what I call the 'Czech solution', which is to maintain sufficiently tight control of wages to ensure that after price liberalization a significant number of SOEs retain profitability, while at the same time discouraging excessive reallocation of credit from old to new customers by the commercial banks. Instead of banks subsidizing bad enterprises, workers (in all enterprises) do.
5. I am grateful to Dr. Largo of the EBRD for this point.

6. The only exception has been the GDR, where Western banks have been admitted *en masse* onto the domestic market and where the old enterprise debts to the banks have been effectively transferred as assets to the government (they continue to be SOEs' and privatized SOEs' liabilities, unless taken over by the state on a case by case basis).

7. Calvo (1991) develops a similar model which requires, however, that real inventories continuously accumulate for inflation to be generated.

8. If the one-off nature of the increase in nominal credit is credible, then prices will increase no more than (and possibly less than) nominal credit.

9. Calvo and Coricelli (1993) seem to be tending towards such an interpretation when they say that capitalized interest should not be included in any calculation of real credit. However, it is unclear why *any* interest on loans, be it capitalized or not, should be included in real credit. If a firm actually pays interest due, it has that much less liquidity available, and this should be subtracted from the additional liquidity obtained by another firm, which is now the recipient of a new loan partly made possible thanks to the interest payment made by the first firm. Only a net flow of funds from other sectors of the economy, or from the external sector, should count as a 'liquidity increasing increment in real credit', and therefore relevant in the 'credit crunch' framework.

10. Even non-commercially allocated credit is likely to be related in some way to the amount of gross output (and, in the short term, even value added) which an SOE produces.

11. It should be noted that such a net outflow of real funds from the enterprise sector could take place after stabilization even if Calvo and Coricelli's 'once and for all' increase in nominal credit were successfully applied, in such a way that real credit did not decline. This is because a net outflow occurs as long as real credit increases less than the capitalization of interest rates would require.

6

Labour Markets and Wages Policies during Economic Transition

1. Introduction

Arguments in favour of wage controls in post-communist economies have changed considerably since the issue was first addressed in the late 1980s (Chapters 2 and 3). Then it was suggested that Latin American experience showed that wage controls were necessary during stabilization (Fischer, 1988). Two kinds of argument were put forward: the first centring on the danger of increases in the real wage upon stabilization (discussed in Section 2), the second on controls (both wage and price) as a mechanism for co-ordinating expectations (Section 3). Indeed, it was believed that if such controls were combined with the fixing of the exchange rate, balancing the budget and bringing monetary emission under control, then 'virtually costless stabilization is possible'.

While price controls were rejected as inappropriate for PCEs, wage controls in the form of tax based incomes policies (TIPs) with very high marginal tax rates became almost standard in the Central European stabilizations (e.g. Poland 1990, Czechoslovakia 1991). The justification given was often that, whatever the case in other regions such as Europe or Latin America, the absence of private owners interested in maximizing returns on capital meant that, in the absence of wages policies, real wages would be excessive given the requirements of stabilization. We shall examine these claims in Section 4. Once stabilization was largely completed by the mid-1990s, those arguing in favour of wage control claimed it continued to be necessary as long as a large part of manufacturing industry remained in state hands, in order to prevent the decapitalization of the economy (i.e. effec-

tively negative net investment). We shall examine the argument for wage control in the longer term in PCEs in Section 5.

2. The Pazos-Simonsen Mechanism: Short-Term Wage Controls as a Means of Abrogating Existing Wage Contracts

For any group of workers in an inflationary situation the real wage reaches a peak of w^* at the beginning of each period of h months for which the nominal wage is fixed (Dornbusch and Simonsen, 1988). As inflation occurs at a rate p percent a month, the real wage declines in value until the end of h, when it is once again increased to w^*:

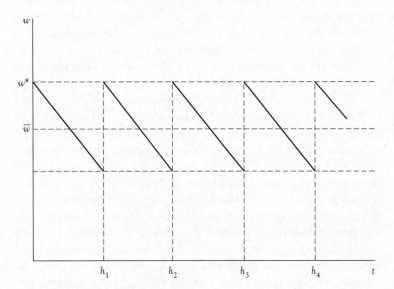

Figure 11 *Evolution of real wages*

The average real wage is given by:

(1) $\mathbf{w} = w^*((1+p)^{h+1}-1)/((h + 1) p (1 + p)^h)$

So that an increase in the rate of inflation p, or the lengthening of the period of indexation h, leads to a fall in the real wage (Modiano, 1988).

If the indexation period is synchronized across the economy, so that different groups of workers start h at the same time, then if inflation is stopped overnight at t^* at the beginning of h_i, then the average wage of all workers in the economy will increase to its peak value w^*. Such an increase will obviously be unsustainable if the economy is an open one. If the exchange rate is fixed, the country will begin to run a current account deficit which will ultimately become unsustainable. If the exchange rate floats, the currency will depreciate, raising prices, reducing the real wage, and causing demands for nominal wage increases at the end of h, which will feed into further inflation.

Nor does the increase in the average real wage depend on stabilization happening at the beginning of a new indexation period. If nominal wage increases occur automatically—as a result of pre-existing wage contracts—to compensate workers for the inflation which occurs between the beginning of h and the moment of stabilization, then the average real wage will increase irrespective of when the stabilization takes place relative to the beginning of h. Under the circumstances described in this paragraph wage control is needed above all as a mechanism for abrogating pre-existing wage contracts (Fischer, 1988).[1]

If the indexation period is not synchronized across the economy, so that different groups of workers start h at different times t_1, t_2, etc., then if inflation is stopped overnight at t_i and at the same time pre-existing contracts result in nominal wage increases to compensate those workers whose indexation period started before t_i for the inflation which occurred between the beginning of their h and t_i, then the average wage of all groups of workers will again increase to their peak value w^*. As a result, the average real wage in the economy will rise sharply, with the consequences described earlier, unless inflationary wage contracts are abrogated through wage controls.

The above justification of wage controls has been used to justify price controls, on the grounds that otherwise trade unions will not argree to the abrogation of wage contracts (Bruno, 1988). The logic, though, is unclear. If trade unions understand that their members, average real wage has not been w^* but in fact **w**, and if they are prepared to accept the

latter, then there is no need for price control. With the old wage agreements abrogated and the authorities stopping inflation through suitable financial policies, real wages will settle automatically at **w** (effectively prices will adjust to the frozen nominal wages to generate the correct average real wages).[2] If on the other hand trade unions are unwilling to accept **w**, then no agreement on the level at which prices are to be frozen will be possible in any case.

A critical, and usually unspoken assumption, of advocates of wage controls is that monetary and fiscal policies are simultaneously tightened, so as to ensure that the equilibrium wage is not higher than that embodied in the controls. If this were not the case, the authorities would find themselves trying to maintain the controls against a market in which both suppliers of labour and its purchasers were willing to settle on a higher wage. Achieving such a goal is, however, likely to be far from easy. Policy makers are unlikely to know what equilibrium average nominal wage corresponds to what degree of fiscal and monetary tightness. This is particularly the case when the inflation being stabilized is very high. The argument for wage control is often, therefore, phrased in terms of *forcing* nominal and real wages *below* equilibrium level, and therefore achieving stabilization at a lower cost in terms of unemployment and lost output. The question then comes down to whether one believes that the government is in fact able to enforce such a wages policy. The experience of many countries (including the UK in 1973 and 1979) has shown that success is very unlikely.

Even if demand management policy is such as to ensure that the controlled wage is at or above equilibrium (i.e. the wage controls acts exclusively to abrogate outdated contracts and not to repress wages), the question remains which of the potential equilibrium average real wages should be chosen. This is mainly a question of the economy's external balance. The higher the real wage the smaller the payments surplus:

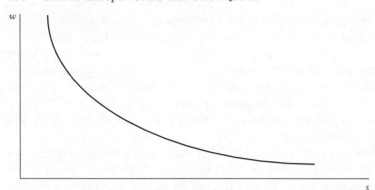

Figure 12   *Real wages and the external balance*

3. Short Term Wage Controls as a
Mechanism for Co-ordinating Expectations

Fischer (1988) makes this point strongly. If the government sets a low inflation rate when economic actors expect it to continue at a high rate the result is recession. This is essentially the case with a non-credible stabilization programme. The possible actions of government and expectations of economic actors, together with the economic outcomes that result from each combination are given in Table 15.

Since the government cannot know whether economic actors will believe in its programme, i.e. whether the result will be stabilization or recession, it should impose wage (and price controls!) as well as fixing the exchange rate. In this way it guarantees to the economic actors that in the short term infla-

Table 15 Interaction between government policies and expectations of economic actors

| Economic Actors expect: | Government causes: | |
	High inflation	*Low inflation*
High inflation	Hyperstagflation	Recession
Low inflation	High employment hyperinflation	Stabilization

Source: Fischer (1988).

tion will indeed be low. The economic actors supply and demand quantities—and also set any free prices—accordingly, and stabilization without recession is achieved. The argument in this case is rather different from that in the previous section: it is not just a matter of abrogating pre-existing contracts which would otherwise lead to disequilibrium prices, but rather of changing expectations which would cause new contracts to be set in such a way as to generate a high unemployment/low output outcome.

Two problems arise. The first is that unlike in Latin America or Israel, the bulk of prices in communist economies before transition had been controlled for decades. As a result in many countries there was a large monetary overhang, while in others relative prices had become so distorted that there was a generalized expectation that they would soon be freed. This expectation aggravated the already existing shortages, making perseverance with price control impracticable. Far from helping to change inflationary expectations, in post-communist economies price controls actually fuelled them. This is because they increase demand and reduce supply by pricing goods at the old low prices, which are certain to be raised in the future. Also, after decades of price controls, it is unrealistic to imagine that the authorities could know at what level to set relative prices.

Second, with prices free it is not clear that wage controls would be likely to add significantly to the authorities' ability to affect economic actors inflationary expectations. Although wages might affect prices in the medium term, in the very short term other factors, such as the exchange rate or increases in administered prices of important inputs such as energy, are likely to be more important. Indeed, in Poland in 1990 prices soared far ahead of wages during the first quarter of the stabilization programme, so that wage controls are unlikely to have been important in forming inflation expectations.[3]

4. *Short-Term Wage Controls in Semi-heterodox Stabilization Programmes in PCEs*

Stabilization programmes have conventionally been classified according to whether they are shock or gradual, orthodox or

heterodox. Of course, there has been considerable disagreement as to what constitutes orthodoxy or otherwise. Orthodox plans must include: (1) balancing the budget; and (2) bringing nominal monetary growth under control—although real money balances may increase sharply as a result of remonetization of the economy (Chapter 10). If inflation has been very high, orthodox plans must also include the fixing of the exchange rate (Chapter 3). Heterodox plans on the other hand must include: (1) price and wage controls; and (2) fixing the exchange rate. However, it is admitted by supporters of the heterodox approach that if such plans are to be successful in the medium term they must also include responsible—that is orthodox—fiscal and monetary policy. Of the three attempted 'heterodox shock' stabilizations of 1985, those in Argentina and Brazil failed because they did not 'get the fundamentals [fiscal and monetary policy] right', while Israel was successful because it did (Bruno, Di Tella, Dornbusch, and Fischer, 1988). Thus, the key difference between orthodox and heterodox plans is the presence in the latter of price and wage controls.

How then should we classify the various stabilization programmes in PCEs? All the countries which stabilized (and some which did not) freed prices rather than controlled them. Poland (January 1990) and Czechoslovakia (January 1991), which had wage controls and fixed exchange rates, can be thought of as semi-heterodox shocks—because prices were freed. Bulgaria (February 1991) had wage controls and a *floating* exchange rate, so that one can only call it semi-heterodox/semi-orthodox shock! Hungary (1990–2) was 'gradualist semi-heterodox' as it had wage controls,[4] and its exchange rate float was dirty. Estonia (June 1992) was orthodox shock (fixed exchange rate, no wage controls), while Latvia (October 1992) was maybe 'super-orthodox' shock (no wage controls and a floating—though dirty—exchange rate). Russia's failed stabilization of January 1992 was also 'super-orthodox'—even the exchange rate float was only minimally dirty, as the authorities had hardly any reserves. Here was the curious case of an orthodox stabilization programme which failed because it did not 'get the fundamentals right'.[5] Much the same is true of the Russian attempt of 1994.

As can be seen, the variety of approaches in the region has been considerable. Nevertheless, the semi-heterodox shock stabilization of the Polish and Czechoslovak type was an innovation unique to the region, and it has been justified as being particularly suited to the nature of PCEs. In PCEs prices have to be liberalized so as to 'get relative prices right', and in order to eliminate any monetary overhang that may exist. Thus stabilization must be accompanied by price liberalization rather than price control. The argument in favour of wage controls in PCEs therefore owes little to the idea that inflationary expectations need to be co-ordinated.

The main arguments in favour of wage controls in Central Europe were as follows. First, there was the feeling, particularly strong in the Polish case where wages were set monthly by managements highly dependent on workers' councils, that very tight wage controls at the beginning of the programme would help to break inflationary inertia of the kind discussed in Section 2. Nevertheless as we have seen, in Poland wages failed to increase up to the thresholds permitted by the TIP, indicating that the policy did not in fact fulfil this function. Second, there was a crude cost-push view of inflation, which was particularly widespread among officials inherited from the communist regime. The weakness of this approach has been discussed at length in Chapter 2.

Third, there was a slightly more sophisticated version of cost-push (which was widespread among politicans, officials and advisers) which rested on the belief that enterprises might play a game of 'chicken' with the authorities, paying out large wage increases and financing these either by running up bank or inter-enterprise debt (Chapter 8). The authorities would then be in a position in which they would have either to countenance the bankruptcy of a large part of industry, or to validate enterprise behaviour by creating domestic credit (making any subsequent stabilization attempt even less credible). This danger requires that there be at least a tacit 'conspiracy of enterprises', since the authorities can afford to close down any enterprise on its own, or a small number of enterprises. This was a particularly worrying danger as, at this early stage of the transition,

there were practically no mechanisms to select enterprises according to whether their financial problems were fundamental (solvency) or transitory (liquidity). The problem with this argument is that the mechanism used to control wages, the TIP, provides no real protection against the threat it is supposed to meet. If enterprises raise wages excessively, then their obligations under the TIP (which are not paid immediately) involve an even greater likelihood of bankruptcy and mean an even greater climbdown by the authorities if they are forgiven.

The fourth argument used is that wage controls reduce the cost of the marginal worker and therefore reduce unemployment. This was clearly not relevant in Poland in 1990, when enterprises could choose whether the TIP should apply to their average wage or to their wage bill. The bulk chose the latter, and were thus encouraged to increase average and marginal wages while reducing employment. Indeed, the authorities allowed this quite consciously, realizing that many enterprises were grossly overstaffed. This is quite typical of what has happened in successful PCE stabilizations. Stabilization and liberalization have occurred simultaneously with the first appearance of unemployment, with the latter being the unavoidable by-product of the new regime in the labour market which allows labour to be reallocated to more efficient uses, particularly in the private sector (Chapter 14). Furthermore, one should not try to discourage the growth of unemployment at the beginning of a stabilization programme, as unemployment must reach—and probably exceed—the NAIRU if inflation is to be stopped (Chapter 2).

5. Medium-Term Wage Controls in Semi-Shock Stabilization Programmes in PCEs

With the exception of Yugoslavia (1994), none of the stabilizations in PCEs have been 'full shock' stabilizations in the sense that inflation was stopped completely in a matter of a few months. In this they differ from the stabilizations of the 1920s (Rostowski and Shapiro, 1992), and from the Bolivian hyperinflation of 1985 (Morales, 1988). The reason for this is that in

the PCEs none of the inflations, again with the exception of Serbia-Montenegro (1994), reached rates at which prices were so flexible (both up and down) that the inflations could be stopped almost overnight by fixing the exchange rate and backing the currency (Chapters 3 and 4). In all these cases, inflation continued at rates above 20 per cent per annum for at least two years after the stabilization programme began. It is therefore useful to think of the standard PCE programmes as 'semi-shock', in which inflationary concerns remain at the heart of policy making for a number of years after the initial stabilization.

Thus, in this medium-term context of a year and more after the beginning of the stabilization programme, the effects of wages policies in distorting labour markets become important. Freezing wages over a number of years would clearly destroy the functioning of the labour market completely, and is thus impossible in PCEs where one of the main requirements during the transition is to restructure the economy. However, even TIPs have an important distortionary effect in the medium term, although less so than wage freezes.

In order to see this we must first clarify a number of technical points regarding TIPs. If the economy is in a period in which inflation is declining, then any indexation built into the TIP should be foreward-looking, i.e. wages in the firm should be allowed to rise by some fraction of the inflation in the period for which the wages are paid before the wages tax becomes payable, so that the tax free wage is given by:

(2) $W^*_t = W^*_{t-1} * aP_t$, where $a<1$

If instead the wages free of wage tax were index by the inflation of the previous period, then nominal wages in any given period would be higher, real wages would be higher in the short term and inflation would be higher in the medium term. Instead of equation (2) we would have:

(3) $W^*_t = W_{t-1} * P_{t-1}$.

The TIP would be binding only on the exceptional firms which wished to raise wages by more than inflation in the previous

period (when it was higher than in the present one). The TIP would cease to be an anti-inflationary tool, and for good or ill reducing inflation would have to be left to orthodox tools (monetary, fiscal, and exchange rate policy). On the other hand, the more one wishes to 'bear down' on inflation by use of the TIP the lower should one set the parameter a in eq. (2). Thus in Poland in 1990 a was set at 0.3 in January, 0.2 in February and March, and 0.6 for the rest of the year (except for August when it was set at 1.0).

Thus, if $a << 1$, as the vigorous use of the TIP as an anti-inflationary instrument requires, then given 'forward-looking' indexation as in eq. (2) the real wage which is free of the TIP must decline continuously. As a result, firms would only be able to respond to positive opportunities in the goods market in one of two ways before crossing the TIP threshold: (1) if the tax was based on increases in the total wage bill, firms could hire better workers by increasing the average wage in the firm by reducing the number of employees; or (2) if the tax was based on increases in the average wage in the firm, they could hire more workers with the same (or a lower) mix of skills, while ensuring that the average wage did not increase (or actually fell by the amount required by the parameter a).[6] Thus firms could not expand both employment and improve the skill mix of their labour force without paying a price as a result of the TIP.

The above is not too much of a problem in the very short term, since PCEs start the transition from full employment, and thus almost all firms are overstaffed. Even in the short term, though, private sector firms can be expected to have the potential to expand—and this is one reason why the Polish authorities excluded the private sector from the operation of the TIP in early 1990. But in the medium term it can become a serious problem, since some state firms should continue to reduce output and employment, while other state firms should be increasing both and also the skills of their workforce.

It can, of course, be argued that if—as is the case in Poland but not in Czechoslovakia[7]—the private sector is free of the TIP, then firms which wish to expand in ways discouraged by the TIP, can avoid the TIP if they become privatized. In this way

the TIP can become an inducement for privatization. Although this may work in practice to induce some firms to co-operate in the privatization process, it is very much a second best argument, which confuses two separate issues: firms should be privatized irrespective of whether they wish to expand or contract production and employment, and those firms which have the opportunity to expand should do so irrespective of whether they are privatized.

Given these costs of a TIP in the medium term what are the arguments which have been advanced in its favour? The most important argument is probably that, even in the medium term, the TIP helps to either sustain investment in state owned firms (SOEs), or at least to hinder their decapitalization. SOEs are either worker controlled as in Poland, or suffer from the absence of real owners who would have a clear pecuniary interest in resisting wage demands and defending the interests of capital within the firm. Even where managers of SOEs are appointed by the state as in the Czech Republic,[8] the state officials who appoint the managers are not personally interested in the return on capital, so the managers are similarly motivated. Even if managers received profit linked bonuses experience has shown that these count for little when weighed against the likelihood of losing one's job for having provoked a strike by resisting wage demands.

At the same time workers will wish to appropriate the whole of the firm's revenue. As Ward (1958) showed, they will wish to pay out their average product rather than their marginal product. If workers expect to remain in control of the firm for a significant period of time, then they may wish to pay out only average revenue after allowance has been made for the depreciation of the capital stock. In such a case the SOE will not have sufficient resources to expand through net investment. If workers expect to lose control of the firm soon, either because of privatization, redundancy, or because they intend to depart for the private sector, then they will not even amortize the capital they consume during production. The firm will engage in negative net investment and will be decapitalized. In fact, the workers may sell off parts of the physical assets of the SOE so as to

generate revenue which they can then divide among themselves. In this way they can accelerate the rate of decapitalization of the SOE above the rate of depreciation of its physical assets.[9]

Thus the argument is that the TIP, by increasing the cost of wages when these exceed a certain threshold, increases the cost to workers of a zloty or crown going towards wages costs (apart from the tax, the cost of paying out a zloty in wages can be thought of as the reduction in investment, which reduces job security). In this way the TIP increases the attractiveness of spending that same zloty on investment in the firm.[10] In Fig. 13 the TIP introduces a tax wedge between the marginal cost of wages (MCW) and the marginal benefit of wages (MBW), which is downward sloping as one would expect (both schedules hold revenue and employment constant). The result is to reduce W/R, the share of wages in the firm's revenue.

This argument has two weaknesses. The first is that it assumes that the effective wage within the firm can be controlled by controlling the nominal wage. In the context of the distribution of a firm's income between labour and capital, the effective wage can be defined as the money wage/unit of time × units of effort. In labour managed or dominated firms the workforce can get around the restrictions resulting from a TIP either by reducing the hours they work every day (either

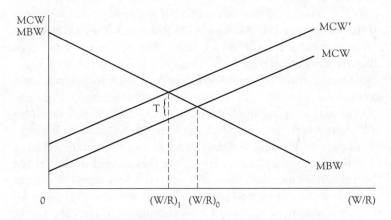

Figure 13 *Tax based incomes policies and the wage share*

openly or covertly), or by reducing the effort they make during the hours worked. In both cases production and revenue will decline. Thus although nominal wages remain the same so as to avoid the TIP, they will be obtained in exchange for a smaller number of hours worked with less effort.

The hours or strength saved may be used to earn additional income in a second job or may be spent on leisure. Wages (W) as a share of revenue (R) may reach much the same level as in the absence of a TIP. The difference is that $R-W$ approaches zero not as a result of a high W, but because of a low R. Although it is not the only reason, such an 'effort effect' may well have been partially responsible for the fact that output fell so much more than employment in Polish industry in 1990. Clearly, $R-W$ may remain somewhat above the level at which it would be without the TIP for two reasons: first, it may be hard to find part-time work outside the firm; second, the marginal cost of working with a given amount of effort when one is in the workplace may be relatively small. However, both kinds of rigidity are likely to decline over time, so that in the medium term the TIP is unlikely to act as an effective barrier to the decapitalization of SOEs.

The second weakness of the decapitalization argument is that it assumes that nominal wages can be controlled effectively. We noted in Section 2 that governments which tried to maintain wages below equilibrium levels through wages policies usually found themselves unable to make the policies stick. This is because although employers are unwilling to pay wages above the marginal product of labour, they are also unwilling to pay below the marginal product of labour, if that means being unable to hire as much labour as they desired at a given moment. Thus only the government defends the wages policy if the controlled wage is below equilibrium.[11] In an economy dominated by labour managed or dominated firms, a government which attempts to prevent decapitalization of SOEs by use of a TIP also has no allies within the firms (and often no allies outside the firms either!). This is because the equilibrium wage for each firm is determined by the employees themselves, and as we have seen, depends mainly on their expected employment in, and control of, the firm. This does not mean that the

government cannot control wage growth in SOEs, but that it can only do so through restrictive demand management. In doing this the authorities reduce firms' revenue, leading to their decapitalization at a given wage.

Of course, the question needs to be asked whether the decapitalization of SOEs is such a bad thing during transition. When such decapitalization takes the form of divestment of assets by SOEs it leads to the 'asset privatization' which has played a very important role in private sector development, for instance in Poland (Chapter 14). It is far from clear that such assets would be used more efficiently if they were privatized as part of an ongoing business. Even if the use of assets were known to be more efficient after enterprise privatization than after asset privatization, which is not the case, asset privatization might still be preferred on the grounds that it happens far more rapidly.

It is often argued that the decapitalization of SOEs leads to an increased share of consumption and a reduced share of investment in GDP. However, workers are more likely to decapitalize their SOE if they expect to cease working for it soon. Such workers are the ones who are particularly exposed to the risk of unemployment, and will therefore tend to have particularly high propensities to save, so it is far from clear that the consumption rate need rise. These savings may not be efficiently invested if the banking system lacks skills (Chapters 11 and 13), but it is not clear why ploughback into SOEs should be much better than even the inefficient allocation of capital achieved by the banking system. A more serious problem is that the proceeds of asset privatization go to the SOE rather than to the state. A TIP ensures that a part (maybe even most) of the proceeds of asset privatization go to the state (unless the workers raise effective wages by reducing hours and effort).

A quite different argument in favour of TIPs has been advanced, based on the optimand of the labour managed firm. If workers expect to remain in control of the firm for a long period of time and to remain personally associated with the firm, then they may in fact engage in net investment. In such a case, however, they will tend to invest in more capital intensive technologies than would a capitalist owner. In this way, an

economy consisting of labour managed or labour dominated firms will generate a higher level of unemployment than a capitalist economy. A TIP which has as its object the average wage within firms, will help to counteract this tendency by increasing the cost of additional income for existing workers generated by new investment. Unfortunately, this is a weak argument in favour of the TIP as it will achieve this effect by discouraging the workers from investment altogether, rather than by encouraging them to invest in more labour intensive technologies.

Another argument often advanced in favour of wage controls in the medium term in PCEs relates to so-called 'wage chim-neys'. These are enterprises which have extremely high capital labour ratios, so that if wages were completely unconstrained they could rise within the firm to levels which would be out-landishly high. An example is the Płock Refinery in Poland, which at one time employed 10,000 people, but whose turnover was equivalent to 5 per cent of the industrial sales of the whole country. When capital/employee is as vast as at Płock there is little danger of workers being able to achieve a significant decap-italization of the firm over a short period of time by reducing work effort or hours. A TIP is therefore likely to succeed here. The question is whether it is sensible to impose a TIP on all SOEs just because it is justified and workable in few massively capitalized firms. The TIP could be restricted to such firms, or alternatively, they could be made to pay a large capital charge.

There is one argument in favour of wage controls which is relevant, but which has not—to my knowledge—been advanced. This is that wage controls, be they in the form of a TIP or not, provide a mechanism by which the authorities can precommit themselves strongly to stabilization. If the wages policy is brea-ched, then such a government defeat is visible to all, possibly leading to the fall of the government itself (as happened in the UK in 1973). Thus, when a government announces a wages policy it is forced to adopt monetary and fiscal policies which ensure that the controlled wage is at or below the equilibrium wage (i.e. that the policy is not binding), so as to help it to win any conflict with workers over the wages policy.

This is very much the role played by the TIP in Poland on at least two occasions: first in the autumn of 1990 and then in early 1991. The first episode occurred after a period when financial policies had been excessively loosened in June 1990.[12] Combined with the political uncertainty resulting from the presidential elections, this led to severe strike pressure and the danger that SOEs would grant wage increases and incur wage tax liabilities which they would be unable to meet. As a result, the government urged a sharp tightening of interest rate and credit policy on the National Bank of Poland, to which the bank acceded after considerable hesitation.[13] A second wave of labour unrest occured in early 1991 as a result of expectations that the new Bielecki government would fulfil President Wałesa's intimations that the TIP would be abolished. Again, monetary policy was tightened to protect the TIP.[14]

Of course, the question arises as to whether precommitting to the exchange rate is not better than precommitting to a set of nominal wages implicit in a TIP. A very strong commitment to the exchange rate, as with the kind of 'high powered money board' arrangement discussed in Chapter 11 and implemented in Estonia and Lithuania, is probably superior to precommitting to a TIP. But if a country has not followed the Baltic path it is probably better for it to precommit to a TIP and a weakly fixed exchange rate than to precommit (weakly) only to the exchange rate. It is also possible that in countries with a strongly organized working class it may be advisable to precommit to something which makes it clear from the start that attempts by trade unions or workers' councils to undermine the stabilization programme will be faced down by the government.

6. *Reducing Inflationary Inertia by Lengthening the 'Indexation Period' of the TIP*

If we accept that a TIP will help to reduce inflation directly (i.e. not just through the 'precommitment effect'), then the period for which the TIP thresholds remain constant in nominal terms should be lengthened as much as possible as inflation declines. In Fig. 11 we saw that a shortening of the period of indexation

of wages *h* resulted in an increase in the real wage (at a given rate of inflation). Not surprisingly as inflation increases and the real wage falls, workers demand a shortening of *h* as compensation. As a result indexation periods become very short (often a month or less in very high inflations), with the result that any increase in prices is quickly transmitted to wages, thence to price and so on. The economy becomes very fragile as regards any resurgence in inflation.

In PCEs we are concerned with wages in SOEs. Since these are labour managed or dominated, they will shorten indexation periods as much as workers desire. The only way of controlling this is through the TIP. The object of the TIP is defined as either the wage bill or the average wage, and the threshold value of this variable at which the TIP begins to be paid is revalued in nominal terms every so often. In very high inflation countries this is often once a month, as was the case in Poland in 1990–1. By lengthening the period of indexation of the TIP threshold as inflation declines one achieves an effect similar to that of lengthening the contract period in a capitalist market economy (Blanchard and Layard, 1991), reducing in this way the economy's inflation fragility.[15]

NOTES

The first draft of this chapter appeared as no. 22 of the *Studies and Analyses* Discussion Paper series of the Centrum Analiz Społeczno-Ekonomicznych, Warsaw, 1994.

1. 'This is the serious reason for intervention in the wage setting process.' Of course, if wage contracts were abrogated and if inflation were stopped just halfway through h, then the average real wage would remain constant, and if this happened just before t_i the average real wage would fall.
2. However, it is important that the frozen nominal wages and the fixed exchange rate be compatible with **w**.
3. Wages also rose less than the amount permitted by the wage controls— a point to which we return below.
4. Wage increases in excess of a government determined threshold were included in profits for tax purposes (the corporate profits tax was 54 per cent).
5. Wages in firms where the average wage is in excess of six times the minimal wage are taxed as profits. The difference between this and the Hungarian system (n. 4) is that the classification of wages as profits does

not depend upon their rate of increase (which qualifies as a TIP), but on their level, which qualifies as a very high marginal rate of payroll tax.

6. In Poland, enterprises had to choose between the total wage bill or the average wage as the 'object' of the TIP before the beginning of the tax year in 1990. Their choice would clearly be determined by their expectation as to whether they would be expanding or reducing employment. In 1991, the TIP for all enterprises was based on the average wage. The intention was to reduce the incentive to sack workers. The effect on unemployment seems to have been noticeable but very transitory, even though the previous choice was not restored.

7 And after mid-1993 also not in the Czech Republic.

8. And previously Czechoslovakia.

9. Macieja (1993) has calculated that about 17 per cent of the net profit of SOEs in Poland comes from the sale of capital assets. Although this is less than 1 per cent of sales, revenues from the leasing of SOE floorspace, which Macieja believes to be much more significant, is not reported.

10. On the assumption that the worker expects to be associated for at least some time to come with the firm. Those workers who expect to leave or be sacked will not be affected by the TIP, but will usually be in a minority.

11. The wage controls can be brought in line with the equilibrium wage by tightening demand, but then the controls are no longer binding.

12. A government may, of course, not understand this fact. This was the case in Britain in 1973, when wages policy was accompanied by an expansionary demand management policy with catastrophic results. It was also the case in Poland in the summer of 1990, when monetary and fiscal policy were sharply loosened, while the wages policy remained unchanged. This resulted very quickly in significant labour unrest, and the reversal of financial policy.

13. The government wanted the refinance credit interest rate increased from 35 per cent per annum to 50 per cent in October. The NBP raised the rate to 45 per cent in October with the result that it then had to increase the rate to 56 per cent in November, one week before the presidential elections.

14. This time the NBP was in favour of increasing the refinance interest rate to 75 per cent, while the government had doubts. Both sides were agreed that monetary policy had to be tightened, the question at issue was whether credit limits or interest rates should be the main instrument of that policy.

15. I was one of the advisers recommending such a course in Poland from March 1990 on. Although I returned to the subject each time the TIP was discussed, and it was changed in form and object several times during 1990–1, for some unknown reason the lengthening of the indexation period was the one change which it was impossible to get the bureaucracy of the Ministry of Finance to accept, though it was probably the only change in the TIP which would actually have been a clear improvement.

PART TWO

Disintegration and Inflation in the Former Soviet Union

Drought, Relief, and Inflation in

Introduction
to Part Two

Part II deals with inflation and economic disintegration in the former Soviet Union. Chapter 7 analyses the reasons for the failure of Gaidar's 1992 attempt at stabilization. Apart from weaknesses in the design and implementation of policy, the main cause of failure was the combination of a particularly high level of structural distortion (over-consumption of raw materials, above all energy, a particularly large military-industrial complex) with the collapse of key state structures (customs borders, monopolised money creation at the central bank). Russia has shown that the populist policy of 'transformation without stabilization' is possible. However, this has happened at a particularly high cost in terms of income inequality, capital flight, criminality, and output depression. Moreover, the chaos which high inflation brings strengthens authoritarian, anti-democratic politicians. Chapter 8 deals with the inter-enterprise debt explosion which has a key factor in forcing Gaidar to retreat from stabilization. Lack of credibility of the stabilization programme is identified as the main reason for such explosions, and securitization of the debt (without any government guarantee, explicit or implicit) is proposed as a solution when doing nothing is either politically or economically unfeasible. Solutions involving the multilateral clearing of the debt are rejected as either inflationary or ineffectual.[1]

Chapter 9 (written in June 1992, before the introduction of the Lat) proposed a mechanism for a smooth decoupling of Latvia from the rouble zone through the introduction of a secondary domestic currency to circulate in parallel with the hyperinflating rouble.[2] Such an approach would have allowed the gradual replacement of the inferior currency with the stable one, allowing the avoidable output costs of stabilization to be reduced. This advice was not followed, but it is impossible to

say what proportion of the 60 per cent fall in industrial output which subsequently occurred in Latvia could have been avoided. Chapter 9 also proposed that the new stable currency should be administered through a currency board type of system, something which was later done in Estonia and Lithuania, but not in Latvia. Finally, 100 per cent reserve banking was proposed so as to ensure that monetary stability was not only achieved but maintained.

Chapter 10 examines the dilemmas which were predicted to confront Russia once macroeconomic stabilization is achieved. In particular the problems arising out of the post-stabilization growth in money supply are discussed. These come not just from the well-known post-stabilization increase in the demand for real balances, but also from the increase in the supply of money as a result of the increase in the money multiplier (which is rarely mentioned in the literature). This latter process also augments the post-stabilization bad debt problem. However, the likely dimensions of post-stabilization bad debt were not expected of themselves to be large enough to undermine stabilization. The problem is rather the moral hazard introduced into the banking sector if the authorities recapitalize the banks. The predictions in Chapter 10 were largely confirmed during 1994 and 1995, when a partial stabilization occurred in Russia: a banking crisis did occur, but because of the lack of credibility of the stabilization, de-dollarization was very limited and there was no increase in the money multiplier.

NOTES

1. Unless nominal money is increased, in which case they are only inflationary.
2. Latvian rouble notes were already in circulation as a 'cash substitute', since Russia refused to supply Latvia with cash roubles, although Latvia could create as many non-cash roubles as it desired. These latter had purchasing power throughout the FSU, as the non-cash banking and payments systems remained unified.

7

What Went Wrong?
The Reasons for the Failure of
Stabilization in Russia in 1992
with Marek Dąbrowski*

1. Introduction

When the Gaidar team took over the running of the Russian economy in November 1991, its intention was to introduce a stabilization/liberalization programme very similar to the one which had been implemented with considerable success in Poland in 1990 under Leszek Balcerowicz.[1] Two years later this aim had still not been achieved, and most of the radical reformers and 'Westernizers' had left the Russian government after the elections of December 1993. We examine four main kinds of reason for Gaidar's failure: (1) problems arising from the process of designing the programme; (2) failures of implementation; (3) problems arising from Russia's economic structure; (4) problems arising from Russia's political structure. In a final section we consider the sequencing debate regarding whether stabilization or privatization should take place first.

2. The Design of the Liberalization/Stabilization
Programme in Russia

The Gaidar team had two months for the preparation of the Russian stabilization programme—significantly less time than did their counterparts in other PCEs.[2] Furthermore, it was not until the end of November 1991 that the absolute political primacy of Russian Ministers over their Soviet counterparts was finally established.[3] Most important, however, was the

informational and conceptual chaos which reigned at the time. Part of this chaos was due to the fact that many of the definitions used in government were unsuited to a market economy. Thus, to give one example out of dozens, in Soviet practice budget revenues were defined to include the increase in savings deposits of the population which were then automatically passed on to the government, although these should have been classified as financing of the deficit. On the other hand, revenues and expenditures resulting from the purchase and sale of foreign currency at various prices in the multiple exchange rate system (including all export tax revenues) were excluded from the state budget and included in a special 'foreign trade budget'.[4] The problem was not that the new team was incapable of understanding what the correct classification of various items was, but rather that they had so very little time in which to do it.

Further massive confusion was caused by the ending of the USSR. The Russian Ministry of Finance had to decide just which of the expenditures of the USSR it would take over, and in what amount. The same, of course, went for the revenue side. Budget planning under such circumstances became almost impossible, particularly as these difficulties were laid on top of the usual difficulties of estimating the budget under conditions of high inflation resulting from the so-called Tanzi effect, which makes the real value of revenues highly sensitive to variations in inflation and in tax payment delays.[5] Additional budget planning problems arose from the fact that much of budget revenue was to come from a completely new tax, the VAT.

Equal confusion existed on the monetary planning side. A key instrument of monetary policy is the planning of the evolution of the liabilities of the central bank—so-called 'high powered money'.[6] The Central Bank of Russia (CBR) took over the State Bank of the USSR (Gosbank) in early December 1991, yet it was to take over a year for it to integrate the balance sheets of the two institutions. Thus although the Gosbank ceased operations at this time, there was enormous confusion as to what the liabilities of the CBR actually were. As a result of this, for any

given absolute increase in high powered money, it was very difficult to know what the rate of increase was.[7]

Because of the informational and conceptual chaos, the IMF felt it had little understanding of what the current situation regarding the budget and the money supply was, and what is more, it felt unable to follow the evolution of key macroeconomic variables over time. It felt unable, therefore, to define criteria against which to measure Russian performance, so as to determine whether any commitments the Russian government made were being adhered to or not. As a result, no agreement was in place between Russia and the IMF when the stabilization programme began in January 1992.[8] Such agreements had, of course, been agreed with both Poland and Czecho-Slovakia before their programmes were initiated. Such a programme would have provided two things: a very large stabilization fund (of $5 billion in the Russian case) to support a fixed exchange rate for the rouble, and a coherent framework in which stabilization policies could have been assessed and if necessary adjusted.

If the Russian government had had the $5 billion stabilization fund available to it in the first quarter of 1992, there is a very good chance that the stabilization programme would have succeeded. M2 at the end of January 1992 was about 1050 billion roubles, or about $9 billion at the current exchange rate. The stabilization fund would thus have provided the Russian government with backing for over half of the money supply. Since such backing was clearly unnecessary, the international value of the rouble could have been fixed at a far higher rate, say 30 roubles/US$.[9] As it was, even with practically no reserves available, the rouble maintained its international value unchanged between January and mid-June, in spite of a tenfold increase in prices. On the back of a rapidly nominally appreciating rouble, domestic inflation would have been quickly limited, with positive effects on the budget and most important, on the political situation. What is more, true internal covertibility[10] for the rouble could then have been introduced at the beginning of the programme. Finally, with a nominally appreciated rouble the increases in energy prices necessary to bring these closer in

line with world prices would have been far smaller. As a result, the supply shock to the economy resulting from such nominal price increases (Chapters 5 and 6) may have been proportionally smaller, reducing—at least somewhat—the fall in industrial output. The economic policies of the pro-Western government, supported critically by Western aid, could have been shown to be successful. There is thus little doubt that the absence of an agreement with the IMF played an important part in the failure of stabilization in Russia in 1992.[11]

The question which arises is whether, given these circumstances, the beginning of the stabilization/liberalization programme should not have been delayed well past 1 January 1992. The argument from failure is always strong. However, the reasons for not delaying the programme were also convincing. It was generally known that the main plank of the new government's economic policy was the freeing of almost all prices in Russia. As a result, the degree of repressed inflation increased sharply, in anticipation of high inflation after liberalization. There was a massive flight from money by households and enterprises: everyone wanted to buy, no one wanted to sell at the fixed prices. Furthermore, massive repressed inflation was causing the economic disintegration of Russia, as 'oblast'i' and even cities introduced 'export' bans on the transfer of goods—particularly consumer goods—outside their region. Such policies resulted in retaliation by other regions, and a spiral of 'export protectionism' seemed to threaten the dissolution of the state.[12]

Given the absence of sufficient state power to impose physical output and delivery orders, and the failure of the market mechanism to function because of fixed prices and generalized excess demand, most of the economy had shifted into barter already in 1991. By the end of the year a very large proportion of government time was taken up with organizing barter argreements between various sectors of the economy.[13] The only way for the government to avoid being bogged down indefinitely in such crisis management of a barter economy was to liberate prices immediately. The original intention was to free prices on 15 December 1991. The two week delay

which occurred (with price liberation delayed until 2 January 1992) resulted in the almost complete emptying of all shops—particularly in the politically vital cities of Moscow and St. Petersburg.[14]

Price liberalization required stabilization, both for economic and political reasons. As we have seen, rapid inflation can become self-accelerating. The Tanzi effect reduces the real value of tax revenues, increasing the real budget deficit. The increasing inflation tax on holding money reduces the demand for real money balances, increasing any given budget deficit as a proportion of the real money supply, and therefore increasing inflation (Chapters 4 and 10). If a significant part of government expenditures result from subsidies to the production of goods whose prices are fixed, then inflation increases the costs of production of these goods, requiring increased subsidies, as was the experience of Poland in 1989.[15] In order to limit the increase in the deficit resulting from this source, administered prices have to be increased from time to time, and if inflation is rapid, these increases must be by large amounts. As a result, relative prices become highly variable, causing severe disruption to economic activity. Last but not least, high inflation makes it hard for market participants to know whether any given price change is the result of an increase in the relative price of the good concerned or in the average price level. As a result, the price elasticities of supply and demand decrease, reducing the efficiency of resource allocation and output. In Fig. 14 an external shock which increases demand by AB, causes output to increase only to Q_1 (the intersection of S_O' and D_1'), instead of to Q_2, which is what the non-inflationary supply and demand curves (S_0 and D_1) would indicate.

Politically, inflation undermines the authority of government, which is seen as incapable of fulfilling one of its basic functions, while the various actions which are necessary to manage inflation at a very high level (and prevent an exponential increase in prices), will repeatedly bring government into conflict with various powerful groups in society.[16]

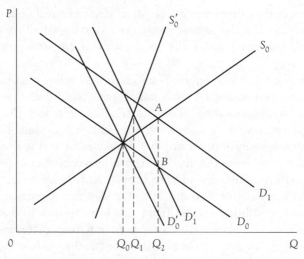

Figure 14   *Hyperinflation and output decline*

3. The Implementation of the Programme

As a result of the situation described in the previous section, the liberalization/stabilization programme introduced in Russia on 1 January 1992 was very rudimentary. There was a budget for the first quarter of 1992, a commitment by the CBR not to increase the quantity of its refinancing credit by more than 15 per cent per month during the first quarter, and a commitment to the freeing of most prices. There was also a desire to see the rouble appreciate significantly, or at the very least to maintain its international value. However, there were practically no reserves available for this purpose.

In general outline, and in its intentions, the Gaidar 'programme' was very similar to the Polish and Czecho-Slovak programmes which had preceded it. However, in its details the Russian plan was far less thorough in its implementation of the principles it espoused. This could be seen quite clearly from the very beginning in the systemic changes relating to liberalization. Later it also became evident in the implementation of stabilization policy.

Price liberalization was 'contaminated' to a large degree from

the start. Thus, the drafting of the decree liberalizing prices was entrusted to the old Price Commission! The result was a law of such complexity that it was quite some time before it became clear which prices had been liberalized and to what extent. Furthermore, retail margins in state shops were not to exceed 25 per cent over wholesale prices. This meant that often shortages actually had to appear (or inventories decline) causing retailers to increase orders, before suppliers would increase their prices, making it possible for the retailers to raise their prices in turn.[17] Finally, the prices of many basic food products were centrally administered until March 1992, after which local authorities often continued to fix their prices, and state retail chains found it easier to set a single price in all their shops. Price control was in the interest of shop staff, who in its absence would be unable to sell 'deficit' products 'under the counter'. The control of profit margins of so-called monopolistic producers was also very widespread, and was only given up at the end of 1993.

The result was that while liberalization led to a definite improvement in supply, the situation on the market continued to be one of 'semi-shortage', with many consumer goods completely or mostly unavailable. Thus the Russian Government's Centre for Economic Reform's index of availability of goods stood at between 60 and 65 as late as the last quarter of 1992.[18] The result was that the political benefits to the government of the improvement in the supply of consumer goods were limited. This may have been one reason the conservative counterattack against government economic policies started in April 1992, far earlier relative to the beginning of the programme than in either Poland or Czecho-Slovakia.

Formally, a significant degree of quantitative planning remained, with the maintenance of 'state purchase orders' (*goszakazy*) in the energy sector, and particularly in the oil industry.[19] The government argued privately that these orders would have no effect, as to become enforceable they required the delivery of inputs to the energy producers which the Ministry of Economy (the old Gosplan) was incapable of effecting. At the very least, they caused confusion for actors as to whether

they were operating under a centralized barter system or under a market system. The *goszakazy* also encouraged the central bureaucracy to believe that it could maintain its traditional directive power, at least in some areas of the economy.

Finally, the whole area of foreign trade was riddled with price and quantitative controls. On the export side, a part of export earnings had to be sold to the authorities at half the market exchange rate, with the proportion varying from 80 per cent for oil and gas to 40 per cent for manufactures in the first half of 1992.[20] This was the equivalent of a variable export tax. More seriously, there were also dozens of export ceilings, affecting almost all of Russia's exportables. The most important single item here was oil. The controlled domestic price was so low, at about 5–15 per cent of the world price,[21] that even the very high export tax on this commodity (equivalent to 40 per cent of the world price) would have been insufficient to prevent a surge in exports, and massive domestic shortages.[22] Instead of raising the domestic price closer to world levels, the Russian authorities tried to restrict oil exports through export quotas (additional to the export tax). In the case of many goods the agency granting the export quota was also the main domestic purchaser of the product: thus exports of medicines had to be approved by the Ministry of Health! These export barriers made it harder for Russian enterprises to respond to the fall in domestic demand accompanying the stabilization by increasing their exports, as Polish, Czecho-Slovak and Hungarian enterprises did under similar circumstances. A key safety valve present in well designed stabilization programmes was effectively shut off. This in turn made it harder for the Russian authorities to resist the political pressure to increase domestic demand; and indeed they gave way to it in June 1992.

In the Central European countries, increased export earnings increased the supply of foreign currency and thus strengthened demand for the domestic currency, while at the same time financing increased imports from the West, improving consumer goods supply and variety with positive political effects, and also reducing or eliminating monopoly power in the traded goods sector. Freedom to import resulting from internal con-

vertibility facilitated the growth of the private sector (Chapter 14) and increased efficiency as a result of imports of Western capital goods. All of these benefits were available to Russia in far smaller degree because of its export and import controls.

In Russia, on the other hand, in the first half of 1992, 40 per cent of all imports were centrally administered, the foreign currency being provided to the importer initially at a rate of 5 roubles/US dollar (at a time when the market rate fluctuated between 110 and 230 roubles). As a result of inflationary expectations the rouble was so massively undervalued in real terms, that in the first quarter of 1992 imports were the equivalent of about 135 per cent of national income (NMP)[23] at the market rate of exchange for non-cash roubles. In the second quarter, when the rouble had appreciated very significantly in real terms this share was 60 per cent.[24] Thus, centralized imports were equivalent in value to about 65 per cent of NMP in the first quarter and 30 per cent of NMP in the second quarter, if one priced them at the market rate of exchange, which is what purchasers would have had to pay if they had proved unable to obtain the foreign currency at massively favourable rates from the government. These figures give us some idea of the degree of resource misallocation resulting from the controls, but also of the degree of microeconomic power retained by the central bureaucracy.[25]

In one respect, moreover, the Russian programme differed fundamentally from its Polish and Czecho-Slovak predecessors: wage controls were very weak.[26] In spite of this, statistical real wages crashed in January 1992 and then increased slowly during the rest of the year, very much as in Poland and Czecho-Slovakia during the analogous periods in their programmes (Fig. 15). This close similarity is the more surprising as unlike the Central European countries (including Hungary) which formally had tight wage controls, unemployment remained vestigial in Russia. What is more, wages are not generally believed to have been the direct motor of inflation in Russia, particularly in the first quarter of 1992 when the ratio of profits to wages increased by 22 per cent.[27] Such cost-push pressures as existed seem to have been mainly initiated by

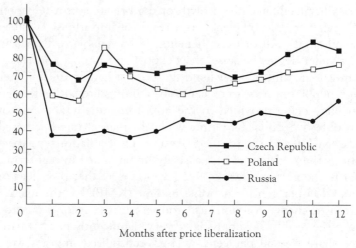

Months after price liberalization

Figure 15   *Real wages in the Czech Republic, Poland, and Russia*

enterprise managements aggressively pushing up prices, with wages largely following somewhat passively. This is reflected in the inter-enterprise debt explosion (Chapter 8) and the far faster growth in producer prices than in consumer prices (Fig. 16). Thus, paradoxically, the point on which the Russian programme seems to have differed most in principle from its Central European predecessors, seems to have been the one which was least important in practice for its divergent outcome.

The main outlines of macroeconomic policy and performance are given in Fig. 16 and Tables 16–19, which trace the evolution of producer and consumer prices, high powered money, M2, the budget deficit and nominal and real exchange rates. Essentially, the year can be divided into two periods, corresponding roughly to January–May and June–December of that year. Until June, monetary policy was relatively restrictive (Table 16), and the consolidated general government's budget was actually in surplus in the first quarter (Table 17).[28] In May the budget began to deteriorate, and in June high powered money grew by 68 per cent and M2 grew 28 per cent (compared to an average of 17 per cent and 12 per cent

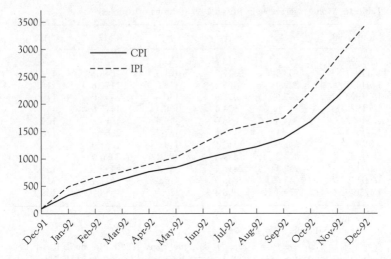

Figure 16   *Consumer and industrial prices in Russia, 1992*

respectively during the first five months of the year). The change can be seen not only in policy, but also in economic outcomes, though with a slight delay. After the initial 'price flare' following liberalization, inflation was on a downward trend which continued until August, but then it reignited rapidly, exceeding 20 per cent in every month from October 1992 to April 1993. The nominal exchange rate for non-cash roubles appreciated from 230 roubles/US$1 on 28 January 1992 to 113 roubles/US$1 on 2 June 1992. After that the nominal exchange rate depreciated rapidly, reaching 309 roubles/US$ on 1 October and 416 in mid-December 1992. The real exchange rate appreciated from an index of 140 at the beginning of January to one of 25 at the beginning of June (i.e. a real appreciation of 460 per cent)[29], after which it depreciated some 45 per cent to mid-October.

The change in macroeconomic policy has been explained in different ways. According to Gaidar[30] political pressure by the industrial lobby for a massive expansion of credit became irresistible in May. The source of this pressure was the vast amount of trade credit the SOEs had granted each other, and which they could not pay off because monetary policy, though in fact quite

Table 16 Money aggregates in Russia 1992 (billions of roubles)

Month/1992	MO	H	H[a]	M2	M2[a]
1/1/1992	165.9	313.3	n.a.	924.4	n.a.
1/2/1992	183.8	317.5	101.3	1046.1	112.7
1/3/1992	209.3	365.2	115.0	1172.6	112.1
1/4/1992	247.6	476.9	130.6	1338.0	114.1
1/5/1992	317.5	574.4	120.4	1477.6	110.4
1/6/1992	365.6	686.0	119.4	1614.2	109.2
1/7/1992	455.1	1150.6	167.7	2066.8	128.0
1/8/1992	642.8	1312.1	114.0	2593.9	125.5
1/9/1992	804.0	2599.0	198.1	3396.0	130.9
1/10/1992	949.5	2418.7	93.1	4465.1	131.5
1/11/1992	1145.6	2836.9	117.3	5671.4	127.0
1/12/1992	1379.8	3498.4	123.3	5968.7	105.2

[a] previous month = 100
n.a. = not applicable

Source: Tekushchie tendentsii v denezhno-kreditnoi sfere, Tsentral'nii Bank Rossiiskoi Federatsii, vypusk no. 1 (Moscow, January 1992); no. 2 (Moscow, April 1993).

Table 17 Consolidated budget of the Russian Federation 1992 (billions of roubles)

Months of 1992	Consolidated budget			Budget balances	
	Revenue	Expenditure	Balance	Republics	Local
1 & 2	196.6	184.4	12.1	−1.2	13.4
3	185.6	176.3	9.3	−3.5	12.8
4	231.5	227.9	3.6	−48.2	51.8
5	211.1	253.1	−42.0	−70.2	28.2
6	216.3	415.3	−199.0	−178.2	−20.8
7	374.9	524.7	−149.8	−191.6	41.8
8	375.7	675.7	−300.0	−327.0	27.0
9	516.1	394.2	121.9	103.6	18.3
10	1022.9	675.3	347.6	182.6	165.0
11	813.4	851.5	−38.1	−88.9	50.8
12	1183.8	1591.1	−407.3	−335.2	−72.1

Source: Document of the Ministry of Finance of the Russian Federation.

loose, was tighter than they had expected (Chapter 8). In order to save the general thrust of the reforms, Gaidar not only agreed to a change in the stance of macroeconomic policy but also accepted the appointment of four anti-reformist Deputy Prime Ministers and in July the proposal for a multilateral clearing of inter-enterprise debts.[31] Anisimova, Sinelnikov, and Titov (1993) draw attention to the massive increase in government

expenditure which was one expression of this shift in policy. As a percentage of GDP, expenditures of the consolidated budget (Federal and local) increased from 25.7 per cent in the first quarter to 40.6 per cent at the end of August.[32] By sector of expenditure the changes were as follows:

Table 18   Russia: share of Federal expenditure in GDP in 1992 (%)

	1 April	1 September
National economy	7.9	13.3
Social safety net	6.8	9.3
Defence	4.2	6.3

Source: Anisimova, Sinelnikov, and Titov (1993).

Revenues remained unchanged relative to GDP at about 28 per cent, giving rise to a deficit of about 12 per cent of GDP (compared to 2 per cent of GDP in the first quarter).[33] This corresponds to Gaidar's description of events: there was a conscious, if enforced, shift in budgetary and monetary policy, and the consequences for inflation and the exchange rate followed naturally.

Table 19   Russia 1992: nominal and real exchange rates (end of month)

	nominal rate (R/US$)	real rate
December 1991	144	275.6
January 1992	180	100.0
February	170	68.3
March	161	49.9
April	155	39.5
May	128	29.1
June	119	22.8
July	136	23.5
August	163	25.8
September	204	28.9
October	338	38.9
November	448	40.9
December	418	30.5

Source: Russian Economic Trends, nominal rates for the middle of the month, real rates are deflated by the CPI.

4. *Russia's Economic Structure*

A commonly held view before the beginning of the transition in Russia was that the highly monopolized nature of Russian industry made a stabilization of the Polish kind impossible. This is a version of the structuralist belief common throughout developing countries (but particularly in Latin America), that—whatever the case in the rest of the world—inflation in one's own country is a monopolistic phenomenon.

In considering this question we need to distinguish monopoly in the non-traded and the traded sectors. In the former, the high level of monopolization of wholesale trade in basic consumer goods was a serious problem which required forceful government intervention, which did not in fact materialize. In the retail sector, small privatization and private sector development resulted in far reaching demonopolization, but not until the second half of 1992 at the earliest. The decree on the freedom to trade of 28 January 1992 was an attempt by the authorities to weaken monopolistic trade and wholesale organizations by strengthening the rights of the ordinary people who were taking to street trading in their thousands.[34] However, the local authorities were powerful enough to largely ignore the decree if they wished, and maintain the position of the trade networks they owned.

As regards internationally traded goods, at the beginning of the transition Russia does not seem to have been potentially less open to international trade than Poland. The authors estimate that in 1992 exports outside the FSU were about 12.5 per cent of GDP (at purchasing power parities) compared to 8 per cent for Poland before the transition began.[35] The problem therefore lay with the host of export controls described in the previous section. In fact, as we shall see below, Russia as an exporter mainly of raw materials, was likely to face very strong penetration of her manufactured goods markets by imports, providing strong competition for domestic producers. What we have little information about is the degree of concentration of domestic production of tradable goods. Anecdotal evidence suggests it was higher than in Poland, where a degree of demo-

nopolization of the state sector had been undertaken by reform communists in the 1980s.[36] Certainly the Russian anti-monopoly office did little to split up producer cartels, or even to prevent their formation, concentrating instead on attempts at price control in cases in which it believed monopolistic behaviour had been identified (Fornalczyk and Hoffman, 1993).

More fundamentally, we need to consider why monopoly should inhibit anti-inflationary policy. Monopolists maximize profits by setting output at level at which marginal cost=marginal revenue, but both of these are effectively *relative* prices, which should therefore have nothing to do with inflation. It is true that monopolists who have previously had their prices controlled may increase them sharply on liberalization, but this would be a once and for all change (Berg and Blanchard, 1994). Also, Soviet-type economies suffered from many sole purchasers as well as sole producers. Where these buy from sole producers you have a bilateral monopoly with no implication for the price level. Where they are monopsonists, they are actually likely to force prices down.

However, there is another way in which Russia's economic structure did indeed make the whole transformation process (and stabilization as part of that process) particularly difficult. Russia is suffering today from what was known in the 1970s as the 'Dutch disease', but on a continental scale. This results from the way in which the Soviet economic system since Stalin was directed primarily at supplying the industrial base on which Soviet military power rested. Therefore, the economy was based on exploiting the vast natural resources of the north Eurasian land mass and transforming them into relatively efficient weapons and low quality machinery and consumer goods. The Soviet manufacturing sector was far too large, based as it was on underpriced raw materials (particularly energy), and almost completely protected from foreign competition by the planning system and the inconvertibility of the currency.

A significant part of Russian manufacturing was therefore bound to be uncompetitive when world prices for traded goods were introduced into the economy. The country as a whole would gain, exporting more raw materials than it otherwise

could, and using the revenue to buy better and cheaper foreign manufactures. But the problem for manufacturing enterprises as purchasers of raw materials was bound to be severe.

One of the apparently paradoxical aspects of this issue was that the energy producing enterprises themselves were opposed to the freeing of the prices of their products. The reason for this was the property rights structure of these firms: the managements could make large amounts of money by exporting oil which they claimed had been sold domestically, and pocketing the difference.[37] Thus, a major problem with stabilization in Russia is that the basic mechanism of the Soviet economy was privatized *before* the end of the 'perestroika' period and before the transition to capitalism began. With the collapse of the Soviet system this mechanism became one by which individuals and companies use their access to natural resources to transform them into private wealth. In the absence of legitimate private property rights to these natural resources, distorted prices are a key element in this process, but so is high inflation as it makes it easier to obtain cheap financing for such operations. Fraud is also made easier by the chaos which accompanies very high inflation, as is capital flight.

The raw materials pricing problem was compounded by the massive reduction in arms procurement which Gaidar implemented.[38] A democratic and peaceful Russia clearly did not need the level of weapons production of the USSR.[39] A similar situation held in some of the former Soviet satellites, but to a smaller degree, first because these countries were less well endowed in raw materials than was Russia, and secondly because their economies were generally less directed to weapons production.[40]

With so many SOEs threatened by the introduction of world prices, a significant part of elite and public opinion was susceptible to claims that monetary policy had to be loose to make possible the provision of cheap credit to threatened enterprises (and that fiscal policy had to be loose so as to provide subsidies). Export taxes and quotas, and especially favourable exchange rates for imports were justified on the same grounds.[41] This does not, of course, mean that it was the

most threatened or the most deserving of temporary support who actually got it. Moreover, instead of 'maintaining production' as was intended, cheap credit was often used to buy foreign currency in order to avoid the inflation tax, and thus effectively to speculate against the rouble.

5. *Russia's Political Structure*

What made the Gaidar attempt at stabilization unique was that at the beginning of 1992 Russia was a state without frontiers, sharing a common currency with fourteen other countries—it was in fact a state in the process of being born from the ashes of the USSR. At the end of 1991 Russian leaders were faced with an insoluble dilemma. They could, as Grigorii Yavlinsky proposed,[42] try to devise a stabilization programme which would have the support of at least the major post-Soviet states. The problem was that most of these (and in particular Ukraine) were not prepared to accept a general liberalization of prices, let alone the shock stabilization programme that had to accompany price liberalization. Alternatively, as Gaidar proposed, Russia could go it alone. This meant accepting that the USSR was an empty shell, its republics effectively independent states, and devising an economic policy for Russia alone, which would take into account only Russia's interests.

Gaidar's problem was that neither Russia's frontiers nor her currency were under the control of the state. There were few border and customs posts because these were on the external borders of the USSR, and were now mostly in the territory of foreign countries, so that the Russian Government did not have any authority over them.[43] As a result it was difficult for the state to raise the export taxes which could have been an important part of its revenue.[44] Indeed, in the first two months of 1992 export taxes were simply not levied. Furthermore, during the first nine months of 1992 the states of the FSU (excluding the Baltics) received Russian energy at domestic Russian prices. Since then these have been increased, but still not consistently to world levels.

The situation was equally serious as regards money creation.

The central banks of all fifteen successor states were able to create non-cash roubles without any restraint. In such a situation, it is in the interest of each central bank to create as much money as possible, and in this way to give the residents of its state purchasing power over goods produced in other states. The only constraint was that only Russia had the printing presses. This has meant that if a non-Russian central bank created so much deposit money that the demand for cash exceeded the amount made available to it by Russia, a cash shortage would develop in that state. Most central banks were eager to avoid such a situation, and this imposed some restraint on their behaviour.[45] On the other hand, they were also eager to prevent a differential in price levels between their country and others in the rouble area, so as to avoid a trade surplus which would represent the payment of seigniorage. This was in effect the exchange of goods and services for a book entry in the central bank of the importing country. Such a system inevitably led to an 'inflation race' between the states of the FSU.[46]

The only real solution was for Russia to 'nationalize the rouble', i.e. to treat the non-cash roubles created by the central banks of the other states as foreign currencies, and effectively to force these states to introduce their own currencies and decide on an exchange rate regime *vis-à-vis* the Russian rouble and other currencies. Although this step was discussed within the Russian leadership from as early as October 1991, it really happened only on 11 November 1992 when Ukraine finally left the rouble zone, and a system of *daily balancing of payments between the two countries* was made effective.[47] The automatic overdraft facilities which the non-Russian states had at the CBR until June 1992, and the massive 'technical credits' supplied to them by the CBR under Gerashchenko's governorship from then until November cost Russia the equivalent of between 8.6 and 10.9 per cent of GDP (Dąbrowski, 1993b).[48] Since the Russian state was unable to raise this money through taxation, it had to be paid by Russian savers through the inflation tax.

Why did nationalization of the rouble take so long to happen? Certainly the interests of those Russian firms whose main export markets were in the countries of the FSU played an

important role. There was also the fear that, deprived of this massive subsidy (equivalent to 12–18 per cent of the GDP of the recipients), the economies of the non-Russian states would collapse, with grave effects on the welfare of the 25 million ethnic Russians living there. The effect could then have been a massive emigration of these Russians to the Federation.[49] Ironically, Russia which had given up territory was in a similar position to Germany which had gained the former GDR, and which was also spending very large sums to avoid mass migration into its heartlands. However, a major motive was also imperial—the desire, particularly by Gerashchenko, to hold the former Soviet Union together at least economically, if this could not be done politically.[50] Unlike Germany, Russia proved incapable of sustaining the burden, and by the second half of 1993 the crediting of the non-Russian states had effectively ceased (and prices charged for Russia's raw materials were also sharply increased). Interestingly, the catastrophic effects for ethnic Russians outside the Federation failed to materialize.

6. The Stabilization vs. Privatization Debate

As 1991 turned into 1992 and the Gaidar programme was being launched, one of the major criticisms levelled at it was that price liberalization and stabilization, which were based on the assumption that enterprises would respond to market forces,[51] failed to take into account the nature of the SOE. It was therefore argued that privatization had to precede a liberalization/stabilization package. The Gaidar team, including those directly engaged in privatization, argued correctly that Polish experience showed this was not the case, and that a liberalization/stabilization package was feasible in an economy dominated by SOEs (though it is preferable to implement such a programme in an already predominantly private economy). It was felt, again probably correctly, that the majority of those arguing for privatization first did so because they knew that privatization would be a lengthy process, and hoped in this way to delay liberalization and stabilization.

The opponents of the Gaidar policy were unable to prevent price liberalization but, for the reasons described in the previous sections, they were able to severely limit liberalization in the wider sense, and to prevent stabilization. They were not, however, able to prevent privatization.[52] The bulk of state assets outside the natural monopolies and the defence industry was privatized by the middle of 1994, i.e. within two and a half years of the beginning of the transition. No other post-communist country has achieved a comparable result in so short a time, not even the Czech Republic, and this in spite of the far greater organizational and political difficulties encountered in Russia. It happened because of the bold decision to base privatization in Russia on vouchers and auctions, and thanks to the enormously privileged position given to insiders within the privatized firms by Anatoli Chubais, the Deputy Prime Minister in charge of privatization (Frydman, Rapaczynski, and Erle, 1993).

Thus, despite the intentions of the Gaidar team, in Russia privatization has preceded stabilization.[53] The reason for this seems clear: unlike liberalization and stabilization, which required painful adjustment by the SOEs to changes in relative prices and to a reduction in liquidity, Chubais' privatization programme was in the interests of the most powerful groups in Russian society, i.e. the insiders in the SOEs, and in particular their managements (workers have been politically far weaker in Russia than in Central Europe). The result is that during 1992–4 Russia has experienced 'transformation without stabilization', very much along the lines advocated by easy money populists. Few would dispute that this has happened at a particularly high cost in terms of capital flight, income inequality, criminality, and general chaos, which has strengthened authoritarian and anti-democratic politicans.

7. Conclusion and Postscript

It is impossible to assess which of the four groups of causes for the failure of stabilization in 1992 were critical. Weakness in the implementation of the programme resulted from both the political pressures which emerged from the economic and political

structure of Russia, and also from the lack of a clearly thought out programme well supported by Western finance. The counter-factual one will never be able to answer is whether such a programme could have developed enough economic and political momentum to make it effectively irreversible, as has happened for example in Poland. Unlike with privatization, however, it is difficult to imagine that it could have been possible to develop a liberalization-stabilization programme which would have been in the interest of the dominant producer groups in Russia (Layard and Richter, 1994 and Section 4). Thus the only way to stabilize in Russia in 1992 was to take these groups by surprise by the speed of stabilization, as happened in Poland.[54]

By 1994 this situation had changed somewhat because of the completion of mass privatization. Very high inflation reduced the price insiders had to pay for control of their SOEs to very low levels, and was thus in their interests. Now that the privatization programme has been completed, this reason for opposing stabilization has gone, and this (together with the nationalization of the rouble and the establishment of effective borders) may be one reason why stabilization has been somewhat more effective in 1994. On the other hand, as we noted in Section 4, a major problem is that the fundamental mechanism of the Soviet economy (the exploitation of natural resources) was privatized *before* the end of the 'perestroika' period and before the transition to capitalism began. In the absence of legitimate private property rights, high inflation and distorted relative prices for raw materials facilitate the process of expropriation of the state which is at the base of much of the larger scale private sector activity in the country. At present there is little indication that this process is abating, or that the groups which benefit from it are losing their power.

NOTES

*Centrum Analiz Społeczno-Ekonomicznych (CASE), Warsaw.

1. The success of the very similar Klaus programme of 1991 in Czecho-Slovakia strengthened their conviction that this was the right approach.

2. Four months in the Polish case and over a year in the Czecho-Slovak.
3. The agreement to dissolve the Soviet Union came on 8 Dec. 1991 at Bialovezha, and followed upon the Ukrainian presidential elections and referendum on independence of 1 Dec.
4. The purpose was to hide the surplus which was expected on this budget in 1992, so that the 'internal' budget could register a deficit, which was expected to appeal more to the populist parliament.
5. With a given delay between the time a given economic activity takes place and the time the tax due on it reaches the exchequer, the higher the rate of inflation the lower the real value of the tax revenue raised. Furthermore, the incentive to delay tax payments as long as possible increases as inflation increases, augmenting the Tanzi effect. During stabilization the Tanzi effect is reversed, increasing the real value of budget revenues. The problem is that it is very difficult to forecast either effects quantitatively, yet doing so is vital for effective budgetary planning.
6. Mainly cash and deposits of the commercial banks with the central bank.
7. Another example was the problem of how to treat the hard currency accounts of state enterprises at the Vneshekonombank (the Foreign Trade Bank of the USSR), which had been frozen by the Soviet authorities (and which the Russian authorities did not have enough international reserves to unfreeze for the foreseeable future). These amounted to $6 billion. The devaluation of the official exchange rate of the rouble on 1 January 1992 from roubles 5/US dollar to roubles 130/US dollar, meant a hypothetical increase in the value of these accounts from 30 billion roubles to 780 billion roubles—an increase of 750 billion roubles, or a further 70 per cent on the money supply for January 1992!
8. A key problem for the IMF was that neither Russia, nor the USSR before it, were actually members. However, this difficulty need not have stood in the way of the G7 acting outside the formal context of the IMF.
9. If the exchange rate regime chosen had been a floating one in the initial period, the value of the rouble would probably have soared, either as a result of intervention by the authorities, or as a result of an understanding by the markets of the strength of the rouble given the available backing.
10. This is very similar to current account convertibility. The failure to do this was an important reason for the failure of the stabilization (Sec. 3).
11. It is therefore not unimportant to know where the fault lies for the failure of Russia and the IMF to reach agreement. For if Russia is 'lost to democracy' one will be able to trace the causes back to this very moment. My own belief is that the smallest amount of blame attaches to the Russian government, which was in the midst of a political and economic hurricane. There was, however, a tendency to underestimate

the usefulness of an IMF agreement. The IMF itself is to blame on two main counts: first, that it wasted much of the early months of the Gaidar period on negotiating on debt on behalf of its Western members, and second, its attempt throughout 1992 to keep the rouble area in existence. But most of the blame attaches to the G7 governments, which failed to understand that the USSR was finished and which, once they did understand this, were more concerned with safeguarding their loans than with supporting radical reform—which would have been in any case the best way of ensuring that their loans would ultimately be repaid. The decision to leave the organizing of Western support for democracy and reform in Russia to the IMF was similar to leaving peacemaking in the former Yugoslavia to the UN and the EC, and with similar results.

12. Export bans had popular support in the regions. They were also contributing to declining output.

13. On finally getting to see Gaidar, after having waited for 12 hours one Sunday in December 1991, while the government arranged an exchange of clothes and diesel for grain from the kolkhozy, he said to me: 'You see before you the Walrasian auctioneer of Russia'.

14. It was these two cities which were the main targets of export bans by neighbouring agricultural regions.

15. If such subsidies are not increased, shortages of the goods will increase.

16. Members of the Gaidar team expected an 'industrialist' government headed by A. Volsky to precede their own. They expected such a government to pave the way for transformation and stabilization by freeing many prices and most entrepreneurial activity, in much the same way that the last communist government, headed by M. Rakowski had done in Poland. Possibly unfortunately from the viewpoint of the success of transformation in Russia, the August 1991 coup 'accelerated history', causing the reformist team to come to power 'too early', so that it had to be responsible for both the first price liberalization in Russia and to attempt stabilization. In an irony of fate, it may be that the 'industrialist' government of Viktor Chernomyrdin will succeed in implementing the stabilization which the reformists have not been able to.

17. The justification was originally that the 25% margin would not apply to those shops which left the state owned retail monopolies. It was thus supposed to induce the break-up of these monopolies. As it turned out, no exception was in fact made for the 'leavers' in the decree.

18. The index measures the availability of 70 food items and 28 non-food items in 132 cities in Russia. 0 indicates that none of the items are available anywhere, while 100 means that all are available everywhere. As can be seen, it is not a very demanding measure of market saturation!

19. Coal prices were only freed in July 1993.

20. This was made uniform in the second half of the year.
21. This varied with oil price and exchange rate changes.
22. This did not prevent export smuggling of oil from taking place on a very large scale (see Sec. 4).
23. Net Material Product (NMP), see Russian Economic Trends vol. 1.
24. The figures for exports are very similar: about 110 per cent and 60 per cent of NMP in quarters 1 and 2 of 1992.
25. In the second half of 1992 the share of imports to which a preferential exchange rate was applied fell from 40 per cent to 10 per cent. The implicit subsidy was supposed to be funded by the budget, but this did not in fact apply to imports financed by foreign credits.
26. Wages above 3 times the minimum wage are not counted as costs, and cannot therefore be set against enterprise income tax. Effectively this means that they attracted a further 30 per cent tax, on top of the payroll tax paid on all wages. This was a very mild regime compared with the Polish one, where wage increases which were more than 5 per cent above the permitted threshold increase (itself generally considerably less than inflation) attractive 500 per cent tax on top of the payroll tax (Ch. 7).
27. This does not mean that the NAIRU analysis does not hold for Russia. If financial policies had been sufficiently tight in Russia, the policy of aggressive price increases practised by enterprise managers in the initial months of the reform would have led to large-scale unemployment, and forced the enterprise managers to desist.
28. This was according to Russian methodology, which counted foreign loans as income.
29. April 1991 = 100.
30. Lecture at the London School of Economics, 7 May 1993.
31. The present author presented Gaidar with a proposal for a market based solution to the inter-enterprise debt problem—which would have avoided the need for additional money creation—in May 1992. It is contained in the last two sections of Ch. 8.
32. In real terms this increase was about 60 per cent.
33. However, revenues were smaller than they might have been because of the difficulties the authorities had in properly indexing tax prepayments (an example of the Tanzi effect).
34. This phenomenon had dramatically increased retail competition in Poland in 1990. The decree was the result of advice by a number of advisers who had been involved in the Polish programme (including the present authors).
35. Russia's per capita GDP at purchasing power parities (PPP) before the transition began is assumed to have been 2/3 of Poland's, giving a total GDP of $240 billion compared to $90 billion for Poland. Exports were respectively $30 billion and $7.5 billion.
36. And where the revision of the law on state enterprises of March 1990 (as part of the Balcerowicz plan) gave component entities the right to leave SOEs without the agreement of the latter.

37. Viktor Chernomyrdin was brought into the Government in May 1992 as Deputy Prime Minister in charge of energy production as a concession to this interest.

38. Said to be 80 per cent in 1992 alone.

39. Gaidar was politically astute in cutting weapons procurement far more than the personnel budget of the army. One area where the generally pro-Western stance of the Government may have made things harder was the disapproval of the United States for Russian arms exports to certain countries. However, many of the most unpleasant customers of the former USSR were even more broke than Russia, and arms deliveries to them were more in the nature of gifts than sales.

40. Part of the impact of the collapse of the Council for Mutual Economic Assistance (CMEA) was due to the cheap raw materials obtained by the Central and East European satellites, which helped to sustain their manufacturing industry (and in the case of some countries—such as Slovakia—into weapons for the Warsaw pact to a significant degree). Similar effects—but far stronger—were felt by the more industrialized of the newly independent states of the former USSR, such as Ukraine and Bielarus.

41. Thus in the first half of 1992, Aeroflot was paying 25 roubles/US dollar, at a time when the market rate was 120 roubles/US dollar (Dąbrowski, 1993a).

42. At the time Deputy Prime Minister of the USSR.

43. Some 'internal border posts' had been established before the dissolution of the USSR (for instance on the frontiers with the Baltics) so as to 'defend the domestic market' from the purchasing power of residents of these republics. But these frontiers remained highly porous.

44. A very rough calculation shows just how large these revenues could have been. Exports in the first quarter were $7 billion. We assume that half the exports consisted in energy products, of which half was oil and half gas (these figures are taken from the actual shares in Q1 1993 quoted by *Russian Economic Trends*), and that the difference between the domestic and world prices was (1) 90 per cent of the world price for oil, and (2) 50 per cent of the world price for gas. If the whole of this difference had gone to the federal budget, as should have been the case, then these two items alone should have brought in 288 billion roubles, i.e. over ten times as much as total 'earnings from foreign economic activity' actually did, and about 21 per cent of GDP in that quarter! However, it needs to be noted that these difficulties were to some extent anticipated and the budget of 18 Dec. 1991 left all such revenues out of account (one of the purposes being to prevent the populist parliament from spending this revenue).

45. Some non-Russian central banks (in early 1992 particularly those of Lithuania and Ukraine) tried to escape from this dilemma by emitting 'emergency cash' of their own. This had the additional advantage of

limiting non-residents' access to consumer goods on the domestic market.

46. A similar mechanism operated in 1991 in Yugoslavia in the run up to the formal disintegration of that country, and indeed during the Serbo-Croat war which followed.

47. This system had formally been introduced in July, but the automatic overdraft facilities and technical credits issued by Gerashchenko meant that it had little bite.

48. The last overdraft facilities and technical credits for FSU republics were only abolished by Finance Minister Boris Feodorov in May 1993.

49. This could have been either as a direct result of economic collapse in their countries, or because of a violent reaction against them by local inhabitants. This line was put forward to the authors by highly placed Russian officials.

50. A second irony of history is that it was only once the rouble was nationalized that the non-Russian states realised their true economic weakness, and the states of the FSU began to come under renewed Russian domination. The exception are the Baltics, which were prepared themselves to cut the umbilical cord of CBR transfers, and with it their economic dependence on Russia, by creating their own currencies on their own initiative and stabilizing inflation. The third, and final, irony is that Lithuania, the last of the Baltics to stabilize and thus to prove itself capable of independent statehood, did so under the auspices of the post-communist (so-called Socialist Party) government, while the previous more nationalist Sajudis government had not had the courage, or maybe the understanding, to take this step.

51. Both at the micro level (e.g. enterprises would respond to relative prices) and at the macro level (e.g. the money supply would affect the aggregate price level).

52. Though the attempts to do so were on occasion desperate (Chubais, 1993).

53. Thus implementing the proposed sequencing of the 500 day plan, so heavily criticised by reformers for its lack of radicalism.

54. An important element in Poland was that producers were profoundly divided, with power divided between workers councils, trade unions, and the managements. This so-called 'Bermuda triangle' was much lamented by Balcerowicz as a break on the restructuring of enterprises, and Gaidar said to one of the present authors that Russia's great advantage was that it did not have Solidarity. It seems to us that the case was quite the opposite: the internal conflicts within Polish SOEs played a vital role in inhibiting producer mobilization against stabilization. And, as is claimed in Ch. 1, little restructuring will happen in the absence of stabilization anyway.

8

The Inter-Enterprise Debt Explosion in the Former Soviet Union: Causes, Consequences, Cures

1. Introduction

Inter-enterprise debt (IED) has long been perceived to be a problem in market socialist economies,[1] and it has resurfaced as an acute anxiety for policy makers in many post-communist economies attempting to implement so-called 'big bang' liberalization/stabilization programmes. However, it is in the states of the former Soviet Union (FSU) that the phenomenon has attained truly epic proportions. Between 1 January and 30 April 1992, IED in Russia grew from a few dozen billion roubles to 1800 billion roubles, the equivalent of total GNP generated in the first four months of the year.[2] Roughly the same relationship of IED/GDP held in Latvia in June 1992. This suggests that in both countries about half of transactions were not being paid for.[3] By the end of June the stock of IED in Russia had reached 3000 billion roubles. In Romania at the end of 1991, IED amounted to about 50 per cent of GNP (Khan and Clifton, 1992). On the other hand, in the Central European PCEs the ratio of IED to GNP is much smaller, and seems to have increased at a far slower rate—or not at all—upon initiation of 'big bangs'. Thus in Czecho-Slovakia, IED constituted about 18 per cent of GDP at the end of 1991,[4] a level to which it had merely doubled from the beginning of the year (Table 23). In Poland at the end of 1989 IED/GDP ratio was also around 18 per cent, after which it declined (see Table 22).[5]

2. The Causes of Inter-Enterprise Debt Explosion

As Begg and Portes (1992) point out, the ratio of IED to bank credit in Central European PCEs is not out of line with that in advanced capitalist countries, where the two categories of credit are roughly of equal size. This is the case in Poland, whereas in Czecho-Slovakia the IED/bank credit ratio only reached 25 per cent at end 1991, although it was rising quite rapidly. In Poland during 1991 the average period of payment delay was 62 days (GUS, 1991, and GUS, 1990–2), whereas the corresponding figure in the West ranges from 45 days in Germany and Scandinavia, through 80 days in the UK to 90 in Italy and 110 in France.[6] Under central planning IED was strictly controlled by the authorities and severely discouraged as a symptom of enterprise independence. It is therefore clear that an important reason for IED growth in Central European PECs is adjustment to levels suitable for market economies.

Begg and Portes suggest further microeconomic reasons for IED growth in PCEs: First, enterprises with liquid assets and low costs of monitoring other enterprises in their own sector may effectively join the banking business by extending credit to their customers (interest, often at penal rates, is due on payments delayed beyond the credit days granted by the seller).[7] Second, taking action against debtors may signal to one's creditors that one is oneself in financial difficulties. Third, there is an option value in waiting before closing down a major customer—his financial health may improve. The last two are reasons for what Begg and Portes call 'creditor passivity', which can be perfectly rational in such circumstances.

However, these explanations, although they may contribute to the phenomenon, cannot—severally or jointly—be adequate to account for the difference in the magnitude of the IED explosion in the FSU and Romania as compared to the Central European PCEs. First, as described in the previous section, the magnitude of IED is of a different order in the FSU and Romania.[8] Second, the growth rate of IED has also been much greater. IED increased by about 130 per cent in nominal terms and 50 per cent in real terms in Czecho-Slovakia in the first six

months of the stabilization programme in 1991. In Poland during the first six months of the stabilization programme in 1990, IED increased by 70 per cent in nominal terms and fell 36 per cent in real terms. On the other hand, in Russia in the first six months of 1992 the nominal increase was almost 100 times, and the real increase was about eight and a half times, while the ratio of IED to bank credit increased from almost zero to over two.[9] In Romania the increase was similar, but not quite to rapid. In 1991, IED increased six times in nominal terms and three times in real terms while the ratio of IED/bank credit increased from 0.2 to 2 (Table 24). Second, it would be stretching the meaning of words to suggest that Russia or Romania are market economies in anything like the way in which Poland or Czecho-Slovakia are.

The intuition has to be that in the FSU and Romania the main reasons for the IED explosion are macro, not microeconomic. Williamson (1992*a*) has provided a useful taxonomy of the various kinds of macroeconomic shock to which PCEs have been, or may have been, subject over the last three years (see Table 20). Some of these categories of shock could have caused IED growth because their effects on purchasers' cash flow was not anticipated by suppliers. The latter provided goods before they realized that payment would not be forthcoming. Once this had happened the reasons for 'creditor passivity' described by Begg and Portes could have come into play. This scenario could explain IED growth where purchasers were affected by a fall in demand for their products for one of the following reasons: a fall in foreign demand because of the collapse of CMEA trade; a shift in domestic demand (e.g., as a result of a fall in government's share of national income, which seems to have taken place in Czecho-Slovakia); the elimination of forced substitution with the disappearance of excess demand as a result of price liberalization; a fall in domestic demand for purchasers' products as a result of foreign trade liberalization (resulting in foreign competition); input dislocation making it impossible for purchasers to complete their output and sell their product, in spite of provision of inputs by some suppliers, because of the complementarity between inputs. Note that

most of these reasons were as much present in the Central European PCEs as in the FSU and Romania.

Sachs and Lipton (1993) point to a number of technical causes of arrears specific to the FSU. First, and most important, is the breakdown of bank payments mechanisms leading to long delays in receiving payments.[10] Enterprises which have not yet received payments cannot pay their own suppliers. The fact that in the FSU non-cash roubles are not convertible into cash means that payment delays in the banking system cannot be avoided by resorting to cash payment in exchange for a discount on the price.[11] It is natural that arrears have grown faster in the FSU where this is the case, than in Romania where SOEs are free to shift into cash to effect payments.[12] However, the slowdown in payments through the banks has itself been a result of accelerating inflation (banks wishing to obtain part of the inflation tax), and therefore caused by macroeconomic conditions. Second, according to Lipton and Sachs, the cash shortage which existed until May of 1992 meant that final goods purchases were squeezed more than intermediate goods purchase, and final goods producers were unable to pay their suppliers. Intermediate goods producers, who had more access to the non-cash money which was more easily available, then extended inter-enterprise credit (IEC) to final goods producers. While this factor may have played some role, there is no evidence that IED is concentrated in retail trade enterprises, or that the expansion of IED slowed after the elimination of the cash shortage in mid-May 1992.[13] Finally, in the FSU, VAT is paid on goods sold only when the money due for them is received. Thus some of the losses from payment arrears are borne by the treasury rather than the supplier.[14]

3. *Credibility and the IED Explosion*

The most likely cause of massive growth in IED in the FSU and Romania thus seems to be simply a lack of credibility of the stabilization component of a 'big bang' transition programme.[15] A reduction in the rate of growth of bank credit in nominal terms is always announced as part of such a programme, and a

fall in the rate of growth of real credit is usually part of its initial phase.[16] State owned enterprises (SOEs) which do not believe in the durability of the reduction in the rate of growth of nominal credit will behave entirely rationally if they extend credit to their customers. They expect these customers to shortly obtain sufficient bank credit to be able to repay the credit which suppliers have provided. However, in order to protect them-selves from the inflation which can be expected to accompany the loose monetary policy which is implicit in such an expecta-tion, they have to set prices sufficiently above what they would otherwise be for the real value of the payment they receive to compensate them for the goods they deliver on credit, adding even more to inflation in the short term.[17]

This seems to be a good description of what has happened in the FSU in 1992 and Romania in 1991 (see Tables 21 and 24). Khan and Clifton, consider that it is the faster growth in prices than in the money supply which is the cause of the increase in IED (to provide liquidity which compensates for the fall in real money balances or real bank credit). For the present author the direction of causation goes the other way: a lack of credibility in the stabilization programme leads to a growth of the IED/money ratio, to increased inflation, and finally to a fall in the real stock of money. The lack of credibility of stabilization policy in Russia can also be seen in the maintenance of produc-tion of military hardware by the Russian defence industry, in spite of the very sharp cutback in budgetary spending under this heading. Because defence industry enterprises are not being paid by the budget they cannot pay their suppliers, yet they continue to be supplied (Sachs and Lipton, 1993).

In contrast, at the beginning of the stabilization programme in Poland in 1990, the real value of IED fell 40 per cent from December 1989 to January 1990, after which it remained at roughly the same level for the ensuing two and a half years (Table 22). The ratio of IED to bank debt exhibited much the same pattern. In December 1989 it was 1.54 and it rose over the two first months of the stabilization programme to 1.75. It then fell almost continuously, reaching 0.95 in June 1990, 0.75 in January 1991, after which it has fluctuated in the 0.75 to 1.0

range through to the summer of 1992. In other words there was no IED explosion in Poland after stabilization in 1990, showing that the stabilization was credible.

Let us look in more detail at behaviour at the microeconomic level in such a situation. If stabilization is not credible and rapid IED expansion is taking place, then the prices charged by suppliers need to be higher than they would otherwise be as a result of two effects: first, without the credit purchasers could not afford to pay as high a price; second, the price incorporates an implicit interest charge for the expected delay in payment, which itself reflects expected inflation during the period of non-payment. Effectively, for any given level of sales to a particular customer, a supplier is making a choice between a low price with immediate payment and a high price with delayed payment. If the authorities capitulate and abandon their stabilization programme, the extension of the inter-enterprise credit (IEC) is justified to the extent to which the price charged for the goods was sufficiently high to compensate the supplier for the opportunity cost of the money he failed to obtain at the time of delivery.

In such a framework, what are likely to be the determinants of the expansion of IED? These will include: (1) the expected length of time before the authorities reverse the credit crunch they have engineered; (2) the expected rate of inflation in this period; (3) the rate of interest on deposits; (4) the cost of financing inter-enterprise credit.

Given the expected values of these variables, the SOE, contemplating the extension of inter-enterprise credit, needs to choose an optimal price, quantity, and IEC combination. In the short term, the system can be unstable: the larger the amount of IEC extended, the higher both price and quantity can be; if many enterprises decide on high levels of IEC expansion this will lead to higher inflation, which may induce each creditor to charge higher prices and extend even more credit. Moreover, higher inflation means a reduction in the opportunity cost of IEC for any given rate of interest on deposits and of the cost of financing IEC for any given nominal rate of interest on loans. Thus there is the possibility of an inflationary bubble developing.

The bubble can be burst by a number of developments: an increase in the credibility of the stabilization programme; an extension in the expected period before the credit crunch is reversed; the introduction of *ex ante* positive real interest rates (on loans, deposits or both); or the unavailability of financing for IEC expansion. As yet, none of the above conditions for bursting an IED driven inflationary bubble seems to hold in Russia or the other countries of the FSU. This is a major difference between the FSU on the one hand and Poland and Czecho-Slovakia on the other. In the latter two countries, during the first six months of the stabilization programme, real *ex post* rates of interest on loans were positive[18] and real *ex post* interest rates on deposits were massively positive in terms of foreign currency.

How do SOEs finance the IEC they extend to customers? To a large extent this is done by not paying their suppliers, i.e. by the amount of IED they accumulate. This makes the calculation regarding the optimal amount of IEC to extend even more complex, in that the optimal amount of IED to contract becomes part of the calculation, so that the prices charged by suppliers (which incorporate their implicit interest charges) ought to be taken into account. Indeed, the calculation now becomes so complex that one must doubt whether SOE managers in fact behave in such a sophisticated way in deciding whether to extend IEC.

The true explanation may be cruder: when a Soviet-type economy (STE) becomes a PCE, state enterprises become free to extend inter-enterprise credit. If this is followed shortly after by a credit squeeze as part of a stabilization programme, SOEs may initially be willing to muddle through and avoid adjustment by both taking on IED and extending IEC, without much concern about whether this is financially optimal or not, as long as there is a general belief in the impermanence of the credit squeeze. The reasons for such apparently suboptimal behaviour may not be far to find. First, one must remember a key microeconomic fact: in the initial stages of a big bang stabilization/liberalization package in a PCE there is unlikely to be an effective bankruptcy system in operation.[19]

SOE managers are therefore unlikely to be very concerned about the effect on their income statements of extending or taking on IEC.

Furthermore, in the initial stage of a stabilization programme in a PCE, managers of SOEs are likely to have a particularly short time horizon because of the high level of uncertainty, and may therefore attempt to avoid the conflicts with the workforce over nominal wages which could arise from a need to econo- mize on money balances so as to be able to pay suppliers. Money or bank credit are indispensable to SOEs in the short term only for the payment of wages and the purchase of foreign currency (in order to buy imports).[20] All other purchases can be financed by IEC provided it is made availabe. Thus not only may enterprises be unwilling to 'waste' money on intermediate inputs when contracting IED is possible, but also they may not insist on money payment as long as their money revenues[21] suffice for those expenditures for which money is essential. There may, therefore, be a widespread willingness to extend IEC, as long as the opportunity cost of doing so is not very high due to low *ex ante* real interest rates on deposits.[22]

Every enterprise can thus, for a short time, effectively create liquidity on a base of money as a reserve asset (which is needed to ensure wage payments etc.).[23] If domestically produced inter- mediate inputs constitute, for example, 60 per cent of expendi- tures then, as long as purchases of these inputs can be financed with IED, SOEs could use all their money holdings to finance remaining expenditures, i.e. wage costs, payments for imports of intermediate inputs and tax payments.[24] In the aggregate the nominal value of transactions in the economy can increase rapidly when IED begins to grow, even if the money supply is constant. Thus:

(1) $PT = M(1/a)V$

(2) $PT = MV + D$

where a is the ratio of transactions in which the medium of exchange is money to total transactions (which are financed using either money or by the extension of additional IED),

and D is the increment in IED. If M and V are constant then as long as IED is increasing a < 1, so that 1/a > 1. We can have a number of patterns of change in PT (with M and V constant). One such pattern would be the following:

1) when IED is forbidden by central planners, D = 0, a = 1 and PT is constant;

2) when D is a constant > 0, a = some constant < 1, so that PT jumps to the higher level which can be accommodated by M(1/a)V or D > 0, until IED reaches its maximum level;

3) once IED reaches its maximum level D = 0 and a = 1, so that PT jumps down to its previous level.

Maximum IED is determined by expected inflation, the nominal interest rate, expected changes in the money supply and in the velocity of circulation.[25] The above pattern would be consistent with the extreme case of a completely incredible stabilization policy combined with a constant money supply. In phase (1) IED was banned by central planners. During phase (2) SOEs are convinced that the authorities will soon increase M. In phase (3) SOEs suddenly become convinced that the authorities will not increase M after all.

Alternatively, if the stability of the economy is credible, then once IEC is legalized, it will rise to some level which is the aggregate of the decisions regarding how much trade credit lenders and borrowers decide is optimal. While D is growing, a is declining and the velocity of circulation of money with respect to all transactions—(V/a)—is increasing.[26] Once D stabilizes a also stabilizes. Once IED stabilizes, D = 0, a = 1, so that PT falls back to its previous level of before the increase in IED. Thus, even if the stability of the economy is credible, IED will only grow if an increase in M or V are anticipated.[27] Otherwise the growth in IED will merely cause a 'bubble' in PT (and in inflation).[28]

Finally, if there is no maximum for IED, because SOEs are prepared to extend unlimited credit to their inter-enterprise customers, then D can remain constant indefinitely (financing at the limit all inter-enterprise transactions), and PT can remain stable. The need to pay for final goods and primary inputs in money, together with a fixed M and V, is what constrains PT

and thus inflation even in this extreme case. This is on the assumption that the prices of intermediate goods relative to final goods and primary inputs remain unchanged. It is possible, however, that the unlimited availability of IEC (e.g. because of an expectation of repeated multilateral clearing of IED)[29] will lead to the relative prices of domestic intermediate inputs rising considerably in the short term. D would then rise without a falling. PT would continue to grow, while PY remained constant. However, lower prices would come to be charged for cash on delivery, requiring the calculation of PT in 'cash prices' (see below).

The situation may be clarified further if we assume that some enterprises are 'downstream', some are 'intermediate', while others are 'upstream'. The ratio of final sales/intermediate sales is relatively high in downstream enterprises (e.g. retail networks and exporters), as is the ratio of final sales/primary inputs. In a retail network for example, 100 per cent of sales may be 'final', and thus involve the receipt of cash money, 10 per cent of expenditures may be primary and thus require the payment of cash money, while 90 per cent of expenditures may be intermediate, which can be paid for either with non-cash money (on the assumption that, as in the rouble zone, the difference between cash and non-cash money still exists), or by taking on IED. If all domestic intermediate inputs are financed with IED, then such a downstream enterprise will deposit its money revenues at its bank. In order to avoid this money being paid out in response to a payment demand order, it may deposit the money in a hidden account, which its suppliers do not know about.

Then there are the 'intermediate' enterprises. Let us assume that these have no final sales but only inter-enterprise sales. They can supply their customers on credit and receive domestic intermediate inputs from their suppliers on credit. However, they do have some, relatively small, amount of primary inputs (wages and imported intermediate inputs), which they have to pay for with money which they borrow from the banking system. Finally, there are the 'upstream' enterprises, which sell most of their output to inter-enterprise customers, but

most of whose inputs are primary (labour, imports). They too have to borrow money from the banks.

The banking system thus acts as the conduit for money from 'money rich' downstream enterprises to 'money poor' intermediate and upstream enterprises. Since the 'money poor' enterprises cannot service their debts, let alone repay them, once such a situation arises the banking system is effectively bankrupt.

If, upon liberalization, intermediate and upstream enterprises begin to finance all purchases by their inter-enterprise customers by extending IEC, then the effects of IED on PT can follow the following three phases:

1) when IED is forbidden, $D = 0$ and PT is constant;

2) when IED is permitted, $D > 0$ and PT jumps to the higher level at which all M is used exclusively for transactions involving final sales or primary inputs, while all intermediate transactions are financed by IEC;

3) if, in this situation, there is no limit on the growth of IED, then the relative prices of domestic intermediate products can continue to rise, causing continued growth of PT, increasing paper profits among upstream (and possibly intermediate) enterprises, and declining paper profits or even paper losses among downstream enterprises.

The point is that in this configuration it is far from clear what mechanism would, in the short term, prevent IED from increasing indefinitely. Indeed, D could grow over time so that IED grew at a constant (or even at an accelerating) rate. If M was not increased, final goods producers' unit costs would rise while their revenues remained constant. The result could be falling sales of final output.

Sachs and Lipton (1993) have suggested that a similar process, in which the supply of non-cash money expands more rapidly than the supply of cash, may be one of the causes of the current Russian depression. Just as IEC is not convertible on demand into money so, in the rouble zone, non-cash money is not convertible into cash (except for certain categories of payments, such as wages, which are usually those required to obtain primary inputs). Furthermore, non-cash money is received mainly

by intermediate and upstream enterprises, as a result of sales to other enterprises or as bank credit. Cash money is received mainly by retailers, and is spent mainly by very upstream enterprises which have high labour costs. The difference between non-cash money and IED is that non-cash money is created by the banking system, whereas IED is created by the enterprises.

In both cases, however, the more rapid expansion of the inferior and inconvertible means of payment (IED as against money, non-cash money as against cash), if it continues unchecked, must ultimately lead to its depreciation. Prices will be quoted both for cash or money payment and (higher ones) for non-cash or delayed payment (involving the extension of IEC by the supplier). Once it has been recognized by all that there are in fact several means of payment in use within the country and that output price formation, profit calculation, and taxation must take this fact into account, the real effects of IED or non-cash money growing faster than money or cash will disappear. The relative prices of intermediate goods will continue to rise in non-cash roubles or when sold on credit, but will remain constant in cash or money terms. As regards the accumulation of IED, the result would be a real devaluation of the stock of debt to the level which suppliers wish to hold. Once this had happened the real value of IED could not grow unless suppliers wished to hold more of it, real $D = 0$, and PT denominated in 'money prices' (as opposed to those charged when IEC was extended) would be constant: this would be the long-term result in phase (3) above. One can thus see that the problems associated with excessive IED growth (and excessive non-cash money growth) are those of a transitional period, in which it has not been openly admitted that an SOE's debt may not be worth its face value, or that non-cash roubles are not worth cash roubles.

There is, of course, an important difference between IED and non-cash money. Since there is an implicit government guarantee of all bank deposits, actors need know only one price: the exchange rate of cash into non-cash roubles. In the case of IED, suppliers need to assess the likely payment delay specific to each customer.

4. Consequences

As we have seen, the disappearance of administrative constraints on IED may lead to a temporary expansion of liquidity (money plus increases in IED) in the economy with little increase in the money supply.

A number of macroeconomic consequences follow. First, prices can rise more than expected if the expansion of IED was not foreseen (Khan and Clifton). Second, since the 'liquidity' provided by IED is of a very specific sort (i.e. unlike bank debt it is not usually accepted as a means of payment by third parties), the steady state nominal value of transactions in the economy remains unchanged.[30] As a result, although the increase in liquidity allows prices to increase more than they would have done, once liquidity is again stable then either prices or real transactions, or both, have to fall, so as to return nominal transactions to their previous level. These processes might therefore help to explain both price 'overshooting' and the large output falls during stabilization/liberalization programmes in PCEs.[31]

Policy makers implementing a stabilization programme in a PCE thus have to choose between, on the one hand, an initial reduction followed by an increase in real money balances, together with an increase in the size of the money multiplier as the ratio of high powered money to deposits in the structure of bank balance sheets declines (Chapter 11) during a successful disinflation, and on the other hand the expansion of inter-enterprise liquidity discussed here, when the stabilization is not credible (see Calvo, 1992, for a useful framework within which one can consider these options).

A second round consequence of such an unsustainable increase in nominal transactions is that when SOEs come to understand the nature of the process, they put pressure on the monetary authorities to increase the money supply, the velocity of circulation, or the multilateral 'clearing' of IED, so as to validate the price increases they have generated (see Section 5).

Apart from the macroeconomic drawbacks resulting from an IED explosion, there is also a complex of microeconomic

problems, which are described by Begg and Portes. The first is that uncertainty regarding the liquidation value of individual enterprises is increased. Second, systemic risk arises because of the creation of an interlocking network of enterprise commitments. Third, liquidity is redistributed from sound to potentially unsound enterprises, which impedes exit and restructuring of the unsound.

5. Proposed Solutions to the IED Problem

The simplest solution to the IED problem is to reverse the conditions which have given rise to it. This solution is usually favoured by those who are opposed to macroeconomic stabilization on the grounds that the cost, in terms of reductions in output and employment, is unacceptable. This implies making available as much bank credit—via an expansion of central bank credit or a reduction in reserve ratios—as is needed to ensure that the current level of PT can be financed by the new money stock M.[32] In economies which require macroeconomic stabilization this can be the route to uncontrolled hyperinflation: the increase in bank credit would confirm the expectations of loose monetary policy which make the stabilization incredible. Additional bank credit would then be needed not only to finance old IED, but also the new inter-enterprise credit which SOEs would extend more willingly once they knew that bank credit was once again easily available. A race between the growth rates of bank credit, inter-enterprise credit and prices would develop.[33]

Alternatively, there can be a 'multilateral clearing' of IED, without any additional money creation. As we shall see in Section 5.2, such an approach is likely to be less expansionary than money creation. Nevertheless, it does present serious difficulties: there is nothing wrong with cancelling out mutual obligations between pairs of enterprises; however, there is a fundamental difference between such 'bi-lateral' netting out and the 'multi-lateral' netting out (Section 5.1).

An approach which is intermediate between the two described above, consists in first 'cancelling out' as much IED

as possible, and then providing central bank credit to finance remaining net IED. Such a solution was implemented in Romania in December 1991 and in Russia in July 1992. Providing bank credit to finance the remaining net IED means that the authorities effectively validate the previous credit policies of SOEs. It means that SOEs are allowed to have effectively determined the level of bank credit growth in the period up to the emission of the new bank credit, i.e. to have determined monetary policy. The effects of such a mechanism then depend crucially on the extent to which the clearing is credible as a 'one off' event. We explain in Section 5.4 why we consider this to be unlikely.

5.1. The Russian Schemes

The Russian Government's proposed solution to the IED problem in the summer of 1992 was of the 'multilateral clearing without bank credit creation' variety. The first step was to cancel out the debts among enterprises, and then use the assets of net debtors to pay net creditors. Net debtors were thus to be fully or partly liquidated. As the bankruptcy system is not operational, and will not be operational for some time, a special centralized debt management agency was to have been set up to administer the realization of net debtors' assets (see Sachs and Lipton, 1993, for a description of how such a system might work).[34] While such an approach was less dangerous than that advocated by the Central Bank of Russia and in effect finally adopted (see below), there are still a number of serious problems involved.

First, the very act of multilaterally 'netting out' IED is not a neutral, technical undertaking which merely ensures that mutual liabilities can be settled more quickly and conveniently—even though it is sometimes presented as such. The multilateral clearing of IED implies that all the IED 'cleared' is given an equal value in the clearing process, with the result that the authorities change the true underlying (and as yet possibly unrevealed) values of the IEC extended by different enterprises. This value depends on the true, also possibly as yet unrevealed, creditworthiness of the borrowers. If the 'multilateral clearing' did

not take place, the IEC extended to purchasers who are expected to pay relatively quickly would be worth more than that extended to those who are expected to pay later—or possibly never. By setting all IED cleared equal to its nominal value, the authorities eradicate these differences in the value of IEC extended and then cleared.

It is true that only cleared IED benefits from this 'equalling up' in this approach, with the result that the proposal of the Russian government was less inflationary than the CBR's in which, after 'multilateral clearing', bank credit is injected to pay off all remaining net IED. How much less inflationary in the short run 'multilateral clearing without bank credit creation' is than its 'with bank credit creation' cousin, depends on how much multilateral clearing of IED can be effected: the more IED is successfully cleared the smaller the difference between the two approaches in the short run (in the long run IED growth depends on increases in M or V—see Section 3). The amount that can be cleared may vary considerably, depending on the proportion of IED owed by net debtors. Thus, in 1991 the Comercny Banka of Czecho-Slovakia cleared IED and as a result reduced it by 20 per cent (Begg, 1991), whereas the Romanian multilateral clearing operation of end January 1992 resulted in the clearing of 75 per cent of all IED.[35]

It is also worth considering the political economy of the 'multilateral clearing without bank credit creation' approach: the more IED has been cleared by 'multilateral clearing' the greater the likelihood that the small additional amount of bank credit required to avoid unpleasant consequences for net debtors (and net creditors!) will somehow be created.[36]

The similarity between the 'multilateral clearing' of IED and the creation of money so that IED can be serviced is highlighted by the technique which was used for 'multilateral clearing' in Russia in 1992: special accounts were created for each enterprise on which its inter-enterprise assets and liabilities were registered. Those enterprises with positive balances could then use their 'special accounts' to pay off their IED. SOEs which received such payments could in turn use them to pay off their own IED.[37] The close similarity of this procedure to

money creation is evident. If the 'special accounts' had not been created, money would have had to be used to service the IED. In this way, ordinary money was freed to be used for other purposes.

In the event, in Russia net creditors' positive balances on the special accounts were subsequently turned into money by making them useable for tax payments and for the servicing of bank debt, thus turning the earmarked money on the special accounts into ordinary money.[38] This has effectively meant the triumph of the Central Bank of Russia approach to IED clearing. The CBR wished to combine multilateral IED clearing with injections of central bank credit. In Romania also, the multilateral IED clearing exercise of December 1991 has involved an increase in the money supply.

5.2. The Inflationary Effect of Different Solutions

It is useful to compare the expansionary/inflationary effects of the three mechanisms:

1) multilateral clearing without bank credit (i.e. money) creation;

2) increasing M sufficiently to allow the money stock to service the new, higher, level of nominal transactions—PT in equation (1)—resulting from the extension of IED, without engaging in any multilateral clearing;[39]

3) multilateral clearing with bank credit creation.

If all IED could be multilaterally cleared, the approach excluding bank credit creation would then be the equivalent of temporarily increasing the velocity of circulation of money (V) to the extent required to allow all IED to be paid off while maintaining the quantity of money (M) constant. In terms of equation (1) therefore, PT can be sustained at its new, higher, level $P'T'$ (determined by the optimal IED/M ratio), because domestic intermediate inputs can be purchased through the accumulation of new IED, i.e. $D > 0$ in equation (2) once again. As a result the constant money stock M can continue to be used to finance exclusively transactions in final goods and primary inputs, i.e. $a < 1$ in equation (1). Under these circumstances comprehensive multilateral clearing is equivalent in the very

short term to an increase in M which would have the same effect on PT.[40]

However, there is an important difference between multilateral clearing and increasing the money supply when we take into account the effects of expectations on post-clearing events. We have noted that for transactions to be sustained at the higher level P'T' after a multilateral clearing of IED, IED must be allowed to grow after the clearing exercise. Thus, expectations of repeated multilateral clearings, far from fuelling accelerating inflation, are actually necessary if the aim of preventing nominal transactions from falling is to be achieved. However, the situation is quite different when there has been an increase in M. If this increase was sufficient to sustain transactions at P'T' in the presence of a belief among SOEs that M will not be increased further (and that there would be no multilateral clearing of IED), then if SOEs in fact expect further increases in M (or multilateral clearing), the result will be not just the maintenance of transactions at P'T', but instead an increase in transactions to a new, even higher level P''T''. Thus in the presence of a lack of credibility, increasing M will be more inflationary than multilateral clearing.

The mechanism involving the creation of bank credit to eliminate net IED, which would only need to be applied if it were impossible to multilaterally clear all IED, would involve both a temporary increase in V and a permanent increase in M. Thus, the expansionary effect of this approach will be greater than that of multilateral clearing of all IED without bank credit creation. However, the inflationary effect of this mechanism may actually be greater than that of increasing M and not having a multilateral clearing of IED. This is, first, because the increase in M required to make the elimination of all net IED possible may be greater than the increase in M required to allow the stock of money to service the new level of nominal transactions P'T'. What one might call the 'money supply base for the creation of IED' would be increased (see equation (1)), so that IED could reach a higher maximum level than before (as determined by the aggregate of the optimum IED/M ratios for individual SOEs). Second, even if this is not the case, part of the

stock of IED will have been cleared, allowing part of $P'T'$ to be financed by increases in IED, so that a smaller increase in M together with the multilateral clearing of part of the old IED could have a stronger inflationary effect than a larger increase in M unaccompanied by any clearing of IED. Multilateral clearing without money creation is thus the least inflationary of the three mechanisms discussed, with the relative position of the remaining two being ambiguous.

The situation looks rather different if we assume that 'downstream' enterprises are money rich while 'intermediate' and 'upstream' enterprises are money poor, and that the banking system acts as the conduit from the former to the latter, as we did in Section 3. If IED becomes grossly excessive, such a situation results in the banking system becoming effectively bankrupt, because the 'money poor' enterprises can never be expected to be able to service, let alone repay, the credits they have obtained from the banking system. In this case, multilateral clearing without money creation will not suit, as the IED of net debtors is large. Money creation then not only provides the finance for commercial banks to be able to continue crediting intermediate and upstream enterprises, but by causing inflation, it reduces the real value of their past debt. As such, the policy can be thought of as being directed at saving the banks as much as the 'money poor' SOEs. In this case, reducing the nominal value of IED by securitizing it (as described in Section 7) might need to be accompanied by a once and for all increase in bank liquidity and a once and for all recapitalization of the banks.

5.3. Perverse Incentives Resulting from Multilateral Clearing

These occur if SOEs expect that a 'multilateral clearing' of IED is due to take place, even if the clearing is to involve no bank credit injection whatsoever. In such a case, SOEs which are net debtors can improve their position by extending more IEC (which will then be set against what they owe). As long as they can do this there is no reason for them to attempt to achieve balance by reducing the IED they owe. Equally, net creditors will try to achieve balance so as to avoid being left

holding the possibly valueless assets of the net debtors. However, they need not try to do this by reducing the IEC they have
extended, but may rather do so by taking on additional IED—
particularly since reducing IEC one has already extended may
not be easy. Ceasing delivery to a debtor will not reduce the
level of IEC an SOE has extended if the debtor ceases servicing
his debt. As we have just noted, there will be net debtors happy
to accommodate net creditors in this desire.

Once all SOEs had achieved rough balance of their IE assets
and liabilities, then even if every SOE insisted on maintaining
this balance, no technical limit would be set on IED growth if
SOEs knew that a multilateral clearing exercise (even without
money creation) was due to take place.[41] This is similar to the
situation under free banking: the 'law of reflux' and a bank
clearing system are not of themselves sufficient to prevent
excessive note issue by the banking system (Smith, 1990).[42]
Multilateral clearing will thus bias the economy towards the
expansion of IED. The root cause of this bias has already been
discussed: it stems from artificially setting the value of one unit
of each SOE's IED equal to that of every other SOE in the
clearing process.

Although the nominal value of final goods and primary
inputs should not be affected if M remains constant, nevertheless, the effects on the economy will be deleterious, as SOEs
will compete for domestic intermediate inputs, driving up the
prices of these relative to other goods (while their volume
remains constant). The effects on the redistribution of profits
among enterprises have already been discussed in Section 3.
Alternatively, the real value of final goods could fall together
with an increase in their price, due to the increase in the prices
of intermediate goods. SOEs, not being profit maximizers might
operate on a cost plus basis, at least in the short and medium
terms.[43] The expectation of multilateral clearing, and the IED
growth it leads to could, in such a case, cause accelerating
stagflation.[44] This would happen both in the short term, i.e.
when SOEs know that a clearing of IED is to take place soon,
and in the long term, if they come to believe that such clearings
will be a permanent feature of the economic system. In such a

situation, in which IED has severely distorted relative prices, multilateral clearing is no solution whatever to the difficulties the economy is encountering as a result of excessive IED.

If a multilateral clearing with money creation is expected, then SOEs do not even need to ensure that their expanding IED is balanced by their IEC, so that the strength of the bias towards the expansion of IED is strongly augmented. Moreover, money creation will result in an increase in the money supply base for subsequent IED expansion.

All the above objections have far less force if multilateral clearing is voluntary and there is no money creation. In that case there is no imposition of equal value on assets which may intrinsically have very different values. Nevertheless, even here, the multilateral clearing of IED speeds up the velocity of circulation of money, something which authorities in a country with near hyperinflation may wish to avoid. They would certainly need to try to allow for the resulting increases in velocity when determining monetary policy.

5.4. The Romanian Scheme

We saw in Section 5.2 that it is right to attach some importance to the relatively small size of the increase in broad money which was part of the multilateral IED clearing in Romania.[45] However, it is far more doubtful whether the Romanian authorities have been on the right track when, in order to convince SOEs that the clearing exercise was 'one-off' and thus to avoid the moral hazard problem, they attempted to sharply restrict IED after the multilateral clearing exercise of end 1991 by making failure to pay invoices within 30 days sufficient grounds for declaring a debtor insolvent.[46] Quite apart from ones doubts regarding the effectiveness of the Romanian measures, which depend on the voluntary actions of suppliers (creditors), it is dubious whether they are in fact desirable on either macro- or micro-economic grounds.

If there is a comprehensive multilateral clearing of IED accompanied by a minimal increase in the money supply, then if we were initially in a situation in which the existing money stock was insufficient to effect the current level of

nominal transactions (including intermediate transactions), then we remain in that situation after the multilateral clearing. Therefore, in spite of the clearing, either a combination of prices and output must fall or a combination of money supply and IED must increase. Not very surprisingly, therefore, in spite of the restrictions, IED in Romania increased from zero to 800 billion lei in the first six months of 1992, compared with an increase from 100 billion lei to 600 billion lei in the first half of 1991 (Table 24).[47]

From the microeconomic perspective, it seems very doubtful whether one month's trade credit is enough for a market economy: as we saw in Section 2 average trade credit in the West ranges from one and a half months in Germany and Scandinavia to three and one third months in France.

We have already seen that once multilateral IED clearing with central bank credit injection begins to be seriously discussed, SOEs will know that in the run-up to the clearing they can effectively force the creation of bank and central bank credit by extending IEC.[48] This is exactly what happened in Romania in 1991. Khan and Clifton therefore suggest that the preparation of a multilateral clearing of IED should not be a long drawn out process. However, it is difficult to imagine the first (and supposedly last) such exercise in any country taking less than the few months which were required in Romania. Furthermore, once a multilateral clearing of IED had taken place, it is not in fact likely to be credible that it will not be repeated. SOEs are therefore likely to believe that they can effectively force the creation of bank and central bank credit by extending IEC. Naturally, they could in fact do so only if central bank policy proved to be accommodating. However, the costs of convincing SOEs of central banks' determination not to accommodate IEC extension could be very large.

5.5. *Other Proposed Solutions*

A number of authors (e.g. Calvo and Frenkel 1991; Williamson, 1992*b*) have suggested that the IED problem could be solved by forgiving or consolidating the debts. Forgiveness differs from creating sufficient bank credit to allow all IED to be paid off to

the extent that net creditors loose in proportion to their net asset position. However, the idea that such an outcome would be politically acceptable is at the least doubtful. As Calvo and Frenkel admit, it is more likely that after such debt forgiveness either the treasury would have to reimburse net creditors, or the central bank would have to create credit to provide liquidity to cover net creditors' losses. In both cases there would be little difference between debt forgiveness and increasing the money supply.[49] As for consolidation (i.e. rescheduling), under conditions of high inflation, it differs little from debt forgiveness unless the real value of IED is maintained through indexation.[50]

6. Market Based Solutions

The first of these is simply to do nothing about IED, as was done in Poland in 1990–2, and as Begg and Portes recommend. By the middle of 1990, IED had fallen to 95 per cent of total bank credit, compared to 154 per cent before the beginning of the stabilization programme in December 1989, and through to the summer of 1992 it never exceeded 100 per cent (Table 22). On the other hand, real bank credit exceeded its December 1989 level by August 1990 and then stayed at about that level for the next two years.

If nothing is done, Polish experience shows that a number of mechanisms may begin to operate to limit IED expansion (and even to cause contraction). The most important, of course, is that suppliers simply cease supplying those who are particularly slow in paying, unless they pay cash. Second, resumption of supplies can be accompanied by a cash settlement of outstanding IED at some (often considerable) discount. Third, a secondary IED market develops in which financial intermediaries begin to trade IED at a discount. In Poland this market began to operate in early 1990 (i.e. soon after the beginning of the stabilization programme) when one of the state commercial banks began to purchase the IED of its clients from their suppliers. As a bank, it had the right to deduct money owed to it from its clients' bank accounts and was therefore in a much better position to enforce payment than were the suppliers

themselves. However, as could be expected, clients responded to this by moving their accounts elsewhere, and the bank concerned had to give up its activity on the IED market. By 1991 a number of private firms were acting on this market as brokers, bringing together creditors and debtors of an enterprise which was particularly bad at servicing its IED. The debtor of such an enterprise can buy his creditor's inter-enterprise liabilities from his creditor's creditors at a discount, and set them against his own liabilities. The bad debtor's creditors gain liquidity, while its debtors save money, the brokers charge a commission.

Setting real interest rates at realistic levels is an important part of 'doing nothing' about IED. As described in Section 3 this increases both the opportunity cost and the cost of financing of IEC. A sharp increase in interest rates can thus be an important instrument in bursting a 'IED-price-IED' bubble. However, making it mandatory for creditors to charge penal rates on IEC is not likely to be helpful. In the first place, where IEC is extended voluntarily the authorities' intention can easily be avoided by post-dating invoices. Second, where debtors cannot pay, pushing them even faster into a debt trap is not useful. Special high rates on IED are an attempt to affect directly the financial relationship between supplier and purchaser.[51] Since this relationship may already be unhealthy, in the sense that it exhibits a large element of creditor passivity, it may not respond much to such changes in the price of credit. It is therefore better to affect the supplier's (lender's) financial environment through economy wide interest rates.

However, some developments which one might have expected to occur on the basis of Western experience may in fact be unlikely. In Poland in early 1990, when IED was thought to be a serious problem, much hope was placed on its voluntary securitization. It was hoped that suppliers would insist on immediate payment with bills of exchange (*weksle*). Such bills have the advantage that, if they are not honoured by their term date then the failure to do so becomes a sufficient reason for a court to declare the bankruptcy of the issuer.[52] Not surprisingly, purchasers were unwilling to voluntarily transform the undated liabilities which IED constitutes into strictly regulated

commercial bills, so that the use of bills has not increased significantly.

Thus if the stock of IED is of approximately the magnitude observed in established market economies and if its rate of growth is not excessive—as has been the case in Poland and Czecho-Slovakia—then doing little about IED is probably best.[53]

7. Forced Securitization

However, doing little may not be an adequate response if, due to the lack of credibility of the stabilization policy, IED has expanded to such an extent that the existing level of nominal transactions (including IED servicing) is too large to be effected by the existing stock of money, requiring a sharp fall in prices or output or both. In other words: what should be done if the stabilization has not been credible, the stock of IED is excessive relative to the money supply, but the authorities are determined to stabilize, and we wish to minimize the cost of their doing so? Moreover, as Khan and Clifton point out, falling output, which is the result of the lack of credibility of the stabilization, may itself increase the lack of credibility.

We thus come to the final possibility—a market based reduction in the nominal value of IED. As we have seen, a reduction in nominal IED should not take the form of a multilateral clearing of IED imposed from above. This is above all because it is very unlikely that the 'one-off' nature of a multilateral clearing of IED will be credible. There will be a bias in the economy towards the expansion of IED, as a result of the lack of credibility and the setting of the value of all IED equal to par, both in the run-up to the first clearing exercise and subsequently. This bias will be stronger if multilateral clearing of IED is combined with money creation. As a result, the situation after clearing is likely to revert rapidly to what it was before, with a level of nominal transactions which is unsustainable with the given money supply without a further multilateral clearing of IED. If IED expansion has led to a serious distortion of relative prices in the economy, then multilateral

clearing provides no solution and merely perpetuates this situation. Furthermore, measures which have been suggested to
strengthen the credibility of clearing as a 'one-off' event are
likely to involve considerable microeconomic costs—if they are
at all effective.

The securitization of IED, by which it would be continuously
'marked to market' would not have the same undesirable
effects. There would be no credibility problems, because no
concession would have been made (in the sense of bailing out
SOEs which had imprudently extended IEC or taken on IED).
Once the market mechanism for revaluing IED had been established, it would function continuously. Thus there would be no
problem of whether revaluation was to be repeated or not.
Finally, the value of the liabilities of borrowers of varying
quality would not then be made uniform and effectively set
equal to their nominal value.[54] What would be the effects of
this approach on the prices and output of goods and services?
To make the situation more realistic, let us assume that the
economy we are discussing conforms to our second model
from Section 3, in which enterprises are either 'downstream',
'intermediate' or 'upstream'. Unlike our first 'average enterprise' model, downstream final goods producers have high
levels of IED and significant amounts of money in their bank
deposits. Intermediate enterprises have large amounts of IED,
but have also granted large amounts of IEC, while upstream
primary input purchasing enterprises have granted large
amounts of IEC, but have large borrowings from the banking
system. As we noted in Section 5.2, revaluing IED on the
market might then cause problems for the liquidity of the
banking system, as final goods producers would finance more
of their purchases from 'intermediate' enterprises by buying
the IED of the latter from SOEs further upstream for money.
This money would not then be deposited as before in banks. A
once and for all increase in bank liquidity might therefore be
needed. There might also be a need for a once and for all
recapitalization of the banks to compensate them for the losses
they might suffer if purchasers of primary inputs found that

they had to sell their IEC at such low prices that they were unable to service their bank debt.

However, revaluing IED on the market should make it easier for all three kinds of enterprise to go the route of price rather than output reduction in their adjustment to the shortage of liquidity in the economy at the given level of nominal transactions. Let us take the case of intermediate goods producers first (i.e. both 'intermediate' and 'upstream' enterprises according to the classification we adopted in Section 3). A supplier of such goods who is owed a large amount of IEC by his customers has relatively little interest in reducing his sales price. If his inter-enterprise assets are equivalent to several months' worth of sales then, even if the demand curve for his product is elastic, any reduction in his sales prices will result in increased revenue only once the IEC outstanding at the time he makes the decision has been paid off—and this is several months away. However, it is not only a matter of there being a long delay between price reduction and increased liquidity for the supplier. There is the more fundamental problem of the credibility of the purchaser, who has not been paying promptly and who now states that he is willing to accept larger deliveries if the price of the goods he purchases is reduced (it needs to be remembered that this in an institutional environment in which the bankruptcy system is not operational). In fact, for the liquidity of the supplier to improve once the goods delivered now at a lower price are paid for at a future date, then the IEC extended by the supplier to the purchaser must actually increase in the period until these lower priced goods are due to be paid for! Many suppliers may be unwilling to take this risk.[55]

This problem can, of course, be solved if the supplier concerned offers a lower price for his products subject to immediate money payment on delivery for the newly lower priced items. In that case, by voluntary agreement between the parties a temporary moratorium is effectively placed on the customer's IED. This is quite similar to marking the IED concerned to market, something which becomes explicit if these moves are accompanied by an agreement on how the

outstanding IED is to be serviced or paid off at a discount. The advantage of creating a market for all IED, however, is that a price is generated for each SOE's IED in that market, allowing creditors to obtain money in exchange for their inter-enterprise assets if they so wish. Also time-consuming bilateral debt rescheduling or reduction negotiations can be avoided. Once this has happened, suppliers are freer to decide whether to offer lower prices, and whether to demand payment on delivery or to extend new IEC to their customers. They thus operate in a more transparent environment than previously.

The situation with regard to final output is somewhat different. With a given money stock and a given velocity of circulation suppliers as a whole cannot increase their cash flow by reducing prices. But unless suppliers can enter a cartel, many individual suppliers will be able to increase revenue by reducing price, or will be able to maintain revenue in the face of price reductions by others only by reducing prices themselves.

As suppliers of final goods are generally paid immediately in cash, the problem of customer creditworthiness does not arise. However, it may be hard to reduce output prices in order to improve one's liquidity if one's suppliers are unwilling to reduce their prices. Producers of final goods may be unwilling to sell products at significantly below cost, even if their cash flow improves temporarily as a result and even when there is no effective bankruptcy system. If they do so they may make it more likely that they will not be able to service the IED they owe their suppliers in the long run, unless these latter themselves reduce their prices. Yet, as we have seen, there may be good reasons for intermediate goods producers not to reduce prices, unless this is accompanied by some credible settlement of the IEC they are owed. Thus, marking their IED to market may be essential for final producers also to be able to reduce their output prices.[56] What is more, given the existence of a secondary IED market, intermediate input suppliers might be more willing to reduce their own prices as described previously, which would mean that

more final goods producers could individually improve cash flow without worsening their profitability.

To summarize: the creation of a secondary IED market would not be sufficient to result in the (constant) money supply becoming fully adequate to finance the higher level of nominal transactions which has resulted from an excessive expansion of IED. Prices or quantities, or some combination of both, would still have to fall. However, prices could fall more and output could fall less than in the absence of a secondary IED market.[57] Furthermore, the stock of money needed for the servicing of IED might be smaller, as much of the debt settlement which took place would happen on the basis of the setting off against each other of the assets and liabilities of given SOEs.[58]

Last but not least, an excessive stock of IED has effects which are similar to those of a debt deflation, and this applies both to intermediate and final goods producers (Fisher, 1936). In this situation falling product prices, which are essential if output is not to fall and the money supply is not to be increased, result in increases in the real value of the inter-enterprise component of SOEs' liabilities. Given a constant money supply, reductions in prices can have no effect in the aggregate on SOEs' cash flow nor on the ratio of that cash flow to their IED. Nevertheless, it does increase the real value of that debt, possibly to a degree which might be considered unrepayable, even in the absence of interest charges on IED. If this were the case, suppliers would be unwilling to continue supplying such customers.[59] In such a situation output would fall even if prices were fully flexible downwards. Of course, as with a standard western debt deflation, one can either accept the output effects for the sake of the anti-inflationary results, or one can try to reduce the real value of the debt through an inflationary policy (or prevent it from increasing through an anti-deflationary policy). The difference is that in a PCE in transition, loose financial policy may cause expectations to become not merely inflationary but hyperinflationary. If there were a secondary market on which the value of IED could be reduced in nominal terms, the danger that persistence with stringent monetary policy would lead to a debt deflation would be reduced.[60]

8. Inter-Enterprise Debt Auctions

However, for all this to happen IED must be tradeable, i.e. securitized. As we have seen, the Polish experience shows that SOEs are unlikely to voluntarily securitize their debt quickly: the securitization therefore has to be forced if it is to be rapid. What is more, we noted that it is the absence of an efficient bankruptcy system which causes the IED problem to arise in the first place: the exact nature of the instruments into which IED would be transformed would therefore have to take this key institutional fact into account.

Fortunately, a good instrument is to hand in those countries which have the good luck to have maintained the 'payment demand' system which existed under central planning. Under this system, demand for payment is not sent directly to the purchaser in the form of an invoice, but instead is sent by the seller's bank to the purchaser's bank in the form of a 'payment demand'. Once the payment demand reaches the purchaser's bank it is automatically paid out of the purchaser's account. If there is no money to fulfil the payment demand it is filed in the so-called 'second file' (*kartoteka dva*) of the account in the order in which it arrives.[61]

The existence of this payment demand system allows the elimination of an excessive stock of IED through the simple expedient of IED auctions. Since all payment demands in the *kartoteka dva* are dated, it is simple enough to decide to auction off each month all the demands which are, let us say, more than three months overdue.[62] All commercial banks, on instructions from the central bank, would be obliged to organize such auctions. This would be necessary to avoid the defection of customers to banks which were not forcibly securitizing IED. Settlements would have to be by banker's cheque or cash. Initially one would expect three kinds of bidders to appear on the market: the creditors (who would be setting a reserve price), the debtors (who would be offering to settle their debt at a discount), and debtors' debtors, who by buying their creditors' liabilities at a discount could reduce their own liabilities to their creditors by setting off the newly acquired assets against

their own liabilities. With time, however, one could expect the emergence of professional arbitragers, who would buy the liabilities of a particular SOE on the basis that its debtors' debtors at several removes would be willing to purchase this security as a cheap way of settling their own liabilities.

How efficient would such a market be? For efficiency, each of the players should have equal access to information about the financial position of the SOE in whose debt he wishes to trade. Since this depends in turn on the financial position of the debtors of the SOE concerned, and their position depends on that of their own debtors, and so on, one could argue that for the market to be efficient all players have to have equal access to information about the financial position of all SOEs. Not only is this clearly impossible, it is also unnecessary. The players likely to be initially involved in trading an SOE's debt are, as already mentioned, the firm itself, its creditors and its debtors. A considerable amount of information about the firm and its environment will be available to all these players acting together (and against each other). The price for the IED of the SOE concerned will be the result of the bids of the players involved, and will be a reflection of the information held by them.[63] In setting a price for IED, the bidders will be making the information they hold available to others, including players involved in pricing another SOE's IED. Although the market for an SOE's IED cannot be efficient, it is the attempt by those with privileged information to benefit by it from participating in the market which generates and spreads information regarding the SOE concerned.

The fact that no effective bankruptcy system exists, and that it is very unlikely that such system can be created in the time frame required,[64] means that it would be pointless to set a term by which the newly securitized IED had to be repaid, since there are no sanctions which can be effectively applied in the case of non-compliance. Unpaid payment demands are already overdue liabilities, and it seems unnecessary to pretend otherwise by setting a new, later, time limit. Equally, since it is the purpose of such securitization to make it possible for equal nominal values of IED debt to be set off against each other

(whatever the discount they may have been bought at), one should no longer require debtors to meet the payment demands in chronological order.[65] There remains the fact that the secondary market value of IED might increase as the prospect of effective bankruptcy procedures approaches. This need not be a problem, as it will induce debtors to settle for cash all the more quickly. Also, the main stabilization problems, which are the primary source of excessive IED, should have been settled by the time an effective bankruptcy system is in place.

As a final twist, it is possible to widen participation in the securitized IED market considerably by making debt to equity conversion possible, either on the basis of negotiation between creditors and debtors or, preferably, through rules relating nominal IED to the book value of SOEs. In this way the secondary IED market, in which private persons would be allowed to participate on equal terms, could become a powerful instrument in the privatization process.[66]

What can be done in countries in which the 'payment demand' system has already been abolished? One possibility is to oblige suppliers to obtain a confirmation of delivery which would show the value of the goods delivered. In the absence of such a confirmation, suppliers would be denied recourse to the courts to enforce payment. Effectively, all deliveries for which such a confirmation had not been obtained would be gifts by the supplier to the customer from the legal point of view.[67] Such 'confirmations' would then be made tradable, and banks could be required to organize monthly auctions of them. Obviously, since the 'confirmations' would not be all deposited at the banks as are 'payment demand orders' under the *kartoteka dva* system, it would be an entirely voluntary matter whether suppliers delivered their unhonoured 'confirmations' to the banks for auction or not.

It may be objected that a secondary market in IED involves a high degree of moral hazard, in that debtors can affect the value of their own liabilities (by not servicing them) and then buy them back at a lower value. However, it needs to be remembered that because of the non-existence of an effective bankruptcy system, debtors already have full control over the true

value of their liabilities due to their power to decide when (and whether) they will fulfil their obligations. The only choice facing creditors is whether to continue expanding the credit they have already extended. If IED is securitized it is creditors' options which are expanded—not those of debtors. Creditors can then obtain payment from their debtors' debtors at an appropriate discount, and base their decision on whether to continue supplying a particular customer on the effective price (net of discount) which they expect to receive for the goods.[68]

9. Conclusions

There are a large number of possible reasons for IED growth in PCEs. One can distinguish healthy expansion of IED from the pathological (or excessive). The former is mainly the result of previous repression of trade credit by central planners (an example is IED growth in Czecho-Slovakia in 1990 and 1991). The latter occurs when IED growth leads to a level of nominal transactions in the economy which is unsustainable at the given money supply, velocity of circulation, and relative prices of domestic intermediate goods with respect to other goods. The FSU in 1992 and Romania in 1991 seem to provide examples of such pathological IED expansion.

The most important cause of excessive IED growth seems to be a lack of credibility of macroeconomic stabilization policy in the absence of an effective bankruptcy system. In such a situation, it is quite rational for firms to extend large amounts of IEC, as long as implicit interest charges are included in the price. Thus the fall in the real value of IED in Poland at the beginning of the stabilization programme suggests strongly that stabilization was credible in that country from the very beginning. In countries in which stabilization is not credible, an IED-price-IED bubble can develop, leading to levels of transactions which cannot be sustained.

If the authorities are determined to stabilize, but their will or ability is not credible, what should they do to minimize the costs of incredible stabilization (which will take the form of falls in ouput)? A one-off increase in the money supply, which is the

best solution from a purely technical point of view, is unlikely to be credible. The greater money supply will merely be perceived as providing a higher base for further IED expansion. Multilateral clearing of IED is no solution if nominal transactions are already at an unsustainable level: further multilateral clearings or increases in the money supply will be required in due course, if reductions of output are to be avoided.

The least bad solution seems to be the forced securitization of IED, which allows the development of secondary IED markets, enabling creditors to improve their liquidity and debtors to improve their balance sheets. As a result the unavoidable downward adjustment of nominal transactions to a level consistent with the money supply should involve a greater reduction in prices and a smaller reduction in output than otherwise. Above all, this solution involves no additional liquidity provided to the economy from the outside. All that the authorities do is make certain trades possible. Flexibility is increased without increasing liquidity. The problem of establishing the credibility of the one-off nature of the intervention does not, therefore, arise. Countries which still maintain the 'payment demand order' system and the *kartoteka dva* are particularly well placed to forcibly securitize IED through regular auctions of unhonoured payment demand orders carried out by the banks.

Table 20 Possible causes of output collapse in the economies in transition

Cause	Countries
External demand:	Bulgaria, Hungary, CSFR
—exogenous decline	Poland, Romania, East Germany
—overvalued currency	East Germany
Internal demand:	
—Keynesian	CSFR, Poland?
—FX shortage	Bulgaria, Romania, FSU
—Demand shift	CSFR, Poland
—Unwanted goods	Russia, all
Supply:	
—Exogenous shocks	Russian oil
—Uneconomic output	Widespread
—Input dislocation	FSU
—Credit squeeze	Poland? CSFR? Hungary?

Source: Williamson (1992*a*).

Table 21 Credit and inter-enterprise arrears in Russia 1992 (billions in roubles)

End Month		Nominal bank credit	Real bank credit	Nominal arrears	Real arrears	Arrears/bank credit
12	1991	450	450	39	39	0.078
1	1992	510	148	141	41	0.277
2	1992	700	147	390	82	0.558
3	1992	920	149	800	129	0.870
4	1992	1050	139	1800	239	1.710
5	1992	1050	125	2050	243	1.952
6	1992	1400	140	3000	299	2.143
7	1992	2300	207	1190	107	0.517

Source: Russian Centre for Economic Reform.

Table 22 Credit and inter-enterprise arrears in Poland 1989–92 (trillions of zlotys)

Month	Nominal bank credit	Real bank credit[a]	Nominal arrears	Real arrears[a]	Arrears/bank credit
12/1988[b]	11.1	11.11	7.0	7.00	0.63
3/1989[c]	13.0	10.00	6.8	5.20	0.52
6/1989[c]	15.3	9.46	9.2	5.68	0.60
9/1989[c]	21.5	6.49	15.9	4.80	0.74
12/1989	30.7	4.15	47.4	6.41	1.54
1/1990	30.2	2.27	50.3	3.78	1.67
2/1990	37.7	2.28	66.1	4.01	1.75
3/1990	44.8	2.61	75.1	4.37	1.68
6/1990	70.7	3.54	81.5	4.08	1.15
9/1990	95.5	4.33	77.3	3.51	0.81
12/1990	113.1	4.38	103.0	3.99	0.91
3/1991	133.8	4.11	109.1	3.35	0.82
6/1991	154.5	4.30	126.2	3.52	0.82
9/1991	178.1	4.72	143.0	3.79	0.80
12/1991	192.0	4.65	179.8	4.35	0.94
3/1992	208.3	4.52	177.1	3.48	0.85
6/1992	220.2	4.35	190.6	3.77	0.87

[a] In December 1988 zlotys.
[b] Calvo and Coricelli (1992*a*).
[c] Coricelli and Thorne (1992).

Source: GUS (1992*a*).

Table 23 Credit and inter-enterprise arrears in CSFR 1989–91 (billions of crowns)

Month	Nominal bank credit	Real bank credit	Nominal arrears[a]	Real arrears	Arrears/bank credit
12/1989	578	578	7	7	0.012
3/1990	569	569	11	11	0.019
6/1990	579	579	14	14	0.024
9/1990	588	588	28	28	0.048
12/1990	583	490	54	45	0.093
3/1991	618	358	77	53	0.125
6/1991	664	367	123	68	0.185
9/1991	694	391	147	83	0.212
12/1991	732	407	155	86	0.212

[a] These are overdue arrears. Before the beginning of the transition, normal terms of payment in Czechoslovakia were one month, so that at end 1989 the ratio of total arrears (overdue and not overdue) to bank credit was about 0.2. Since normal terms of payment do not seem to have changed during the transition, and at the end of 1991 overdue arrears were equivalent to one month's payment lag (Schaffer, 1992*a*), the ratio of total arrears to bank credit at the end of 1991 was 0.4. As a result total arrears/bank credit and the real value of total arrears increased significantly less between end 1989 and end 1991 than follows from the table.

Source: Begg and Portes (1992).

Table 24 Credit and inter-enterprise arrears in Romania 1990–92 (billions of lei)

Month		Nominal bank credit	Real bank credit[a]	Nominal arrears	Real arrears[a]	Arrears/bank credit
12	1990	684	486	100	71	0.146
3	1991	756	419	400	222	0.529
6	1991	811	332	600	245	0.740
9	1991	749	235	800	250	1.068
12	1991	954	215	1777	400	1.863
3	1992	1270	193	400[b]	61	0.316
6	1992	1274	158	800[b]	99	0.627

[a] In October 1990 lei.
[b] National Bank of Romania.

Source: Khan and Clifton (1992), International Financial Statistics, IMF, for prices.

NOTES

This Chapter was first published in *Communist Economies and Economic Transformation*, vol. 5, no. 2 (1993), 131–59. It initially grew out of a memorandum written in April 1992 to Yegor Gaidar, then Deputy Prime Minister of Russia, on what to do about what was perceived as an explosion of inter-enterprise debt in the spring of 1992. The key policy proposal

of the chapter, that IED should be marketized, was incorporated in the Decree of the President of the Russian Federation on Payment Arrears of November 1993, which was never implemented. I am grateful to Marek Dąbrowski, Fabrizio Coricelli and Geoff Davison for comments.

1. Peter Wiles (1973*b*) describes it with regard to Yugoslavia.
2. The figures are those reported to the IMF by the Russian Government. According to figures provided by the Bank of Latvia, in that country IED had reached 25 billion roubles by June, showing that Latvia, which had traditionally accounted for about 1 per cent of the USSR's population and GDP, now accounted for approximately the same proportion of IED.
3. In Poland the ratio of transactions to GNP in industry is about 2, and I am assuming a similar ratio for Russia.
4. Hrincir and Klacek (1991) give the figure for Jan. 1991 as 8.5 per cent of GDP. Assuming this to be the same as for Dec. 1990 and taking the figures for the real value of IED at the end of 1991 from Table 23, then we arrive at 18 per cent if we accept a 10 per cent fall in GDP during 1991.
5. Calvo and Coricelli (1992*a*) make the mistake of comparing end 1989 IED with nominal GDP for 1989 as a whole, and get 47 per cent. Since prices rose 740 per cent (Dec. to Dec.) during 1989 this is not suitable. I have crudely re-estimated 1989 GDP in Dec. 1989 prices by assuming that real output was the same in all twelve months of that year. I get a value of 260 trillion zlotys (as opposed to the 100 trillion at average 1989 prices), and therefore an IED/GDP ratio of 18 per cent.
6. C. Batchelor, *Financial Times* 11 Feb. 1991.
7. Even if credit is formally free, interest can be effectively charged by being incorporated in a higher price for the goods delivered, which the purchaser would refuse to pay in the absence of the credit.
8. Romania seems to be closer to the countries of the FSU in this respect than to Central Europe. Thus at the end of 1991, IED amounted to 1.8 trillion lei, or 50 per cent of GNP (Khan and Clifton, 1992).
9. Russian data in Table 2 show the sharp fall in IED in July 1992 which resulted from the effective closing of the 'second file' on bank accounts to new payment demands (see Sec. 8 for a description of the system). Banks were no longer obliged to accept payment demands, with the result that the stock of IED on the 'second file' declined as old payment demands were honoured. The clearing exercise of August then eliminated some 60 per cent of the IED that remained. This does not, however, mean that IED is now close to zero. It now merely takes the form of unregistered unpaid invoices.
10. Delays are particularly long for payments between republics.
11. It is legal to pay for goods in cash, but it is not legal for banks to allow SOEs to withdraw deposits in the form of cash except for specified, justified, purposes. These include wage payments but exclude the payment of suppliers. Thus the expansion of the use of cash in inter-enterprise transactions is severely inhibited.

12. Thus, unlike in Russia, the shift to cash transfers probably helped to compensate the Romanian economy for the slowdown in payments through the banking system, and thus helped to mitigate the fall in output caused by growing arrears. This does not emerge clearly from Khan and Clifton (1992), who take the view that the shift into cash delayed payments further, which seems unlikely in a country in which payments through the banking system take between 15 and 21 days (Coricelli and Thorn, 1992).

13. The absence of bills of exchange and letters of credit appeared as much in Poland and Czecho-Slovakia as in the FSU. Moreover, unsecuritized and uninstrumentalized trade credit remains the norm in domestic transactions—as opposed to international ones—in Western market economies (see n. 6).

14. Information from the Ministry of Finance of the Russian Federation.

15. Khan and Clifton's failure to note this in the case of Romania is of a piece with their mistaken belief that: 'The rapid growth of arrears poses a serious policy problem in all the transforming economies of Eastern Europe.'

16. Sometimes, as in Poland in 1990, there is also a reduction in the level of real bank credit. See Calvo and Coricelli, 1992*a*.

17. In Romania arrears were effectively indexed in 1991. When not paid on time, suppliers would re-bill debtors at new higher prices (Khan and Clifton).

18. If one excludes the first month's once and for all price jump.

19. Bankruptcy laws are only a necessary, but far from sufficient, condition for the existence of a bankruptcy system. If courts have no experience of bankruptcy cases and of how to rule on their complexities a high 'R&D' cost is borne by the first to use them. Also there will be few, if any, trained liquidators for the courts to hire: in Poland in mid-1991, i.e. 18 months into the big bang programme there were six such people in the whole country.

20. Taxes also have to be paid in money, but it may be possible to accumulate arrears here also.

21. I use this term so as to avoid the question of whether payments are made in cash or bank money (which is not convertible into cash in the FSU).

22. As Begg and Portes point out, there may also be a 'strategic' reason for SOEs to extend IEC. Those which are not 'too big to fail' on their own, may hope to create an interlocking network of inter-enterprise commitments, so that all the enterprises in the IEC chain together are indeed 'too big to fail', and the failure of any one SOE in the network threatens the failure of all.

23. Thus Khan and Clifton report that in Romania, as a result of the growth in IED, the income velocity of broad money rose from 1.8 in 1990 to 3.9 in September 1991. The ratio of GDP to broad money plus gross IED (i.e. the income velocity of 'liquidity') was 1.7 in

September 1992. In other words it had hardly changed compared to 1990, when there was very little IED (see Table 24).

24. Note that within the rouble zone in 1992 enterprises could extend IEC to each other across state boundaries.

25. As long as a is declining inflation can increase independently of increases in M and V.

26. Here, V is the velocity of circulation of money with respect to transactions financed with the use of money (i.e. excluding those financed with the use of IED).

27. This may result from an anticipation of a natural increase in V as a result of increased efficiency of the bank payments system as a result of reform in the absence of very high inflation (this may have been the case in Czecho-Slovakia).

28. As long as SOEs' debt is not accepted as a means of payment by third parties. This would presumably only happen to those enterprises which were scrupulous in meeting their obligations on demand—i.e. to those SOEs which effectively became banks. This is unlikely to happen in many cases.

29. See Sec. 5.

30. In the absence of increases in money stock or velocity.

31. Price overshooting both relative to government expectations and 'objective overshooting' which requires downward price adjustments after initial increases. This process cannot, of course, be the only reason for price overshooting in PCEs since we have seen that IED expansion was not a major source of liquidity growth in either Poland or Czecho-Slovakia in the aftermath of 'big bang' stabilization. Moreover, in these two countries the 'bust' phase followed immediately upon stabilization rather than with some delay, as one would expect if the main cause of recession were excessive IED expansion in the face of tight monetary policy. Such a mechanism may, however, be part of the explanation of output declines in Romania in 1991 and Russia in 1992.

32. An alternative would be the banning of IED and the return to physical command planning. It is interesting how few people suggest this at present. This is probably due in the FSU to the main opposition to stabilization coming at present from the industrial lobby. That lobby has no desire to see a return to direct control from the centre. Rather, it wishes the freedom of a market economy without the need to control costs. The impossibility of business functioning effectively in a hyperinflation (see Auerbach, Davison and Rostowski, 1992) has not yet been understood by many industrial managers.

33. Calvo (1992), therefore suggests wage (and possibly price!) control as a way of ensuring that the real value of additional bank credit is not eroded by inflation. The question is whether wage control can be effective in the face of expansionary monetary policy (for it is of that which we speak). Price controls are unlikely to be a good idea

in PCEs, whose distorted relative price structures are an important source of waste.

34. It is not clear what the incentives would be for the employees of such an institution to brave the opprobrium which liquidating enterprises would bring on them—and all for the benefit of the net creditor enterprises.

35. The rest was financed by credit from the banking system of which about 10 percentage points came from the National Bank of Romania (Khan and Clifton).

36. As happened in Russia in September 1992 and in Romania in June 1991.

37. In fact, since 'multilateral clearing' takes place in time, new IED would be contracted even as the clearing was taking place.

38. A similar thing happened in Romania in May and June 1991, when banks extended 15.5 billion lei in credits to enterprises on special accounts which were to be used exclusively to pay off arrears, and were then to be repaid to the National Bank of Romania. They never were repaid. In Russia, as a result of this change it is not clear at present what the status of net debits on the IED clearing accounts is. Some 300 billion roubles worth of the net positive balances on these accounts was used to pay tax arrears in September of 1992, significantly improving the appearance of the Russia's budgetary accounts (information supplied by the Russian Ministry of Finance).

39. We need to distinguish between increasing M so that the existing level of PT can be financed and attempting to increase M sufficiently to eliminate IED altogether. Trying to do the latter implies an even looser posture. This is because M has then to increase sufficiently to finance PT and to pay off all IED.

40. Naturally, if not all IED can be cleared multilaterally then the failure to provide the bank credit required to clear the IED of net creditors will result in PT having to fall from $P'T'$, and would make this option less expansionary than either increasing M or multilaterally clearing IED and supplying bank credit to clear net debtors' IED.

41. IED would stabilize only if there were some maximum IED/M ratio above which SOEs were not prepared to expand IED. Furthermore, if there are net debtors whose position is hopeless—i.e. SOEs whose net IED already exceeds all their assets, and who are therefore inevitable bankrupts—these would be willing to take on unlimited quantities of additional IED, concentrating the net debts of all SOEs in their own hands. In this way, they gain the possibility of effectively creating money. This would give a new twist to the usual situation in which central banks cannot go bankrupt—here bankrupts would temporarily become central banks! Non-bankrupt net debtors would not need to deliver goods of any significant value to the bankrupts—they would merely need to invoice them appropriately. In this situation net creditors would try to escape their exposed position, and this would act as

the only brake on IED expansion. Yet, it is a rather weak break, given the difficulty a net creditor has in reducing IED unilaterally.

42. The limit on note issue was banks' need to maintain convertibility into gold. Over-issue was possible, however, in the sense that convertibility could become threatened.

43. This could then feed through to lower demand for primary inputs in real terms, so that the prices of these could also rise.

44. IED, effectively inconvertible into money, would thus play a role which was similar to non-cash money in the FSU in contributing to stagflation (Lipton and Sachs).

45. As Khan and Clifton do. The money supply increased as a result of the clearing exercise of January 1992 by only 17 per cent.

46. This in itself is then a basis for creditors to enforce payments through the courts. The World Bank has, following its usual dirigiste instinct, effectively approved this approach: it has made its Structural Adjustment Loan to Romania subject to the condition that IED should not exceed 7.5 per cent of SOE turnover (Khan and Clifton).

47. In real terms the level of IED in June 1992 was 40 per cent of that in June 1991. However, real bank credit was also less than 50 per cent of its June 1991 level.

48. The inflationary effects of 15 central banks in a single currency area have already been observed in the FSU—the effects of tens of thousands of emission centres can readily be imagined.

49. However, if the authorities succeed in refusing to maintain the liquidity of net creditors, then SOEs would probably become very careful not to extend any IEC in the future, which would ensure that the IED problem did not recur for quite some time. The question is whether there is any benefit in having net creditors' illiquidity legitimized in this way?

50. Indexation would make the debtor's position worse than it is at present in Russia, where real interest rates on IED are massively negative.

51. There may also be further effects due to the tax system. Thus in Poland, until the second half of 1991 penal interest rates due (but not paid) on IEC counted as part of the supplier's revenue—but not as part of the purchaser's costs!

52. The fact that commercial bills need to be endorsed by two or more non-bank firms before being discounted by a bank means that they can constitute a sophisticated mechanism for assessing the creditworthiness of the issuer.

53. A modest proposal regarding what to do even in this situation, so as to help the secondary market in IED to develop, is put forward at the end of Sect. 8.

54. With multilateral clearing without bank credit injection it is also the case that this does not happen with regard to net debtors. However, as we have seen in Sect. 5, such a system creates strong incentives for there to be few of these.

55. Of course, lowering the price may attract new, credible, customers.
56. Also final goods producers may find that by reducing their prices they cause their suppliers to doubt their ability to pay, which may cause these suppliers to cut them off, rather than to reduce their own prices.
57. In practice some increase in the money supply might be countenanced. This would need to be less than the preceding price increases so that the real money stock should fall, first, in order to ensure the disappearance of any monetary overhang which might exist, and second, so as not to accommodate all of the SOEs' 'price push'.
58. These would be set off against each other at par, although they would have been bought by their current owners at varying discounts depending on the status of the debtor (see the description of the auction system suggested below).
59. This gives us an additional reason as to why SOEs might decide to keep prices high in the absence of a secondary IED market. Doing so may not improve one's cash flow compared to price reductions, but it signals to suppliers that one continues to consider the current credit crunch as temporary, and that once it is reversed one's IED will be of manageable proportions.
60. However, the nominal value of bank debt owed by SOEs could not be reduced.
61. The 'first file' (*kartoteka odin*) consists of paid payment demands. In the traditional system, the payment demands in the *kartoteka dva* were paid in strict chronological order as money became available. Nowadays, even where the payment demand system has survived, enterprises have the right to decide in which order the payment demands should be met.
62. As the system proved effective ever 'younger' payment demands could be forcibly securitized in this way.
63. Clearly some players will be more liquidity constrained than others, but this in itself is an important piece of information.
64. This was still the case in Poland two years into the reforms.
65. On a purely technical note: evidence of delivery of goods, confirmed by the purchaser and accompanying the payment demand, should be required for its validity to be accepted by the banking system and the courts. Suppliers could avoid forced securitization in this way, however, only at the cost of losing all legal claim to payment. Suppliers can, furthermore, avoid securitization by setting the reserve price of their IEC at its nominal value. To discourage this, one could require the original owners to actually pay in money for their own IEC if it failed to reach the reserve price, so that they would lose the use of the money involved for a certain amount of time.
66. Khan and Clifton's view that IED is a contingent liability of the budget because SOEs belong to the state is mistaken. In market socialist

economies, such as are most PCEs, the state's liability in SOEs is limited, whether these are formally limited liability nationalized firms or the more traditional 'state enterprise' (with or without workers' control).

67. In the 1970s in Yugoslavia, the so-called *weksel* was introduced as a confirmation of delivery.

68. Thus the shorter the period of delay before IED is auctioned the better from the supplier's point of view.

9

A Proposal on how to Introduce a Currency Board-Based Monetary System in the Republic of Latvia

1. *Historical Background*

The Republic of Latvia is now an independent state, completely outside the Commonwealth of Independent States (CIS) established by most of the other successor states of the Soviet Union. Nevertheless, as far as monetary matters are concerned, Latvia is fully integrated into the post-Soviet monetary and banking system. The means of payment in Latvia, as in most of the CIS, is the rouble and at the time of writing the Latvian banking system is still fully integrated with that of the CIS. This means that the customers of Latvian banks in Latvia can use their rouble deposits to pay for goods from suppliers in any of the post-Soviet states, and vice versa. The money is sent via the Latvian Central Bank and the central bank of the other state to the account of the supplier at its commercial bank.

Furthermore, all the central banks of the successor states have been able until now to create roubles without any formal restraint. In such a situation, it is in the interest of each central bank to create as much money as possible, and in this way to give the residents of its state purchasing power over goods produced in other states. The only constraint is that only Russia has the printing presses. This has meant that if a non-Russian central bank creates so much deposit money that the demand for cash exceeds the amount made available to it by Russia, a cash shortage develops in that state. Most central banks have been eager to avoid such a situation. On the other hand, they have also been eager to prevent a differential in price levels

between their country and others in the rouble area, so as to avoid a trade surplus which would in effect represent the payment of seigniorage. This has led to what has been described as an 'inflation race' between the states—a race in which, however, Russia has an enormous advantage.

Since non-Russian central banks have still been able to create deposits which have purchasing power in Russia through interbank payments as described above, the Russian supplier of a Latvian purchaser can obtain cash in Russia in exchange for the deposit money he obtains as a result of his sale of goods to Latvia. This has led Russia to impose export quotas on sales to Latvia and the other CIS states. The single currency area has thus been destroying the single economic space of the ex-Soviet Union. Russia is in the process of putting an end to this situation by obliging the central banks of the successor states to open correspondent accounts at the Central Bank of Russia. Those who draw these accounts down to zero will no longer be able to purchase anything from Russia. This means that the non-Russian states will be unable to pursue monetary polices which are laxer than those of Russia itself.[1] Those who renounce the introduction of their own currency for at least the next year will share in the seigniorage revenue of the Central Bank of Russia. Effectively, the non-Russian states must accept Russian monetary policy or create their own currency.

Latvia, like the other Baltic states, has been committed to the introduction of its own currency since it obtained independence in August 1991. Apart from the importance of an independent currency for political reasons, Latvia has been dissatisfied with Russian monetary policy. However, whereas some of the CIS states have objected to Russian policy as being too tight, Latvian authorities view it as too lax. The Latvian authorities see the monetary reform as a two stage process: in the first stage a 'Latvian rouble' would be introduced (this would be a freely floating, independent, partially internationally convertible currency),[2] in the second stage the Latvian rouble would be exchanged for the Lat,[3] which would be fully internationally convertible at a fixed rate against some Western

currency (probably the Deutsche Mark), and would be administered by a currency board.

Finally, it is important to note that Latvia, in common with most non-Russian successor states has been running a very large balance of trade deficit at world market prices, and that it will therefore be subject to a large terms of trade shock once all its trade with the outside world (including the post-Soviet successor states) comes to be conducted at world prices (Hanson, 1992).

2. Why a Currency Board?

Successful stabilization of very high or hyperinflation usually involves fixing the exchange rate of the domestic currency, at least for a short period of time. The reason is simple. Very high inflation causes people to save on the real balances—on which they have to pay the inflation tax—which reduces demand for the domestic money, so that the real stock of the domestic money becomes very small. Fixing the exchange rate means that, for at least a short period of time, people know that the foreign exchange value of the domestic currency will be stable. This can cause the demand for the domestic money to increase sharply, so that a virtuous circle develops: increased demand for domestic money ends the 'flight from domestic money' which is fuelling very high inflation—as inflation falls the demand for money increases further—and so on (Dornbusch, 1987).

One problem is how to maintain credibility for the new fixed exchange rate without starving the economy of the greatly increased real balances it needs once inflation has fallen sharply. The sudden elimination of inflation through the stabilization means a large increase in the demand for money. If the authorities fail to accommodate this increased demand by increased supply they will cause very high real interest rates to prevail. These can only be avoided if prices fall to such an extent that the given nominal money supply satisfies the demand for real balances at the new rate of inflation.[4] If, on the other hand, the authorities increase the supply of money on a large scale the

danger is that they will undermine the credibility of the stabilization (Dornbusch and Simonsen, 1988). Caught on the horns of this dilemma the authorities usually try to steer a middle course, with the result that post-stabilization real interest rates tend to reflect a mixture of causes: both the overall shortage of liquidity and depreciation and default risk premia. This in turn causes an information and control problem for the authorities, which do not know whether high interest rates mainly reflect liquidity shortage (in which case the nominal money supply should be increased), or the lack of credibility of the exchange rate (in which case the nominal money supply should be tightly controlled). The result is that the authorities are likely to conduct either too restrictive a policy—leading to unnecessary recession—or (which is more likely) too loose a policy, which makes the fixed parity unsustainable and, if not reversed, leads to a re-ignition of inflation.

A solution to this problem would be the establishment of a currency board based monetary system. Hanke and Schuler (1991) have proposed such a system as the solution to Yugoslavia's chronic high inflation problems. In a currency board system all domstic currency has to have a fixed amount (over 100 per cent) of backing in foreign currency denominated assets or foreign cash. The board always stands ready to exchange domestic currency into the foreign currency to which the domestic currency is fixed (henceforth called the 'metropolitan currency'). A pure Humean mechanism then ensures that in the medium term prices cannot change other than as in the 'metropolitan country'. In the short term, if prices of traded goods are lower than in the metropolitan country, the reserves of the currency board will increase, increasing domestic cash and therefore—through the standard money multiplier[5]—the domestic money supply and thus the prices of traded goods. If the process goes too far and prices of traded goods exceed those in the metropolitan country, this mechanism goes into reverse, causing the domestic money supply to decline (grow less fast), so that prices (inflation) fall. The fact that only a fraction of the cash backing is held in foreign cash, while the rest is held in foreign interest bearing assets, means that the

costs, in terms of seigniorage paid to the metropolitan country are significantly lower than they would be otherwise.[6]

It is, of course, possible to implement a 'fractional currency board system' or a 'marginal currency board system'. In the first, the domestic currency would be only fractionally backed by foreign currency (say 50 per cent), while in the second, only increases in domestic currency would be backed, but these would be 100 per cent backed. The advantage of both systems over the true currency board is that a far smaller amount of foreign currency has to be obtained by the country, so that a smaller balance of payments surplus needs to be generated, resulting in lower inflation and less recession during the period of reserve accumulation (see next section). The disadvantage of both systems is that confidence in the domestic currency and the fixed exchange rate would be much smaller, as a decision to depart from the principles governing domestic money creation could rapidly leave the domestic currency only very slightly backed. The proposal put forward in Section 4 has many of the advantages of the 'marginal currency board' while avoiding its disadvantages.

3. Defining the Problem

There are two key problems in establishing a currency board: the first is deciding on the exchange rate, the second is obtaining the reserves required for the 100 per cent backing of the currency. If the aim is to establish a proper currency board with 100 per cent foreign currency backing of the domestic currency, the initial exchange rate may need to result in an initially very undervalued currency, so that the board can accumulate enough reserves from an initial position of almost zero reserves, as is the case in Latvia.[7]

In an economy, such as the Latvian, in which the currency has for a long time been inconvertible and where prices have been state administered, finding the right level at which to fix the exchange rate is particularly hard. The fact that most prices have been fixed by the state means that a degree of 'corrective inflation' resulting from the adjustment of prices to market

clearing levels is unavoidable. Yet the degree of corrective inflation will itself depend on the exchange rate, as the domestic
prices of traded goods will depend on world prices and the
exchange rate. The greater the initial undervaluation the greater
will be the corrective inflation required before the prices of
traded goods stabilize at world levels.[8] At the same time, the
larger the initial devaluation, and the more it is the case that
additional money can only be created as a result of surpluses in
the balance of payments (i.e. that the money multiplier is low),[9]
the larger will the initial recession in the country be, as the
demand for the domestic money soars and therefore domestic
demand for goods and services declines, simultaneously generating a surplus on the current account of the balance of payments and high domestic interest rates.[10] Thus greater
devaluation, while ensuring adequate backing of the currency
for a currency board system to be established, causes both
higher inflation and higher recession for a transitory period.[11]

Latvia is faced with choosing whether to move to a stable,
convertible currency administered by a currency board in one
step or in two. If it proceeds in one step, there is a greater
danger that the exchange rate will be fixed at the wrong level:
either too high, in which case insufficient international reserves
will be accumulated to back the domestic currency fully,[12] or
too low, in which case recession, inflation, and international
reserve accumulation will be higher than was necessary.

On the other hand, if Latvia proceeds in two steps as is
intended at present, first introducing its own currency in the
context of free prices and convertibility[13] and only subsequently fixing the exchange rate and establishing the currency
board, then there will be other, though equally serious problems. The partially convertible Latvian rouble will presumably
be initially exchanged within Latvia for 'Soviet roubles' (both
cash and bank deposits) on a one to one basis. Once the
exchange is complete, however, the Latvian rouble would float
against all other currencies, including the Soviet rouble. One
can therefore expect that this initial period will be characterized
by high inflation, as the new currency will have a floating
exchange rate and prices will still be subject to 'corrective

inflation' resulting from price liberalization and the newly introduced convertibility of the currency, in a situation in which the country will be suffering from a severe terms of trade shock which it will be unable to amortize with the use of international reserves.[14] The benefits of introducing the Latvian rouble are that Latvia will cease to be in the 'inflation race' with the rest of the rouble area, its monetary policy will no longer be effectively determined in Moscow, and it will be able to remove export barriers on trade with other post-Soviet states and these states will be more likely to do the same with respect to Latvia.

Having achieved internal market equilibrium, a partly convertible currency, and balance of payments equilibrium, the Latvian authorities would then have to sharply devalue and fix the exchange rate of the Latvian rouble (which will be simultaneously exchanged for Lats at a fixed rate), so as to generate a sufficient balance of payments surplus to accumulate the international reserves required to provide the backing to the domestic currency required by the currency board system. The advantage of this two stage approach is that it should be easier to guess the right exchange rate once the microeconomic distortions resulting from price control, inconvertibility of the currency and distorted prices in intra-rouble area trade have been removed. There are three disadvantages: first, there is a, possibly extended, period of high inflation, which may result in the adaptation of institutions to inflation via indexation. This results in so called 'inflation inertia', as a result of which the costs of stopping inflation increase. Second, the economy would be required to make two adjustments to external conditions in a relatively short space of time: first, to achieve balanced international payments under the floating Latvian rouble regime, and then to run a significant surplus under the fixed Lat regime.

Although such gradualism is probably advantageous economically, the second shock, undertaken just for the sake of achieving a fully backed currency, may be politically unfeasible. Third, and most important, the right exchange rate still has to be guessed, and although this should be easier than in the single step approach, there is still bound to be some error.

4. *The Proposal for the Introduction of the Lat*

However, many of the disadvantages of both the single step and the two step approaches to the introduction of a currency board in Latvia can be avoided. This can be done by initially allowing two currencies to circulate side by side in Latvia—the so-called bi-paper standard.[15] One currency would be the rouble (initially the Soviet rouble, later the independent Latvian rouble) which would float freely against foreign currencies. The second currency would be the Lat whose parity would be fixed to a foreign currency, and which would be emitted by the currency board only to the extent to which Latvians wished to exchange any hard currency they had earned for Lats at the fixed exchange rate. The rate of the rouble (initially Soviet and then Latvian) against the Lat would also float freely. Such a bi-paper standard is not an end in itself. It is merely a tool which allows the growth in the use of Lats to proceed gradually and organically, in response to market conditions, rather than as a result of imposition of the exchange of Lats for Latvian roubles from above.

Since there would be no initial stock of unbacked Lats there would be no need for the Latvian Currency Board to guess correctly which exchange rate would be low enough for Latvia to ensure an international payments surplus sufficient to fully back the whole stock of Lat notes with international reserves. Any exchange rate of the Lat to the currency of the 'metropolitan country' would be acceptable. The rate should simply be such as to ensure that Lats would be in such denominations as to be convenient for use within Latvia. Ten Lats to the Deutsche Mark might be a sensible rate.

During the transitional period of corrective inflation and adjustment to world prices for traded goods, rouble inflation would be high. Latvian households and firms would therefore prefer holding Lats to holding roubles (Soviet or Latvian), as this would allow them to avoid the inflation tax. As a result, the market itself would determine what trade surplus Latvians wished to run with the rest of the world so as to build up their stock of stable Lats. The risk of fixing the exchange rate either

too high or too low, and getting too small or too large a stock of international reserves, and also the risk of generating too large a recession and inflation in Latvia (as described in the previous section) would thus disappear. Also, the authorities would not be accused of having created high inflation and deep recession just so as to achieve 100 per cent backing of the currency.

The Latvian authorities could encourage the holding of Lats by requiring that all foreign currency earned after the introduction of the Lat as a result of the sale of merchandise exports had to be converted either into Latvian or Soviet roubles or Lats.[16] However, a more liberal attitude, allowing Latvian residents to hold foreign currency would do little more than slow down the process of 'Latization' of the economy, while at the same time increasing the population's confidence in the authorities' commitment to free market principles and respect for property rights.

It is, of course, true that the introduction of the stable Lat will, other things being equal, reduce demand for the other currency circulating in Latvia. This will have different consequences, depending on whether the other currency is the Soviet or the Latvian rouble.

In the first case, the Lat would have an effect similar to the Ukrainian coupon, in that it will 'push' the roubles into the other post-Soviet successor states, and effectively allow Latvia to earn seigniorage at the expense of its neighbours. This would appear to be contrary to the agreement on the introduction of independent currencies which was reached at Brussels by the post-Soviet states in February 1992. There would be, however, an important difference between the Lat and the Ukrainian coupon: the Lat would be at least 100 per cent backed, so that introducing it should have no more effect on the outflow of Soviet roubles to other post-Soviet states than allowing the holding and circulation of foreign currency within Latvia, which is certainly not against the Brussels Agreement. What is more, the Ukrainians made the coupon the only currency for which consumer goods could be bought. This would not be the case as regards the Lat in Latvia. In this scenario, the exchange

of Soviet for Latvian roubles, when it came, would take place on the principles agreed to at Brussels.

The question arises whether there really is a need for the exchange of Soviet for Latvian roubles if Latvia is to operate on a bi-paper standard. The answer was partly given in the last section: unless there is an exchange, Latvia's monetary policy with respect to the rouble stock would be made in Moscow. Furthermore, the Russians have, quite reasonably, made clear that, once the system of correspondent accounts is introduced, only those states which commit themselves not to introduce their own currency for a year would share in the seigniorage revenue which the Central Bank of Russia obtains from printing rouble notes. The Latvian Treasury would thus be completely deprived of the seigniorage revenue it now obtains as a result of the, rather limited, transfer to the Latvian Central Bank of rouble notes. Nevertheless, as we have seen in the previous paragraph, there is no need to wait with the introduction of the Lat for the exchange of Latvian for Soviet roubles. Indeed, an introduction of the Lat before the introduction of the Lat-vian rouble would have the advantage of avoiding a situation in which the Latvian Treasury became too accustomed to obtain-ing emission revenues from the Latvian Central Bank.

5. *The Effect of the Lat on Demand for the Latvian Rouble*

As regards the effects on the demand for the Latvian rouble of the introduction of the Lat, much will depend on the rate of depreciation of the Latvian rouble. If this is relatively low, demand for the Latvian rouble may not decline very sharply. Even if the demand for the Latvian rouble did fall sharply, this would result from growth in the stock of Lats in the economy, which after all is the aim of the policy. However, even with very rapid inflation, it is not clear that demand for the Latvian rouble must necessarily be lower as a result of the presence of the stable Lat. This was shown in Russia during the hyperin-flation of 1922–4, when the introduction of the second, rela-tively stable, 'chervonets' currency in 1923 actually initially resulted in an increase in the real value of the hyperinflating

sovznak currency, although of course the stock of chervontsy grew far more rapidly (Rostowski and Shapiro, 1992). While the real stock of chervontsy increased to 28 per cent of the real sovznak currency stock in the five months after the introduction of the chervonets, the sovznak currency far from declining, as the orthodox view of currency substitution would indicate, also increased by some 23 per cent (compared to a fall of 56 per cent in the same period of 1922, the previous year).

The theoretical explanation for the failure of the introduction of a stable secondary currency to necessarily reduce demand for the depreciating domestic currency can be developed by taking the simple monetary model of hyperinflation in a single currency economy which is presented by Dornbusch (1987). Rational expectations are assumed, as is the full monetization of the budget deficit:

(1) $\mu m_a = \lambda y$

where

μ = the growth rate of nominal primary money
$m_a = M_a/P_a$ = real primary money balances
λ = the budget deficit as a share of output
y = real output

There is also a linear velocity equation:

(2) $y/m_a = \alpha + \beta\pi_a$

where

π_a = the rate of inflation of prices denominated in the primary money

Assuming a steady state in which $\mu = \pi_a$, substituting (1) into (2) and rearranging gives:

(3) $m_a = y(1 - \beta\lambda)/\alpha$

The real money supply thus depends on the budget deficit and the two parameters of the velocity equation. An increase in α, brought about by a flight from the primary money (the Soviet or the Latvian rouble) due to an increase in the use made of

the secondary money (the Lat) will thus reduce m_a, the real primary money supply. This in turn increases the growth rate of nominal primary money required to finance the given budget deficit, leading to an increase in inflation.

However, when the indirect effects of a secondary currency via the budget deficit and output are taken into account, the presence of a secondary currency may possibly even increase the demand for real primary currency balances, rather than reduce it. In the simple Dornbusch framework it is explicitly assumed that the budget deficit is fully monetized, as is likely during a high inflation. Dornbusch, however, assumes that the deficit is exogenously given. However, with lags in tax collection, inflation erodes the real value of tax revenues via the Tanzi effect, and thereby exacerbates the inflation even further. If taxes on economic activities using the secondary currency are raised in the secondary currency, or in the primary currency at the spot rate of exchange at the time of payment, then the Tanzi effect on these activities is eliminated, which reduces the budget deficit.[17] Furthermore, legalization of currency substitution means that transactions in which the secondary currency is used are legal. Such activities are therefore less likely to go unreported to the tax authorities, helping to reduce the budget deficit.[18]

The question, therefore, is whether the overall budget, including inflation tax revenue, is affected more strongly by the Tanzi and legalization effects or by the reduction in the inflation tax base caused by currency substitution. Thus a country may be on the upward sloping part of its inflation tax Laffer curve as regards gross inflation tax revenues, and yet be on the backward sloping part of the curve when inflation tax revenues net of the legalization and Tanzi effects on other revenues are taken into account. In such a case, currency substitution will result in a lower inflation tax rate being needed to balance the budget, which will in turn lead to an increase in the demand for real primary currency balances. If a country is on the upward sloping part of its 'Tanzi and legalization effects-adjusted net inflation tax Laffer curve' then the overall budget imbalance will indeed be worse in the presence

of currency substitution, a higher inflation tax rate will be required to finance expenditures, and the ensuing higher rate of inflation will result in declining output of those economic activities which involve the use of the primary currency in transactions.[19] However, it is important to note that as regards the overall output of the economy, such a reduction will be transitory, as the higher inflation will cause an acceleration of the shift in activities to the secondary currency using sector of the economy, in which output is protected from the disruption caused by higher inflation.[20] The negative effect of currency substitution on the budget will therefore also be transitory. At the limit, if the secondary currency is foreign or provided by a currency board, and if almost all activities use the secondary currency, then the government will be forced to balance the budget without recourse to the inflation tax.

In much of the above we have assumed that the use of secondary currencies can be banned successfully. In fact, in most high inflations in which secondary currencies have been banned they have been used extensively in spite of their illegality.[21] The advice to ban is thus advice to render the use of such currencies less widespread, rather than to eliminate it altogether. In such cases, the impact of lifting the ban will be smaller, both as regards the undesirable effect on the demand for the primary currency and the desirable direct effect on output. However, the desirable effects on the budget deficit, inflation, and the demand for the primary currency which result from the retention of secondary currency financed activities within the tax base and from the elimination of the Tanzi effect on part of the tax base through the 'Latization' of tax revenues are not reduced.

6. When and How to Withdraw the Latvian Rouble

The bi-paper standard proposed above is, of course, intended merely as a transitory measure to ease the introduction of the 100 per cent backed Lat. The question therefore arises how to withdraw the Latvian rouble once it has performed its function.

As described in the previous section, the demand for the Latvian rouble will depend on the tightness of monetary policy. However, given the availability of the stable Lat and the fact that a significant amount of corrective inflation will be occurring with respect to both domestic and international market conditions in the early days of the existence of the Latvian rouble, one should not expect that the Latvian Central Bank will find it worth while to expend great efforts on stabilizing the value of the Latvian rouble, particularly as rapid depreciation of the Latvian rouble will increase demand for the Lat.[22]

The simplest way for the Latvian authorities to withdraw the Latvian rouble is for them to announce at the appropriate time that no more roubles will be printed, and at the same time to announce a fixed exchange rate between the Latvian rouble and the Lat (which would simultaneously fix the exchange rate between the Latvian rouble and foreign currencies). As a result, a proportion of the Lat stock would now no longer be backed, but all additional money demanded over and above the now fixed stock of Latvian roubles would have to come from increases in the stock of Lats, i.e. from the accumulation of international reserves. This approach differs from the 'two stage' approach described in Section 3 in a number of important ways. The increase in international reserves required to satisfy increased demand for money as a result of the reduction in the inflation tax to metropolitan country levels will be smaller relative to the proportion of the total money supply in the form of Latvian roubles at the time of this last stage of the monetary reform. Upon this 'unification' of the Latvian currency, the stock of Latvian roubles should be a small proportion of the total money supply in Latvia. Equally, the smaller this proportion, the smaller will be the degree to which the Lat is not fully backed on withdrawal of the Latvian rouble. Over time, of course, the degree of backing will asymptotically approach 100 per cent, as all increases in the stock of Lats will be fully backed.

Western aid for the stabilization of the Latvian currency could be used to ensure that, after its unification, the whole stock of Latvian currency was in fact fully backed. The amount

of Western aid, the exchange rate of the Latvian rouble, and the share of the latter in the total Latvian currency stock could then determine the moment at which it was judged that stock of Latvian roubles was sufficiently small for unification to take place. Given very high inflationary expectations, it is possible that a full backing of the Latvian rouble by a Western provided stabilization fund would be possible before the use of the Lat had spread significantly. However, it would be preferable for the use of the Lat to be widespread and the share of the Latvian rouble in the total currency stock to be relatively small, so as not to generate a sudden and massive increase in Latvia's payments surplus upon unification. The avoidance of such an increase is in fact one of the main purposes of the bi-paper approach.

Of course, the authorities are still faced with a trade-off. For a given differential between Latvian rouble and Lat inflation, the longer the bi-paper system lasts the smaller the proportion of Latvian roubles in the total money supply, which is desirable. On the other hand, the longer this system persists, the longer will Latvia have to bear the costs of using two currencies, one of which is depreciating quite rapidly.

7. Backing Bank Deposits

The banking system typical of post-communist economies makes the implementation of the classical currency board system in its unadulterated form, as proposed by Hanke and Schuler, impossible in Latvia.[23] In the Hanke and Schuler approach, only the domestic currency is backed, and banks are entirely free to decide on their own reserve ratios—i.e. it is entirely up to them to decide to what extent they will back their deposit liabilities with domestic currency (which itself is to be 100 per cent backed by foreign currency) and to what extent they will back deposits with the credits which they extend to borrowers. Banks could, of course, be obliged to maintain some obligatory reserve ratio. But at reserve ratios common in the Western world (in the 10–15 per cent range) this would probably be insufficient to ensure a stable monetary

system in a post-communist economy (PCE) such as Latvia's. This is because in PCEs, banks are not capable of allocating credit on a commercial basis among borrowers, as they do not have the skills to assess the creditworthiness of clients, the likely profitability of a project requiring financing, or the riskiness of the project and the client.[24]

With a low level of credit assessment skills in the banks[25] the monetary system becomes potentially highly unstable as the degree to which deposits are backed by reserves at the central bank declines. Yet a rapid reduction in reserve backing of deposits is characteristic of post-communist banking systems once market oriented reform begins in earnest. Soviet-type banking systems tend to operate with very high ratios of reserves to deposits. This is partly the result of the fact that they start out as monobank systems with 100 per cent reserve backing of deposits, partly because of the extreme inefficiency of the payments system, which requires the maintenance of large commercial bank deposits at the central bank, and partly because of the great ease of obtaining central bank credit by commercial banks in the pre-stabilization period. Thus in the Soviet Union in June 1991, enterprise deposits were almost 60 per cent backed by reserves, whereas household deposits at the Savings Bank were 100 per cent backed by reserves. In Poland, just before the beginning of tight monetary policy at the beginning of 1990, more than three quarters of deposits were backed by reserves (mainly voluntary) at the central bank. A year later, however, this ratio had fallen to 30 per cent, and after seventeen months it stood at 20 per cent. Thus Poland moved rapidly from a situation in which central bank money was easily obtainable and backed a very high proportion of deposits to one in which it became far less available, yet was substituted for by deposits at commercial banks backed by credits of dubious quality.

Latvia, like other post-Soviet successor states is in danger of repeating the Polish experience. The backing for bank deposits will become highly uncertain because the true value of the bank assets (excepting reserves held at the central bank) is likely to be significantly less than the deposit liabilities which they are

supposed to back because of the low quality of credit allocation. In such a situation the rigorous application of market
principles would lead to the bankruptcy of many banks, and
a reduction in the money supply resulting from depositors
receiving only a fraction of their claims and from less use of
banks by a population concerned about the possibility of
further bank failures, leading to a fall in the money multiplier
and a 'multiple contraction of deposits effect'. The potentially
disastrous effects on the real economy of such a run on the
banking system are well known (Friedman and Schwartz, 1963).
On the other hand, bailing out the banks through government
recapitalization of their equity bases will create a severe moral
hazard problem, as the banks will be confirmed in their belief
that they can continue irresponsible and incompetent lending
practices safely. Such a set up would be intrinsically inflationary, as banks would offer excessively high interest rates on their
liabilities and grant credits as rapidly as possible on the asset
side of their balance sheets, knowing that bad loans would be
made good by the authorities. Unless the money for bank
recapitalization was obtained through taxation or government
borrowing this would merely be a roundabout way of printing
money.[26]

It would thus be largely futile to introduce a monetary system
which ensured the stability of the value of Latvia's currency,
while at the same time failing entirely to ensure the stability of
the value of bank deposits which constitute a large proportion
of the money supply, and what is more, a proportion which will
grow as the market economy develops in Latvia. In the long
run, the problem of the quality of commercial bank assets can
best be solved by the development of credit assessment and
other banking skills in the Latvian banking system, and bank
supervision skills at the Latvian Central Bank.[27] The question is
what to do in the short run.

One way of dealing with this problem is initially to set very
stringent capital adequacy ratios and obligatory reserve requirements for banking operations conducted in Lats, so as to ensure
adequate backing for Lat denominated deposits. Banks wishing
to conduct Lat operations would have to establish special sub-

sidiaries for this purpose. These 'Lat banks' would have to have paid in capital equal to say 25 per cent of total liabilities. If average obligatory reserve ratios were also 25 per cent non-reserve assets could be written down by one third before depositors suffered as a result of bank losses. Since a proportion of reserves would be held by the Latvian Currency Board in interest bearing foreign assets (Hanke and Schuler), reserves could bring a modest return to commercial banks. As a result the high reserve ratio would not constitute as high a tax on banking services as would be the case in a system with a central bank and zero interest on obligatory reserves.[28]

The high reserve ratio and high capital adequacy ratio would together act as very strong restraints on the size of the Lat money multiplier, with the capital adequacy requirement to pay in 1 Lat of capital for every 3 Lats of deposits accepted acting particularly strongly. The low money multiplier will inevitably mean that a larger part of the Lat money stock will be in the form of currency than would otherwise have been the case, so that a larger accumulation of international reserves by Latvia will be necessary. Nevertheless, this is the unavoidable consequence of aiming for a highly backed, stable and safe monetary system, which appears to be the aim of the Latvian authorities. Such an approach would, moreover, probably be less of a problem for a PCE such as Latvia than for an economy which had been operating on a market basis for a long time, because Latvia will be starting from a situation in which its deposits are highly backed by central bank reserves, albeit reserves which are easily obtainable. The purpose of initially maintaining high reserve and capital adequacy ratios in the 'Lat banks' is to ensure that the backing of deposits by commercial bank credits only increases in line with the ability of the banks to assure the quality of their assets, and thus to enable Latvia to avoid the 'internal bank debt trap' into which Poland has fallen.

Even with high capital adequacy and reserve ratios, the Lat banks will be at risk as long as their equity belongs to bodies which themselves are ultimately state owned, as the state and state owned entities will not be effective owners. This is why the rapid privatization of the Lat banks is desirable. However, the

high capitalization proposed here will at least ensure that when it comes to privatizing the Lat banks this will not be hindered by being effectively bankrupt as a result of bad loans, as has proved to be the case in other PCEs. New private Lat banks should also be licensed, so that the development of a privately owned Lat bank system should not depend exclusively on the, inevitably slow, process of divestment of equity in existing banks by the state and state owned institutions.

What about bank operations in Latvian roubles? These could continue in the present commercial banks on the current basis, that is to say with deposits highly backed by central bank reserves, which would be relatively easily available. Latvian rouble depreciation would mean that if deposit interest rates continued to be kept negative in real terms, demand for Lat deposits would grow quite rapidly. Rouble deposits would wither on the vine, as there was a shift to Lat deposits and Lat cash.

NOTES

This chapter first appeared in the Discussion Paper series of the *Centre for Economic Performance, London School of Economics*, no. 83, 1992. It grew out of a paper written for Einars Repše, Governor of the Bank of Latvia in June of 1992, when Latvia was considering how best to introduce its national currency. I am grateful for discussions on this subject with Geoff Davison.

1. Since they are unwilling to amass roubles, they will not wish to pursue a policy which is tighter.
2. There might initially be a multiple exchange rate regime as in Russia at the beginning of 1992.
3. Such a two stage procedure was adopted when the Lat was introduced in newly independent Latvia after the First World War.
4. To make things more difficult the domestic inflation rate may be negative for a certain period as prices fall.
5. With or without obligatory minimum reserve requirements. Hanke and Schuler assume that liquid reserves are set voluntarily by banks.
6. And lower than if foreign currency was actually used as money within the country.
7. Yet an excessive initial devaluation will lead to 'redundant backing' (the cash stock may become several hundred per cent backed). A number of additional problems arises: the first is that in a country wishing to establish a currency board system, but starting from a position of zero

reserves, the stock of currency must increase more slowly than reserves, so that by the time reserves have stopped growing the currency is at least 100 per cent backed. Second, the growth of the total money stock (currency plus bank deposits) must also be constrained in some way, so that with free convertibility of deposits into domestic currency and of domestic currency into foreign currency, there is an assurance of adequate backing for the whole of the domestic money supply (see Sect. 4 on regulation of the banking system).

8. Of course, this problem applies to any fixed exchange rate regime, independent of whether the currency is administered via a currency board or not.

9. Which is desirable for other reasons, see Sect. 6.

10. These might be largely offset if there were a significant inflow of capital which, however, is unlikely initially in the Latvian case because of a likely lack of credibility of the new regime, particularly to foreigners.

11. Greater undervaluation means that the gap between the prices of domestically produced tradable goods and world prices for those goods is larger. This means that the amount by which these prices must increase will be greater. As these prices do not adjust instantaneously there will be a period of inflation, and this inflation will be higher the higher the initial undervaluation. At the same time, the desire of the population to build up money balances will reduce demand for both tradable and non-tradable domestic goods. In equilibrium total demand for tradables would be unaffected by a fall in domestic demand for them (it would be compensated one to one by increased foreign demand)—but equilibrium takes time to achieve, and on the path to equilibrium which is what we are describing here, demand for tradables will initially fall causing recession, before foreign demand compensates. Moreover, the demand for non-tradables will also fall, and this cannot be made up by exports.

12. At the limit, no reserves may be accumulated and the Lat would have to be devalued immediately, with disastrous implications for the credibility of the whole policy.

13. At least on current account and on capital account internally (so-called 'internal convertibility'). Most prices will have been freed as a result of price liberalization in Russia even before the 'Latvian rouble' is introduced.

14. Even if Latvia had reserves, these should not be used until the authorities are ready to fix the exchange rate under this 'two stage' strategy.

15. See Rostowski and Shapiro (1992) on the functioning of the bi-paper standard in Russia in 1922–4.

16. The requirement to surrender all export earnings to the Central Bank at the fixed rate of exchange was part of Poland's introduction of 'internal convertibility' in 1990.

17. If the latter mechanism is chosen, we do not even have a fall in the demand for the primary currency as a result of the elimination of the demand for it for the purpose of paying taxes.

18. I am grateful to Paul Auerbach for this point.
19. Inflation reduces output as the informational function of prices declines, both as regards relative prices between goods and intertemporal prices (see Auerbach, Davison, and Rostowski, 1992). As a result, we would not necessarily have even a 'direct' positive effect of currency substitution on the budget via increased output and therefore increased tax revenues. All would depend on whether reduced output of primary currency using activities was greater or less than increased output of secondary currency using activities (on the assumption that both kinds of activities were subject to the same tax rates).
20. In a single currency economy the decline in output resulting from high inflation is likely to be larger than in one in which a secondary currency is permitted, because the secondary currency provides the information generating services, both as regards relative prices between goods and intertemporal prices, which only a stable currency can supply (see Auerbach, Davison, and Rostowski, 1992).
21. Thus in the absence of Lats it would be foreign currency which would be used with Latvia as a stable money if the rouble (Latvian or Soviet) was depreciating rapidly.
22. This is not, of course, to advocate the intentional acceleration of Latvian rouble inflation, as this will augment the instability of inflation, which causes high uncertainty for economic actors, and will ultimately result in hyperinflation. But maintaining a stable inflation rate once most of the corrective inflation has occurred should be a sufficiently restrictive policy for the Latvian rouble in the bi-paper system advocated here.
23. This may be less the case in Yugoslavia than in other PCEs, particularly the less advanced ones such as Bulgaria, Romania and the ex-USSR.
24. The reasons for this state of affairs are that most banks in PCEs are not only state owned, but until recently were effectively part of a monobank system which had two main functions: a) a control system by the state over state enterprises, both as regards current payments and in order to direct financial resources for investment; b) as a savings bank system. Even where banks are owned mainly by state institutions rather than by the state itself, as is the case in the post-Soviet successor states, the skills of bank staff are predetermined by the nature of the Soviet-type banking system which existed prior to the 1989 banking reforms.
25. And a very low level of bank supervision skills at central banks.
26. Poland now finds itself in exactly this situation.
27. Under a currency board system the Central Bank would only have this supervisory function.
28. If half the reserves were held in interest bearing assets by the currency board, and if the interest received was passed on to the commercial bank concerned (with the exception of a small margin), then a 25 per cent reserve ratio would be almost equivalent to a 12.5 per cent ratio with non-interest bearing reserves.

10

Dilemmas of Monetary and Financial Policy in Post-Stabilization Russia

1. *Introduction*

Stabilization of high inflation is hard, not only because the political conditions conducive to such an undertaking are not always present, but also because such stabilizations are 'regime changes' par excellence. Relationships between variables which existed before the stabilization are violently changed to quite different ones almost overnight. What is more, the new relationships are initially unknown (particularly as regards their quantitative aspect), and yet economic policy cannot cease until the new relationships have been identified. Stabilization is thus technically as well as politically difficult, and it is likely that as many attempted stabilizations have failed as a result of technical errors as from an unconducive political environment. Certainly, if technical mistakes increase the costs of stabilization they can be expected to undermine such political support as there is for the policy.

This is why this paper is concerned with such technical problems. I take as given the 'acquis' of stabilization programmes in PCEs: the abolition of central planning, price liberalization, convertibility at a unified exchange rate, low trade barriers, moves towards world prices for key raw materials, sharp reductions in subsidies, budget equilibrium, and an end to accommodative monetary policy. Instead, I concentrate on a number of monetary and financial problems with regard to which it seems less evident just what should be done: the techniques of monetary control (Sections 2 and 3), the choice of the exchange rate (Section 4), bad bank debt (Section 5), and inter-enterprise debt (Section 6).

2. The Behaviour of the Money Supply after Stabilization

A number of countries which experienced very high inflation followed by stabilization in the 1970s, 1980s, and 1990s have exhibited a characteristic pattern of behaviour of the money multiplier: as inflation accelerates, the ratio of reserve money (the monetary base) to one's chosen money aggregate increases—i.e. the money multiplier falls and the proportion of the money supply which consists in central bank liabilities becomes large. Upon stabilization this process is reversed, with the ratio of central bank liabilities to commercial bank liabilities in the composition of the money supply falling, so that the money multiplier increases. Figs. 17–22 show that this typical pattern for the M1 multiplier was exhibited for the periods before and after stabilization by Argentina (June 1985 and July 1989), Brazil (February 1986), Poland (January 1990), Uruguay (October 1978), and Yugoslavia (January 1990). Figs. 23 and 24 show that the domestic M2 money multiplier[1] exhibited the same pattern in Poland (1990) and Yugoslavia (1990). Figs. 25 and 26 show that during the high inflation which began with price liberalization in January 1992, Russia has gone through the first part of this typical pattern, and can therefore be expected to experience the same post-stabilization increase in the money multiplier which occurred in the other examples.[2] A number of recent episodes of very high inflation followed by stabilization have failed to exhibit this pattern: these cases, and possible explanations, are discussed in the Appendix.

Two consequences result from the increase in the money multiplier after stabilization: first, the conduct of short-term monetary policy is made harder; second, in post-communist economies (PCEs)—which suffer from a severe shortage of banking skills—the increase in the real value of commercial bank liabilities is likely to create a 'bad debt' overhang, which either adds to the contingent national debt, or increases the instability of the monetary system (as a result of the increase in the ratio of commercial to central bank liabilities in the composition of the money supply). We shall address the first question later in this section and the second in Section 5.

But first, let us examine the reasons for the money multiplier's 'typical pattern' during high inflation and stabilization. Essentially it stems from the decline in the willingness of households and firms to hold bank deposits as the inflation tax increases, with nominal interest rates falling relative to the inflation rate. Thus such a flight from bank deposits will not occur if real deposit interest rates do not fall as a result of the increasing inflation.[3] Fleeing bank deposits, households and firms shift into foreign currency, foreign currency deposits, and in some cases—paradoxically—cash. The shift into cash can occur when payment delays through the banking system are such that the effective inflation tax on using cash is lower than on bank deposits (because of the lower velocity of circulation of the latter). Of course, the length of payments delays is not a purely exogenous variable—banks tend to increase delays as inflation increases, as this allows them to take for themselves a larger part of the inflation tax revenue.

Thus in Russia, between February 1992 and March 1993 the real value of currency in circulation (deflated by the consumer price index) increased by almost 20 per cent, whereas the real value of bank deposits fell by 17 per cent deflated by the consumer price index, and by 44 per cent deflated by the wholesale price index (*Russian Economic Trends*, May 1993). A similar phenomenon took place in Poland in 1989: the real value of deposits fell 66 per cent during the year,[4] and the share of cash in zloty broad money increased from 28 per cent to 37 per cent. In Russia as a result of this change in the composition of the broad money stock in 1992, the structure of financing of total credit (to government, non-government, and to the other CIS states)[5] has shifted sharply away from bank deposits and towards CBR credit. In February 1992 this structure was 75:25 (bank deposits: CBR credit), by March 1993 it was 46:54.[6] Thus, as households and firms are driven out of bank deposits by high inflation and massively negative real interest rates, the CBR is sucked ever more deeply into becoming the lender of first resort to the government, Russian enterprises, and foreign (CIS) governments, as well as the dominant source of financing for the banking system. Again a similar phenomenon occurred in Poland,

with central bank credit accounting for 60 per cent of bank financing in December 1989.

The increased financing of commercial banks by the central bank was accompanied in both Poland and Russia by a sharp increase in voluntary reserves held by commercial banks at the central bank.[7] The most probable reason for this is that with easy access to central bank credit[8] banks are not particularly concerned about maximizing the use of the financing they have.[9] The result of this increase in voluntary bank reserves in Poland and Russia was that total credit (commercial plus direct central bank credit) increased by significantly less than commercial bank deposits plus total CBR credit. A second vicious circle thus developed, in which the accommodating central bank, wishing to increase total real credit in the economy found that a larger and larger proportion of the credit it creates ends up 'uselessly' deposited back with itself.

Upon stabilization the shrinking of the money multiplier is reversed. The reduction in the degree to which real interests rates are negative[10] causes an increase in households' and firms' desire to hold bank deposits and thus an increase in the money multiplier. Thus in Poland after stabilization, between January 1990 and July 1991, the zloty money supply increased *sevenfold* without any increase in central bank credit during these nineteen months.[11] There were two reasons for this: First, thanks to the real undervaluation of the zloty at the new fixed exchange rate, a large amount of base money was coming into the economy through the non-interest current account surplus, so that there was less call for base money creation by the central bank. Second, the increase in the money multiplier allowed a given amount of base money to support a growing amount of deposit money after stabilization.

3. The Dilemmas of Post-Stabilization Monetary Policy

Thus, during the stabilization of a high inflation the money supply is a 'doubly geared' instrument, which makes it difficult to use with any kind of precision. The first 'gear' is the well known effect by which stabilization leads to an increase in the

demand for money (reduction in the velocity of circulation), so that a given increase in the money supply will have a smaller effect on the price level given a lower expected rate of inflation (e.g. Dornbusch and Simonsen, 1988). Of course, the expected rate of inflation is not entirely independent of increases in the money supply, which makes for interesting dilemmas for policy makers! The second 'gear' is the increase in the money multiplier after stabilization, which results in an increase in the money supply which can be far greater than the increase in base money. This second gear is, of course, a result of the first, as it reflects an increase in the demand for domestic deposit money relative to domestic cash and/or foreign currency (cash and deposits).[12]

Clearly, the two gears work in 'opposite directions', the one increasing the demand for money, while the other increases its supply. Is there a 'Say's law' in reverse in operation in the monetary sphere during the stabilization of high inflation, with increases in the demand for money creating its own supply? Does this mean that policy makers can count on the effects of these two gears cancelling each other out? To the extent that this is the case, it follows from the institutional fact that during a high inflation most bank deposits are interest bearing. The inflation tax rate is then given not by the rate of inflation, but rather by the rate of inflation less the nominal interest rate.[13] When the degree to which real deposit interest rates are negative is reduced sharply (or eliminated), then both the demand for (interest bearing) money and its supply increases as non-bank actors shift out of cash (and foreign currency)[14] and banks shift out of reserve money, until the maximum size of the money multiplier has been reached. However, the question arises: since in such a case the supply of money is largely endogenous, even when the exchange rate is floating, what then determines the rate of inflation?

A number of monetary policy regimes are possible in practice. The first is to combine the traditional 'fine tuning' approach to the determination of the money supply with a flexible exchange rate regime. Guesses are made regarding the amount by which the demand for money is likely to increase and of the level of the money multiplier in the next period, and

base money is adjusted accordingly.[15] Attempts to limit increases in the multiplier may be made by fixing quantitative credit limits for individual banks.[16] Because of the gearing which results from the negative relationship between expected inflation and the demand for real money balances, overshooting is likely in both directions (i.e. policy is likely to be excessively tight when it needs to be tightened and excessively loose when it needs to be loosened). Overshooting is certain if the 'gearing' is not taken into account, as in the proposed Ukrainian monetary policy rule for 1993 (Savchenko, 1993), which intended limiting money supply growth to 80–90 per cent of expected inflation in the next period. Even if the rule simply sets a decelerating rate of growth of the money supply, errors in the predicted inflation path will be cumulative, probably causing severe problems with the real values of planned nominal variables such as budget expenditures or the budget deficit/surplus.[17]

The second regime is based on a fixed exchange rate. With a convertible currency this means that the money supply becomes endogenous. However, if convertibility is limited to current account operations plus internal capital account ones (so called 'internal convertibility'), then this is only true in the medium term. Although the money supply has to end up at the level at which prices of domestically produced tradeables are the same as world prices, this will not happen instantaneously with internal convertibility, because it takes time for the requisite amount of money to enter or leave the country through the current account.[18] In the short term monetary policy still matters. If a country begins with an undervalued exchange rate, then if domestic money creation is too rapid there is a serious danger that the equilibrium price level will be overshot, because today's money supply may determine next month's prices and the current account several months later.[19] Once the current account shifts from surplus to deficit there is the likelihood that the currency will be devalued, creating room for further domestic money creation and the possibility of further overshooting. This was the experience of Poland during 1990–1, mainly because of the policy of the National Bank of Poland, whose policy aimed at a continuous increase in the real money stock.

If the exchange rate can be sustained the money supply will fall as a result of a loss of reserves, as long as further domestic money creation ceases. The result will then be full stabilization (at a rate of inflation at which the country's international reserves are stable). However, reserves may be insufficient to sustain the exchange rate. More probably, the loss of competitiveness and the increase in unemployment resulting from the maintenance of an overvalued exchange rate may result in irresistible political and economic pressure (the latter in the form of capital flight) for a devaluation. Once this has happened monetary policy once again becomes important as a means of ensuring that overvaluation does not recur.

For countries in Russia's situation there seem to be two possible styles of monetary policy: the 'controlling' and the 'laisser aller', the former can be best applied to a fixed exchange rate regime while the latter can be applied to either regime. The 'controlling' approach attempts to ensure that the broad money supply evolves in line with international reserves, so that as domestic prices of tradeables rise towards world prices, reducing the rate of increase of international reserves, the rate of increase of broad money declines proportionately. Thus the central bank behaves like a pseudo-currency board of the marginal-fractional kind, with each one rouble increase in international reserves leading to a given number of roubles of increase in the money supply (Chapter 11). The advantage of such an approach is that it allows the economy itself to decide how much nominal money it wishes to hold, as it can always obtain more by running a balance of payments surplus.

The problem, as we have seen, lies in ensuring that the money supply actually increases by the amount desired, as the central bank controls base money but not the money multiplier. As we have noted, quantitative credit limits will help the authorities to control broad money, although at significant microeconomic cost. A better solution are high reserve requirements (possibly only at the margin) for commercial banks and a high ratio of increases in international reserves to increases in the domestic money supply. The first sets a low upper limit to the money multiplier,[20] and also reduces the extent to which

deposits are backed by credits, which will reduce the post-stabilization bad debt problem (see Section 5). If it is impossible to raise reserve requirements on existing deposits, the growth of the money multiplier can be effectively limited by high reserve requirements on increases in deposits.[21] A high incremental international reserves/broad money ratio ensures that if broad money increases much more than intended by the authorities, and the result is that prices of domestically produced tradables exceed world levels, then at least the international reserves are available to defend the exchange rate.

The alternative style of monetary management during stabilization available is what I call 'laisser aller': it can be applied under both fixed and flexible exchange rates, and it may be that Russian circumstances (and national character) might predispose one to this style. It consists in taking advantage of the fact that both the demand for and the supply of broad money will increase as inflation falls, the latter even when the supply of base money remains constant. Combined with a flexible exchange rate regime the 'laisser aller' approach would simply consist in terminating the creation of CBR credit overnight. A number of things would then happen more or less simultaneously: (1) real interest rates (both loan and deposit) would increase; (2) both the demand for and supply of money would increase; (3) inflation would fall; (4) the exchange rate would appreciate.

The question is whether the maximum increase in the supply of money would be sufficient to satisfy the increased demand for money? Clearly, the larger the difference between the pre-stabilization size and the maximum size of the money multiplier the less danger there is of this. On the other hand, the greater this difference the greater the danger of a 'bubble' developing, in which the demand for and supply of money increase to such a degree that inflation re-ignites temporarily, and/or the stability of the banking system becomes threatened through an asset price boom-bust cycle.[22]

If there is doubt as to whether the difference between the pre-stabilization and maximum money multiplier is large enough, an additional element of flexibility can be introduced by adopt-

ing a fixed exchange rate regime. This allows the economy to increase the stock of base money. The first problem is that if it turns out that there is in fact considerable room for the money multiplier to increase, then the money supply may grow to such an extent that it undermines the fixed exchange rate.[23] The second problem is that one has to choose what level to fix the exchange rate at.

4. Choosing the Exchange Rate

Excessive undervaluation of the currency is deflationary, because the costs of imported inputs increase rapidly causing a negative supply shock, while the domestic money supply can only expand relatively slowly in accommodation, particularly if tight rules of the kind recommended above are in force. It is in order to avoid this, and the post-stabilization inflation, which is greater the greater the initial undervaluation of the currency, that 'stabilization funds' have become a standard part of stabilization programmes in PCEs.

The difficulties involved were clearly demonstrated in the Polish stabilization of 1990. The options for the exchange rate which were considered ranged from zl.9,000/$1 proposed by the National Bank of Poland (NBP) to zl.14,000/$1 proposed by the Ministry of Foreign Economic Relations (a representative of the exporters' lobby). The IMF proposed zl.10,000/$1 and the final compromise was zl.9,500/$1. The degree of uncertainty was so great that the government would commit itself to this rate only for three months. As it turned out the rate was held for 16 months. Had it not been for the Soviet trade shock of 1991 it could have been held for many months more, even given the NBP's excessively expansionary monetary policy. In these 16 months prices rose 4.6 times. An exchange rate of one third of that chosen, say zl.3,500/$1, should therefore have been sustainable in principle in 1990, which would have allowed Poland to avoid the devaluation driven supply-shock it underwent. Thus a common view has been that, given the degree of uncertainty, the currency may not have been undervalued *ex ante*, but it was definitely undervalued ex post.

It seems, however, that it is far from clear that the rate was undervalued, even *ex post*, if we mean by this that there existed a far lower rate which would have been in fact sustainable given the expectations at the time. The example of the failed Romanian stabilization of November 1991 is instructive here. The chosen exchange rate of lei 180/$1 gave an average monthly wage of $60. This meant that the lei was less undervalued than the zloty at the beginning of 1990, which gave an average monthly wage of $75 in the first quarter of that year. Nevertheless, with the Polish average monthly wage now at some $220, it seems reasonable to suppose that the Romanian 'equilibrium' dollar wage should not be less than $100/month, so that the Romanian exchange rate of November 1991 still had a very significant cushion of undervaluation built in. Yet, the Romanian authorities lost all of their reserves within a few days of fixing the rate with disastrous consequences. First, they confiscated all the hard currency accounts of firms, then when this was not enough to save the rate, they abandoned convertibility.[24]

5. *Bad Debts in the Banking Sector*

As we have seen, stabilization leads to an increase in deposit money relative to currency and to an increase in bank credit relative to commercial bank reserves. Thus the importance of central bank liabilities declines, while those of commercial banks increase. Money becomes less backed by the central bank and more backed by the credits which commercial banks have issued. In PCEs this is a particularly acute problem because commercial banks have practically no experience in allocating credit on a commercial basis.[25] Furthermore, real loan interest rates are often high in absolute terms in the immediate post-stabilization period, resulting in borrowers who might have been creditworthy under stable non-inflationary conditions being unable to service their debts. This happens just at the time when increasing deposits provide the banks with finance, so that the temptation to 'evergreen' loans to dubious borrowers by rolling over interest payments due will be strong.

In this way a significant stock of bad debt can be built up by

the banking sector quite rapidly. In Poland, total credit to non-government was the equivalent of about 8 per cent of GDP in January 1990. By December of that year it was about 17 per cent, a level it has roughly maintained since that time. International audits in mid-1991 showed that about one third of this credit was classified. Firm level data analyzed by Gomulka (1993c) suggests that the proportion of problem loans may be closer to 50 per cent. If the true value of these loans is half their nominal value, then the additional debt which would accrue to government if it recapitalized the banks would amount to 3–4 per cent of GDP.[26] While this is not a very large sum, it could if handled badly lead to severe moral hazard problems in the banking sector, with the government printing money for repeated bank recapitalizations.[27] In Russia, the bank credit to GDP ratio is about 14 per cent, quite similar to the Polish level before stabilization,[28] so that one could expect any bad debt problem to be of a similar, limited, magnitude. A country such as the Czech Republic, where bank credit is about 80 per cent of GDP is potentially in a far worse situation.

The best way of minimizing the bad bank debt problem is to oblige banks to maintain high obligatory reserves and capital adequacy ratios (Chapter 11). The former limits the degree to which deposits are backed by bank loans in favour of a greater share being backed by central bank liabilities. The latter ensures that there is a cushion to absorb loan losses before either depositors or the taxpayer have to suffer.[29] Since capital adequacy ratios require that the quality of the portfolio be regularly examined so that necessary provisions be made, and since such skills are largely unavailable in Russia at present, it seems that high reserve requirements can more easily play a useful role under Russian conditions. This requirement for high reserve ratios, and therefore the maintenance of a low money multiplier, suggests that the 'controlled' rather than 'laisser aller' approach to monetary policy should be preferred, and since it is so hard to determine what the right rate of money growth is during a stabilization, the further implication is that this should be accompanied by a fixed exchange rate regime, to provide a safety valve if the monetary authorities are excessively restrictive.

High reserve ratios mean that for a given level of the money supply there is a lower level of bank credit than otherwise. However, in a PCE in the early stages of transition this is probably an advantage. As Gomulka (1993c) has shown, in Poland 60 per cent of credit ended up with the 12 per cent of firms which have the worst 'quick ratios'.[30] Moreover, the extremely dynamic private sector has had very little access to credit,[31] financing its very rapid expansion through retained earnings (Chapter 14). Thus credit in Poland has gone to those to whom it should not have gone (mainly the state sector losers), and has not gone to the winners, in particular not to the rapidly growing private sector, for whom its lack has—interestingly—not proved an unsurmountable obstacle. Indeed, one can maybe formulate a hypothesis about the microeconomic unimportance of credit in the early stages of transition in a PCE. The explanation for this is probably that liberalization opens up so many new, highly profitable opportunities that the private sector can finance its own rapid expansion with ploughback.[32]

6. Inter-Enterprise Debt: a Non-Problem?

Recently the magnitude of this problem has diminished sharply in Russia. Whereas payments arrears on the *kartoteka dva* accounted for three trillion roubles (about 50 per cent of annual GDP in June 1992)[33] by December the estimate for 'accounts receivable' was five trillion roubles, or only about 16 per cent of GDP.[34] The question is whether the problem will return in its acute form after stabilization. The Polish experience (described in Chapter 8) shows that if a stabilization programme is credible, inter-enterprise debt (IED) will decline in real terms rather than increasing.

Just how likely one believes this is in the Russian case depends to a large extent on one's explanation for the fall in real IED since the summer of 1992. The optimistic explanation for this fall is that, although there was a multilateral clearing of IED in August–September 1992 this came too late to save the enterprises which had extended this credit from severe loss due

to the fall in its real value. In this case, one can be quite optimistic as to the likely behaviour of IED upon stabilization. The pessimistic interpretation would put most of the stress on the very rapid rate of growth of nominal credit since the multilateral clearing exercise. The fact that the ratio of bank credit to non-government/GDP rose only slightly from 12 per cent in June 1992 (which was when real IED reached its peak) to 14 per cent in March 1993 inclines one towards the optimistic interpretation.

Nevertheless, given the quality of the current data it is as well to be prepared for a surge in IED post-stabilization as in 1992 post-liberalization. The worst thing to do about IED is to inject money into the economy. The second worst thing is to do a multilateral clearing, as this is in effect a government sponsored equalization of the value of all debtors inter-enterprise liabilities, and moreover the setting of their real value equal to their nominal value. As such it causes severe moral hazard problems. The best thing to do about a surge in IED is to do nothing: Latvia which had an IED/GDP ratio very similar to that of Russia in May 1992 refused to do a multilateral clearing, and now has inflation of a few per cent per month and a fully convertible currency which has been appreciating against the US dollar.

However, if there are doubts as to the authorities political ability to resist calls for inflationary solutions such as multilateral clearing or money creation, then making IED tradable should be considered. One of the main reasons for the difficulties surrounding IED is that a properly functioning bankruptcy system does not exist in most PCEs,[35] so that inter-enterprise claims cannot effectively be enforced directly against debtors. If IED is made tradable then creditors can obtain liquidity by 'bypassing' their debtors and selling their claims at a discount to the debtors' debtors. The creditor's liquidity gain is the debtor's loss, as he will not then obtain the money he is owed by his own debtor. For this to work the debtor's debtor must be able to set the face value of his creditor's liability against his own liability to his creditor, and only be required to pay any residual. Debtors will, of course, be able to bid for their own liabilities by offering to buy them at a discount

in exchange for immediate payment. Tradable debt is, after all, the solution which has been generated by the market in the other area in which bankruptcy is impossible—sovereign debt.

The simplest way of ensuring that IED is tradable is to require suppliers to obtain a properly made out bill of lading, with the signatures of the relevant authorized persons representing the customer on it. If such a bill is not obtained when goods are delivered, then the goods are deemed by law to be a gift from the supplier to his client. If the bill is obtained it is deemed a formal liability of the client, obliging him to pay within a certain period, and can as such be sold by the supplier at will.

The most important result of such a procedure is that it eliminates the danger of a 'liquidity log-jam', by which whole strings of enterprises can claim that they cannot pay each other or (possibly more dangerously) the budget, because they have not themselves been paid. If IED is tradable it will allow liquidity to flow to where it is most demanded, possibly cutting out whole swathes of non-payers, and at the same time revealing the true revenues of suppliers.[36] In this way, most of the arguments for inflationary solutions to the IED problems will be eliminated. The pressure to increase the money supply so that it can effect the existing nominal mass of payments due should disappear when the nominae value of these payments adjusts itself automatically to the existing money supply.

Furthermore, IED trading will, if public, generate useful information regarding the standing of various enterprises. A firm, its suppliers, and its direct customers are likely to be as well informed about its financial situation as any group of actors in the economy, and in public auctions of IED their collective assessment would become available to all. If such auctions existed and one made IED convertible into equity[37] this could be a powerful tool for the privatization of the economy. Something similar is happening in Poland under the 'Enterprise and Bank Financial Restructuring Programme' (EBFRP): as part of a 'compact' between creditors and a bad debtor. Bank and inter-enterprise debt can be traded and any holder of more than 30 per cent of a bad debtor's liabilities can have them converted into equity at par.[38]

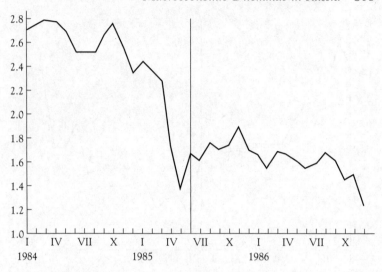

Figure 17   *Argentina 1984–86: reserve money to narrow money*

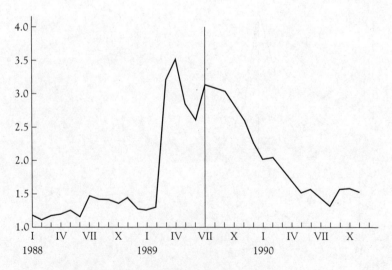

Figure 18   *Argentina 1988–90: reserve money to narrow money*

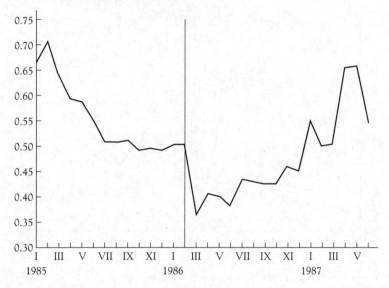

Figure 19   *Brazil 1985–87: reserve money to narrow money*

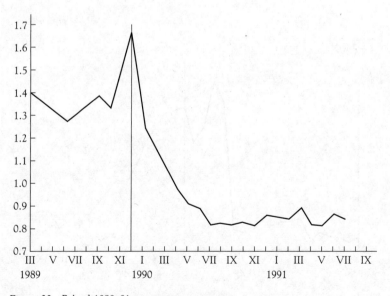

Figure 20   *Poland 1989–91: reserve money to narrow money*

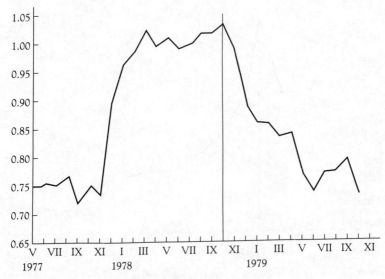

Figure 21   *Uruguay 1977–79: reserve money to narrow money*

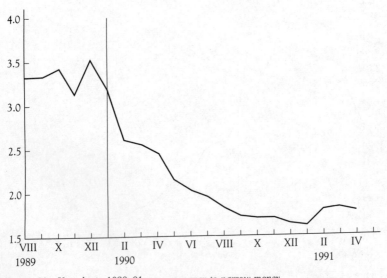

Figure 22   *Yugoslavia 1989–91: reserve money to narrow money*

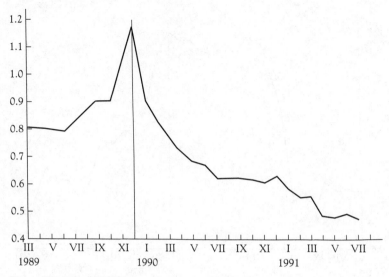

Figure 23   Poland 1989–91: *reserve money to broad money*

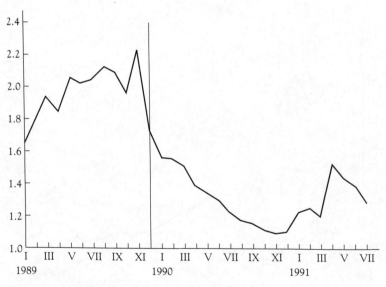

Figure 24   Yugoslavia 1989–91: *reserve money to broad money*

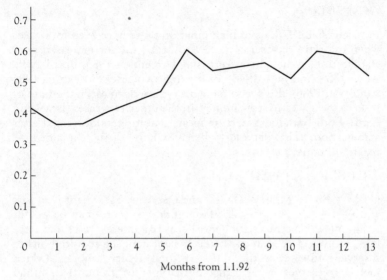

Figure 25   *Russia 1992–93: reserve money to narrow money*

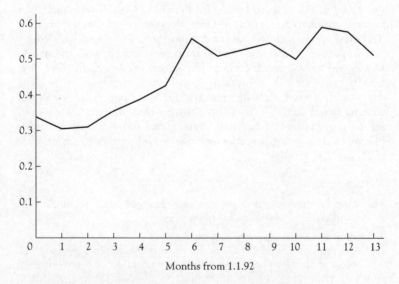

Figure 26   *Russia 1992–93: reserve money to broad money*

APPENDIX

In recent stabilizations of high inflation there have been four cases when the ratio of reserve money to broad money increased after stabilization, rather than decreasing (Argentina 1985, Brazil 1986, Israel 1985, and Peru 1990). In the first two cases (Argentina 1985 and Brazil 1986), this accompanied a typical decrease in the ratio of reserve money to narrow money. In the other two cases (Israel and Peru), both broad and narrow money multipliers decreased after stabilization. This 'atypical' behaviour is easily explained as regards the first two cases:

(1) $BM = TD + SD + C$

BM = Broad Money, TD = Time Deposits, SD - Sight Deposits and C = Cash. As a result of stabilization, there may be a shift from time deposits to sight deposits, as real interest rates may have been more negative on the latter. If sight deposits required higher reserve ratios, then the ratio of total reserve money (which includes reserves held against both types of account) to broad money can increase. At the same time, the ratio of total reserve money to narrow money $(SD + C)$ falls as expected because C remains constant.

A simultaneous fall in the broad and narrow money multipliers upon stabilization (as in Israel and Peru) can occur if the shift into narrow money (be it out of time deposits or foreign currency deposits) is much more into cash than into sight deposits.[39] Since cash is part of reserve money the ratio of reserve money to narrow money $(SD + C)$ can increase. The broad money multiplier also falls because of the reduction in time deposits relative to sight deposits. If a fixed exchange rate regime is in operation, as was the case in Israel in 1985, then both broad and narrow money can increase even though both the broad and narrow money multipliers are decreasing, because reserve money increases faster.

NOTES

This chapter first appeared in *Economic Transformation in Russia*, ed. A. Aslund (Pinter Publishers, London, 1994).

1. Excluding foreign currency deposits.
2. The datum for 1 Sept. 1992 is excluded from the graph. The figure was 0.765, and seems to have been due to the injection of reserve money which took place to complete the multilateral clearing of inter-enterprise debt (Ch. 8).

3. This is the explanation for the failure of the M2 money multiplier to follow the 'typical pattern' in a number of countries (see Sect. 3).
4. When deflated by the consumer price index. The figure using producer prices was almost the same.
5. Which is effectively to Russian exporters.
6. The actual figures are: February 1992: deposits, 964; CBR credit 325; March 1993: deposits, 8331; CBR credit 9646, all in billions of roubles. Unlike other central banks, the CBR engages in a significant amount of direct lending to firms. However, this does not affect what is happening in the monetary system: the ever greater role of the CBR in financing credit.
7. In Poland in December 1989 'money in transit' from payer to payee (a central bank liability) plus commercial banks' deposits at the central bank amounted to 20.5 trillion zloty, or 1.25 times bank deposits, so that the effective reserve ratio was 125 per cent!
8. Directly in the case of the former Spetsbanki in Russia and the state banks in Poland, and via the interbank market in the case of less favoured banks.
9. A second possible reason is that payments delays result in a larger amount of money being held at the central bank, either because there are delays in paying money out by the bank concerned, or because of the need to have a cushion against unexpectedly large payments needing to be made. In both cases payments delays would no longer be the result of a deliberate policy by the banks. The observation that they increase with inflation could then result from either: (1) inflation leading to general economic disorganization leading to payments delays; (2) in PCEs inflation has accompanied liberalization, and liberalization has led to a massive increase in the number of bank account holders in a very brief period, which has in turn led to a sharp increase in payment delays (I am grateful to Miroslav Kerous for this insight).
10. They may become sharply positive, particularly in terms of foreign currency if the exchange rate is fixed, as was the case in Poland in 1990.
11. *National Bank of Poland Monthly Bulletin*, various issues.
12. We have already mentioned how the demand for cash may be relatively higher during a high inflation (as compared to the demand for deposits) because, as a result of payments delays when the banking system is used, the inflation tax can in fact be higher on bank deposits, even though they attract some nominal rate of interest.
13. It is then the repression of deposit interest rates which reduces the demand for real interest bearing money balances, and not just inflation itself. This repression can occur in one of two ways: directly by administrative control, which then calls forth the need for massive central bank credit creation to 'fill the financing gap' left by the disappearing deposits, or indirectly via massive central bank credit creation which depresses the nominal interest rate far below the rate

of inflation, causing a flight from deposits. Real interest rates are not bid up to positive levels by borrowers because the demand for credit does not respond positively to the same degree to highly negative real interest rates as the demand for interest bearing money responds negatively. This results from high nominal rates requiring very rapid repayment of the real value of loans, and there always being the danger that refinancing one's real debt may prove difficult.

14. If the exchange rate is fixed.

15. Fortunately in the relatively unsophisticated financial systems of PCEs it is still possible to control base money directly. In more sophisticated systems it is usually the interest rate at which base money is provided which is the direct control variable. This adds a further 'gear' to the relationship between the central bank's control variable and prices.

16. In Poland this led to periods of excess bank liquidity in 1990 and 1991, and combined with interest rate ceilings on loans it also led to corruption of banks' credit officers.

17. If the predicted monthly inflation path is 100 per cent, 90 per cent, 80 per cent, 70 per cent, etc., and a 10 percentage point fall in the monthly inflation rate leads to a 10 percentage point increase in the demand for nominal money balances whereas the authorities expect an increase of only 5 percentage points, then in period 2 the money supply is increased by 95 per cent, but inflation in fact goes down to almost 80 per cent (the 85 per cent inflation rate which would result from the authorities error requires a further increase in the demand for nominal money of 2.5 per cent, which requires a further 2.5 per cent fall in inflation).

18. Unless there is a very large amount indeed of domestic foreign currency holdings. However, Poland, which had foreign currency deposits equal to twice the zloty broad money supply at the beginning of the stabilization, took about a year to achieve this equilibrium state, and that largely thanks to the negative Soviet trade shock.

19. Unless the exchange is already believed to be overvalued, in which case the effect on the balance of payments may precede that on prices.

20. The multiplier is $(l + d)/(r + d)$, where d is the currency/deposit ratio and r is the reserve ratio, with a 33 per cent reserve requirement and a 25 per cent cash/deposit ratio, the upper limit to the multiplier is 2.

21. Such high marginal reserve requirements have often been used in Latin America for this very purpose, and were used in the UK in the 1970s (the so-called 'corset'). The present author proposed a 'corset' on bank assets in Poland in 1990.

22. Such inflation could not persist as long as no additional base money was emitted. The threat to the stability of the banking system is thus the greater danger.

23. The 'Currency School' were right that overissue is possible under just such circumstances (and the 'Banking School' were wrong to deny the possibility).

24. One of the few consolations is that Romania had very few reserves to lose. It is possible that with very low reserves any fixed exchange rate is undefensible, however low it may be in real terms. If this was the case, then in the Polish context the question becomes: given that Poland did have substantial reserves, how much higher could it have fixed the value of its currency? This is a question to which there will now never be an answer, since it requires the repetition of a non-repeatable event.

25. It is very hard to achieve being unable to repay credits obtained under conditions of massively negative real interest rates such as obtain before stabilization.

26. The actual amount by which the Polish Government intends to recapitalize the banks is about $1 billion, or 1 of GDP. But this may prove quite inadequate.

27. By delaying its response to the problem and being careful to ensure the 'incentive compatibility' of its techniques of recapitalization, it appears that Poland may avoid this problem.

28. I am grateful for the Russian data to Brigitte Granvelle. In March 1993 commercial bank credit to non-government amounted to 8.7 trillion roubles while monthly GDP was 5.2 trillion roubles. In Poland, in December 1989 the ratio of credit to non-government/monthly GDP was about 12 per cent.

29. Of course, if bank capital belongs to the state or to SOEs the owners may not be able to exercise effective supervision over managers to encourage the avoidance of loss. This is why bank privatization is so important.

30. QR = (Cash + Receivables − Bank loans − Payments due)/three months sales. Interestingly, these are not the socialist giants one would expect to find in this category. They account for 8 per cent of sales, and are thus smaller than average.

31. Some 15 per cent of bank credit goes to private firms in Poland, even though the private sector accounts for about 50 per cent of GDP and for 70 per cent of employment outside the budget sector (60 per cent of all employment).

32. But see the contrary view put forcefully by Calvo and Coricelli (1992*b*).

33. At June 1992 prices.

34. I am grateful to B. Granvelle for the figures for monthly GDP in June and December 1992, which allowed the calculation of annual GDP in June 1992 and December 1992 prices through the simple expedient of multiplying by 12. *Russian Economic Trends* vol. 1, no. 3 for the June 1992 figure for inter-enterprise debt. The December 1992 figure for receivables was provided by the Russian Government's Centre for Economic Reforms.

35. The existence of a bankruptcy law is not the same as the existence of a bankruptcy system. Only Hungary has an efficient bankruptcy system. Poland has had a law since the beginning of its reforms and a

system which is still very inefficient, but is slowly improving. The Czech Republic's bankruptcy law only came into force in April 1993!

36. It is, of course, these and not the formal sales price which must be taken into account in calculating profit and sales taxes.
37. At nominal value into the book value of enterprises' 'own funds'.
38. Subject to the approval of the Ministry of Privatization.
39. The reason for the shift out of these kinds of deposits is that with stabilization the inflation tax declines.

PART THREE

Laying the Foundations of
Long-Term Stability

Introduction
to Part Three

Part III looks at how the conditions of long-term macro-economic stability in PCEs can be established. Chapter 11 first describes the evolution of banking systems from monobanks under central planning to two tier systems. This evolution was very different in Central Europe on the one hand (what I call the 'main sequence'), and in the former Soviet Union on the other. The chapter then proceeds to identify the requirements of monetary stability as the creation of a banking system which is able to gradually develop credit allocation skills, and a 'monetary rule' which ensures exchange rate stability. It is argued that the former would be more likely if banks had to maintain 100 per cent—or very high—reserve ratios at the beginning of the transition. I call this position 'banking gradualism'. McKinnon (1991) espoused a similar point of view. There is, however, one key difference: under McKinnon's scheme, banks holding 100 per cent reserves at the central bank are effectively crediting the government. Under the scheme in Chapter 11, the need to back 100 per cent of central bank liabilities with foreign assets means that depositors are ultimately crediting world capital markets (and are therefore more likely to get their money back). The essence of this 'monetary rule', which is the other pillar of the proposed system, is that a key monetary aggregate should depend on changes in international reserves at a fixed exchange rate and at least current account convertibility. As the quality of the banking system improves, the key monetary aggregate to be controlled in this way can become ever narrower.

Interestingly, after the stabilization in Poland there was an initial rapid expansion of credit to non-government (CNG), after which CNG has declined sharply as a share of bank assets. This was the result of caution by the banks, and the ready availability of government paper in 1991–2, due to large budget deficits. Consequently, by 1994 about half of bank assets were non-risk (either

reserves at the central bank or government securities)—very much what a 'banking gradualist' would have advocated. The difference is that the detour via a period in which there was a high loans/deposits ratio would have been avoided, had a policy of gradualism in banking reform been followed. The current situation in China is further grist to the mill of banking gradualists. Deposits of non-state firms and households have been used to provide SOEs with credit, which many are unable to service.

Chapter 12 analyses the sources of the post-stabilization fiscal crisis in Czecho-Slovakia, Hungary and Poland, and concludes that Hungary must cut back its social provision sharply, while the Czech Republic, Poland and Slovakia need to avoid its expansion. Once more, this chapter bears the mark of its time. While these conclusions may be correct as regards these countries' immediate policy needs, they are too modest if one looks at the longer run. Given their level of development, neither the Czech Republic nor Poland can afford their current shares of government expenditure in GDP if they are to continue growing rapidly. Chapter 13 assesses to what extent German-type universal banks—which would play an active role in the corporate governance of non-bank businesses—are suitable for the PCEs. It concludes that they are not, as long as PCEs are characterized by state ownership of most large banks, high inflation, and a tendency to state interventionism at the micro level. Chapter 14 argues that structural change began very early on in the transition in Poland, that the far-reaching structural transformation of the Polish economy, which has occurred thanks to very rapid private sector growth, macroeconomic stabilization, and generalized liberalization of the economy as a whole. It also claims that this structural change occurred without much help from the reallocation of savings by the financial (mainly banking) sector, so that the importance of this sector as a source of adjustment in the early transition should not be overstated. Finally, it is argued that although Poland has progressed rapidly without privatization of SOEs, with time the absence of privatization is likely to become an ever more severe burden. This is because of the political influence—and the access to the treasury which goes with it—which large unprivatized SOEs will retain.

11

Creating Stable Monetary Systems in Post-Communist Economies

1. Introduction

Post-communist economies (PCEs) usually enter the transition to capitalism with a high rate of inflation. This is, first, because price liberalization without a hard budget constraint or unemployment must lead to high inflation (Chapter 2). Second, the weakening of communist political power in the period before the overthrow of communist governments has often led to a weakening of such budgets constraints as there were in the Soviet-type economy—particularly as regards wages. Post-communist governments are thus often faced with the need to tackle high or very high inflation just at the time when they also have to guide the country through the transition to capitalism. Creating stable monetary sytems in PCEs is thus vital both in the short and the long term. Yet a major hindrance in the achievement of this aim is the nature of banking systems in these countries. This paper aims to draw lessons from banking reform in the more advanced countries (particularly Hungary and Poland) for what one can call the 'sedcond wave' reformers (the countries of the former Soviet Union and some of the Balkan states). In particular, we consider whether the present generally accepted 'main sequence' of banking reform is likely to result in the creation of stable banking, and therefore monetary, systems. What we call the 'main sequence' consists in: (1) splitting up the traditional Soviet-type monobank into a number of state owned commercial banks (SCBs); (2) liberalizing entry by private (mainly domestic) banks; (3) trying to privatize the SCBs.

There are two pre-conditions for a stable monetary system: a stable banking system and an anchor binding the domestic

currency to foreign currencies. Adopting a fixed exchange rate is insufficient in itself to achieve this, particularly in the absence of central banking skills. Some kind of 'monetary rule', providing an automatic link between the money supply and reserve holdings of an outside asset is necessary (Simons, 1936). A second question we consider is what kind of monetary rule is suitable for PCEs at various levels of development of their banking systems.

2. Creating a Stable Banking System

2.1. The 'Main Sequence' of Banking Reform in PCEs

In Soviet-type economies, the banking system consisted of a state monobank, which combined the functions of a central bank and of the monopolistic commercial bank. There were specialized banks for savings, foreign trade, sometimes investment, and some other functions such as agriculture, but these were parts of the monobank in balance sheet terms, in that they had to hold 100 per cent reserves against deposits, and received financing for any lending from the central bank in the form of refinance credit.[1]

The main sequence of banking reform was initiated in Hungary in the mid-1980s, and consists in a number of steps. The first is usually the hiving off the commercial operations of the monobank into a number of state owned commercial banks (SCBs). In Hungary there were three of these, and nine in Poland, where the reform took place in 1989. These SCBs and the specialized banks were then required to hold only a fraction of their deposits as reserves, while the state bank concentrated on classical central bank functions.[2] In this way the basic structure of a two tier banking system of the Western kind was created. At the same time, the creation of private banks, both domestic and foreign, has been allowed. The next step in the reform is supposed to be the privatization of the SCBs, once they have developed sufficiently, both organizationally and in terms of their financial health, for this to be feasible.[3]

An alternative path has been followed in Russia and Ukraine. There the monobank first had three specialized banks split from it in 1989. Since these 'Spetsbanki' could create money and were thus effectively central banks, the State Bank encouraged the creation of commercial and co-operative banks, the former belonging to various state enterprises and organs (including Ministries!), the latter to effectively private so-called co-operatives. This trend continued once the republican central banks got their independence from USSR Gosbank, and was strengthened by the creation of independent banks out of local sections of the 'Spetsbanki' during 1991. The result was the creation of thousands of banks in the former Soviet Union (FSU).

Transitional PCE banking systems initially tend to operate with very high ratios of reserves to deposits. This is partly the result of the fact that they start out as monobank systems with 100 per cent reserve backing of deposits, partly because of the extreme inefficiency of the payments system, which requires the maintenance of large commercial bank deposits at the central bank, and partly because of the great ease of obtaining central bank credit by commercial banks in the pre-stabilization period. Thus in the Soviet Union in June 1991 enterprise deposits were almost 60 per cent backed by reserves, whereas household deposits at the Savings bank were 100 per cent backed. In Poland, just before the stabilization programme at the beginning of 1990, more than three quarters of deposits were backed by reserves (mainly voluntary) at the Central Bank. Yet a rapid reduction in central bank reserve backing of deposits is characteristic of post-communist banking systems once stabilization and market oriented reform begin in earnest. Thus, a year after the beginning of the 'big bang' in Poland the ratio of reserves to liabilities had fallen to 30 per cent, and after seventeen months it stood at 20 per cent. Thus Poland moved rapidly from a situation in which central bank money was easily obtainable and backed a very high proportion of deposits to one in which it became far less available, yet was substituted for by deposits at commercial banks backed by credits.

2.2. The Inside Money Problem

In PCEs most banks are not capable of allocating credit on a commercial basis among borrowers, as they do not have the skills to assess the creditworthiness of clients, the likely profitability of a project requiring financing, or the riskiness of either. The reason for this is that most banks are not only state owned, but until recently were part of a monobank system, in which all deposits were effectivley liabilities of the central bank, and thus had their nominal value openly guaranteed by the state. The monobank had two main functions:

a) a savings bank system which funnelled savings either to the state budget or to state enterprises on the basis of central planners' decisions via the monobank, making such loans quasi-budget expenditures;

b) a control system by which central planners could check up on, and direct, the activities of state enterprises, with respect to both current payments and financial resources for investment.

When a PCE switches from a monobank to a two tier banking system, it is moving from a situation in which all money is 'outside money' to one in which most money is inside money, i.e. the liabilities of the banks instead of the state.[4] We saw that upon stabilization there occurs a rapid increase in the ratio of inside to outside money, i.e. the money multiplier increases sharply. This inside money is backed by bank assets, mainly credit to the non-government sector. The problem is that this backing for bank deposits may become highly uncertain as the true value of bank assets (excepting reserves held at the central bank) may become significantly less than the value of deposit liabilities, because of the low quality of credit allocation.

The rigorous application of market principles could then lead to the bankruptcy of many banks, and a reduction in the money supply resulting from depositors receiving only a fraction of their claims.[5] The potentially disastrous effects on the real economy of such a run on the banking system are well known (Friedman and Schwartz, 1963). On the other hand, bailing out the banks through government recapitalization of their equity bases as is being done in Poland will create a severe moral

hazard problem, as the banks will be confirmed in their belief that they can continue irresponsible and incompetent lending practices safely.[6] The resulting regime could be intrinsically inflationary, as banks may offer ewxcessively high interest rates on their liabilities and grant credits without attention to the quality of the borrower/project, believing that bad loans would be made good by the authorities. Furthermore, unless the money for bank recapitalization was obtained through taxation or government borrowing, successive bank recapitalizations could become a roundabout way of printing money.[7] The lack of banking skills in PCEs thus introduces a fundamental instability into their monetary systems. Until this problem is resolved, macroeconomic stability will remain hard to attain.

2.3. *Implications for 'Main Sequence' Reform of the Banking System*

In the long run, the problems described above can be solved in one of two ways. The first is the development of credit assessment, liability management, and other banking skills in the banking systems of PCEs, and sophisticated banking supervision skills in the bank supervisory authority—in other words, through the development of the skills necessary to provide the microeconomic underpinning of a banking system along lines current in the West.

If this is the path followed then it would be prudent for the first principle of banking system evolution to be that in the short term, the stability of the monetary system must have priority over the freedom of action of the banks themselves in the management of their assets and liabilities. In other words, in the initial phases of the 'main sequence', when supervisory and banking skills are rudimentary, bank regulation needs to be rigorous and based on simple rules. This is because of the vital role of macroeconomic stability in successful economic transition from state ownership and central administration of the economy to capitalism.

The usual argument against tight regulation, which stresses that tight regulation leads to disintermediation (Goodhart, 1989) is largely irrelevant in a context in which people have so little possibility of informed choice between risky and safe

banks that the authorities feel themselves obliged to guarantee all deposits. The development of a dual sytem in which deposits at strictly regulated banks are known to be safe, while loans to unregulated non-bank financial institutions are clearly known to be not guaranteed by government seems healthier than the alternative by which all deposits are a contingent liability of a state budget which has no effective control of the degree of risk to its exposure. In the West, the state tries to limit this exposure by sophisticated and light regulation of the whole of the banking system, but in PCEs such regulation is likely to be ineffective for a long time because of a lack of skills.

What methods of rigorous yet relatively simple regulation can central bank authorities in PCEs apply? First, banks can be obliged to maintain some obligatory reserve ratio. However, reserve ratios common in the Western world (in the 10–15 per cent range) would probably be insufficient, and ratios above 25 per cent on current accounts seem closer to what might be initially required to ensure a stable monetary system for a post-communist economy. High reserve ratios reduce the variability of the money multiplier, and thus of the tendency of the money supply to vary in a pro-cyclical way. They also reduce the share of bank assets held in the form of claims against the non-bank sector, which is particularly important in PCEs, since it is these very claims whose value is uncertain because of the shortage of credit assessment skills in banks. If the PCE concerned also had some form of monetary rule (i.e. did not have a lender of last resort), such obligatory reserves (unlike in the West) would have to be available to the banks to meet the liquidity demands of their depositors. Use of reserves by a bank would then trigger stricter supervision by the bank supervisory authority. Second, banks can be obliged to hold high capital/asset ratios, so that losses resulting from bad loans are borne by the owners of the bank's capital and not by depositors or taxpayers (as happens if the bank is bailed out by the state). Again, given low banking skills, capital/asset ratios of 25–30 per cent would seem to be prudent. Finally, banks need to be privatized, as only private owners of bank equity will exercise the requisite degree of control over bank management, so as to secure their equity.

As banking and supervisory skills increased, and as the macro-economic situation stabilized, the stringency of regulation could be reduced by gradual reductions in obligatory reserve and capital adequacy ratios, and the introduction of more sophisticated forms of regulation (e.g. weighting exposure by risk, limiting concentration of exposure, etc.).

In the early stages of banking system evolution, the minimum desired ratio of central bank to inside money in the economy can also be maintained through a policy of tight credit limits on the banks. Whether credit limits or high obligatory reserve and capital/asset requirements are chosen depends on the level of skills of central and commercial bank staff. Control of capital/asset ratios in particular requires an ability to assess the degree to which loans need to be written down.

A dilemma would arise in this case regarding the treatment of Western banks. High capital adequacy ratios reduce the rate of return on bank capital. When applied to domestic banks with low skills they constitute a form of insurance for depositors and for the government, which is the ultimate guarantor of deposits in the regulated part of the system. If applied to reputable Western banks with good banking skills they would be a barrier to entry, and thus a drag on the development of an efficient banking sector. Branches of foreign banks could remain in the unregulated, unguaranteed, part of the system, as long as they were subject to the supervision of their national bank supervisory authorities, and if the capital of the whole bank was legally subject to make good the losses of its domestic branch. The foreign banks might then take over the whole of the domestic market (having higher skills and lower capital costs).

Thus PCEs are faced with four alternatives:

1) an inadequately regulated and excessively guaranteed banking system, which will be microeconomically inefficient and macroeconomically unstable.

2) a dual system, based on domestic banks, part of which is strictly regulated and guaranteed, while the other is lightly regulated but unguaranteed. The stringency of regulation in the strictly regulated sector would decline as skills improved.

Microeconomic efficiency would initially be low, but would slowly improve, while macroeconomic stability would be good.

3) a lightly regulated system based mainly on foreign banks.

4) some mix of (2) and (3).

Which system out of options (2) to (4) a country will end up with would depend on the desire of foreign banks to enter the market, and the rate at which the banking skills of domestic banks developed, as well as the political willingness of the authorities to allow foreign entry.

2.4. The 100 per cent Reserve Banking System

An alternative approach would be to start from the proposition that a banking system which combines the functions of payments system and allocator of savings may be fundamentally unstable whatever the level of banking skills, but that it is certain to be so if such skills are lacking, and that such skills cannot be developed in the time required, given that macroeconomic stabilization is essential for successful economic transformation. Critics of bank based monetary systems often stress the mismatch between the term structures of bank assets and liabilities, with liabilities being extremely short term (i.e. money) and assets being far longer term. One proposed solution, what one might call the traditional 'sound banking' view, is that banks should have more short term assets on their books. The problem is that such assets can never be sufficiently short term to make their maturity correspond to that of bank liabilities, and of course, being liabilities of the private sector, they are subject to the risk of default. Furthermore, as Simons (1936) pointed out, an increase in the amount of very short term liabilities of non-bank businesses to banks actually increases the susceptibility of the economy to sharp fluctuations in the nominal money stock, as banks can relatively easily refuse to roll over short-term debt as it comes due. In the absence of a central bank operating in a discretionary manner (i.e. in the presence of a monetary rule) this susceptibility to money stock fluctuations could become a reality, leading to profound economic depression.

Simons therefore suggested that both the asset and liability

sides of banks' balance sheets be reformed. Those financial institutions whose liabilities would continue to be deposits (i.e. money) would be obliged to keep 100 per cent of their assets in the form of short-term government (or central bank) liabilities. In other words, the payments system function of the banking system would be performed by what was, from the balance sheet point of view, effectivley a monobank system of the Soviet type. If these reserves did not pay interest (the question is discussed below), then users of the payments system would have to pay charges. This would prevent the waste of the resources going into the performance of this function. On the other hand, those institutions which no longer held despoit liabilities (i.e. non-bank financial institutions) would be free of any reserve requirements, and only they would be able to undertake the savings allocation functions of the banking system. Simons was very dubious as to the feasibility proposals for eliminating the imbalance between the term structures of bank assets and liabilities by allowing non-banks to take only long-term deposits and to make only long-term loans (the problem is one of policing or regulatory race). His solution was, therefore, to limit non-banks to granting and taking equity participation (i.e. transforming them into investment trusts or Islamic banks).

If we accept Simons' criticism of Western banking systems, then maybe the finacial systems of PCEs should follow a quite different evolutionary route to that pursued so far in their transformation. PCEs in the early stages of economic transformation do not have banking systems, and they have a single integrated payments system. This payments system is extremely inefficient and urgently needs to be reformed. This could be done either by splitting up the existing monobank into competing money warehousing and payments companies (WPCs) or by allowing new, private, WPCs to be created. All WPCs would be obliged to keep all of their assets either as reserves at the central bank, or at whatever clearing and settlement centre(s) they wished to create (the clearing and settlement centre(s) would then keep its/their reserves at the central bank). The freedom of the WPCs to create their own clearing and settlement centres is vital,[8] as the inefficiency of the monobank in managing the

payments system stems from its state owned nature, and the achievement of payments and settlement times comparable with those in the West is important for the overall economic efficiency of PCEs.

As they would be unable to lend out deposits, WPCs would be obliged to charge for their services, unless the state decided to subsidize the development of the payments system by paying interest on WPCs' reserves. This could be done by allowing WPCs or clearing centres to hold their reserves in treasury bills or bonds. One could argue in favour of this on the grounds of some 'public good' aspect of the payments system. WPCs would then compete for deposits, as these would generate reserves which brought in interest. Those providing the best payments services would get the most deposits, thus the most reserves and the most interest payments. It can be argued that lender of last resort support to a two tier banking system by the authorities is similar to paying interest on reserves to WPCs since it allows banks to take greater risks with their liquidity and asset positions at no cost to themselves. The tab is picked up by the authorities, which then either fund the expenditure through taxes, or by creating more central bank money. In a 100 per cent reserve system there is no liquidity or solvency risk for the authorities. They can therefore afford to pay interest on the reserves, and this will not be inflationary as long as the expenditure is funded through taxation not emission.

As PCEs do not have the investment trusts which the Simons-type system requires, the conditions which make it possible for such trusts to emerge need to be created. However, the legal infrastructure for such trusts is much simpler than that required by Western-type banks. Ordinary company law should be sufficient, as investment trusts can be ordinary companies which issue their own shares and which then use the financial assets they accumulate in this way to buy the shares of other existing companies or to create new companies.[9] It is often pointed out that even in a mature capitalist country, relatively few households own shares: people will first wish to hold property they can directly control, then nominally denominated bank deposits and only last financial assets whose

nominal value is volatile. Given the lack of track record of financial institutions in PCEs, this unwillingness to buy the shares of investment trusts would be understandable. As a result, one can expect investment trusts to develop slowly in PCEs. However, a similar unwillingness to deposit one's money in banks would probably exist, were it not for the assumption of a government guarantee of deposits. In the absence of such an implicit guarantee people would have to chose between depositing their money in WPCs (which would not pay interest and might charge for the services they provided), holding cash, buying nominally denominated commercial paper, and buying shares in investment trusts. Under such circumstances, the relative attractiveness of investment trusts might be somewhat greater than at present, particularly if WPCs were not subsidized by the state.

The fact that as a result of the slowness of the development of investment trusts, a large part of the nation's personal savings would lie 'useless' at the monobank need not be feared. First, it is better for these savings to lie 'useless' than for them to be wasted as a result of incompetent lending by commercial banks. Second, the savings can be exported and invested abroad via foreign investment funds. Third, savings can also be mobilized by the issuing of securitized debt and equity (commercial paper and shares). Initially the demand for such instruments may be relatively small, but the total unavailability under a Simons-type financial system of bank credit, which by definition is 'soft' under PCE conditions—particularly as regards state owned enterprises (SOEs)—might change SOEs attitude to privatization (which would become one of the few ways of obtaining outside financing) and to the issuing of securitized debt.[10]

Finally, if it is not the aim to develop a Western style banking system, but rather to move towards a Simons-type financial system, then the various proposals for a write-off of SOE debt (Begg and Portes, 1992; Schmieding, 1991; Williamson, 1992a) make sense. Writing off the debts of SOEs entails recapitalization of the banks by the state. Once a fractional reserve two tier banking system exists—however immature it

may be—commercial bank managements need to be largely independent of the state as regards their credit decisions. Recapitalization therefore means that the state effectively allows two independent sets of agents (the managements of the banks and the SOEs) to determine its expenditures. Under such circumstances, once the precedent of a supposedly 'one-off' debt forgiveness has been set, the belief that it will be repeated (again and again) may become strong. The costs of proving that the initial debt write-off is not a precedent could be very high.

In the absence of a two tier banking system, and in the absence of any intention of creating one, debt forgiveness becomes a simple matter. SOEs have their debts to the mono-bank written off and replaced by government debt on the asset side of the monobank's balance sheet. Since the SOEs and the monobank all belong to the state this is a pure book-keeping operation without any economic significance, as long as the SOEs did not have a large degree of operational and financial autonomy at the time they incurred their debts (i.e. as long as we are still in the highly centrally planned phase of a PCE in transition).[11] Once the debt has been written off, the monobank is banned from any further lending to non-government.[12] The one-off nature of a debt forgiveness carried out in this way would be fairly credible.

If the PCE has reached the transitional stage in banking system evolution, evolution towards a Simons-type financial system could take place as follows: first, banks could be split into WPC and investment trust operations; second, WPCs would be required to increase their reserves over time until they had achieved 100 per cent backing. At the same time they would transfer non-reserve assets to the investment trust parts of the old commercial banks. Depositors would be required to choose whether their money was to remain on deposit in WPCs, which charged for their services, or to be transformed into shares in the investment trust companies issuing from the original commercial bank. If such a financial system was combined with a currency board one would have a highly stable monetary system.

3. Choosing an Appropriate Monetary Rule

3.1. The case for a Monetary Rule

Ever since the writings of the currency school in England in the 1840s, economists have been aware that the broad money supply tends to vary in a pro-cyclical way, either causing, or at the least increasing, the amplitude of the business cycle (Schwartz, 1989). However, attempts by central bank authorities to counter this tendency through discretionary policy intervention are often mistimed, and result only in its exacerbation. Hence the belief that a rule should be established for the behaviour of the monetary base (or central bank money). These rules assumed the gold standard (i.e. a fixed permanent exchange rate) and suggested a relationship between domestic central bank money and either the level of, or changes in, the international reserves (in gold) of the central bank (e.g. Simons, 1936). PCEs seem to be particularly in need of a monetary rule of this sort to provide a nominal anchor for their monetary systems for two reasons: first, their central banks have little experience in conducting monetary policy in an open economy with a convertible currency, because monetary policy was previously subordinate to physical planning, the economy was closed and/or the currency was not convertible. Second, the transition is the 'macroeconomic regime change' *par excellence*, making the conduct of policy on the basis of behavioural models of the economy impossible. As a result, policy has to consist in choosing values for those parameters which one can determine (inevitably fairly arbitrarily), and establishing rules which ensure that the economy adjusts to these parameters—hopefully as quickly and painlessly as possible. Third, many PCEs enter the transformation in a state of very high inflation.

Successful stabilization of very high inflation usually involves fixing the exchange rate of the domestic currency, at least for a short period of time. This is because very high inflation causes people to save on real balances—on which they have to pay the inflation tax. Fixing the exchange rate means that, for at least a short period of time, people know that the foreign exchange value of the domestic currency will be stable. This can cause the

demand for the domestic money to increase sharply, so that a virtuous circle develops: increased demand for domestic money ends the 'flight from domestic money' which is fuelling very high inflation—as inflation falls the demand for money increase further—and so on (Dornbusch and Simonsen, 1988).

A key problem is how to maintain credibility for the new fixed exchange rate without starving the economy of the greatly increased real money balances now desired. If the authorities fail to accommodate this increased demand for money by increased supply, then in the absence of perfect capital mobility, they will cause very high real interest rates to prevail. These can only be avoided if prices fall to such an extent that the given nominal money supply satisfies the demand for real balances at the new low rate of inflation.[13] If, on the other hand, the authorities increase the supply of money rapidly the danger is that they will undermine the credibility of the stabilization. Caught on the horns of this dilemma the authorities usually try to steer a middle course, which causes an information and control problem. It is impossible to know whether high interest rates mainly reflect liquidity shortage (in which case the nominal money supply should be increased), or the lack of credibility of the exchange rate (in which case the nominal money supply should be tightly controlled).

A solution to this problem would be the adoption of a monetary rule strictly relating the supply of the monetary base to international reserves. However, the kind of monetary rule suitable for a given PCE largely depends on the extent to which its banking system has evolved from the classical Soviet-type monobank towards a fully fledged two tier Western-type system, since this determines the relationship between the monetary base and the broad money supply. We address this question in Sections 7 to 10.

3.2. The Reserve Accumulation Problem

However, the first problem facing a PCE wishing to base monetary system on a monetary rule is how to accumulate adequate reserves to back the currency fully. The exchange rate needed may result initially in a very undervalued currency. In an econ-

omy, such as that of most PCEs, in which the currency has for a
long time been inconvertible and where prices have been state
administered, finding the right level at which to fix the exchange
rate is particularly hard. The fact that most prices have been
fixed by the state means that a degree of 'corrective inflation'
resulting from the adjustment of prices to market clearing levels
and the elimination of the monetary overhang is unavoidable.
Yet the degree of corrective inflation will itself depend on the
exchange rate, as the domestic prices of traded goods will
depend on world prices and the exchange rate. The high degree
of initial undervaluation which is likely to be necessary to
ensure a high level of backing of the money supply may lead
to high inflation and recession during the period of reserve
accumulation (Chaptger 9).[14]

It is, of course, possible to follow different monetary rules, to
establish for example a 'fractional monetary rule' or a 'marginal
monetary rule'. In the first, the targeted money aggregate (e.g.
domestic currency or broad money) would be only fractionally
backed by foreign currency (say 50 per cent), while in the
second, only increases in domestic currency would be backed,
but these would be 100 per cent backed. The advantage of both
systems over 100 per cent backing is that a far smaller amount
of foreign currency has to be obtained by the country, so that a
smaller balance of payments surplus needs to be generated. The
disadvantage of both systems is that confidence in the domestic
currency and the fixed exchange rate would be proportionally
smaller. For a fractional monetary rule to be credible, the
fractionality of the backing has to be maintained also during
periods of contraction of international reserves. In order to
avoid the risk of abrogation of international convertibility of
the national currency, one could have a monetary rule which
was marginal during periods of international reserve expansion,
while during periods of international reserve contraction it
would follow a fractional backing rule. The proposal put forward in Chapter 9 for a currency board for a parallel currency
for Latvia has many of the advantages of the 'marginal currency
board' while avoiding its disadvantages.

3.3. The Monetary Rule for a Monobank

All money in such a system is central bank money, and it can take one of three forms: 100 per cent backed deposits at a specialized bank, deposits at the state bank itself, or cash (also a central bank liability). If there existed an economy with a monobank system and a convertible currency then the monobank could quite easily adopt a monetary rule: it would manage its deposit liabilities so as to ensure their convertibility on demand into domestic currency[15] and also so as to ensure that all domestic currency was fully, fractionally, or marginally backed (whichever approach had been adopted—see next section). An alternative would be for the monobank to adopt some rule for the fractional backing of all money[16] (deposits as well as currency), or for the backing of increases in money, with international reserves. The banking system in Czecho-Slovakia was not dissimilar to such a 'monobank with convertibility' at the beginning of the economic reform in that country in early 1991, with one foreign trade bank, one savings bank, one investment bank, and one commercial bank in each of the two constituent republics of the Federation.

A key question facing policy makers in such a situation is how to combine maintenance of the monetary rule with the evolution of the banking system towards a two tier competitive system of the Western kind? On the other hand, if the ultimate aim is the creation of a Simons-type financial system, then the traditional Soviet-type monobank provides an excellent starting point. The main problem facing the authorities, apart from the development of WPCs described in Section 4, would be obtaining sufficient reserves to back the central bank money in the system.[17]

3.4. The case against a Currency Board in a PCE with a Transitional Banking System

Hanke and Schuler (1991) have proposed a system as the solution to Yugoslavia's chronic high inflation problems.[18] In a currency board system all domestic currency has to have a fixed amount (over 100 per cent) of backing in foreign currency

denominated assets or foreign cash. The board always stands ready to exchange domestic currency into the foreign currency to which the domestic currency is fixed (henceforth called the 'metropolitan currency'). A pure Humean mechanism then ensures that, in the medium term, prices cannot change except as in the 'metropolitan country'. In the short term, if prices of traded goods are lower than in the metropolitan country, the reserves of the currency board will increase, increasing domestic cash and therefore—through the standard money multiplier[19]—the domestic money supply and thus the prices of traded goods. If the process goes too far and prices of traded goods exceed those in the metropolitan country, the mechanism goes into reverse, causing the domestic money supply to decline, so that prices fall.[20] The fact that only a fraction of the backing is held in foreign cash, while the rest is held in foreign interest bearing assets, means that the costs, in terms of seigniorage paid to the metropolitan country, are significantly lower than they would be otherwise.[21]

The low level of banking skills during the transitional period in PCEs makes the implementation of a classical currency board system in its unadulterated form, as proposed by Hanke and Schuler, quite unsuitable. For a PCE to move directly to a currency board means that the monetary system is switched from being one in which the central bank is lender of first resort to one in which there is no lender of last resort whatever.[22] In the Hanke and Schuler approach, only the cash part of the domestic money supply is backed, and banks are entirely free to decide on their own reserve ratios—i.e. it is entirely up to them to decide to what extent they will back their deposit liabilities with domestic currency (which itself is to be 100 per cent backed by foreign currency) and to what extent they will back deposits with the credits which they extend to borrowers.

As a result, irresponsible credit expansion by the banks on an excessively small reserve (cash) base could lead to a run on bank deposits, once it was realized how small the cash reserves of the banking system are. Since a currency board cannot be a lender of last resort to the banking system, the board would then be faced with the choice of supplying unbacked currency

to the banks (i.e. suspending the currency board system), or of allowing the collapse of many banks (and possibly of the banking system as a whole). This is always the problem with a currency board, and indeed it is the key to the discipline it exerts on the banks. However, the danger is magnified when a currency board is grafted onto a banking system with practically no liquidity management skills. The consequence of incompetence on the asset side could be even more dangerous, leading to not just the illiquidity, but the actual insolvency of the bulk of the banking system (see Sections 2 and 3).

3.5. A 'Broad Money' Rule for PCEs with a Transitional Banking System

In PCEs with a transitional banking system of the type described in Section 1, what I call a 'broad money rule' may be more suitable than a classical currency board. This consists in the central bank committing itself to maintain some given level of backing of the whole broad money stock. Under a 'fractional broad money rule' the exchange rate is set so as to generate international reserves which will give a desired level of backing, after which the money supply is allowed to expand, at the margin, at the rate allowing the maintenance of that ratio.[23] Under a 'full' broad money rule, 100 per cent of the domestic money supply is backed by foreign assets. This is the system which obtained in the second half of 1992 in Estonia.

If the relationship between broad money and central bank money depends on an obligatory reserve ratio (augmented by a capital/asset ratio), then the central bank needs to maintain a relationship between central bank money and international reserves such that the relationship between international reserves and broad money to which the central bank is committed is indeed adhered to. So that if the degree of backing of central bank money with foreign assets was more than 100 per cent, then the degree of backing of broad money with foreign assets would be higher than the obligatory reserve ratio. In less sophisticated systems, changes in deposit money can be controlled via changes in credit limits which are themselves dependant on changes in international reserves.

The achievement of high levels of backing for the domestic money supply need not necessarily involve the generation of huge payments surpluses, particularly in countries which have suffered from very high inflation. Thus, in the case of Poland, total broad money (zloty cash and deposits and hard currency deposits) was almost 40 per cent backed by international reserves when it reached its maximum in 1990. This was achieved by Poland running a trade surplus equivalent to some 2.7 per cent of GDP during the year.[24]

Furthermore, as described in Section 9, an arrangement by which a large part of a country's money supply is backed by foreign assets need not mean that the country must pay a large amount of seigniorage to the foreign government whose currency backs the domestic money supply. This is because a significant part of the backing can be held in the form of secure interest bearing assets (e.g. government bonds) of the metropolitan country, so that the backing is not bought from the metropolitan country (seigniorage), but merely constitutes a loan to it. If deposits as well as cash were backed by foreign assets, the assets concerned could be allowed to be less liquid than in the case when they were backing only cash.

An arrangement of this kind does, of course, imply the export of a significant part of a country's household and enterprise savings, as we noted in Section 4. The proportion will depend on the share of savings which actors wish to hold in money form, and the proportion to which broad money is backed. For this reason the 'broad money rule' monetary system is likely to be criticized by those pointing to the great shortage of capital in PCEs, which need to restructure their economies profoundly after decades of misallocation of investment by central planners. However, against this must be set the fact that the original problem which needs to be solved is that the newly liberalized banking system is also incapable of allocating credit efficiently. Savings allocated within the country via the banking system are therefore also likely to be wasted. By reducing the share of deposit money backed by domestic credits, and increasing the share backed by foreign assets, a monetary system based on 'broad money rule' reduces the amount of

waste involved. Until credit allocation skills have been developed in the banking system it is therefore better for an important part of savings deposited in banks to be invested abroad, ensuring in this way at least the stability of the monetary system (and the avoidance of the loss of the domestic savings).

In this initial period domestic investment would be financed mainly by equity participation (i.e. in most cases by ploughback of profits and the establishment of partnerships[25]). If the aim is to develop a Western-style banking system, then the key policy question is at what rate and how to liberalize the tight regulations described above, so that the banks' role in the allocation of savings within the country can grow safely.

Finally, it is worth noting that the difference between a 100 per cent broad money rule and a financial system of the type proposed by Simons is not large. Although nominally denominated assets exist in the former on a large scale and do not in the latter, they are mostly held against foreigners and therefore do not constitute liabilities of domestic economic actors. Fractional broad money rules would be closer to 100 per cent reserve banking, the closer the amount of foreign backing of broad money was to 100 per cent.

3.6. *The Argentine-type 'High-powered Money Rule'*

This is the case where the provision of central bank reserve money to banks is made dependant on the balance of payments position of the country, each dollar of international reserve accumulation generating a given number of dollars of reserve money. If one dollar of reserve money was made available to the banking system for each dollar of international reserves accumulated, one would have something very close to a currency board mechanism, except that not only cash but also commercial bank reserves at the central bank would be backed by foreign assets.[26] If the system were run by a central bank then it could, without any institutional or legal measures, change the rule it was following.[27] If more than one dollar of reserve money was made available to the banking system for each dollar of international reserves, then one would have a 'fractional' or 'marginal' high powered money board arrangement. In either of

these cases the interest rate on central bank loans to commercial banks would be determined exclusively by the need to achieve the pre-announced relationship between reserve money and international reserves (or between the increments in each of these). High reserve and capital/asset ratios would be required to ensure the safety of deposits. In Argentina the reserve requirement on foreign currency deposits is 3 per cent giving a money multiplier of 33. With a fixed dollar/new peso parity of one to one and full convertibility of the peso, the dangers implicit in this arrangement are clear. Indeed, the real appreciation of the peso has recently been so large as to cast serious doubts on the sustainability of the system. This kind of monetary rule would clearly only be suitable for a PCE in which the banking system and banking skills had reached an almost Western level of development, for example Hungary.

4. Conclusions

The stability of the Western banking system since the war still allows one to accept it as the basic model towards which PCE financial systems will probably ultimately evolve.[28] Nevertheless, the experience of PCEs since 1990 and the experience of fragile banking systems subjected to high degrees of political interference in Latin American and African countries, suggests that haste should be made very slowly. In other words, we should be well advised to incorporate significant elements of the Simons-type into the financial system of PCEs. The approach to banking system reform which has become pretty well universal in PCEs, and which consists in creating, usually out of bits of the old monobank, autonomous state owned commercial banks which are supposed to be guided by the profit motive, and which are intended to be ultimately privatized, seems fraught with danger. These state commercial banks (SCBs) not only lack private owners, and therefore the motivation to be truly profit maximizing, they also lack basic banking skills, and are often burdened with the old monobank's bad loans.[29] Being state owned there is an implicit state guarantee not only for their deposits but also for their capital (SCB losses

are part of the quasi budget deficit even if there is no formal write-down of loans or recapitalization). Most important, once the possibilities of extracting money from the state budget have been exhausted, the PCE banking system is often seen as a source of 'directed' soft financing by various populist and lobby groups.[30]

A number of conclusions follow. If the PCE concerned is lucky enough to still have its monobank intact, it should not try to create the standard two tier Western-style banking system by hiving-off SCBs. Rather it should create competitive WPCs, either by splitting the monobank (the provision of warehousing and payments services should not be beyond the ability of the market socialist enterprises which will be created in this way) or, better, by allowing private WPCs to be formed and for these to create their own clearing and settlement centres if they wish. Initially no domestic banks would be allowed. Savings would be mobilized either through equity participation—ploughback, share flotation, investment trusts, foreign direct investment— or through non-intermediated debt (i.e. commercial paper).

Domestic banks would only be allowed to begin operations slowly. They would be obliged to operate subject to very high reserve and capital/asset ratios (from 25 per cent up). Since there would be no lender of last resort in the system, reserves could be drawn down to meet liquidity needs, but such a move would render the bank concerned subject to a tightening of supervision by the bank supervisory authority. It would also be made very clear from the start that deposits at banks (unlike those at WPCs) were in no way guaranteed by the state. If a third tier of non-banks outside the authorities' supervisory system came into existence, the fact that the companies concerned had no legal right to take deposits (but were merely borrowing under the ordinary commercial laws with a promise to repay on demand), should be enough for it to be clear to depositors what risks were involved.

Foreign banks of good repute setting up branches in the PCE, and subject to the supervision of their own central bank, would also be allowed to operate with minimal local supervision, as long as the capital of the whole bank was legally subject to make

good the losses of its local branches. Since they would not be required to satisfy the stringent conditions facing native banks, foreign banks would have a considerable competitive advantage. There is no doubt that the banking system might be taken over by foreign banks. But given the argument that a secure banking system is vital for macroeconomic stability, and that macroeconomic stability is vital for a successful transition to a market economy, then some PCEs may find it most efficient to import foreign banks to create their banking systems, just as they have to import foreign machinery for their productive investments. The law of comparative advantage does not apply only to goods.

In the final stage of banking system evolution in a PCE, reserve and capital/asset requirements for domestic banks could be slowly reduced towards Western levels, as the bank supervisory authority became more confident of its own supervisory skills and of the banking skills of the commercial banks. However, as long as a monetary rule was in force, i.e. as long as there was no lender of last resort, these ratios would need to be higher than in systems with a central bank. A strategic decision would then be needed with regard to the WPCs. Allowing them to reduce their reserve ratios, i.e. to become banks, would mean accepting the transformation of the system into one based entirely on clasical Western two tier banking system lines.

Because the banking system is a major weak point of monetary control in PCEs it is important that any monetary rule which is adopted should embrace a broad money aggregate, as long as the structure and skills of the banking system are such as to render very risky indirect control of the whole money stock through control of currency or high powered money alone. As the skills of the banks improve the monetary rule can be changed from a 'broad money rule', first to a 'high powered money rule' and finally to a currency board.

NOTES

This chapter first appeared in *Europe-Asia Studies*, vol. 45, no. 3 (1993), 439–55.

1. Sometimes (e.g. in the USSR) they did not formally receive financial resources as such, but rather the right to extend credit according to their credit plan which was determined for them by the state bank. Once the credit plan was received there was no need to actually obtain financial resources. These were created by simply debiting the so-called 'inter-branch circulation' (the *mezhdufilialny oborot* in the USSR). In other words the specialized banks, and indeed the branches of the state bank, created their own liabilities just like a central bank. Control of this central bank money was exercised by control of credit creation by State Bank headquarters via the credit plan. Once the Spetsbanki and the Republican Central Banks could draw up their own credit plans (from 1989 and 1990 respectively) they effectively became central banks, because they could still debit the 'inter-branch circulation' to finance the credit they extended.

2. In Poland, the Central Bank still engaged in commercial operations, though on a much reduced scale, at the end of 1992.

3. At the time of writing, none of the Hungarian SCBs has been privatized. In the Czech and Slovak Republics, the SCBs have been partly privatized in the framework of the mass privatization voucher programme, and in Poland two SCBs are 'soon to be' privatized.

4. Unlike SCBs a central bank does not have limited liability, and cannot, even theoretically go bankrupt.

5. And from less use of banks by a population concerned about the possibility of further bank failures, leading to a fall in the money multiplier and a 'multiple contraction of deposits effect'.

6. In the former Czecho-Slovakia the same was done by removing a large part of bad credits from the books of the SCBs and into a 'Consolidation Bank'.

7. Poland now finds itself threatened with exactly this situation.

8. However, to prevent barriers to entry refusal to allow access to a clearing system by its participants, as is happening in Poland, would need to be forbidden under anti-monopoly legislation.

9. These are effectively 'closed end' mutual funds. This is was has happened in Czechoslovakia in response to the opportunities created by the voucher mass privatization scheme. 'Open end' mutual funds on the other hand require a law of trusts and a highly liquid stock market. As such they are likely to be unsuitable for PCEs in the early stages of their transformation.

10. Thus in Poland, for example, SOEs have been unwilling to issue securitized debt, as the failure to repay it when due makes them automatically subject to bankruptcy proceedings, whereas the accumulation of inter-enterprise arrears does not (Ch. 8).

11. This is why debt write-off made much more sense for the ex-GDR and Czecho-Slovakia in 1990 than it did for market socialist economies such as Hungary and Poland.

12. Thus all subsidies to SOEs become transparent, and the central bank covers the budget deficit openly by creating money to extend credit to

government, rather than hiding it by extending unrepayable credit to banks or SOEs. Stabilization is then effected by making central bank lending to government illegal.

13. To make things more difficult the domestic inflation rate then needs to be negative for a certain period as prices fall.

14. The problem resulting from the need for reserve accumulation does not stem mainly from the size of the required payments surplus. Thus during the Polish stabilization programme, by the time international reserves and the real value of the money supply ceased growing in October 1990, cash was 160 per cent backed and cash and foreign currency deposits together were 70 per cent backed. Although Poland did not start its stabilization programme with zero reserves, this was achieved by Poland running a trade surplus equivalent to only some 2.7 per cent of GDP during 1990, which gives an indication that the trade surplus which might be needed by a PCE to back its currency need not be very large.

15. This is not the trivial point it may appear at first sight. In Russia at the time of writing there is a severe cash shortage, resulting from loose credit policy in a hyperinflationary environment, combined with the inability of the printing presses to keep up with the demand for cash. The result is the maintenance by the Central Bank of Russia of the inconvertibility of business deposits into cash for most purposes (exceptions being such uses as the payment of wages).

16. Simons (1936) suggested such an approach for the US (the backing would, of course, have been in gold).

17. 100 per cent international reserve backing of the monetary base would imply the export of a large proportion of domestic savings, which would be likely to be criticized (see Sect. 4 for a discussion of this question).

18. Also Hanke, Jonung, and Schuler (1992).

19. With or without obligatory minimum reserve requirements. Hanke and Schuler assume that liquid reserves are set voluntarily by banks.

20. The simplicity of the mechanism might be largely lost if there were a significant inflow of short-term capital (as has happened in 1991–2 in Argentina). This, however, is unlikely initially in the case of most PCEs because of a lack of credibility of the new monetary regime, particularly to foreigners.

21. And lower than if foreign currency itself were actually used as money within the country.

22. In British colonies which had currency boards most banks were branches of United Kingdom banks and thus had access to the Bank of England as lender of last resort via their headquarters.

23. Under a 'marginal fractional broad money rule' total domestic money is allowed to grow as some multiple of the increase in international reserves (let us say 2). The disadvantage of this system, as stated in the previous section, is that if the country started off with almost no international reserves and if, after a period of increasing reserves and

money there comes a period of loss of reserves due to some external shock, then the money supply needs to be reduced more sharply for a given fall in international reserves than it was allowed to expand while international reserves were increasing, for the maintenance of convertibility at the fixed parity is to be ensured (i.e. if the country is not to run out of reserves).

24. Had the nominal money supply not been allowed to grow after this period, Poland would have saved herself a further 60 per cent inflation during 1991.

25. With both unlimited and limited liability. Public companies with widespread share ownership are unlikely to develop on a large scale initially, because of a lack of track record.

26. A strict currency board would not accept commercial bank deposits.

27. As such, a pseudo-currency board of this kind would have less credibility than a fully fledged board. In Argentina the law would need to be changed for the high powered money rule to be abandoned. Since this would take time, enabling massive capital flight, Argentina seems to be very pre-committed to the rule.

28. Simons was writing in 1936. Readers of this paper in the year 2000 may have a perspective which is closer to Simons' than the one I am able to adopt today.

29. Even when, as in Poland, the bad loans were largely 'liquidated' by the hyperinflation of 1989, the banks reproduced these bad loans during the high real interest rate stabilization period of 1990–2.

30. The hundreds of billions of roubles of credit made available to SOEs in Russia in 1992 are a good example, as are the subsidized credits for agriculture granted throughout Central and Eastern Europe.

12

Fiscal Crises During Economic Transition in East Central Europe: An Overview
with Kálmán Mizsei

1. Introduction

One of the most pressing problems of the transition economies, even the 'first wave' ones (i.e. those that have achieved preliminary macroeconomic stabilization and an important degree of transformation into market economies), is a large and growing gap between public revenues and expenditures (see Fig. 27 at the end of this chapter). This problem affects Hungary and Poland in particular, but, as this introductory chapter argues, the better performance of the Czechoslovak budget was partly (although not entirely) a consequence of the postponement of hard decisions on microeconomic restructuring. This volume analyzes the reasons for growing budgetary gaps in most of the transition economies of East Central Europe; it also tries to assess the longer-term implications of large budget deficits for debt and inflation.

In the short run, the Central European fiscal crisis has been caused by a fall in revenues, while in the long run the major problem is overspending. The latter problem is exacerbated by the fact that the level of budgetary redistribution (especially in former Czechoslovakia and Hungary) is similar to that in the Scandinavian countries, which have some of the highest levels of GDP in the world, rather than to middle-income countries of similar levels of development. Even as regards the 'short-term' problem of the fall in revenue, it is unclear to what extent this is due to the depression in registered output and is therefore

cyclical—so that it can be expected to disappear as output recovers—and to what extent it is mainly structural, resulting from the fundamental changes in the nature of these economies. One example of such changes, stressed by McKinnon (1991), is that the state is no longer able to interfere directly in the management of state owned enterprises (SOEs). Another, stressed by Rostowski (Chapter 14), is the very rapid shift in the composition of GDP from the state sector to the private sector.

2. Problems on the Revenue Side

The short-run cyclical causes of lower revenue levels in Central Europe operate through a number of channels. Tougher monetary regimes (as in Poland) squeeze liquidity on the micro level; lower inflation disburdens the enterprises from the bulk of the previous inflation tax, but simultaneously strains them financially because of a lack of automatic liquidity financing. Moreover, the measures taken by Poland's Balcerowicz plan in 1990 (followed by a similar set of reform steps in Czechoslovakia in 1991) increased domestic *and* foreign competition on internal markets. Finally, the well-known effects of the collapse of the CMEA (Comecon) in 1991 also contributed to the liquidity squeeze, well demonstrated by the Polish data of de Cromburgghe (1994). Similar phenomena occurred in each of the first wave reform countries. The problem, however, is different in the rest of the region. In the Balkan countries as well as in the former Soviet Union—with the exception of Estonia and Latvia—more or less automatic liquidity financing still prevails. Yet this has not saved these 'non-stabilizing' countries from budgetary problems that are of at least equal severity to those of the Central European stabilizers.

Turning to the structural or systemic causes of the fall in budget revenue, we again have a number of elements involved. The disintegration of the system of hierarchical control in the economy left few countervailing forces against SOEs' natural tendency to *minimize* profits. In Poland, managers of SOEs who are responsible to the workforce rather than to owners have

little reason to make profits, 40 per cent of which they would then have to pay in corporate income tax. In fact, it is surprising and encouraging that Polish workforces have sufficiently long time horizons to induce them to maintain the capital of the firm rather than consume it. This can be seen from the fact that the overall profitability of the SOE sector is still positive in spite of quite high depreciation allowances, which are counted as costs (de Crombrugghe, 1994). However, once profit attracts tax at a 40 per cent rate, it becomes pointless for a Polish SOE.

In all three countries, the time horizon of the managers has become very short as the prospect of privatization has approached, or as future enterprise governance became increasingly unpredictable. In all three countries there were, and are, important opportunities for managers to participate as purchasers in the privatization process. Reducing the paper and real profitability of the SOE puts off outside buyers and increases managers' ability to buy a larger share of the firm. If it is believed that an outside takeover is unavoidable, asset stripping to the benefit of an outside company owned by the management may be the optimal strategy. Finally, under most circumstances, the unavoidable lack of clear rules for privatization means that the maximum return to managerial effort is likely to be through what has been called 'property rights seeking behaviour' (Rostowski, 1993). Managerial concentration on this must result in a reduction in the profitability of the ordinary commercial activity of the firm.

Like privatization, restructuring has also resulted in a reduction of taxable enterprise profits. Revealing which enterprises are unprofitable enables them to set operating profits against past losses, which cannot be taxed. One can see this most clearly in Hungary, where the structural reforms are the most advanced. Moreover, there is a rollover effect from the revelation of the true financial state of the real sector compared to that of the financial sector. In Hungary, the latter lost profitability one to two years after the real sector, as the previous profits of the banks were based on the lack of a realistic assessment of low-quality assets. Similarly, market-oriented tax regulations, such as

more realistic reserves against losses and amortization rules, also reduced the effective corporate tax rate.

However, success in completing restructuring can be expected to play an important role in improving the tax base of the economies concerned in the medium term. Here the effectiveness of wage policies can have a crucial significance: the lower a country has been able to keep real wages, the more chance it has to maintain enterprise profits at levels that make the financing of restructuring possible (as well as generating more tax revenue in the short term). The most restraint in this respect has been shown by Czechoslovakia from 1990 to 1993 (and this has been reflected in continuing large revenues from the corporate income tax in that country), although Hungary and Poland have not lagged all that much behind. However, while Czechoslovakia seems to benefit from the highest profitability in the state-owned enterprise sector, providing the resources necessary for restructuring, it also seems to be experiencing the smallest amount of actual restructuring, as can be seen from its very low level of unemployment. This seems to be a result of the absence of financial pressure on SOEs, which is the other effect of low wage pressure in that country. An exception to this apparent lack of industrial restructuring in Czechoslovakia has been the contribution of foreign investors in that country.

While real wages in domestic currencies have decreased, they have increased sharply internationally in these years, as currencies have appreciated in real terms. It seems that the relatively high Polish real wages are both an expression of the successes of Polish transition so far, but also of relatively weak wage restraint due to the strong position of trade unions. Still, on balance the performance of Polish governments in controlling wages in these years is something few expected, given the disadvantageous political system in that country in the early years of transformation.

The explosive growth of the private sector in these countries is a further structural cause of the fall in budget revenues: the tax administration has been faced in a matter of a few years with hundreds of thousands of new tax-paying businesses (a huge

increase), all of which are highly motivated to evade taxes, in place of the several tens of thousands of state enterprises that provided the tax base in the past. The technique of tax administration has had to be completely overhauled: whereas in the past, the accounts of every tax-paying SOE were examined individually, the new circumstances require the development of Western-style random mechanisms of control. The requisite change in systems, organization, and mentality could not happen overnight. However, it does suggest that one may expect a J-curve in effective taxation rates, with a sharp fall as the private sector expands explosively in the first few years of transition, followed by a steady improvement as the tax administration adjusts to the new situation. The danger is that one will have an L-curve rather than a J-curve, if habits of evasion, built up in the first years of the transition, become entrenched. One can also think of implementing much more severe penalties than now exist for tax avoidance; however, one has to keep in mind that the societies of East Central Europe will accept such measures only if they are accompanied by at least some lowering of the marginal tax rates.

Thus, during the early years of transition, general government revenues have decreased sharply; the most spectacular fall has occurred in Czechoslovakia (data are still somewhat confused, but according to what are probably reliable IMF computations, presented in van der Willigen (1994), general government revenues fell from over 70 per cent, to 52 per cent of GDP between 1989 and 1992), while in Hungary the fall was smaller, partly because the basic elements of a market-oriented tax structure has been in place since 1988. Hungary is the only country of the region where personal income tax, profit tax, and VAT were in place before the political turmoil of 1989. Poland, with its history of near-hyperinflation and stabilization, presents a picture rather like a seesaw, with revenue falling in 1989, rising sharply in 1990 and then falling steadily in the subsequent two years (de Crombrugghe).

The tax systems and marginal tax rates show a very strong convergence between the three countries: corporate income tax rates vary at around 40 per cent to 50 per cent as do top

marginal personal income tax rates; VAT has gradually become a more important source of government revenue, with Hungary having the highest rates, but the two other countries have similar structures, and rate differences are actually minor. The social security system is one of the most significant burdens everywhere, resulting in high linear contributions on wages (those in Czechoslovakia being somewhat lower than in Hungary and Poland). Payroll and wage taxes are everywhere a significant component of the revenue side.

3. Problems on the Expenditure Side

Before 1990, the engagement of general government in redistributing the national product was very large in all three countries, though it was smallest in Poland and the highest probably in Czechoslovakia. At present, the most extensive system of expenditures is to be found in Hungary. In that country, the last communist governments had planned, but for political reasons did not introduce, a comprehensive reform of the 'state household'. Its aim was to cut energetically the generous social welfare expenditures that got out of control at the end of the 1980s. However, not only did the last communist governments fail to undertake the necessary measures, but the first democratically elected government also postponed them.

Consequently, while revenues have decreased not only in absolute terms but also relative to the declining recorded GDP, the proportion of expenditure relative to GDP has not changed significantly in the last four years, implying a fall in real government expenditures of about 20 per cent since 1989. Furthermore, only very modest structural reforms have been undertaken in order to disburden future taxpayers. Most striking is the high share (above 10 per cent) of the pension system in GDP; reforms introduced in 1993 are too modest and will not relieve the central budgets' burden in the foreseeable future. Child allowances are also generous. Finally, large-scale unemployment has contributed to the deteriorating budgetary position.

It is instructive to compare the efforts made on the expenditure side by the various countries. As we have seen in Hungary,

real expenditures have fallen by about 20 per cent since 1989; in Poland, the fall has been about 30 per cent, and according to van der Willigen (1994) it has been an astonishing 45–50 per cent in Czechoslovakia. The huge size of the expenditure reduction in Czechoslovakia is partly explained by the enormous share of government expenditure to GDP in 1989 (over 70 per cent). Much of this was cross-subsidization within the state industrial sector, which has proved relatively easy to eliminate in all three countries. In 1992, general government expenditure as a share of GDP was about 55 per cent in Czechoslovakia, significantly below the Hungarian level of about 64 per cent (which has remained roughly constant as a share of GDP since 1989), and significantly above the Polish figure of 45 per cent.[1] However, consolidation of financial transfers between different levels of government is unfortunately still very primitive, even in the three most advanced post-communist economies; as Semjén (1994) shows, general government expenditure varied widely according to different estimates, with the lowest estimate being 57 per cent of GDP. A great degree of caution in interpreting the figures is, therefore, well advised.

The relative size of general government revenues in Poland (approximately 38 per cent of GDP) is much lower than in Czechoslovakia (52 per cent of GDP in 1992) and Hungary (58 per cent of GDP). Thus both Hungary, with the highest share of expenditure in GDP, and Poland, with the lowest, had excessive deficits (roughly 7 per cent of GDP in each country), while Czechoslovakia had a relatively small one in 1992 (3 per cent of GDP according to van der Willigen). The smallness of the Czechoslovak deficit was due on the one hand to the thoroughness with which expenditure was cut in that country, and on the other to the relative buoyancy of tax revenues (in particular corporate income tax revenues). What these figures show is that if deficits are to be reduced (as they need to be—see Section 6), then this must take the form of expenditure reduction in Hungary, but in Poland it may be possible to increase revenues through better tax administration, though probably not through increased tax rates.[2]

4. *The Czechoslovak Paradox*

The markedly different performance of the Czechoslovak fiscal sphere is one of the most interesting developments in Central Europe. Czechoslovakia showed considerable restraint in its social policies between 1990 and 1992. Consequently, the share of these expenditures in GDP has only slightly increased, i.e. their real value has diminished while enterprise subsidies dried up. This is not much different from what has happened in the two other countries, but the Czechoslovaks were marginally tougher than anyone else. On top of this, wage policies were very restrictive in the same period. This has resulted in a situation in which profits have not plummeted the way they have in the other first wave reformers. This is the crucial difference between Czechoslovakia and the other two countries, and it is an extraordinary achievement given that recorded GDP has fallen in the period by 20 per cent. The share of profit tax in GDP has remained virtually unchanged between 1989 and 1992, as the numbers of van der Willigen (1994) indicate.

On the other hand, it is also true that the economic transformation in the former Czechoslovakia is in many respects behind that in Hungary and Poland. Microeconomic restructuring has only started. This has helped enterprises whose output has decreased considerably not to fire employees. In the Czech Republic, unemployment virtually does not exist, therefore it is no large burden on the budget.[3] Unemployment benefits have been constructed from the very beginning to discourage unemployment rather than encourage it. However, there have been no enterprise bankruptcies at all, i.e. the threat of business failure has not pushed firms towards economising labour costs.[4]

Beginning in the fall of 1993, microeconomic adjustment will finally begin to appear in the Czech Republic: the capital market will value the assets privatized with vouchers, and bankruptcy rules will slowly start working. These effects, combined with the abolition of formal wage controls and the unpleasant consequences of the breakup of the country, may increase the pressure on the budget.[5] Deficits, as shown by van der Willigen,

had already started to build up in 1992—particularly in Slovakia—and may increase in 1993. Still, the low public debt inherited from the past may allow the successor states to avoid the
further expenditure cuts (and possible tax increases) required of
Hungary and Poland. There are widespread expectations that in
this respect also the Czechs will do better than the Slovaks.
However, recent events in Slovakia seem to show that expectations about extreme differences between short-term developments in the two countries are probably exaggerated.

5. The Crisis in the Banking Sector

The way the countries will handle the bad debt problem in the
banking sector is an issue that will have a direct impact on the
size of public debt in the years to come.[6] In Czechoslovakia,
the Konsolidacni Banka was formed in the initial phase of
transition to take over working capital financing loans from
the banking sector; subsequently, some of the privatization
revenues were used to recapitalize the banking sector. As of
1993, the bad debt problem has already recurred, as a suitable
incentive structure in the financial sector is not yet in place.

At the end of 1992, Hungary implemented a poorly designed
loan consolidation programme. Bad assets were replaced, to the
value of 150 billion forints (less than \$2 billion) by long-term
government bonds. Again, the bulk of these assets will not be
recovered and the bonds are going to increase the public debt.
Bank recapitalization was supposed to come in 1993, again
without any mechanism or conditionality to secure improvement in bank lending. The government's inability to act on a
complex subject like this on the eve of the 1994 elections has
postponed the new loan consolidation; 'debtor consolidation',
however, is going ahead without much guarantee that this is the
last bailing out of firms. The generous government guarantees
to ailing firms is especially worrying because it implicitly
increases the public debt; its real extent will be faced by the
new, post-election government.

The Polish 'Banking Agreement' regulation, which will be in
effect for three years from early 1993, tries to look at the issue

in a more complex way. Its initial phase is recapitalization of the banks to the level of 12 per cent capital adequacy ratio (according to the Cook Committee weighting). Subsequently, enterprises can apply for financial restructuring at their lead banks (since the courts are generally unable as yet to deal with insolvency procedures sufficiently rapidly or on a sufficiently large scale). The banks then organize the restructuring agreement, and the consent of 51 per cent of the creditors (and of the credits they represent) will be enough to strike the deal. The law also tries to generate a secondary market for debts and provides incentives to concentrate the ownership of bad assets outside the banking system, as debt-for-equity swaps are envisaged for claims exceeding 30 per cent of the capital of the debtor firm.

6. *Implications for Inflation and National Debt*

In spite of the increasing budgetary gap in all three countries, inflation has decreased significantly over the last three years. Each of the countries has experienced a 'corrective inflation', i.e. one that eliminated shortages through price liberalization. The impact of this was obviously less in Hungary (but still noticeable) and the strongest in Poland. Besides price liberalization, the introduction of new taxes, especially of VAT, has caused large price jumps. Over time, however, fewer such one-time operations were left and consequently their effect has been declining. If we take the producer price index as a good indicator of where the consumer price index is tending, then we can expect inflation to decline over the next few years in all three countries. In Hungary, for instance, PPI inflation was 12 per cent in 1992 while CPI inflation was 22 per cent (see Fig. 28). However, the level of 'underlying' inflation cannot be calculated simply by cleaning headline inflation of relative price adjustments and by ending up with something quite close to the producer price index: the deficit and debt levels in the various countries will play a crucial role in its determination.

Hungarian economists believed in the 1980s that the elimination of subsidies to enterprises would close the budgetary gap.

However, as we have seen, the combined effects of the shrinking tax base, as well as increasing expenditures on certain welfare items, have on the contrary resulted in growing deficits. However, the impact of the deficit on inflation has been modest so far. The primary reasons for this are that household savings have soared and, at the same time, the banking sector has reduced credit to non-government. The initial cause of the latter has not been crowding out by government borrowing, but was rather the weak financial situation of the enterprises. Tougher financial regulations have caused a very cautious lending policy by the banks towards enterprises. Consequently, banks have been able to decrease deposit rates to significantly below consumer price inflation. Government paper has been priced only slightly above the deposit rates and yet loan rates have remained high.

In this way, the savings of the households, and to some extent those of the business sector, have financed the budget deficit through the intermediation of the financial sector, while the credit crunch imposed by the banks has resulted in sharply falling deposit and government paper rates through 1992 and the first months of 1993, in spite of the government's growing demand on the money market. As a result, in 1992 the public debt may actually have decreased in real terms (data is quite messy in this respect as well; Semjén, 1994) and has not increased in terms of (the falling) GDP. However, this should be regarded as an exceptional situation. Persistence of high deficits will inevitably lead to further increases in public debt (now about 80 per cent of GDP), increasing interest rates, and growing inflationary pressure. Without serious measures here, one cannot hope that consumer price inflation will in fact fall to the level of producer price inflation. At the time of writing, what one can observe is rather the accumulation of inflationary pressures.

In this respect, the situation is similar in all three countries, although the problem is the most intense in Hungary. Trade balances have deteriorated in 1993, primarily because in 1991 and 1992 exchange rates have increasingly been used as primary tools of anti-inflationary policy. Consequently, domestic

currencies have become increasingly overvalued; the European recession has added to the problem. As devaluations have become inevitable, their impact will add to the pressure of growing public debt.

The situation is similar in Poland to the extent that the bulk of recent government deficits has been financed by the crowding out of credit to non-government. As in Hungary, banks have tightened their lending policies considerably, so that increased government borrowing has been accompanied by falling, rather than increasing, interest rates on government paper. However, it must be remembered that were it not for continuing government borrowing, loan rates could be even lower, improving the profitability of the corporate sector, making it possible for banks to lend more to that sector safely, and possibly even increasing government tax revenue.

Furthermore, at present about 40 per cent of the net domestic assets (NDA) of the Polish banking system consists in credit to government. Since NDA constitutes about 22 per cent of GDP, and has remained at this level since the end of 1990—suggesting that there is no reason to expect it to increase significantly in the medium term—the non-inflationary financing of a deficit of current (1992) dimensions (approximately 7 per cent of GDP) is clearly impossible. It would require a 50 per cent fall in real credit to non-government in the first year, and the total elimination of such credit in the second year of such a deficit.[7]

In order to avoid such a situation, the National Bank of Poland (NBP) tries to ensure that the banking system has sufficient liquidity to finance the deficit without excessive crowding out of credit to non-government. The deficit is thus financed from four sources: crowding out, NBP emission for the purpose of deficit financing (which accounted for about one-third of the deficit in 1992), NBP emission so as to maintain the liquidity of the banking system (increase in rediscount credit made available to commercial banks), and increased nominal money (and therefore credit) creation through NBP acceptance of an increase in the money multiplier. Credit to non-government in Poland is about 20 per cent

of GDP, a very low figure indeed by international standards. If we accept that further real crowding out is therefore possible only to a very limited extent, then in the medium term any large deficits in Poland will have to be financed by emission.[8]

This is how we come up against some very unpleasant monetarist arithmetic for Poland. Zloty M2/GDP is about 23 per cent, and has remained at this level for two and a half years.[9] With a money multiplier of about two, a deficit of 5 per cent of GDP financed through emission implies a rate of inflation in excess of 40 per cent per annum. Sharply growing foreign debt service obligations from mid-1994, as well as recently growing current account deficits, add to the vulnerability of the Polish situation.[10]

The above problems of financing the deficit are smaller in Hungary, where the deficit was approximately the same size as in Poland, but where the money supply was equivalent to 53 per cent of GDP at the end of 1992. For the moment, such problems are effectively absent in the former Czechoslovakia, where the deficit was 3 per cent of GDP, and the money supply was the equivalent of 80 per cent of GDP.[11]

Looking at the question of the impact of fiscal deficits on inflation in a longer-term framework, it is useful to examine the ratio of total national debt to GDP. This ratio may be—surprisingly—quite similar in all three countries. According to official figures, the ratio is about 70 per cent in Hungary (according to our figures, by the end of 1993 this actually might be as high as 80 per cent), 55 per cent in Poland[12] and about 40 per cent in the Czech Republic.[13] However, the picture may change radically once the contingent liabilities of the budget resulting from bad debts in the banking sector are taken into account. Here the fact that the ratio of credit to non-government to GDP is very high in the Czech Republic (roughly 70 per cent) works against that country, whereas Poland's very low ratio of CNG/GDP (20 per cent) works in its favour. Hungary lies in between, with a CNG/GDP ratio of about 55 per cent. If about a quarter of CNG needs to be taken over by the budget, then this would imply a total consolidated national debt relative to GDP of about 60 per cent in the Czech Republic and about 60 per

cent in Poland.[14] In Hungary, the 1992 loan consolidation has already shifted part of the debt to government, but other large-scale operations may take the national debt as high as 90 per cent of GDP. A lower net loss to the banking system would mean a greater differentiation between the three countries, as well as lower consolidated debt levels all round.[15] However, the obverse of high ratios of CNG/GDP is high ratios of money supply to GDP, which, as we have already noted, makes the non-inflationary financing of large national debts far easier in Hungary and the Czech Republic.

We thus end with the conclusion that both Hungary and Poland have probably reached the end of their opportunities for running large budget deficits combined with declining inflation, as has been witnessed since 1989. As we have already noted, clear signs of the reversal are already there. Since accelerating inflation would probably have very severe consequences for medium-term economic growth (particularly through its effect on foreign direct investment), both countries are faced with an absolute need to cut budget deficits sharply. In Poland, this may occur partly as a result of increased revenues due to the ongoing economic recovery and an improved tax structure and administration (1993 has seen the introduction of both a unified personal income tax and of the VAT). However, expenditure cuts are likely to be necessary, particularly as the deficit will be increased by an annual 4 per cent of GDP from mid-1994 because of the need to service foreign debt.[16] In Hungary almost all of the burden will have to be taken by expenditure cuts. However, a heavily unpopular government is waiting for the elections, expected in the spring of 1994, and thus one cannot expect the necessary tough decisions with a long-term structural impact to be launched before early 1995.

The Czech Republic is clearly best placed, with both low deficits and probably the lowest national debt, as well as a very high demand for real money balances. However, even here it requires only a somewhat pessimistic estimate of bad debts in the banking system to suggest that the country is almost at the limit of what can be considered a safe ratio of national debt to GDP.

   The example of Spain (Barchetta, 1994) shows that East Central Europe faces a far harder task than countries that have had
the fortune of not experiencing several decades of communism.
Spain started out after Franco with low taxes, very low public
debt, and a largely capitalist economy—characteristics that not
even the fast tract reformers (with the partial exception of
Czechoslovakia) of East Central Europe share. Spain could
expand its state welfare services and accumulate a manageable
level of public debt while increasing the tax-raising capacity of
the state. The Hungarian and Czech Governments, already tax-
ing away around 60 per cent of GDP certainly do not have this
option; they, as well as the Polish Government, have to let the
capitalist structures develop, and, at the same time, must make
very hard decisions in cutting budgetary expenditures—a task
certainly unprecedented in modern economic history.

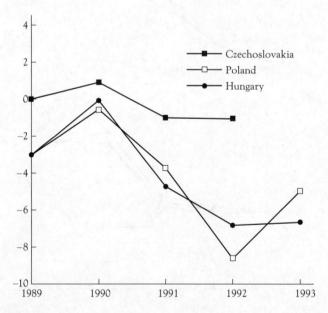

Figure 27   *Government budget balance in Czechoslovakia, Hungary, and Poland*

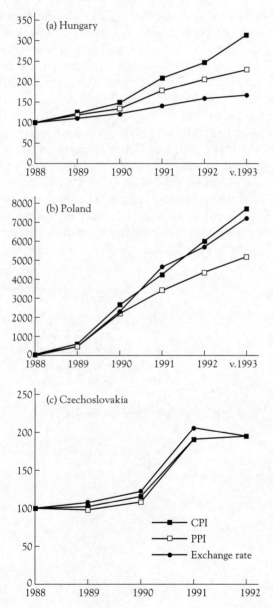

Figure 28 *Prices and exchange rates in Czechoslovakia, Hungary, and Poland*

NOTES

This chapter first appeared in *Developing Public Finance in Emerging Market Economies*, ed. K. Mizsei (Institute of East-West Studies, New York, 1994).

1. Down from about 55 per cent in 1988.
2. The larger size of the Polish agricultural sector, usually difficult to tax, is another problem. However, this should not be overstressed, as agriculture contributes less than 7 per cent of Poland's GDP, as compared to 6.5 per cent in Hungary.
3. Although underemployment is, of course, a burden on the enterprises.
4. Employment has fallen by a quarter, of which 7 percentage points has been due to a reduction in the labour force, and the remaining 19 percentage points to a fall in participation.
5. Before what appears to have been a politically motivated revision, the Statistical Office of the Czech Republic registered a 10 per cent fall in industrial output in the first quarter of 1993. This has now been revised to −2 per cent.
6. The authors do not share the opinion formulated by many Western analysts that the old debts of public enterprises should simply be taken over by the state; their recovery after such a transaction would become more doubtful than ever (see Begg and Portes, 1992; Mizsei, 1993).
7. The deficits in 1993 and 1994 have indeed been far smaller, at about 3.5 per cent of GDP.
8. Increases in the money supply due to increases in the money multiplier have the same effect as emission. Imagine a 50 per cent increase in the nominal money supply as a result of an increase in the money multiplier, of which half goes to finance the deficit: inflation will be 50 per cent. Exactly the same effect would obtain if the money multiplier remained constant at a value of two, and base money were increased by 50 per cent, with all of the additional central bank liabilities constituting additional credit to government. It goes without saying that emission has the same effect whether it results from direct lending by the central bank to government or whether it is due to the central bank maintaining the liquidity of the banking system in the face of government borrowing from the commercial banks.
9. Net foreign liabilities of the banking system (i.e. foreign currency deposits) are roughly equivalent to net foreign assets (i.e. net international reserves), leaving NDA roughly equal to zloty M2.
10. The Polish budget benefited greatly from effectively not servicing the country's international debt in the critical period of 1990 to 1993.
11. The money/GDP ratio is about the same in the two successor states.
12. On the assumption of a $45 billion foreign debt, a $90 billion GDP and an internal debt equivalent to 10 per cent of GDP.
13. The latter figure is based on an estimate of Czech GDP of $30 billion,

and a foreign debt for the Czech Republic of $7 billion, as well as an internal debt of 17 per cent of GDP (see van der Willigen, 1994).

14. This would be the equivalent of a loss of 50 per cent on 50 per cent of the loans made to non-government by the banking system, which may be somewhat over-pessimistic.

15. If the loss is 15 per cent of CNG, then the Hungarian debt becomes 78 per cent of GDP, the Polish 57 per cent, and the Czech 52 per cent.

16. In the absence of any other changes the deficit would then reach 10 per cent of GDP.

13

Universal Banking and Economic Growth in Post-Communist Economies

1. Universal Banks and Corporate Governance

A number of authors with otherwise very different views on the transition of PCEs have postulated an important role for banks in the corporate governance of non-financial firms (e.g. Lipton and Sachs, 1991, and Corbett and Mayer, 1992). The idea is that banks in PCEs should follow the model of universal banks in Germany: owning, and controlling as proxies, large equity stakes in non-financial firms, and having significant representation on their supervisory boards (most PCEs have a two board structure of the German kind for their larger joint stock companies).

The case for the universal bank intimately involved with its non-financial customers has been made most eloquently by Gerschenkron himself (1968), describing the situation in Germany in the second half of the 19th century:

The inadequacy in the number of available entrepreneurs could be remedied or substituted for by increasing the size of plant and enterprise above what otherwise would have been an optimum size. In Germany, the various incompetencies of the individual entrepreneurs were offset by the device of splitting the entrepreneurial function: the German investment banks—a powerful invention, comparable in economic effect to that of the steam engine—were in their capital-supplying functions a substitute for the insufficiency of the previously created wealth willingly placed at the disposal of the entrepreneurs. But they were also a substitute for entrepreneurial deficiencies. From their central vantage points of control, the banks participated actively in shaping the major—and sometimes even not so major—decisions of individual enterprises. It was they who very often mapped out a firm's

path of growth, conceived far-sighted plans, decided on major technological and locational innovations, and arranged for mergers and capital increases (p. 137).

Thus the universal bank is seen as an instrument thanks to which the backward country can catch up with, and maybe overtake, the most advanced—Anglo-Saxon—market economies. The universal bank achieves this aim through 'far sighted plans' which it can elaborate successfully thanks to its 'central vantage point of control' and because its 'capital supplying function' compensates for the 'insufficiency of wealth placed at the disposal of the entrepreneur'. In other words, as was believed to be the case with central planning, the universal bank is supposed to make possible a greater mobilization of savings and their successful application to long-term projects. The aim and the method remain the same, only the institutional instrument is different. The wonder is that Eastern Europe is not awash with state supported (and owned) banks, owning large and concentrated shareholdings in non-financial businesses, and claiming to be budding Deutsche Banks!

How relevant, in fact, is the German-type universal bank to the conditions and needs of PCEs? We need to distinguish between 'German-type' universal banks which are intimately involved in the ownership and control of non-financial firms,[1] and 'non-German' universal banks, which merely provide a wide range of financial services to their clients. Whether banks in PCEs should develop along the lines of 'non-German' universal banks is not one we shall address. The answer depends on whether there are greater economies of scale or scope in the 'financial supermarket' or 'specialist bank' approaches. It has implications for the non-financial sector of the economy mainly to the extent that greater efficiency implies lower costs of financial services, and as such it is not a problem of transition but of final destination of the banking system in PCEs, and thus one which can be addressed at a far later stage in the reform process.

2. The Suitability of German-type Universal
Banks in the Early Stage of Transition

Two key facts have to be remembered about PCE banks in the early stages of transition: very low banking skills and state ownership.[2] Poor banking skills are relevant because medium- and long-term lending is harder than short-term lending since unpredictability (risk) is greater as the term of loans increases. Low banking skills have already led to significant loan losses in spite of the fact that, outside Hungary and the former Czechoslovakia, almost all lending is short term. If PCE banks attempted to engage in a large amount of long term lending the scale of these losses would be even greater. Yet it is the provision of long-term credit which is supposed to justify the close bank-firm relationship of the German model. PCE banks therefore need to learn to allocate credit effectively by first learning to allocate short-term, self-liquidating credit for working capital. It is only once they have mastered this that they can prudently go on to medium- and long-term financing,[3] and it is only once this stage of expertise has been reached that German-style close involvement with customers may be expected to bring benefits.

A high gearing ratio causes a conflict of interests between lender and borrower, increases agency costs and reduces investment relative to the optimum level. Bernanke and Gertler (1987) show that the higher the leverage ratio in a project, the more the interests of the borrower and lender diverge. This is because the return on equity is higher on a riskier project the higher the leverage, while the expected yield to the lender is smaller. The relevance to PCEs is that they suffer from low levels of equity capital among non-financial firms for two reasons. SOEs may have large amounts of equity, but this equity is 'weak' because stakeholders' (the state's, managers' and workers') rights to it are poorly defined.[4] Such equity can act as collateral for loans, but it does not act adequately to motivate SOE borrowers to avoid excessively risky loans, as managers of such firms will not themselves lose much net worth if a project for which they have borrowed to finance proves unviable. New

private sector firms, on the other hand, simply have little equity compared to the amount of capital they could profitably invest in projects because transition opens up a vast array of profitable new projects for the private sector (Chapter 14).

Bernanke and Gertler argue further that the conflict of interests between lenders and borrowers when leverage is high increases the agency costs of the investment process, and hence reduces the level of investment below its optimum level. As we have seen, in PCEs this is likely to be the case both in the new private sector and in SOEs. This may help to account for the widespread populist pressure for 'cheap money' which one observes in the PCEs. Proponents of the German model claim that close control by the bank, and its access to insider information regarding its customers, makes up for the lack of equity capital in the borrowing business and reduces the agency costs of monitoring loans. However, the shortage of equity in SOEs in PCEs is not absolute, but is of a special sort which we have called 'equity weakness'. As a result of this 'weak equity', SOE managements are not to be expected to be as concerned about the net worth of their firms as are managers of private firms. Although German-type access to insider information by lenders might improve the running of SOEs if the lending banks were private, the actual situation in early years of transition is that large commercial banks are almost all state owned so that the equity within these state commercial banks (SCBs) is just as 'weak' as the equity in the SOEs they lend to, and bank managements also cannot be trusted to maximize the net worth of their institutions.

In this situation, 'fuzzy' instruments (such as long-term non-quoted debt or non-quoted equity) which make it harder to assess the value of a firm's liabilities to a bank, but which are so important in the intimate bank-firm relationship of the German model, need to be avoided until after SCBs have been privatized. It is clearly harder to judge whether a loan is good if it is long term than if it is short term, making long-term credit the 'fuzzier' instrument. Even more dangerous would be the ability of SCBs to take equity positions in their customers, a key element of the German model. Non-quoted equity is the

ultimate 'fuzzy' form of financing, whose commercial nature or otherwise is highly opaque and whose true value is only revealed when the shareholder exits by selling his stake. An SCB wishing to hide the fact that it has made a bad loan would find it very convenient if it could purchase part of the borrower's equity thus enabling the servicing, or even full repayment, of the loan.[5] On the other hand, quoted equity—which is not at all 'fuzzy' as regards its value—is highly volatile, putting the bank's capital base potentially at risk. Furthermore, the concentration of both the debt and equity liabilities of a non-financial firm in the hands of a given bank may increase the riskiness of the latter's exposure, unless there are stringent exposure limits.[6]

Altogether, the suggestion that PCEs adopt a German-style relationship between banks and enterprises fails to take into account the fact that, as was stressed in Chapter 5, the main challenge facing SCBs in PCEs is to shift from providing 'systemically bad' (i.e. non-commercial) credit to providing systemically good credit. Everything which reduces the clarity with which a judgement can be made as to whether loans are good or not hampers this vital transformation. If PCEs were to follow the German model there is a real danger that SCBs, which have only recently been created out of departments of the state monobank, and are only finding their feet as true commercial institutions, could become the focal points of large financial-industrial holding companies, which under pressure from governments and from non-financial enterprises, might altogether fail to switch their lending policies to a commercial basis.

Finally, it has turned out to be significantly easier to privatize non-financial SOEs than to privatize the banks in most transition economies. With major banks remaining state owned for quite a few years after the start of the transition in many countries, bank control of the equity of private sector and privatized firms might effectively mean a degree of renationalization of the economy, which is unlikely to be either economically desirable or politically acceptable.

But the unsuitability of German-type universal banks does

not mean that the banking system in PCEs cannot evolve in the direction of efficiency and commercialism. SOEs often have a considerable amount of net worth which can be used to collateralize loans. So that arms length, asset based lending—particularly in the short term—is perfectly feasible. This is the kind of lending which can form the basis for banks in PCEs to develop the skills which they need. It is worth remembering, that this is the kind of lending which first appeared at the beginning of capitalism.

3. The German Model and the Intermediate Phase of Economic Transition

Let us now turn to the intermediate phase of economic transition, during which it can be assumed that banks already have some skill in making medium- and long-term loans.[7] How strong are the arguments in favour of the German model in this context? It seems likely that this phase of the transition in the banking systems of PCEs will more or less correspond to the period of resumed growth of output by non-financial businesses. This would be the time when enterprise adjustment through the cutting back of unwanted output and the cutting out of unnecessary capacity would be giving way, in terms of its overall effects, to accelerating growth in the output of new products and in the creation of new capacity. It would thus be a period of strong and growing demand for capital.

An advantage of the German model in this context is that the average cost of capital would be reduced (debt being cheaper than equity). On the other hand, Aoki (1984) develops a model in which, when banks are shareholders and have control of the capital structure of firms, they opt for a higher level of debt than that which maximizes the value of the shares. In this model banks have no advantage from holding all the shares of a firm. They choose the smallest stake which gives them control over the firm's borrowing decisions. Stakes of 5–20 per cent, such as are often observed in Germany and Japan, seem to optimize banks returns. If control can be exercised through the use of

proxy votes as in Germany, then the benefit of control can be had without the cost of having to own shares.

Moreover, Steinherr and Huveneers (1992) argue that in the German model the leverage ratio of non-financial businesses is raised, not just as a result of the reduction in the cost of debt but also due to the increase in the cost of external equity. Thus the German model provides cheaper long-term debt to firms,[8] at the cost of more expensive external equity. This is because managers of firms controlled by banks have considerable lee-way in allocating free cash flow (what are called 'hidden reserves' in Germany). Since there are few hostile takeovers (i.e. the market for corporate control is weak), there is a major principal-agent problem, so that agency costs for equity holders are high, making equity relatively unattractive to those share-holders who do not participate in sharing out the free cash flow.

One of the key problems of PCEs is SOE privatization. The German banking model would thus make privatization slower, though possibly 'better', as flotations would become harder, leaving only 'trade sales' to other large (presumably mainly foreign) firms as the major vehicle for the state to sell SOEs. However, the political obstacles which can stand in the way of privatization sales to foreigners are well known. Possibly more important in the medium term, the same problem of the high cost of equity would face firms which had already been priva-tized by some 'non-equivalent' method, such as voucher sale or leasing, but which needed a capital injection.

The feasibility of the German model also depends on the inflation record of the PCE concerned. Henderson (1993) points to the UK's weaker record on inflation as a cause of the greater importance of equity markets in financing firms in that country. Higher inflation means higher volatility of nom-inal interest rates, which means higher risk to both lender and borrower, independently of whether contracts mostly involve fixed or variable rates. Given higher inflation, variable nominal interest rates may (but need not) mean more stable real rates. Even if they do, this happens at the cost of greater real amorti-zation of a loan when the nominal rate is high, which can put considerable strain on a borrower's cash flow. At the same time

fixed nominal interest rates in an environment of high (and therefore variable) inflation, mean highly variable real interest rates. Both suppliers and demanders of capital can protect themselves from these kinds of volatility by using equity rather than debt. Thus, the close bank-firm relationship in both Germany and Japan has depended not only on a larger share of long-term credit, but also on a larger proportion of fixed interest loans than in many other countries, and this has in turn been made possible by these countries' superior inflation record. Indeed, one may suspect that the determination of the authorities in both countries to maintain very low inflation has been due to their realization that their bank based financial systems are more vulnerable than others to the disruption even moderate inflation would cause.

In PCEs one can see the likely effects of a country's inflationary past on its ability to adopt the German model by looking at the ratio of bank credit to non-government as a share of GDP. In Czechoslovakia this share was about 75 per cent,[9] in Hungary it is about 40 per cent, in Poland it is about 20 per cent, while in most remaining PCEs it is below 20 per cent. Those countries with a history of very high inflation find that the population minimizes its holdings of domestic money, which reduces the amount of real credit in the economy.[10] High budget deficits and domestic government debt also contribute to the problem, crowding out the amount of credit available to non-government. Moreover, experience shows that post-stabilization remonetization of the economy although significant, remains limited (e.g. in Poland the domestic money supply rose from 12 per cent to 20 per cent of GDP after stabilization). Countries with low credit to non-government/GDP ratios cannot implement the German model, simply because the credit available to their banking systems will be inadequate for the external financing of the capital needs of their firms. Thus, only the Czech Republic together with—possibly—Hungary and Slovakia, could be potential candidates for German-style universal banking, even in the second phase of transformation, when inflation in these countries ought to be down to single figures per annum.

4. The Role of Bank Credit in Economic Transformation of PCEs: The Case of Poland

In Poland bank credit has gone to those to whom it should not have gone (mainly the state sector losers), and has not gone in sufficient quantity to the winners, in particular not to the rapidly growing private sector, for whom its lack has—interestingly—not proved an unsurmountable obstacle (Chapter 14).

Gomulka (1993*b*) has shown that in Poland 43 per cent of credit ended up with the 10 per cent of firms which have the worst 'sales adjusted quick ratios'.[11] Moreover, the extremely dynamic private sector has had very little access to credit. Some 29 per cent of bank credit to non-government went to private businesses (excluding co-operatives) in Poland at the end of 1992.[12] At that time the private sector (excluding co-operatives) accounted for about 45 per cent of GDP and for 60 per cent of employment outside the budget sector.[13] What is more, a very large proportion of credit received by the private sector was misallocated. It was lent to firms which Gomulka places in his 'very bad' category, that is to say with 'sales adjusted quick ratios' of less than −1.5. Out of 22.5 trillion zlotys lent to large private firms at the end of 1992, 16.9 trillion zlotys— or 75 per cent—was to firms in this 'very bad' category! Among medium-sized firms results were not quite so bad, only 50 per cent of loans went to such firms. If the share of loans to 'very bad' businesses was about the same among loans made to small private firms and sole traders, the total amount of lending which went to private sector firms not in the 'very bad' category probably amounted to some 23 trillion zlotys, or under 10 per cent of credit to non-government. Given that ratio of credit to non-government to GDP was about 20 per cent at this time, the ratio to GDP of credit going to private businesses which did not fall into Gomulka's 'very bad' category was about 2 per cent.[14]

It seems very unlikely that this tiny amount of 'good credit' for the private sector could have played an important role in the exceptionally rapid growth of that sector in 1990–3 (Chapter 14). During this period, the non-cooperative private sector's share increased as follows in the various branches of economy:

Table 25 Poland: growth of the share of the private sector in output

	1989	1993[a]
Industry	7.4	32.3
Construction	30.0	80.0
Transport	5.9	39.2

[a] First three quarters of 1993. Guesstimates for the non-cooperative private sector have been obtained by assuming that the co-operative sector's share of output remained constant after the last date for which we have information concerning it, that is Q1–Q3 of 1992. The co-operative sector's share was declining up to that time in industry, increasing in construction and roughly constant in transport (Chapter 14).

Source: Chapter 14 and GUS IoSS-GK (1993).

Moreover, this very rapid growth of the private sector was only marginally due to privatization of state enterprises. In mid-1993 privatized enterprises accounted for 4.4 per cent of the revenue of all current and previously state owned enterprises (GUS *Informacja*, 1993). If revenue and output shares were roughly equal, and if in mid-1993 about 45 per cent of GDP was generated in the private sector,[16] then about 2.3 percentage points of this was accounted for by privatized firms.

To the extent that the state sector has been privatized it is through the privatization of its physical assets, and not through the privatization of organized state owned businesses. In this process—which has been the most important element in the transformation of the Polish economy—bank credit has played a very small role. Indeed, on the basis of the Polish case one can perhaps formulate a hypothesis about the microeconomic unimportance of bank credit in the early stages of transition in a PCE.

What, then, are the actual sources of capital accumulation and economic development in this early phase of economic transition, and what mode of financing is appropriate to them? It seems that in Poland (for which the data seems most detailed) since 1989 private sector expansion has resulted from the ploughback of retained earnings in existing firms and the

establishment of new private sector firms. The market as a selection process has operated through the product market rather than through the capital market. Successful firms have made large profits and thus been able to expand, unsuccessful firms have failed and gone bankrupt. In this way not only successful projects, but also successful entrepreneurs and successful business organizations have been selected, and the information capital of the whole economy under the radically new circumstances of the transition has been increased (Atkeson and Kehoe, 1993). It is difficult to imagine that these selection processes, which are vital if the new capitalist economy is to function successfully in Central and Eastern Europe, could have been undertaken by capital markets, given the very low quality of publically available information regarding projects and the almost complete absence of information regarding entrepreneurs and organizations at the beginning of the transition.

5. Conclusion: Building Appropriate Financial Systems in Post-Communist Economies

What are the lessons from five years of economic transition in PCEs as regards the banking sector? The first is surely that, given how little banking systems have contributed to transformation and economic restructuring in Central Europe, the main motto should be 'safety first'. But safety against what?

The first threat is that of bad debts in the banking system. For old bad debts, the solution is either a global debt write-off, combined with the introduction of 100 per cent reserve banking for banks which benefit from the write off (Chapter 11), or a Polish-style 'Enterprise and Bank Financial Restructuring Project' (EBFRP—Mizsei, 1994). For new bad debts, the answer is very high capital and/or reserve ratios in those parts of the banking system which benefit from implicit deposit insurance. Although such requirements are often thought of as a tax on banking services, they can also be considered as a premium paid for implicit deposit insurance, or as a requirement on the

behaviour of the insured to reduce the insurer's (government's) exposure.[17]

Of the two approaches, high capital ratios make less sense as long as bank capital is state owned (unless, as in Poland, capital adequacy is a criterion for SCB privatization, and bank managements are very interested in privatization), and as long as bank auditing and supervisory skills are rare (valuation of bank equity requires realistic loan classification). High reserve ratios are easier to apply, and as one approaches 100 per cent reserves on deposits the need for high levels of capital to provide a cushion against bad loans disappears.

SCBs should initially concentrate on developing their payments services, which it can be argued, are the most basic and important services they supply in a newly marketizing economy. The first liberalization would then be to allow them to extend the safest kind of credit available (i.e. for self-liquidating working capital). As skills develop, the kind of loan business permitted would become more varied and longer term, obligatory reserve ratios would be reduced while, initially, capital adequacy ratios would need to be increased (to provide a cushion for greater loan risk, and to prepare the SCB for privatization).

Second, there is the question of severe moral hazard developing as a result of successive recapitalizations of the banking system by the state. Much will depend on the success of the Polish EBFRP (Kawalec, Sikora, and Rymaszewski, 1993). If it fails to avoid the moral hazard problem, this will strengthen the arguments for very narrow banking in the first period of the transition. If it succeeds, this will strengthen the view that bad loan losses resulting from excessively 'wide' banking during early transition, though unfortunate, are a mistake which can be successfully corrected at a later stage.

Of course, such a gradualist/conservative approach to banking reform suggests that there is very little scope for the development of German-style universal banks in PCEs for many years to come. This is because the danger of loose financial control of borrowers seems to be augmented when banks become universal while they are still dominated by state owned

equity and have developed few skills even for short-term credit allocation, let alone for the long-term credit allocation and equity finance of clients. Moreover, German-type financial systems require very low rates of inflation indeed, something which is unlikely to be achieved in PCEs for as much as a decade after the beginning of the transition.

The third danger is that of a high level of politicization of credit allocation (this danger persists as long as most banks are state owned, which remains the case in Central Europe outside the Czech Republic).[18] Again, high reserve ratios in the SCBs reduce the scope for such distortions. Furthermore, if SCBs were largely limited to providing payments services and some limited credit for working capital, they might be easier to privatize.[19] Finally, if the SCBs functions are limited in this way, their resistance to the entry of foreign banks (which would be kept out of the payments business) might be reduced.

NOTES

1. Though see Edwards and Fischer (1994) for a dissenting view.
2. In Russia and Bulgaria where many of the large banks are effectively in private hands, they do not seem to be in the hands of 'fit persons'.
3. The attempt to introduce German-type universal banking in PCEs in the early stages of transition reminds one of other attempts in the region to 'speed up history'. Like those, it would be a high risk strategy.
4. To be undertaken, a project must not only be profitable, but there must also exist a way for the stakeholders to benefit from its profitability (something which is hampered by tax based incomes policies, for example).
5. Debt-equity swaps have resulted in Hungarian banks having as much of a problem with the bad equity in their asset portfolios as with bad loans.
6. With SOEs larger, relative to the size of the economy, than large firms in the West and with SCBs' balance sheets relatively smaller than those of Western banks, exposure to large firms has presented a significant prudential hazard to banks during the early transition. If equity holdings are kept in a separate subsidiary, for which the parent bank has limited liability, financial risk is reduced. This is not, however, the German model of the universal bank but rather the French one.
7. This might be 5–10 years into the transition.
8. Although such bank debt is more expensive than securitized debt in Germany (Steinherr and Huveneers).
9. The same ratio holds for the two successor states.

10. Unless a parallel foreign currency based banking system is permitted.
11. SAQR = (Cash + Receivables − Bank loans − Payments due)/three months sales. The actual share of credit going to firms in this 'very bad' group is higher, but in the text I exclude housing co-operatives, which are servicing their debts promptly thanks to budget subsidies, but which have very low sales. I am grateful to Mark Schaffer for pointing out this phenomenon.
12. I arrive at this figure by taking the official figures for credit for the private sector as a whole at the end of 1992 (i.e. 122.9 trillion zloyts) and subtracting Gomulka's (1993b) figures for credit to large co-operatives at the same date (40.9 trillion) as well as credit to households (12 trillion). This leaves a total of 70 trillion, or 28.7 per cent of credit to non-government, which is the upper bound of credit to the non-cooperative private sector. Whether co-operatives generally ought to be classified as part of the private sector is a moot point. In the present context, given that a very large part of co-operative indebtedness is due to housing co-operatives they ought definitely to be excluded.
13. And over 50 per cent of all employment.
14. If we included 'good credit' to co-operatives in this total we might double the figure to 4 per cent of GDP.
15. Guesstimates for the non-cooperative private sector have been obtained by assuming that the co-operative sector's share of output remained constant after the last date for which we have information concerning it, that is Q1–Q3 of 1992. The co-operative sector's share was declining up to that time in industry, increasing in construction and roughly constant in transport (Ch. 14).
16. Allowing 5 per cent of GDP to be generated in the co-operative sector.
17. Analogous to the requirement for fire doors in buildings covered by fire insurance.
18. Even here the National Property Fund owns up to 40 per cent of the shares of the leading Czech banks.
19. See Ch. 12 for a description of how such 'narrow banks' (or 'Money Warehousing and Payments Companies' as they are called in the chapter) might generate income.

14

Private Sector Development, Structural Change and Macroeconomic Stabilization: The Case of Poland 1988–1993

1. *Introduction*

Changes in the ownership structure in Poland—which have occurred mainly as a result of private sector development rather than privatization of state owned enterprises (SOEs)—have been a key part of the economic transition in that country. The usual tendency to concentrate either on macroeconomic variables or on the progress of privatization of SOEs, fails to take into account what has been the most important part of the transformation in Poland. Key aspects of this process can be formulated as four simple propositions:

1) This rapid growth of the private sector would not have occurred in the absence of generalized liberalization of the whole economy (and not just of the private sector itself), as we can see by comparing the relatively slow private sector growth of 1989 in Poland with that in subsequent years.

2) Private sector development was a central part of the process by which structural change, as between one digit sectors of the economy, took place in Poland.

3) Stabilization contributed *directly* to private sector development (this is what I call the *anti-populist* proposition).

4) Very rapid structural change (taking the form of a large shift of resources from SOEs to *de novo* private firms within two digit sectors), began not more than 18 months after the generalized liberalization of the economy at the beginning of 1990. The idea that the supply side of PCEs responds slowly to 'big bang' liberalization is clearly wrong.

After a brief statistical overview (Section 2), this Chapter deals first with three topics which are important for a discussion of macro-micro linkages during transition: the impact of stabilization on ownership and structural change (Section 3); the role of credit in private sector development (Section 4); and the implications of the Polish experience for privatization policy in general (Section 5). Section 6 gives a fairly detailed description of ownership and sectoral change in Poland, which corroborates the conclusions arrived at in Sections 3–5.

2. Statistical Overview

In 1989, at the beginning of the transition to capitalism in Poland, the private and co-operative sectors together accounted for 28 per cent of GDP according to official statistics, of which 18 per cent of GDP was accounted for by the private sector proper. By 1992, the share of the two sectors together exceeded 47 per cent, and was expected to exceed 50 per cent by the end of 1993.[1] Employment in these two sectors had reached almost 60 per cent of the labour force in the first half of 1992.[2]

To achieve such levels, growth rates have been very high. Thus non-agricultural private and co-operative economic activity has increased by almost 90 per cent in real terms between 1989 and 1992, implying an average annual rate of growth of

Table 26 Poland: shares in GDP

	1989	1992
Public	72	53
Private	18	42
Co-op	10	5

Source: Polish Statistical Yearbooks and author's calculations. Co-operatives share in GDP in 1992 was obtained by taking their share in sales in industry, construction, agriculture and transport and applying this to the share of these sectors in GDP (both GUS, 1994). The share of co-ops in commerce was obtained by applying their share in the sales of wholesale commerce (also GUS, 1994). This probably overestimated their share significantly, as co-ops were far more important in wholesale trade than in retail.

almost 24 per cent.[4] Since the share of co-operatives has been declining, the growth of the non-agricultural private sector has been much faster, almost 50 per cent per annum.[5]

To put these figures in historical context, one should note that, according to official figures, between 1985 and 1989 the share in national income of the private and co-operative sectors taken together remained unchanged.[6] Even more striking, during these four years the real output of the private and co-operative sectors[7] together increased at an annual rate of only 3 per cent—whereas, as we have seen, during 1990–2 it increased at an annual rate of 24 per cent.

Most important, very little of this change was due to conventional privatization of state owned enterprises. By the end of 1992, the total number of employees in all privatized SOEs was 187,000. This compares with an increase in non-agricultural private sector employment from 1,766,000 in mid-1989 to at least four million at the end of 1992.[8]

3. Impact of Stabilization on Ownership Change and Structural Change

The view has often been expressed that the supply response to macroeconomic stabilization and liberalization was slow in Eastern Europe. Thus Bruno (1992), defending shock programmes, writes: 'A distinction is drawn between stabilization of prices and exchange rates, which can be achieved fairly rapidly, and the responses of production structure, investment, and ownership patterns to sharp changes in *relative* prices, all of which tend to be extremely slow.' Poland's experience with private sector growth shows that such a view is far too pessimistic, particularly as regards changes in ownership patterns (see for example the very rapid effect of the freeing of commercial rents on the retail sector discussed in Section 6), but also as regards the structure of production and even the structure of investment (see the discussion of changes in the construction industry, also in Section 6).

The expansion of private industrial production in 1991 and 1992 is particularly interesting. It shows that in spite of the

absence of much reallocation of resources between two digit branches of industry (Borensztein and Ostry, 1992), there was a strong supply response *within* many of the industrial branches, which took the form of the establishment and expansion of private firms at the expense of state enterprises. Since it is reasonable to assume that the private firms were not producing identical goods to the state enterprises, this is also indirect evidence of an important change in product mix at a greater level of disaggregation than the two digit industrial branches used by Borensztein and Ostry. The more rapid response of the private sector to changes in the economic environment can, presumably, be traced to the superior property rights structure of private firms as compared to state enterprises and co-operatives.

Atkeson and Kehoe (1993) suggest that 'reform recessions' are due to the destruction of information capital which results from the large increase in available new technologies. Since it is not known which managers will be efficient in the use of the new technologies, resources are—on average—allocated less efficiently than before the reform, leading to a fall in output. The fact that output has grown very fast in the private sector in Poland while falling in the state sector shows that—given efficient property rights as in the private sector—the destruction of information capital can be made good very rapidly and need not lead to any fall in output.

To what extent did the reforms actually favour private sector development? First, it is important to remember that price liberalization and administrative price increases in late 1989 and at the beginning of 1990 worsened the private sector's terms of trade relative to the socialized sector (Appendix I). This was because it was socialized sector prices which were freed or raised (private sector prices had been free already for a long time in Poland). To the extent that the fall in output during 1990 was the result of a price shock, this shock could be expected to affect the private sector more than it did the socialized sector. Yet, instead of falling, private sector output increased during 1990, and soared during 1991–3.

Also, the private sector's access to credit collapsed at the

beginning of the transition and was minimal during the whole period 1990–3 (see next section), suggesting that liquidity shortage of the Calvo and Coricelli (1992*b*) type had little to do with the fall in output in 1990 in Poland, and that the problem rather lay in the change in the structure of demand, and that the private sector was simply better at responding to these changes.[9] The highly profitable opportunities which opened up in commerce seem to have allowed a significant accumulation of capital, and this capital may have been used subsequently to finance the expansion of private sector industrial production after 1991.[10]

On the other hand, rapid private sector expansion would not have happened in the absence of the macroeconomic stabilization programme, because the financial squeeze on state enterprises was necessary to 'create space' for the private sector to expand (Sections 6.1 and 6.3). As we shall see, the financial squeeze induced SOEs to reduce their demand for intermediate inputs, making it easier for private firms to obtain what they needed. Furthermore, SOEs were obliged to realize part of their fixed assets, thus also making machines and factory space available to the private sector. Also, the financial squeeze helped extend the massive privatization of retail trade in 1990 to those parts of Poland in which most commercial property is socially owned (Section 6.2). The numerous attempts by local authorities at the beginning of 1990 to regulate the activities of shops through rental agreements collapsed in the face of their need for revenue.

A full assessment of the Polish transition programme would need to answer whether the gain in terms of restructuring of the economy and private sector growth was worth the cost in terms of unemployment and output decline in the state sector, and whether the same benefits could have been obtained at smaller cost by pursuing a fundamentally different policy. As of 1995, GDP has fallen least in Poland out of all the economies in transition as compared to its 1989 level (Tables 26 and 27 show the effects of transition on GDP and production in the region). This evidence suggests that the costs of transition in Poland have not been higher than in those countries which

pursued more gradual liberalization policies (e.g. Hungary, Romania, and Bulgaria), or than in those countries which had failed to stabilize by 1994 (e.g. Romania and Russia).

4. The Role of Credit in Private Sector Development

Bank credit to private firms and households increased from 10 per cent of total credit to non-government in June 1989 to 14.5 per cent in December 1990 and 24 per cent in December 1991 (IFS, 1992).[11] Nevertheless, by December 1991 only 20 per cent of credits to non-government had been lent to private firms (the remaining 3.5 per cent had been lent to households). Of the 20 per cent, some 4 percentage points was accounted for by Art B, the private conglomerate which was defrauded of most of its money by its owners in 1991. Credit which could actually have helped private borrowers to expand their economic activity was therefore no more than 16 per cent of the total extended to non-government. This contrast between the private sector's share in credit to non-government and its almost threefold larger share in GDP is very striking.

One can thus see that the development of the Polish private

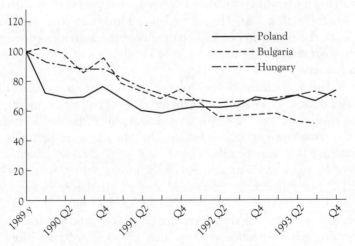

Figure 29   *Quarterly industrial output in Bulgaria, Hungary, and Poland*

Figure 30   *Quarterly industrial output in Poland, Romania, and Russia*

sector confirms the point made by McKinnon (1993) regarding China, where non-state enterprises have expanded rapidly in spite of very restricted access to bank credit.[12] But Poland provides an even more extreme example, in that total credit to non-government in Poland constitutes only about 20 per cent of GDP, whereas in China it is about 90 per cent. Thus outstanding credit to the non-state sector in China is the equivalent of about 18 per cent of GDP, while in Poland it is the equivalent of about 3 per cent of GDP! Almost all financing in the Polish private sector thus comes either from retained earnings or from non-intermediated lending, so that the sector has been able to grow very fast with practically no support from the banking system at all. This conclusion is important because there is evidence that in 1992 most (about two-thirds) of Polish bank lending may in fact have been bad (Gomulka, 1993b).[13] If this was so, then it strengthens the case of those arguing for tight controls on bank lending during the initial stages of the economic transformation of PCEs (McKinnon, 1993, this book Chapter 12): not only is bank lending by banks with very low credit assessment skills dangerous (in terms of the macroeconomic instability it is likely to cause)—but it would also appear to be largely unnecessary.

5. Implications for Privatization Policy

While Poland's failure to privatize many SOEs, and in particular the large ones, has definitely been a weakness in its reforms, we should consider whether there may not be some advantages in the Polish approach of putting private sector development first, and privatization of SOEs second. The primary purpose of privatizing SOEs is to increase their efficiency. Revenue considerations are congruent with efficiency ones: it is only if profitability is expected to increase after privatization that capitalists will be prepared to pay a purchase price higher than the net present value of the enterprise to the state.[14] The question is whether there are greater profit opportunities for entrepreneurs in privatized SOEs or outside the state sector altogether. A number of considerations suggests the latter: first, it may be more efficient to assemble one's own firm by buying the machines and transport equipment and hiring the labour and floorspace which one definitely needs, rather than buying these inputs 'bundled' together, particularly as the bundle was initially designed with operation within a completely different environment in view. Second, inheriting an existing labour force with its own working habits and traditions may be far more troublesome than selecting one's own. The above does not mean that SOEs should not be privatized—after all if entrepreneurs expect higher profits from the creation of their own firms they will merely bid down the price of SOEs. It suggests rather that, at least in the short run, the costs of failing to privatize may not be very large.

A more serious problem will arise in the longer term: if SOEs have not been privatized, at least formally, early on in the transformation process it may become harder to do so later. As the transition proceeds, the economy begins to grow and tax systems are reformed, tax revenues begin to increase. Under such circumstances, SOEs may regain access to public financial support, so that it may become harder to induce them to accept privatization or to close them down. Each larger privatization would then require the SOE to be restructured while in public ownership, on the British model, slowing the privatization pro-

cess down even further. This is why mass privatization of the Czech kind is urgently needed, even if management by financial intermediaries turns out to be very passive and not very successful. At least in the Czech Republic there are private owners and their representatives available, rather than government ministers, to decide on liquidation.

6. Review of the Polish Experience with Private Sector Development

6.1. The Years of Distorted Growth

The late 1980s were a period of considerable liberalization of the restrictions facing private business in Poland, and in consequence of accelerated growth in private sector activity. As Rostowski (1989*a*) shows, private economic activity began to fulfil many of the needs which the state sector was unable to satisfy, from providing a large range of services to maintaining the liquidity of the current account of the balance of payments. One of the things which made this development possible was the reintroduction of the pre-War Commercial Code in 1983. Although the Code of 1934 was amended to maintain many of the privileges of the SOEs, it provided a legal framework for corporate private businesses. Nevertheless, much private activity consisted in either open or hidden arbitrage (namely, the notorious case of Poland's export of tropical flowers),[15] and also presented opportunities for members of the *nomenklatura* to transform their privileges into capital, both physical and financial, in preparation for the change of economic system which many foresaw (although the change in political regime was foreseen by fewer observers).

Rostowski (1989*a*) calculated that privately generated incomes constituted about 35–45 per cent of all personal incomes, and estimated that private activity, both black and official, had grown rapidly in the 1980s. However, as we have seen, according to *official* statistics the share of the private sector in national income (net material product) increased only very slightly between 1985 and 1988.

An important breakthrough came with the 'Law on

Economic Activity', which came into force on 1 January 1989, and which swept away practically all restrictions on, and regulation of, the private sector. The intentions of the communist authorities in passing this law were to liberate the forces of private entrepreneurship, while at the same time avoiding the need to tackle the country's fundamental macroeconomic, ownership, and management problems which lay in the state sector. The expectation was that the private sector would develop rapidly, supplying the shortage ridden market with goods and services, allowing the difficult problems emanating from the state sector to be put off to a later date. Private sector growth was to be harnessed to economic development and thus to political stabilization and the maintenance of communist power. This is very similar to what has since become known as the 'Chinese Way' (i.e., the reforms carried out under the auspices of Deng in the 1980s).

As a result of the 'Law on Economic Activity', in 1989 real NMP generated in the private sector (excluding co-operatives) increased by 12 per cent, at a time when NMP generated in the socialized sector fell 3 per cent.[16] Maybe more significant was the fact that the private sector's share of services, excluding trade, provided to the population and to other private businesses, increased from 34 per cent to 42 per cent in that year.[17] In real terms the value of these services increased by 55 per cent. Non-agricultural private sector employment (end-year) increased from 1.25 million to 1.78 million. Much of this growth was in industry and construction.

Nevertheless, this 'Polish Way' failed on two fronts: first, the macroeconomic disequilibria generated in the state sector continued to accumulate in an unsustainable way—above all through the budget deficit which was stoking up hyperinflation; second, state control over the economy as a whole was such as to prevent the private sector from expanding as fast as the strategy required. The key constraints on private sector expansion arose from the continuation of generalized excess demand due to extensive price control in the socialized (state and co-op) sector, and from the multiple exchange rate system, by which

favoured importers were allocated hard currency at preferential rates.

This brings us to *Proposition 1*:

The rate of growth of the private sector achieved in Poland in the 1990s was made possible by the generalized liberalization of the whole economy which occurred in 1990.

One of the problems resulting from the absence of generalized liberalization in 1989 was that a large—though probably declining—part of private sector activity continued to be based on arbitraging differences between controlled state prices (often for inputs) and the free prices which the private sector could charge. At the time of the semi-free parliamentary elections in Poland in mid-1989, 55 per cent of prices were still controlled, and by the end of the year this was still true of 25 per cent of prices (Ministry of France, 1990).

6.2. The Initial Effects of the Balcerowicz Plan

The general liberalization of the economy introduced at the beginning of 1990, consisted in: the freeing of most remaining controlled prices,[18] the liberalization of foreign trade with the introduction of current account convertibility for the Polish zloty at a fixed exchange rate, and the freeing of commercial property rents. Apart from this, there was the mass de-etatization and de-monopolization of the co-operative sector, which affected some 2.2 million people in 1990 (Schaffer, 1992b). These reforms together with the macroeconomic shock stabilization programme which accompanied them, resulted in two phases of private sector development.

First, in 1990, there was a massive growth of private commerce (initially retail—later also wholesale, initially mainly relating to domestic goods—later also encompassing foreign trade) and private transport. During this period, private industrial output grew only slightly (although this compares well with the very large fall in state sector industrial output given by the official statistics, of which more below).[19] Then, in the second phase, from 1991 the expansion of private commerce slowed down, while that of private industry and construction

accelerated sharply (private transport continued to expand at about the same rate).

Although official statistics show the private sector expanding only moderately if at all in 1990, a more reliable picture of what happened can be gained by looking at such indicators as the number of private businesses and the size of the private sector workforce (see Appendix II). The numbers working in the non-agricultural private sector increased from 1.78 million to 2.33 million, an increase of 30 per cent, while the number of private limited companies increased almost threefold, from 11,700 to 29,700 (all figures apply to end-year).[20]

The structure of the expansion of the private sector in 1990 is particularly interesting. Unlike 1989, when the largest increase had taken place in industry and construction, in 1990 the overwhelming bulk of the increase was in commerce.

We also see the extraordinarily rapid growth of private trade if we look at the increase in the number of private shops (see Appendix II).

Thus a profound restructuring of demand took place in Poland in 1990, changing the structure of the private sector, just as it did that of the economy as a whole. These changes were central to the restructuring of the Polish economy. Indeed, the fact that private sector industrial output did not grow very fast in 1990 confirms the rapid adjustment story, since much of this output in 1989 had been the result of the distorted prices which held at that time. These facts are the basis for *Proposition 2*:

Private sector development was a central part of the process by which structural change took place in Poland as between 1 digit sectors of the economy.

Table 27 Poland: private sector employment ('000)

	Mid-1988	End 1989	Change	End 1990	Change
Industry & Const.	854	1,240	45%	1,332	7.4%
Commerce	90	141	57%	574	407.1%

Source: Polish Statistical Yearbooks

The depth and speed of structural changes in Poland can be gauged by looking at the changes in employment in the main branches of the economy, excluding agriculture:

Table 28 Employment in the main branches of the Polish economy in 1993 (1989 = 100)

Industry	79.1
Construction	85.0
Transport	72.2
Commerce	116.0
Education	101.1
Health	96.3
State administration	144.2[a]
TOTAL	84.4

[a] The need to expand the state administration had three causes: (1) much of the bureaucracy in Communist times was actually the Party apparat (which ceased to function in relation to state matters); (2) another large part of the bureaucracy was in the state enterprises, which could no longer fulfill social or other administrative functions; (3) the transition required the state to take on many new functions (e.g. privatization) just as it was abandoning others.

Source: GUS, IoSS-GK 1993.

Apart from price liberalization, it was the freeing of commercial rents, and the ensuing creation of a rented property market, which was the key event in the private retail trade boom of 1990. Poland had a fairly deconcentrated structure of commercial property ownership. In those territories which had been part of Poland before the war much of the commercial property remained in private hands. In what had been German territory and in Warsaw, most commercial property belongs to 'socialized' entities. However, in most localities these consist of a mix of municipal, housing co-operative and state enterprise property, with there usually being a significant number of different landlords in the latter two categories. This decentralized ownership structure, together with a severe drop in revenues from other sources (such as government subsidies), forced the socialized commercial property owners to try to maximize rental income. Private property owners naturally did the same. The

result was a wholesale termination of tenancies held by the monopolistic co-operative trade networks which had until then dominated both retail and wholesale trade.[22]

This story of private growth amid public collapse (according to official statistics gross industrial output fell 24 per cent in 1990), leads one to ask to what extent there really was a shortage of demand in Poland in 1990? Can an economy which generated sufficient demand for the number of shops to have almost doubled in one year, have been an economy with insufficient domestic demand? Moreover, the sufficiency or otherwise of aggregate demand depends on the elasticity of the supply side of the economy. A perfectly elastic economy would obey Say's Law perfectly, and no shortage of demand could ever exist in it. The private sector's record of rapid growth in 1990 shows that this sector was sufficiently flexible for the general fall in demand not to affect it at all (with the exception of private construction).[23]

We have already described how price and rent liberalization in 1990 increased supply elasticity in retail trade dramatically. However, the preponderance of supply side over demand side effects was true even in private industry which had benefitted from the shortages and hyperinflation of 1989.[24] How do we account for this, especially as all formal barriers to entry had already been removed in 1989? Three factors may have played a role:

1) private sector firms, being more entrepreneurial (and usually less capital intensive) than their socialized sector competitors, were better placed to take advantage of shifts in the structure of demand at the micro level which accompanied the big bang, as forced substitution disappeared together with generalized excess demand (see Chapter 1 and the Introduction to Part 1);

2) much harder budget constraints on state owned enterprises forced these to begin to sell off equipment and sell or rent out factory and warehouse space, so that the market for fixed capital inputs for private business became far freer;[25]

3) strapped for cash, SOEs had not only to sell to whoever would buy, but also had to buy from whoever offered the best

price, so that the long standing practice of discriminating in one's supply policy against private entrepreneurs unconnected with an SOEs management largely disappeared.

Thus, whereas the regime of generalized excess demand favoured SOEs, because they were the ones with the softest budget constraints and because it meant that forced substitution allowed them not to adjust their production to consumer preferences, so the sudden elimination of excess demand in 1990 was of benefit to private industry, dramatically increasing its supply elasticity. For the private sector this benefit outweighed the general reduction in demand which accompanied it, and even the deterioration in its terms of trade with the state sector (see Appendix 1). This justifies *Proposition 3*:

Stabilization contributed directly *to private sector development in Poland.*

Nevertheless, it was probably the deterioration in the private sector's terms of trade with the state sector which accounts for the unpopularity of the Balcerowicz plan among private farmers[26] and many businessmen (particularly those involved before 1990 in arbitraging state sector products sold at controlled prices).

6.3. The Acceleration of 1991–93

In 1991 there was a dramatic breakthrough in the ownership structure of the Polish economy. According to official statistics value added in the public sector[27] fell by 26 per cent, while it increased by 33 per cent in the non-public (private and co-operative) sectors taken together.[28] As a result of these changes the private and co-operative sectors' share of value added rose from 31 per cent to 45 per cent.

The almost 50 per cent expansion in private industrial output in 1991 was the most remarkable aspect of this acceleration, particularly as it took place in the context of the shocks to the Polish economy caused by the sharp increase in the price of imported Soviet energy and the collapse of Soviet imports from Poland.[29] As a result of these shocks, state sector industrial output continued its second year of sharp decline, experiencing

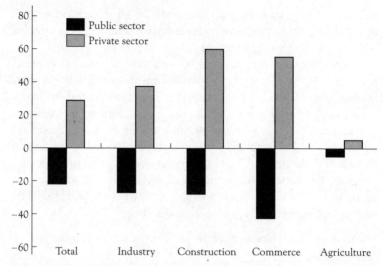

Figure 31   *Poland 1991: change in value added in the public and private sectors*

a fall of 20 per cent during 1991, a fall which was only somewhat smaller than the 24 per cent reduction in 1990. This brings
us to *Proposition 4*:

*Structural change within 2 digit sectors of industry began on a large
scale within 18 months of generalized liberalization of the economy,
taking the form of a large shift of resources from SOEs to de novo
private firms within sectors.*

The rate of growth of private and co-operative industrial
output slowed down slightly in 1992 (to a still very respectable
23 per cent), before accelerating again in 1993:

Table 29 Poland: Industrial production, % change on previous year

	1990	1991	1992	1993
Total industry	−24	−12	−4	−6
State industry	−24	−19	−3	−7
Private industry	8[a]	48	41	—
Private & co-operative industry	27[b]	−25	23	35

[a] see footnote 24.
[b] Due to a massive fall in co-operative output.

Source: GUS, *IoSS-GK*, various issues.

The growth of the private sector's share of industrial output is given in Table 32.

Construction was another sector in which the private sector did far better than in 1991 than in 1990:

Table 30 Poland: construction, value of sales, % change on previous year

	1990	1991	1992	1993
State	−18	−30	−39	−30
Private & co-operative	−19	63	35	20
TOTAL	−18	9	8	9

Source: GUS, *IoSS-GK*, various issues.

In 1991 the private sector accounted for 50 per cent of sales in construction, the co-operative sector for 5 per cent and the state sector for 45 per cent. By 1993 the state sector's share had declined to 14 per cent[30] (see Table 32). Reportedly (GUS, *IoSS-GK* 1992), the main reason for the collapse in the state sector, and the growth in the private sector in construction, has been the fall in the demand for new capital intensive construction for industrial and infrastructural projects. Demand has shifted to refurbishment and modernization of existing buildings, and this is particularly the case as regards the new private sector customers of the construction industry. Private sector construction firms were better at providing such services. It is worth remembering that one of the major problems in the sector prior to 1990 was the tendency to favour large new projects over refurbishment and modernization.

There was a similar pattern in transport:

Table 31 Poland: transport, value of sales, % change on previous year

	1990	1991	1992	1993
State	−13	−23	−17	−16
Private & co-operative	−21	35	39	19
TOTAL	−14	−14	−3	−4

Source: GUS, *IoSS-GK*, various issues.

Table 32 Poland: shares of private and co-operative sectors in output, 1989–1993

	1989[b]	1990	1991	1992	1993
Industry	16.2	17.4	24.2	31.8	37.4
Construction	33.4	32.2	62.2	78.7	85.8
Transport	11.5	14.2	25.2	39.3	44.3

[a] Shares at current prices.
[b] GUS, 1992.
Source: GUS, *IoSS-GK*, various issues.

As a result of these changes by 1993 the private and co-operative sectors accounted for 44 per cent of all transport services sold, in spite of the weight of the state railways in this sector (Table 32).[31]

The implications of the Polish experience are that the declines in statistical output which accompany the economic transition can be mitigated by rapid private sector growth, but that for this growth to achieve its full potential, macroeconomic stabilization and the creation of an enabling environment for the private sector are vital. Above all, the latter consists not only in the creation of the necessary legal framework, but also in a general liberalization of the economy.

APPENDIX I *Official Statistics and Private Sector Growth*

A few words are needed on the use of official statistics in PCEs in transition. In Poland these were considered relatively reliable compared to those in other communist countries. However, the statistical system was not adapted to dealing with the high rates of inflation which have occurred since 1988. As a result, non-sensical results were obtained both for 1989 and 1990, particularly as regards the measurement of GDP and its components (above all inventory growth and consumption).[32] Under these circumstances figures should be taken as indicative only, particularly as all the usual problems with measuring private economic activity, resulting from tax evasion, also exist. Generally, one may suppose that the more 'processed' a particular statistic is, the more subject it is to error: thus, a figure for gross industrial output is likely to be closer to the truth than one for GDP

produced in industry, and figures on employment or the number of businesses in existence are likely to be more reliable than those for sales (although the former are also likely to differ significantly from the truth because of the failure of many businesses to register). In order to reflect this, I try to avoid blatantly spurious accuracy by rounding percentages to whole percentage points, except where the purpose is to discuss the significance of particular statistics (as in n. 6 above).

According to official statistics the private and co-operative sectors' share of GDP increased only slightly in 1990, from 29 per cent to 31 per cent, in spite of far reaching liberalization of the economy. However, these statistics disguise much of what was really happening. The shares of the private and co-operative sectors in GDP are only given in current prices, and in 1990 there was a very large fall in agriculture's terms of trade. As a result, the agricultural private sector's share of GDP fell from 9.6 per cent to 5.9 per cent. Yet in constant prices agricultural GDP fell only 10 per cent (i.e., slightly less than total GDP). At the same time, the private and co-operative sectors outside agriculture increased their joint share of GDP in current prices from 19 per cent to 25 per cent.

We can arrive at a 10 per cent increase in real non-agricultural private and co-operative sector GDP by assuming that the only relative price change in 1990 was the deterioration of agriculture's terms of trade: if this was so, then the 1990 share of the non-agricultural private and co-operative sectors needs to be adjusted downwards by the amount by which non-agricultural 1990 GDP has been overestimated in terms of 1989 prices. This is done by taking this share not out of total GDP but out of GDP adjusted downwards by the number of percentage points by which agriculture's share of GDP fell in 1990 as a result of the shift in the terms of trade, i.e., out of 0.954 of 1990 GDP (agriculture's share in 1989 GDP was 11.8 per cent, compared to 7.2 per cent in 1990, giving a 4.6 percentage point fall in agriculture's share in GDP in 1990 compared to 1989 due to the shift in the terms of trade). This gives us the share of the non-agricultural private and co-operative sectors in 1990, GDP adjusted to eliminate the shift in the terms of trade as 23.9 per cent (instead of 25 per cent). If we accept the official figure for the fall in real GDP in 1990 of 12 per cent, then this 1990 share in terms of real 1989 GDP would have been 21 per cent, compared to the actual 1989 share of 19 per cent—very roughly the 10 per cent real increase I suggest above.

In fact this assumption is probably conservative, as all private and many co-operative sector prices had been free during 1989 (an important exception in the co-operative sector being milk), whereas many state prices were freed or sharply raised in 1990. Thus the non-agricultural private sector's terms of trade with the state sector probably worsened, which in turn suggests that there was an even larger increase in the private sector's real output than the 10 per cent increase calculated above.

APPENDIX II Private Sector Development vs. the Privatization of Co-operatives in Commerce

During 1989 the number of private shops increased from 24 thousand to 29 thousand, but during 1990 the increase was about 170 thousand.[33] This development has transformed not only the appearance of Polish localities, but also the convenience of living in them. The number of inhabitants per shop fell from 250 in 1989 to 160 in 1990 and 123 in 1991, in other words there was a doubling in the number of shops in two years! Thus, not only was there a massive transfer of shops from the socialized to the private sectors, but also a huge increase in the total number of shops, all of which were private.[34] The magnitude of this phenomenon, in an economy which has been widely considered to have been subject to a significant shortfall of domestic demand in 1990, throws the degree of repression of retail trade in pre-transition Poland into stark relief.

In the light of these figures the official increase in 1990 in GDP generated in trade of 0.7 per cent, is entirely incredible. It seems to be based on the total number of the registered workforce in commerce, which increased by exactly 0.7 per cent in 1990 (mid-year to mid-1989). The implication is that the 56 per cent increase in the number of shops and the improvement in the cleanliness and quality of most of the remainder in 1990 (which was evidently market driven) had no effect on customer utility and therefore on national income. GUS assumed that output per head was not a whit higher than when the vast majority of the workforce in commerce were employed in dirty, empty, overstaffed, monopolistic pseudo-co-operative and state shops. Even more strangely, when in 1991 total employment in commerce increased by 16.7 per cent this was officially accompanied by an increase of only 7.9 per cent in GDP generated in the sector.

Wholesale as well as retail trade was affected by rapid private

sector development. Official figures show that by 1991, 30 per cent of wholesale trade was in private hands. However, these figures exclude companies employing fewer than 20 people, and as the bulk of private wholesalers did indeed employ fewer than 20 people, the real share is higher. The development of private wholesalers was particularly important in 1990, as state and co-operative wholesalers still had strong monopoly positions at the beginning of the year.[35] They tended to price on a cost plus basis. Competition from the private sector thus reduced cost-push inflationary forces (and therefore inflationary inertia). An important aspect of this competition promoting behaviour by private wholesalers was the import of consumer goods: 17 per cent of total imports in 1990 were effected by the private sector, and the vast majority of these imports were of consumer goods.

During 1990 the dissolution of the national, monopolistically organized, 'centrale' of co-operatives which under communism had been effective transmission belts for party-state control over co-ops, and the application of the rule of law (as opposed to the rule of the party) to the co-ops, gave power back into the hands of the 'members' (effectively the employees) (Schaffer, 1992*b*).

Schaffer also suggests that the explosion of private sector commerce in 1990 was largely a result of co-operative shops leaving the co-operative legal structures and thus becoming private, or of the workforce of co-operative shops becoming the owners of the new private shops. In support of his argument Schaffer points to the minimal change in the size of the workforce in commerce in the private and co-operative sectors taken together. The difficulty with this interpretation is that the joint total of private and co-operative shops increased from 125,000 at the end of 1989 to 223,000 at the end of 1990, while the number of state shops fell by 13,000 to 14,000. At the same time anecdotal evidence is unanimous in ascribing a small role to employees of retail co-operative shops as owners of the new private shops. It is, of course, likely that many of them became employees in different new private shops. A significant hiatus typically occurred between the closing down of the old and the opening of the new private shop, because of the need to refurbish, which broke any continuity between the old and the new undertaking. Generally, new owners do not seem to have even undertaken the same line of business as their predecessors.

APPENDIX III Private Sector Development vs. *Privatization in Industry*

There are clear indications that the massive increase in private sector industrial production in 1991 was due to the privatization of state enterprises in only a very limited degree. The total number of employees in privatized enterprises in industry was 78,000, which amounted to 2.8 per cent of employment in state industry, i.e. nowhere near enough to account for the difference in the fall in industrial output between state industry (19.5 per cent) and total industry (12 per cent). Furthermore, the fall in employment in state industry is 'point to point' during 1991, while the fall in state industrial production is average 1991 to average 1990. Thus only that part of the privatization of SOEs which had already taken place at any time during 1991 would have reduced state industrial output and increased private industrial output. The relevant reduction in state industrial employment as a result of privatization is thus closer to 1.4 per cent. Furthermore, and most important, of the 78,000 employed in privatized SOEs during 1991, some 48,000 were employed in SOEs which were 'privatized through liquidation on the basis of the law on state enterprises'. These SOEs were in severe financial difficulties, with an average pre-tax profit margin over costs of minus 30 per cent. Although upon liquidation the physical assets of these enterprises were leased to private companies (usually belonging to the managers and workers of the previous SOE), nevertheless, the condition of the companies on privatization was poor, and the number employed after liquidation usually fell sharply.[36]

Finally, the increase in 'old' private sector industrial production in 1991 is unlikely to have been significantly affected by the re-registration of co-operatives as private companies. In 1991 co-operatives share of total industrial output increased slightly to 6.6 per cent from 6 per cent in 1990. This implies that their real output remained roughly constant, as total industrial output fell 12 per cent in 1991, thus very little transformation of co-operatives into private firms seems to have happened in 1991 in industry. Even if co-operatives' output was growing as rapidly as that of firms in the 'old' private sector, i.e., at about 50 per cent per annum, which is an unlikely proposition, this would still mean that—at most—entities producing one third of the co-operative sector's output in 1990 could have transformed themselves into private firms for 1991. This could then at most account for 17

percentage points of the 48 per cent increase in 'old' private sector industrial production.

NOTES

This chapter is an extensively rewritten version of a paper which appeared in the Discussion Papers series of the *Centre for Economic Performance, London School of Economics*, no. 159, 1993.

1. Moreover, the co-operatives have lost much of their monopolistic and socialized character (which had often made them even less market oriented than state enterprises). Furthermore, these figures exclude all black and grey activity, which was probably as large as co-operative activity at the beginning of the transition (Rostowski, 1989*a*).
2. Excluding the black economy and the half million or so illegal workers from the former Soviet Union.
3. Co-operatives' share in GDP in 1992 was obtained by taking their share in sales in industry, construction, agriculture, and transport and applying this to the share of these sectors in GDP (both GUS, 1994). The share of co-ops in commerce was obtained by applying their share in the sales of wholesale commerce (also GUS, 1994). This probably overestimated their share significantly, as co-ops were far more important in wholesale trade than in retail.
4. We assume no change in the relative prices of non-public and public sector output. In fact, as we see in Appendix 1, the relative prices of non-agricultural private sector output probably fell compared to the rest of the economy, implying an even faster rate of growth in real terms.
5. In 1989 almost 10 per cent of GDP was accounted for by private agriculture, a figure which declined to 5.5 per cent in current prices and 9 per cent in constant prices by 1992. This gives the non-agricultural private sector going from 8 per cent of GDP in 1989 to 33 per cent in 1992, while GDP fell 20 per cent according to official statistics.
6. This is the share in net material product (i.e. excluding so-called non-material services). Figures for shares in GDP are not available, but the shares of the two sectors on both definitions of national income, which we have for 1989, are strikingly similar at 28.5 per cent and 28.3 per cent. The share of the private sector (excluding co-ops) in the net material product (NMP) measure of national income also increased only marginally between 1985 and 1989, from 18.2 per cent to 19.2 per cent.
7. Again in terms of NMP.
8. This figure was obtained by subtracting agricultural private sector employment from private and co-operative employment at the end of 1992. Then a further adjustment was made to subtract co-operative employment: this had fallen to 390,000 outside commerce by the end of 1991 and to 625,000 in commerce by the end of 1990, down from a

total of 2.2 million in mid-1989. I therefore guesstimated that this figure could have been at most 850,000 for all co-operatives at the end of 1992.

9. For the changes in the structure of demand to occur, an elimination of generalized aggregate demand was first required.

10. We will only know the truth of these conjectures once proper surveys of the private sector have been carried out. We do not at present know whether enterpreneurs who made money in trade during 1990 shifted into production in 1991–2. On official figures private sector activity has not been very profitable in Poland throughout the period. Nevertheless, given the very rapid rate of growth of the private sector, and particularly its rapid growth in industry, the assumption has to be that this is due to a failure to report profits in order to avoid taxes. Black profits breed black (undeclared) capital, which of its nature is unregistered, but which may be revealed in the statistics on output growth (although this also can be under-reported for the same reasons). Some indication of capital accumulation by the private sector appears in the investment statistics. The sector's share (including co-operatives) increased from 28 per cent in 1989 to 44 per cent in 1992.

11. In January 1990 this figure stood at 4 per cent, showing the massive collapse in real credit to the private sector which accompanied stabilization. On the other hand this meant that there was practically no indebtedness by the private sector at the beginning of the programme.

12. They obtained about 20 per cent of total credit to non-government.

13. In September 1992, 60 per cent of all credit to non-government had been lent to 13 per cent of all businesses (employing above 20 employees), which accounted for 8 per cent of all sales, and which had the worst quick ratios. The quick ratios are defined as cash plus receivables minus bank credit and trade credit received divided by one quarter's sales. The businesses concerned had quick ratios of between -1.5 and minus infinity.

14. Tax revenue also needs to be part of this calculation, and indeed is one of its two main components when privatization is to take place through free distribution (the other is the increase in national income as a result of increased efficiency).

15. Reported in Williamson (1992*a*). This was due to the underpricing of coal used in private greenhouses.

16. State plus co-operative sectors. However, the private sector's share in NMP at current prices hardly increased at all: i.e., it went from 18.9 per cent to 19.2 per cent during 1989, as a result of the shift in the terms of trade against the private sector as state and co-operative prices were slowly liberalized.

17. After having increased quite slowly from 25 per cent in 1980.

18. Those which remained controlled were increased sharply, so as to bring them closer to world levels.

19. Private sector construction was also reported to have fallen sharply in this phase. However, see n. 26.

20. GUS (1992) and GUS (1990–2).

21. The need to expand the state administration had three causes: (1) much of the bureaucracy in communist times was actually the party *apparat* (which ceased to function in relation to state matters); (2) another large part of the bureaucracy was in the state enterprises, which could no longer fulfill social or other administrative functions; (3) the transition required the state to take on many new functions (e.g. privatization) just as it was abandoning others.

22. Out of 96,000 shops held by these co-operatives, some 57,000 were privatized during 1990 alone (information from the Ministry of Internal Trade on the number of shops privatized, and from GUS on the number of co-operative and state shops in 1989 and 1990).

23. Construction, may have been hit because the role of housing as a hedge against hyperinflation was greater than that of durable industrial products. According to official figures (GUS, *IoSS-GK* 1992) there was a real fall of 19 per cent in private construction in 1990, slightly more than that in the state and co-operative sectors. However, these statistics are puzzling, given that there was actually a small increase in employment in private construction at this time.

24. Private sector real industrial global output increased by about 19 per cent in 1990 (obtained from the levels of total real industrial output in 1989 and 1990 and the 'old' private sector's share in each of these years in the statistical yearbooks). This compares to a growth rate of 22 per cent in 1989 (calculated from private sector shares and changes in total real output). These are the right statistics if we wish to compare what happened in socialized and private industry in 1990 as compared to 1989. Then the relevant figures are indeed the fall in socialized industry of about 28 per cent and the increase in private industry of about 19 per cent. These are all annual averages, and they agree well with the increase in average private sector industrial employment in 1990 compared to 1989, which was also 19 per cent. The problem is that much of the increase in private employment in fact took place in late 1989. When we look at the increase in employment from end-1989 to end-1990 we get a far smaller (8 per cent) increase. It seems likely that this is a better indicator of what happened in private industry *during* 1990 itself.

25. This was particularly the case in transport, where SOEs sold off a large part of their road haulage fleets in 1990, when they no longer needed as many trucks to send long distances for inputs of which there was no longer a shortage.

26. This shift in the terms of trade was with respect to industrial inputs into agriculture. It does not necessarily mean that farmers were actually worse off. Very striking is GUS's household survey data showing an increase in the percentage of peasant families owning cars from 30.4 per cent at end-1989 to 36.4 per cent at end-1990, with the corresponding levels for freezers being 33.7 per cent and 42.9 per cent, and for colour TVs 19.8 per cent and 28.4 per cent. What

made these improvements possible was the increase in the real dollar value of the zloty in 1990.

27. This is the state enterprise sector plus the budgetary sphere.

28. In industry value added in the state sector fell 31 per cent while in the non-state sectors it increased 42 per cent. In construction value added in the state sector fell 31 per cent, while in the non-state sectors it increased 64 per cent. In commerce the equivalent changes were: state sector −46 per cent, non-state +60 per cent; and in agriculture: state sector −9 per cent, non-state +10 per cent (Figures 1 and 2). While it is possible (though dubious) to claim as Schaffer (1992*b*) does that much of the private sector growth in 1990 was the result of the transformation of co-operatives into private firms, this process was completed by 1991.

    In spite of its very rapid growth in 1991, the private sector's expansion in domestic commerce was actually much slower than in 1990, while growth accelerated rapidly in private industry, foreign trade, construction and (possibly) transport. Thus the rate of increase in the total number of shops fell from almost 60 per cent in 1990 to 30 per cent in 1991, while the rate of increase in the number of private shops fell from over 700 per cent to under 40 per cent. These are true private shops, i.e. co-operative shops are excluded. The number of sole trading businesses in commerce (both retail and wholesale) rose in 1990 from 72,000 to 346,000 and in 1991 only to 550,000.

29. Poland had to pay in hard currency for Soviet oil deliveries from September 1990. From January 1991 this applied to Soviet gas as well. In addition, from January 1991 Soviet enterprises either stopped importing from Poland, or stopped paying for what they did import.

30. There is no reason to suppose that any of the non-state sectors' increase was due to co-operatives.

31. In 1991, the last year for which we have disaggregated figures, the private sector accounted for 19 per cent of sales and the co-operative for 5 per cent, a share which had slightly declined since 1989.

32. Given this lack of reliable information, the 12 per cent fall in GDP in 1990 was imposed on the Polish Statistical Office by the IMF. The Polish Statistical Office (GUS) initially reckoned the fall at between 17 per cent and more than 20 per cent. Understandably, the IMF were unwilling to accept that with such large falls in GDP, inventories had continued to accumulate rapidly, as GUS claimed. The IMF therefore insisted on a smaller fall in GDP. Even on revised figures increases in inventories were given as 4.3 per cent of GDP (in the midst of a profound recession!). Higher inventory accumulation also implied lower consumption for a given level of real GDP.

33. Again, we have no figures for the private sector alone as from 1990. However, we do know that the number of co-operative shops fell very sharply from the 96,000 there were at the end of 1989. By counting only the total increase in the number of private plus co-operative shops, which amounted to 98,000, and then adding the number of

co-operative and state shops privatized during 1990, which was 70,000 (information from the Ministry of Internal Trade) we arrive at an adequate estimate.

34. These figures do not include the hundreds of thousands of street traders who appeared in Polish cities at the beginning of 1990.

35. At the end of 1990 there were 35,600 registered enterprises in wholesale trade. Of these 29,600 were private traders, 3,600 private companies and 2,400 socialized entities (Government of Poland, 1992). The same source states that financial difficulties forced socialized wholesalers to rent warehousing space to their private sector rivals.

36. It is worth noting that even the 22 enterprises which were privatized outright were barely more profitable than the average of SOEs upon privatization (though this improved considerably subsequently).

REFERENCES

Akerlof, G., Hesenius, H., Rose, A., and Yellen, J. (1991), 'East Germany in from the Cold', *Brookings Papers on Economic Activity*, no. 1.

Anisimova, L., Senelnikov, S., and Titov, S. (1993), 'Fiscal Policy', in *The Gaidar Programme*, ed. M. Dąbrowski (Centrum Analiz Społeczno-Ekonomicznych (C-A-S-E) and Freidrich Ebert Stifftung, Warsaw).

Aoki, M. (1984), *The Economic Analysis of the Japanese Firm* (North Holland).

Åslund, A. (ed.) (1994), *Economic Transformation in Russia* (Pinter, London).

Atkeson, A., and Kehoe, P. (1993), 'Industry Evolution and Transition: the role of information Capital', *mimeo* (Feb.).

Auerbach, P., Davison, G., and Rostowski, J. (1992), 'Secondary Currencies and High Inflation: Implications for Monetary Theory and Policy', Discussion Paper no. 58, (Centre for Economic Performance, London School of Economics).

Barchetta, P. (1994), 'The Lessons from Fiscal Reform in Democratic Spain' in *Developing Public Finance in Emerging Market Economies*, ed. K. Mizsei (Institute for East-West Studies, New York).

Bartholdy, K. (1995), 'Statistical Review', *Economics of Transition*, vol. 3, no. 4.

Baykov, A. (1946), *The Development of the Soviet Economic System* (Cambridge University Press, Cambridge).

Begg, D. (1991), 'Czechoslovakia', *Economic Policy*, 13 (Oct. 1991).

Begg, D., and Portes, R. (1993), 'Enterprise Debt and Economic Transformation: Financial Restructuring in Central and Eastern Europe', *mimeo*.

Berg, A., and Blanchard, O. (1994), 'Stabilization and Transition: Poland 1990–1', in *The Transition in Eastern Europe*, eds. O. Blanchard, K. Froot, and J. Sachs, vol. 1, NBER (Chicago University Press, Chicago).

Berg, A., and Sachs, J. (1992), 'Structural Adjustment and International Trade in Eastern Europe', *Economic Policy*, 14 (Apr.).

Bernanke, B., and Gertler, M. (1987), 'Financial Fragility and Eco-

nomic Performance', Princeton University Woodrow Wilson School, *mimeo* (Mar.).

Bhaduri, A., and Laski, K. (1993), 'The Relevance of Michael Kalecki Today', Vienna Institute for Comparative Economic Studies, *mimeo*.

Blanchard, O., and Layard, R. (1991), 'Post-stabilization Inflation in Poland', *mimeo*, London.

Blanchard, O., and Summers, L. (1987), 'Histeresis in unemployment', *European Economic Review,* vol. 31 (Feb./Mar.).

Blanchard, O., and Summers, L. (1988), 'Beyond the natural rate hypothesis', *American Economic Review* (Proceedings of the AEA), vol. 78, no. 2 (May).

Borensztein, E., and Ostry, J. (1992), 'Structural and Macroeconomic Determinants of the Output Decline in Poland: 1990–91', *IMF Working Papers* (Oct.).

Bruno, M. (1988), 'Opening up: Liberalization with stabilization', in *The Open Economy,* eds. R. Dornbusch and L. Helmers (Washington, DC, OUP and World Bank), 223–48.

—— (1992), 'Stabilization and Reform in Eastern Europe', *IMF Staff Papers*, vol. 39, no. 4 (Dec.).

—— Di Tella, G., Dornbusch, R., and Fischer, S. (1988), *Inflation Stabilization: the Experience of Israel, Argentina, Brazil, Bolivia and Mexico* (MIT Press, Cambridge, Mass).

—— and Fischer, S. (1990), 'Seigniorage, Operating Rules, and the High Inflation Trap', *Quarterly Journal of Economics* (May).

—— and Sachs, J. (1985), *The Economics of Worldwide Stagflation* (Harvard University Press, Cambridge, Mass).

Buchanan, J. (1989), 'Post-Reagan political economy', in *Reaganomics and After*; ed. A. Seldon (Institute of Economic Affairs, London).

Bufman, G., and Leiderman, L. (1992), 'Simulating an Optimizing Model of Currency Substitution', *Revista de Analisis Economico* (June).

Cagan, P. (1956), 'The Monetary Dynamics of Hyperinflation', in *Studies in the Quantity Theory of Money,* ed. M. Friedman (University of Chicago Press, Chicago).

Calvo, G. (1991), 'Financial Aspects of Socialist Economies: from inflation to reform' in *Reforming Central and Eastern European Economies: Initial Results and Challenges*, eds. V. Corbo, F. Coricelli, and J. Bossak (World Bank).

—— (1992), 'Interenterprise Credit in Previously Centrally Planned Economies: a simple analytical framework', *mimeo*, IMF (July).

362   References

—— and Coricelli, F. (1992a), 'Stagflionary Effects of Stabilization Programs in Reforming Socialist Countries', *World Bank Economic Review*, vol. 6, no. 1.

Calvo, G. and Coricelli, F. (1992b), 'Stabilizing a Previously Centrally Planned Economy', *Economic Policy*, 14 (Apr.).

—— —— (1993), 'Output Decline in Eastern Europe', *IMF Staff Papers*, vol. 40, no. 1 (Mar.).

—— and Frenkel, J. (1991), 'Credit Markets, Credibility and Economic Transformation', *Journal of Economic Perspectives*, vol. 5 (Fall).

—— —— (1992), 'Transformation of Centrally Planned Economies: Credit Markets and Sustainable Growth, in *Central and Eastern European Roads to Growth*, IMF and Austrian National Bank (Washington, DC).

Cardoso, E., and Fishlow, A. (1989), 'The macroeconomics of the Brazilian external debt', in *Developing Country Debt and the World Economy*, ed. J. Sachs (Chicago University Press and NBER, Chicago).

Central Planning Office of the Republic of Poland (1992), 'The Economic and Social Situation of Poland, First Half 1992' (Warsaw).

CESMECON (1993a), *Economic Developments in FR Yugoslavia: a Country Report*, prepared for the UNECE (Belgrade, Sept.).

—— (1993b), *Program Makroekonomske Stabilizacije* (Belgrade, Dec.).

—— (1994), *Economic Developments in FR Yugoslavia: a Country Report*, prepared for the UNECE (Belgrade, Jan.).

Chow, G. C. (1987), 'Money and price level determination in China', *Journal of Comparative Economics*, vol. 11, no. 3 (Sept.).

Chubais, A. (1993), 'The Politics of Mass Privatization', presentation at the *Annual St. Petersburg Conference*.

Corbett, J., and Mayer, C. (1992), 'Financial Reform in Eastern Europe: Progress with the wrong model', *Oxford Review of Economic Policy*, vol. 7, no. 4.

Coricelli, F., and Thorne, A. (1992), 'Creating Financial Markets in Economies in Transition: an Overview', paper presented at the *EBRD Conference on Banking Reform and Regulation in Eastern Europe* (London, 19–20 Oct.).

de Crombrugghe, A. (1994), 'The Polish Government Budget: Stabilization and Sustainability' in *Developing Public Finance in Emerging Market Economies*, ed. K. Mizsei (Institute of East-West Studies, New York).

Cukierman, A. (1983), 'Relative Price Variability and Inflation: a

survey and further results', in *Variability in Employment, Prices and Money*, eds. K. Brunner and A. Melzer *Carnegie Rochester Series on Public Policy*, 19.

Dąbrowski, M. (1993a), 'Monetary Policy and Inflation' in *The Gaidar Programme*, ed. M. Dąbrowski (Centrum Analiz Społeczno-Ekonomicznych (C-A-S-E) and Freidrich Ebert Stifftung, Warsaw).

—— (1993b), 'The State Without Borders: the Gradual Collapse of the Ruble Zone and its Consequences' in *The Gaidar Programme*, ed. M. Dąbrowski (Centrum Analiz Społeczno-Ekonomicznych (C-A-S-E) and Freidrich Ebert Stifftung, Warsaw).

—— and Antczak, R. (1994), 'Economic Reforms in Kirgizstan', *Studies and Analyses*, 28 (Centrum Analiz Społeczno-Ekonomicznych (C-A-S-E), Warsaw).

Daianu, D. (1992), 'The Changing mix of Disequilibria during Transition—a Romanian background', *mimeo* (Sept.).

Daniel, Z. (1985), 'The effect of housing allocation on social inequality in Hungary', *Journal of Comparative Economics*, vol. 9, no. 4 (Dec.).

Davies, R. (1958), *The Development of the Soviet Budgetary System* (Cambridge University Press, Cambridge).

Dixit, A. (1993), 'A Simplified Treatment of the Theory of Optimal Regulation of Brownian Motion', in *Optimal Pricing, Inflation, and the Cost of Price Adjustment*, eds. E. Sheshinski and Y. Weiss (MIT Press, Cambridge, Mass.).

Dornbusch, R. (1987), 'Lessons from the German Experience of the 1920s', in *Macroeconomics and Finance*, eds. R. Dornbusch and S. Fischer (MIT Press, Cambridge, Mass.).

—— and de Pablo, J. C. (1989), 'Debt and macroeconomic instability in Argentina', in *Developing Country Debt and the World Economy*, ed. J. Sachs (Chicago University Press and NBER, Chicago).

—— and Simonsen, M. (1988), 'Inflation Stabilization: The Role of Incomes Policy and of Monetization', in *Exchange Rates and Inflation*, ed. R. Dornbusch (MIT Press, Cambridge, Mass.).

The Economist, London, 7 May 1994, p. 49.

Edwards, J., and Fischer, K. (1994), *Banks, Finance and Investment in Germany* (Cambridge University Press, Cambridge).

Engle, R. (1983), 'Estimates of the Variation of U.S. Inflation based upon ARCH model', *Journal of Money, Credit and Banking*, 15, 867–97.

Fisher, I. (1936), 'The Debt Deflation Theory of Great Depressions', *Econometrica*, vol. 1, 337–57.

Fischer, S. (1988), 'Comments on Helpman and Leiderman', *Carnegie Rochester Series on Public Policy*, 28.

Flanagan, R. J. (1987), 'Labour Market Behaviour and European Economic Growth', in *Barriers to European Growth: a Transatlantic View*, eds. R. Z. Lawrence and C. L. Schulze (Brookings, Washington, DC).

Fornalczyk, A., and Hoffman, R. (1993), 'Demonopolization and Deconcentration of Russia's Economy', in *The Gaidar Programme*, ed. M. Dąbrowski (Centrum Analiz Społeczno-Ekonomicznych (C-A-S-E) and Freidrich Ebert Stifftung, Warsaw).

Friedman, M. (1978), 'Inflation and Unemployment: the New Dimension of Politics' (the 1976 Nobel Lecture), *Institute of Economic Affairs Occasional Paper*, 2nd impression (London).

—— (1981), 'Unemployment vs. Inflation?', *Institute of Economic Affairs Occasional Paper*, 4th impression.

—— and Schwartz, A. (1963), *A Monetary History of the United States 1867–1960* (Princeton University Press for the NBER).

Frydman, R., Rapaczynski, A. and Erle, J. (1993), *Privatization in Russia, Ukraine and the Baltic States* (Central European University Press, Prague).

Gedeon, S. J. (1987), 'Monetary disequilibrium and bank reform proposals in Yugoslavia: paternalism and the economy', *Soviet Studies*, vol. 39, no. 2.

Gerschenkron, A. (1968) *Continuity in History and Other Essays* (Harvard University Press, Boston).

Gomulka, S. (1993a), 'Economic and Political Constraints During Transition', *Europe-Asia Studies*, vol. 46, no. 1.

—— (1993b), 'The Financial Situation of Polish Enterprises 1992–3 and its Impact on Monetary and Fiscal Policies', paper presented to the IIASA Conference on Output Decline in Eastern Europe (November, Laxenburg, Austria).

—— and Rostowski, J. (1984), 'The Reformed Polish Economic System 1982–83', *Soviet Studies*, vol. 36, no. 3.

Goodhart, C. (1989), 'Disintermediation', in *The New Palgrave Dictionary of Economics: Money*, eds. J. Eatwell, M. Millgate, and P. Newman (MacMillan, London).

Government of Poland (1992), 'Letter of Intent to the International Monetary Fund'.

GUS (1991), '*Informacja o Sytuacji Społeczno-Gospodarczej w Kraju: rok 1991*' (Główny Urząd Statystyczny, Warsaw).

—— (1990–2), '*Biuletyn Statystyczny, Miesięcznik*' (Monthly Statistical Bulletin), various issues (Główny Urząd Statystyczny, Warsaw).

—— (1992), *Rocznik Statystyczny 1991* (Główny Urząd Statystyczny, Warsaw).

—— (1993), *Rocznik Statystyczny 1992* (Główny Urząd Statystyczny, Warsaw).

—— (1994), *Rocznik Statystyczny 1993* (Główny Urząd Statystyczny, Warsaw).

—— IoSS-GK (1992), *'Informacja o Sytuacji Społeczno-Gospodarczej Kraju: 1992 r.'* (Główny Urząd Statystyczny, Warsaw, Jan.).

—— —— (1993), *'Informacja o Styuacji Społeczno-Gospodarczej Kraju: 1992 r.'* (Główny Urząd Statystyczny, Warsaw, Jan.).

Hanke, S., and Schuler, K. (1991), *Monetary Reform and the Development of a Yugoslav Market Economy* (Centre for Research into Communist Economies, London).

—— Jonung, L., and Schuler, K. (1992), *Monetary Reform for a Free Estonia: a Currency Board Solution* (SNS Forlag, Stockholm).

Hanson, P. (1992), 'Trade and Economic Co-operation: the Baltic States and their Neighbours', Paper presented to the *Conference on the Re-integration of the Baltic States into the World Community* (RIIA Chatham House, London).

Hayek, F. (1976), 'Denationalisation of Money', *Hobart Paper*, no. 70 (Institute of Economic Affairs, London).

—— (1986), *The Road to Serfdom* (Routledge and Kegan Paul, London).

Helpman, Elhanan, and Leiderman, L. (1988), 'Stabilization in high inflation countries: Analytical Foundations and Recent Experience', *Carnegie Rochester Series on Public Policy*, 28.

Henderson, R. (1993), *European Finance* (McGraw-Hill, Toronto).

Hrincir, M., and Klacek, J. (1991), 'Stabilization Policies and Currency Convertibility in Czechoslovakia', *The Path of Reform in Central and Eastern Europe, European Economy*, Special Edition no. 2, 17–40 (Commission of the European Communities, Brussels).

IFS (1992), *International Financial Statistics* (International Monetary Fund, Washington, DC).

Kawalec, S., Sikora, S., and Rymaszewski, P. (1993), 'Dealing with Bad Debts: the Case of Poland', paper presented to the IMF and World Bank Conference on Building Sound Finance in Emerging Market Economies (Washington, DC, June).

Khan, M., and Clifton, E. (1992), 'Inter-enterprise Arrears in Transforming Economies: the Case of Romania', *IMF Paper on Policy Analysis and Assessment*.

Kornai, J. (1979), 'Resource-constrained versus demand-constrained systems', *Econometrica*, vol. 47, no. 4 (July).

—— (1980), *The Economics of Shortage*, 2 vols. (North-Holland, Amsterdam).

Kornai, J. (1986), 'The Hungarian reform process: visions, hopes and reality', *Journal of Economic Literature*, vol. 24 (Dec.).

Korzec, M. (1988), 'Contract labour, the "Right to work" and new labour laws in the PRC', *Comparative Economic Studies*, vol. 30, no. 2.

Kowalski, P. (1987), 'Pauperyzacja ludności i pogorszenie jakości życia w PRL', *Libertas*, no. 8.

Layard, R., and Nickell, S. (1986), 'Unemployment in Britain', *Economica*, vol. 53 (Feb.).

—— and Richter, A. (1994), *Who Gains and Looses from Credit Expansion?*, Special Report no. 1 (Centre for Economic Performance, London School of Economics).

Lipton, D., and Sachs, J. (1991), 'Privatization in Eastern Europe: the case of Poland', in *Reforming Central and Eastern European Economies: Initial Results and Challenges*, eds. V. Corbo, F. Coricelli, and J. Bossak (World Bank).

Macieja, J. (1993), 'Zaangażowanie Rozwojowe Przedsiębiorstw Sektora Publicznego w 1992r' in *500 Największych Przedsiębiorstw Sektora Publicznego w Przemyśle Przetwórczym w 1992r* (Instytut Nauk Ekonomicznych, Polska Akademia Nauk, Warsaw).

Madzar, L. (1993), 'The Art of the Impossible: Economic Policies in the New Yugoslavia', *Communist Economies and Economic Transformation* vol. 5, no. 3.

Matthews, K., and Minford, P. (1987), 'Mrs Thatcher's Economic Policies 1979–87', in 'The Conservative Revolution: a Special Report', eds. D. Begg and C. Wyplosz, *Economic Policy*.

McKinnon, R. (1991), *The Order of Economic Liberalization* (Johns Hopkins UP, Baltimore).

—— (1992), 'Taxation, Money and Credit in a Liberalizing Socialist Economy' in *The Emergence of Market Economies in Eastern Europe*, eds. C. Cleague and G. Rausser (Blackwell, Oxford).

—— (1993), 'Gradual versus Rapid Liberalization in Socialist Economies: Financial Policies and Macroeconomic Stability in Russia and China Compared', World Bank Annual Conference on Development Economics (May 4, Washington, DC).

Mencinger, J. (1983), 'Otvorena nezaposlenost i zaposleni bez posla', *Privredna Kretanja Jugoslavje*, 128 (Apr.).

Ministry of Finance (1990), 'Założenia do Budżetu Państwa, 1990' (Warsaw).

—— (1992), 'Uzasadnienie do ustawy o restrukturyzacji finansowej przedsiębiorstw i banków' (Warsaw).

Ministry of Industry (1990), *Zarys Polityki Przemysłowej*, *mimeo* (Warsaw).

Mizsei, K. (1993), *Bankruptcy and the Post-Communist Economies of East Central Europe* (Institute for East-West Studies, New York).

—— (ed.) (1994), *Developing Public Finance in Emerging Market Economies* (Institute of East West Studies, New York).

—— (1994), 'Lessons from Bad Loan Management in the East Central European Economic Transition for the Second Wave Reform Countries', in *Banking Reform in Central Europe and the Former Soviet Union*, ed. J. Rostowski (Central European University Press, Budapest).

Modiano, E. (1988), 'The Cruzado First Attempt: The Brazilian Stabilization Program of February 1986', in *Inflation Stabilization: the Experience of Israel, Argentina, Brazil, Bolivia and Mexico*, eds. M. Bruno, G. Di Tella, R. Dornbusch, and S. Fischer (MIT Press, Cambridge, Mass.).

Morales, J.-A. (1988), 'Inflation Stabilization in Bolivia', in *Inflation Stabilization: the Experience of Israel, Argentina, Brazil, Bolivia and Mexico*, eds. M. Bruno, G. Di Tella, R. Dornbusch, and S. Fischer (MIT Press, Cambridge, Mass.).

Murrell, P. (1992), 'Evolution in Economics and in the Economic Reform of the Centrally Planned Economies', in *The Emergence of Market Economies in Eastern Europe*, eds. C. Cleague and G. Rausser (Blackwell, Oxford).

Naishul, V. (1994), 'Economic Reforms: a Liberal Perspective', in *Economic Transformation in Russia*, ed. A. Aslund (Pinter, London).

National Bank of Hungary (1993), *Annual Report 1993* (Budapest).

Naughton, B. (1987), 'Macroeconomic policy and response in the Chinese economy: the impact of the reform process', *Journal of Comparative Economics*, vol. 11, no. 3.

Nuti, D. (1985), 'Hidden and Repressed Inflation in Soviet-type Economies: Definitions, Measurements and Stabilisation', *European University Institute Working Paper*.

—— and Portes, R. (1993), 'Central Europe: the Way Forward', in *Economic Transformation in Central Europe: a Progress Report*, ed. R. Portes (CEPR and EUROP, London).

Nyers, R., and Lutz, G. (1993), 'Development of the Financial Sector in Hungary During the Transition Period', *mimeo* (Budapest).

Pejovich, S. (1994), 'A Property Rights Analysis of Alternative Methods of Organizing Production', *Communist Economies and Economic Transformation*, vol. 6, no. 2.

Portes, R. (1993), 'From Central Planning to a Market Economy', in *Making Markets: Economic Transformation in Eastern Europe and the Post-Soviet States*, eds. S. Islam and M. Mandelbaum (CFRP, New York).

Portes, R. (1994), 'Transformation Traps', *Economic Journal*, vol. 104, no. 426, (Sept.).

Reynolds, B. L. (1987), 'Trade, employment and inequality in postreform China', *Journal of Comparative Economics*, vol. 11, no. 3.

Rostowski, J. (1989a), 'The decay of socialism and the growth of private enterprise in Poland, *Soviet Studies*, vol. 41, no. 2.

—— (1989b), *The Hard Currency Economy in Poland: a Special Report* (The WEFA Group).

—— (1992), 'The Benefits of Currency Substitution During High Inflation and Stabilization', *Revista de Analisis Economico*, vol. 7, no. 1.

—— (1993), Comment on 'Privatization in Russia, the First Steps' Shleiffer and Vishny, in *The Transition in Eastern Europe*, eds. O. Blanchard, K. Froot, and J. Sachs, vol. 1 (NBER Chicago University Press, Chicago).

—— and Auerbach, P. (1986), 'Storming, Cycles and Economic Systems', *Journal of Comparative Economics*, vol. 10, no. 3.

—— and Shapiro, J. (1992), 'Secondary Currencies in the Russian Hyperinflation and Stabilization of 1921–24', *Centre for Economic Performance, London School of Economics*, Discussion Paper no. 59.

Rupnik, J. (1988), *The Other Europe* (Weidenfeld and Nicholson, London).

Russian Economic Trends (1994), Centre for Economic Reform, Government of the Russian Federation and Centre for Economic Performance, London School of Economics (Whurr Publishers, London).

Sachs, J., and Larrain, F. (1993), *Macroeconomics in the Global Economy*, (Harvester-Wheatsheaf, New York) 778.

—— and Lipton, D. (1993), 'Remaining Steps to a Market Based Monetary System', in *Changing the Economic System in Russia*, eds. A. Åslund and R. Layard (Pinter, London).

Sargent, T. (1986a), 'The Ends of Four Big Inflations' in *Rational Expectations and Inflation* (Harper and Row, New York).

—— (1986b), 'Stopping moderate inflations: The methods of Poincare and Thatcher', in *Rational Expectations and Inflation* (Harper and Row, New York).

—— and Wallace, N. (1986), 'Some unpleasant monetarist arith-

metic', in *Rational Expectations and Inflation* (Harper and Row, New York).

Savchenko, O. (1993), 'Extracts Highlighting Key Features of the Economic Reform Program', *mimeo* (Kiiv).

Schaffer, M. (1992*a*), 'The Enterprise Sector in Transition Economies', *mimeo* (Centre for Economic Performance, LSE, London).

—— (1992*b*), 'The Economy of Poland', *The National Economies of Europe*, ed. D. Dyker (Longmans, London).

Schmieding, H. (1991), 'Transforming the Financial System in Eastern Europe's Emerging Market Economies', Working Paper no. 497 (Kiel Institute of World Economics).

Schwartz, A. (1989), 'Banking School, Currency School, Free Banking School' (in *The New Palgrave Dictionary of Economics: Money*, eds. J. Eatwell, M. Millgate, and P. Newman (MacMillan, London).

Semjén, A. (1994), 'Some Fiscal Problems during Economic Transition in Hungary', in *Developing Public Finance in Emerging Market Economies*, ed. K. Mizsei (Institute for East-West Studies, New York).

Sheshinski, E., and Weiss, Y. (1993), 'Inflation and Costs of Price Adjustment', in *Optimal Pricing, Inflation, and the Cost of Price Adjustment*, eds. E. Sheshinski and Y. Weiss (MIT Press, Cambridge, Mass.).

Simons, H. (1936), 'Rules versus Authorities in Monetary Policy', *Journal of Political Economy*, vol. 44, no. 1.

Smith, V. (1990), *The Rationale for Central Banking and the Free banking Alternative* (Liberty Press, Indionapolis).

Srinivasan, T. M. (1987), 'Economic liberalisation in China and India: issues and an analytical framework', *Journal of Comparative Economics*, vol. 11, no. 3.

Statystyka Polski (1992), insert into *Rzeczpospolita*, 2 Feb. (Główny Urząd Statystyczny, Warsaw).

Steinherr, A., and Huveneers, C. (1992), 'Institutional Competition and Innovation: Universal Banking in the Single European Market', in *European Banking*, ed. A. Mullineux (Blackwell, Oxford).

Taylor, J. (1981), 'On the relation Between the Variability of Inflation and the Average Inflation Rate', *Carnegie-Rochester Conference Series on Public Policy*, 15.

Three Institutes (1994), *Rekonstrukcija Monetarnog Sistema i Strategija Ekonomskog Oporavka Jugoslavije*, Doprinosi tri Instituta (Ekonomski Institut, Beograd, Ekonomski Fakultet, Beograd, Institut Ekonomskih Nauka, Beograd((Beograd, Jan.), 57.

Topiński, A. (1989), 'Systemowe uwarunkowania procesów infla-cyjnych', *mimeo*.

Ward, B. (1958), 'The Firm in Illyria: Market Syndicalism', *American Economic Review*, vol. 48, no. 4.

Weiss, Y. (1993), 'Inflation and Price Adjustment: a Survey of Findings from Micro-Data' in *Optimal Pricing, Inflation, and the Cost of Price Adjustment*, eds. E. Sheshinski and Y. Weiss (MIT Press, Cambridge, Mass.).

Wharton Econometric Forecasting Associates (1989), *Medium Term Outlook for Latin America* (Apr.).

Wiles, P. (1973a), 'Cost inflation and the state of economic theory', *Economic Journal*, vol. 83.

—— (1973b), *Economic Institutions Compared* (Blackwell, Oxford).

Williamson, J. (1992a), 'The Eastern Transition to a Market Economy: a Global Perspective', *Centre for Economic Performance, London School of Economics*, Occasional Paper No. 2.

—— (1992b), 'Careful therapy in the special case of Russia', *Financial Times*, 25 Aug. 1992.

van der Willigen, T. (1994), 'Some Lessons from Fiscal Reform in Czechoslovakia', in *Developing Public Finance in Emerging Market Economies*, ed. K. Mizsei (Institute for East-West Studies, New York).

Winiecki, J. (1987), *Economic Prospects East and West: A View from the East* (Centre for Research into Communist Economies, London).

—— (1988), 'Narrow wage differentials between blue-collar and white-collar workers and excess demand for manual labor in the CPEs: causally linked system specific phenomena', *Osteuropa Wirtschaft*, vol. 33, no. 3.

Wood, A. (1989), 'Vietnam's stabilisation policy', *Cambridge Journal of Economics*, vol. 13, no. 4.

INDEX